RELIGIONS OF SOUTH ASIA: AN INTRODUCTION

South Asia is home to many of the world's most vibrant religious faiths. It is also one of the most dynamic and historically rich regions on earth, where changing political and social structures have caused religions to interact through decisive conflicts as well as by sharing their cultural horizons. This textbook introduces the religions of South Asia, from the indigenous Hindu, Jaina, Buddhist, and Sikh traditions, to incoming influences such as the Zoroastrian, Judaic, Christian, Muslim, and newly emerging Bahā'ī religions. In nine chapters, it surveys these belief systems of South Asia and explains their history, practices, values, and worldviews. A final chapter helps students relate what they have learned to current discussions in postcolonial theory and interpretation, preparing the way for future study.

Entirely written by leading experts, *Religions of South Asia* combines solid scholarship with clear and lively writing to provide students with an accessible and comprehensive introduction. All chapters are specially designed to aid cross-religious comparison, following a standard format covering set topics and issues; the book reveals to students the core principles of each faith and its particular place in South Asian history and society. It is a perfect resource for all students of South Asia's diverse and fascinating faiths.

Sushil Mittal is an Associate Professor and the Director of the Mahatma Gandhi Center for Global Nonviolence at James Madison University in Virginia. **Gene Thursby** is an Associate Professor at the University of Florida. They have previously coedited *The Hindu World* (2004), also published by Routledge.

RELIGIONS OF SOUTH ASIA

An introduction

Edited by Sushil Mittal and Gene Thursby

Routledge
Taylor & Francis Group
LONDON AND NEW YORK

First published 2006
by Routledge
2 Park Square, Milton Park, Abingdon, Oxon OX14 4RN

Simultaneously published in the USA and Canada
by Routledge
270 Madison Avenue, New York, NY 10016

Routledge is an imprint of the Taylor & Francis Group

Typeset in Times by RefineCatch Ltd, Bungay, Suffolk
Printed and bound in Great Britain by
TJ International Ltd, Padstow, Cornwall

British Library Cataloguing in Publication Data
A catalogue record for this book is available from the British Library

Library of Congress Cataloging in Publication Data
A catalog record for this book has been requested

ISBN10: 0–415–22390–3 (hbk)
ISBN10: 0–415–22391–1 (pbk)

ISBN13: 978–0–415–22390–4 (hbk)
ISBN13: 978–0–415–22391–1 (pbk)

TO
OUR PARENTS:

MAYA DEVI AND KHYALI RAM MITTAL

AND

MARIELLA ICENHOWER AND GENE FAYE THURSBY

CONTENTS

ILLUSTRATIONS

MAPS

NOTE ON TRANSLITERATION

We have, in general, adhered to the standard transliteration system for each of the Indic languages. Although Indic languages make no distinction between uppercase and lowercase letters, we use capitals to indicate proper names and titles; all other Indic terms, with the exception of those used as adjectives, are italicized and not capitalized. Terms that have been anglicized in form or have come into English usage are nevertheless given in their standard transliterated forms, with diacritics (e.g., Kṛṣṇa, *paṇḍita*, and *karma*). Modern place names are given in their current transliterated forms, but without diacritics. If references to such places are made in a literary or historical context, however, they are given in their standard transliterated forms, with diacritics. Modern proper names are given in their current transliterated forms, but without diacritics. All premodern proper names, however, are in their standard transliterated forms, with diacritics.

The reader is advised to observe carefully four important terms that are similar in their linguistic form but different in their meaning. The four are Brāhmaṇ which refers to a category of people, in general those who are born into one of several high-status castes and in particular some from among their number who regularly perform priestly functions: Brāhmaṇa which refers to a category of Vedic texts. Brahman which is a traditional way to refer to that which is Real, absolutely, ultimately, and in principle beyond all qualifications or descriptive designations; and Brāhmaṇism which refers to an authoritative and highly influential sector of Hindu tradition that is preserved and transmitted, ideally at least, by Brāmaṇs.

ACKNOWLEDGMENTS

It is important to acknowledge that any work of cooperative scholarship, at whatever level of specialization, depends on the good will, assistance, and advice of a large team of people who are crucial to the outcome but are unlikely to see in print an adequate statement of appreciation for their valuable contributions. We are indebted to Lesley Riddle, Geraldine Martin, Julene Knox, and supporting staff at Routledge for commissioning the book and for managing its production. We thank our colleagues at James Madison University and the University of Florida who have offered encouragement at times when we most needed it. In addition to our parents, to whom the book is dedicated and who are a continuing inspiration to us, our extended families and close friends inside and outside the academic community have enabled us to appreciate this project as 'deep fun' – which is the way that one of them refers to transformative learning experiences.

Grants and similar forms of direct assistance from several sources in recent years have made it possible to travel to South Asia, maintain the *International Journal of Hindu Studies*, establish the Mahatma Gandhi Center for Global Nonviolence at James Madison University, and continue work on various projects that indirectly helped to improve this one. Among these sources of individually or jointly received support, we particularly want to acknowledge our respective universities, the American Institute of Indian Studies and Smithsonian Institution, the Infinity Foundation, the National Endowment for the Humanities, Dr J. N. Puri and his family in New Delhi, and Vasant and Carol Carswell Bhide in Jacksonville, Florida.

For permission to reproduce visual materials to illustrate the book, we acknowledge the following artists and agencies: (*Introduction*) P. R. VanderMeer, M.A. (née Miller) for an acrylic on canvas painting of Gaṇeśa (divine patron of libraries and literary ventures and in general the remover of obstacles) that was inspired by an image she saw in Bali which exemplifies Hindu cultural influences that were carried overseas from the subcontinent for many centuries before the modern era and received throughout South and Southeast Asia; (*Hindu Dharma*) Nicola Barsaleau for the linocut 'Prayer to the Ten Incarnations' that represents ten forms of Viṣṇu arranged around Kṛṣṇa at center; (*Jaina Dharma*) John Eskenazi Ltd. for a photograph of an image of the *tīrthaṅkara* Mahāvīra in sandstone from Rajasthan; (*Bauddha Dhamma*) the Ministry of Information and Broadcasting of the Government of India for a photograph that records one instance of the official annual celebration in honor of Dr B. R. Ambedkar by the Prime Minister and President of the Republic of India; (*Sikh Dharam*) Dr Marilyn Pearcy Lange for a photograph of a *granthī* ('reader') who is honoring the installed copy of the *Guru Granth Sāhib* and preparing for an evening worship service at Dukh Nivaran, a *gurdwārā* of historical significance in the city of Patiala in the Punjab in northern India; (*Indian Zoroastrian Tradition*) Professor T. M. Luhrmann for a photograph of the blessing of the foundations for a new fire temple at the place where the Parsi people first landed at Sanjan in Gujarat in northwestern India; (*Indian Judaic Tradition*) Professor Shalva Weil for a photograph of an open Torah scroll from the Bene Israel synagogue in Alibag in the Konkan region along the coast of western India; (*Indian Christian Tradition*) Magnum Photos agency representing Indian photographer Raghu Rai for a photograph of Mother Teresa of the Roman Catholic order of the Missionaries of Charity who almost certainly is the most widely known Christian missionary to India in recent times; (*Indian Muslim Tradition*) Professor Peter Gottschalk for a photograph of a teacher at a *madrasah* in North India who is supervising Muslim boys and girls in the practice of recitation of the Qur'ān; (*Indian Bahā'ī Tradition*) Bahā'ī World News Service for a photograph of the Bahā'ī House of Worship (aka Lotus Temple) near Nehru Place in New Delhi; (*Categories and Interpretation*) Professor Peter Gottschalk for a photograph of a woman (her affiliation or religious identity unknown and not possible to determine from evidence in the photograph) who is praying before the tomb of Ṣūfī Hazrat Maqdum Shāh in a Bihar village in northeastern India.

1. Gaṇeśa, divine remover of obstacles. Courtesy of the artist P. R. VanderMeer (née Miller).

INTRODUCTION

Sushil Mittal and Gene Thursby

This book introduces several religious traditions that for many centuries have deeply influenced the patterns by which people have been living in the region of the world currently known as South Asia, a region that has its geographical and cultural center in the subcontinent of India. It is called a subcontinent because India and its near neighbors are separated from the larger land mass of Asia by the highest mountains in the world as well as by deserts, rivers, marshes, bays, and seas. The religious traditions that are introduced in this book have been (and continue to be) integral to the formation of the cultural identity of people in India and South Asia.

Traditions of South Asia: from inside and outside

It seems impossible to think seriously about South Asia without attempting to think in terms of Hindu, Jaina, Buddhist, and Sikh categories of thought and practice. These traditions originated in India and have deeply informed its core values and the ways in which its people interact with one another. Among South Asians, by far the greatest number identify with Hindu ways of living and modes of religious practice. When and where Hinduism was first practiced is unknown. Many contemporary Hindus prefer to say that it is a timeless wisdom that proceeds from a higher source and becomes evident to human beings again and again through diverse types of sages and saints as well as by direct intervention of divine beings who return things to their proper course from time to time and renew the power of the human spirit. The influential minority traditions of the Jainas and Buddhists are at least 2,500 years old, perhaps more; and the very dynamic practices of the Sikhs have their source in revelations received by Guru Nānak about 500 years ago. In this book these distinctively South Asian or Indic traditions are referred to, as they refer to themselves, with the term *dharma* or its near equivalents *dharam* or *dhamma*. The meanings of these key terms will become clearer to you as you continue reading this book. For now let us simply say that *dharma* refers to the deep nature of reality and the kind of action (ranging from a single act right up to a general pattern of behavior and an inclusive way of life) that is in accord with it and is appropriate to the circumstances in which an individual person is involved at a particular time.

During the many centuries that it has taken for the *dharma*-based traditions from India to spread throughout South Asia and from there to all areas of the world, the subcontinent has been receptive to outside influences, too. Zoroastrian religion was brought to India by Parsi or Persian people who were seeking religious freedom. Other

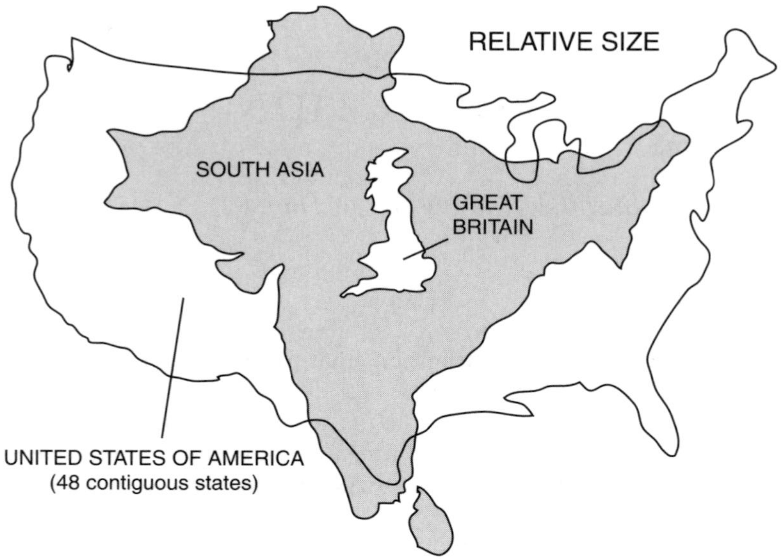

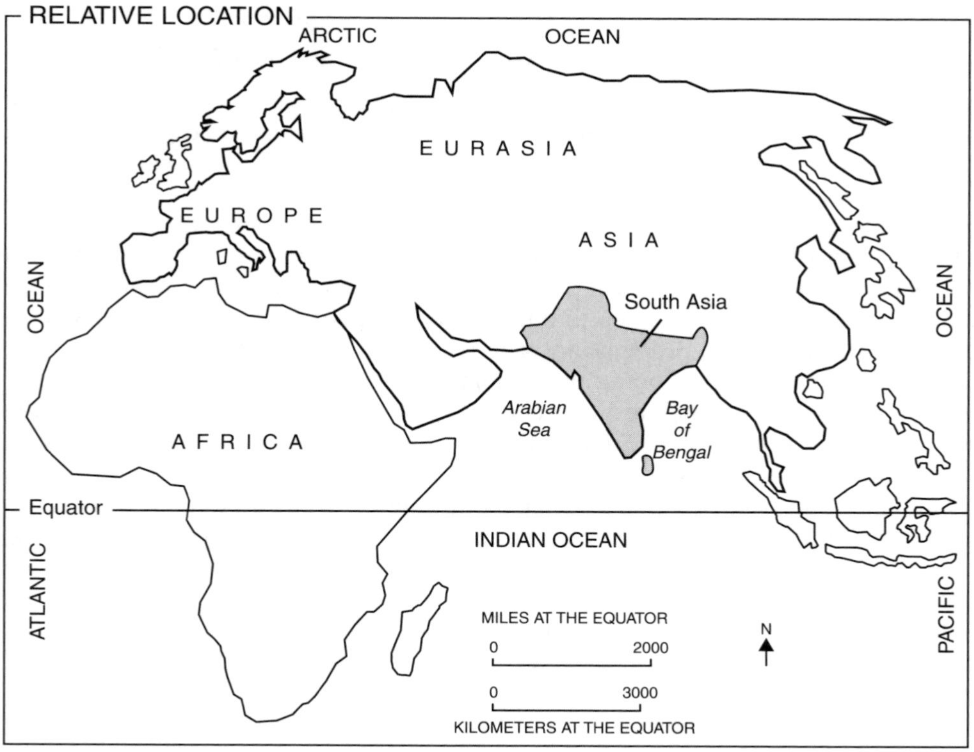

Map 1 – Relative size and location of South Asia

religions from the Near East or Middle East arrived in India in the company of adventure travelers, explorers, traders, missionaries, and invading armies. These religions have included all three main versions of the Abrahamic or Semitic religious traditions – Jewish, Christian, and Muslim or Islamic – and their several subgroups or denominations. Over the centuries, most Christians and Muslims in India have been local converts, and inevitably their adopted traditions 'indigenized' or took on local features and practices. This has happened to a sufficient extent that it would make sense to speak and write about them and the other religions of foreign origin as hyphenated traditions, whether Indo-Zoroastrian, Indo-Jewish, Indo-Christian, or Indo-Muslim. Finally, in addition to these four older religious traditions that found in India a welcome new home, this book also introduces a relatively new religion called Bahā'ī that seems to have potential to find a significant place alongside the others in South Asian cultural life in the years ahead.

South Asia as a region

Tessa Bartholomeusz, the author of this book's chapter on Bauddha Dhamma, the traditions that developed from the teachings of Gotama (or Gautama) the Buddha, was well acquainted with his warnings about the lure of *nāma-rūpa* or names and forms. She was keenly aware, therefore, of the difficulties involved in finding an apt name for the geographical region that is treated in this book and for the religious traditions that developed there. Her reminder to us is to remain aware of the extraordinary variety of physical and cultural terrain in that part of the world and both the value and limitations of each of the alternative ways that could be used to refer to the region, such as India (in the classical and premodern sense), Greater India, or South Asia. The last of these terms has come into wide use after being adopted by modern governments as an administrative classification.

Whatever term may be preferred, we need to be clear that it refers to a large geographical area, the topography of which can include the high mountains of the Himālayas in the north, the sandy beaches of Sri Lanka in the south, the rugged terrain of Myanmar or Burma in the northeast, and the arid deserts of Pakistan in the northwest. Indeed, the complex and varied physical contours of South Asia are a metaphor for the linguistic, cultural, and religious diversity of the region. There is no well-established consensus about how many countries constitute the region, although most specialists would agree that the Indian Subcontinent is almost synonymous with South Asia and certainly is central to it. Yet, because citizens of Pakistan (which was carved out of India in 1947 and has had recurring conflicts with India since then) and of Bangladesh (which became separated from Pakistan by civil war in 1971) might find offensive the dominant placement of India in the term 'Indian Subcontinent,' many scholars today prefer the more recently adopted designation 'South Asia.'

Although more or less a neutral term, the edges of the region it designates remain ambiguous. In scholarly works, Myanmar is sometimes considered to be a South Asian country, while at other times the former British province is classified as part of Southeast Asia. Lack of consensus regarding Myanmar is reflected in the scholarship of Sugata Bose and Ayesha Jalal who argue that South Asia 'encompasses seven diverse sovereign states of very different sizes: India, Pakistan, Bangladesh, Sri Lanka, Nepal, Bhutan, and the Maldives. Some would also include Myanmar' (2004: 3). In his

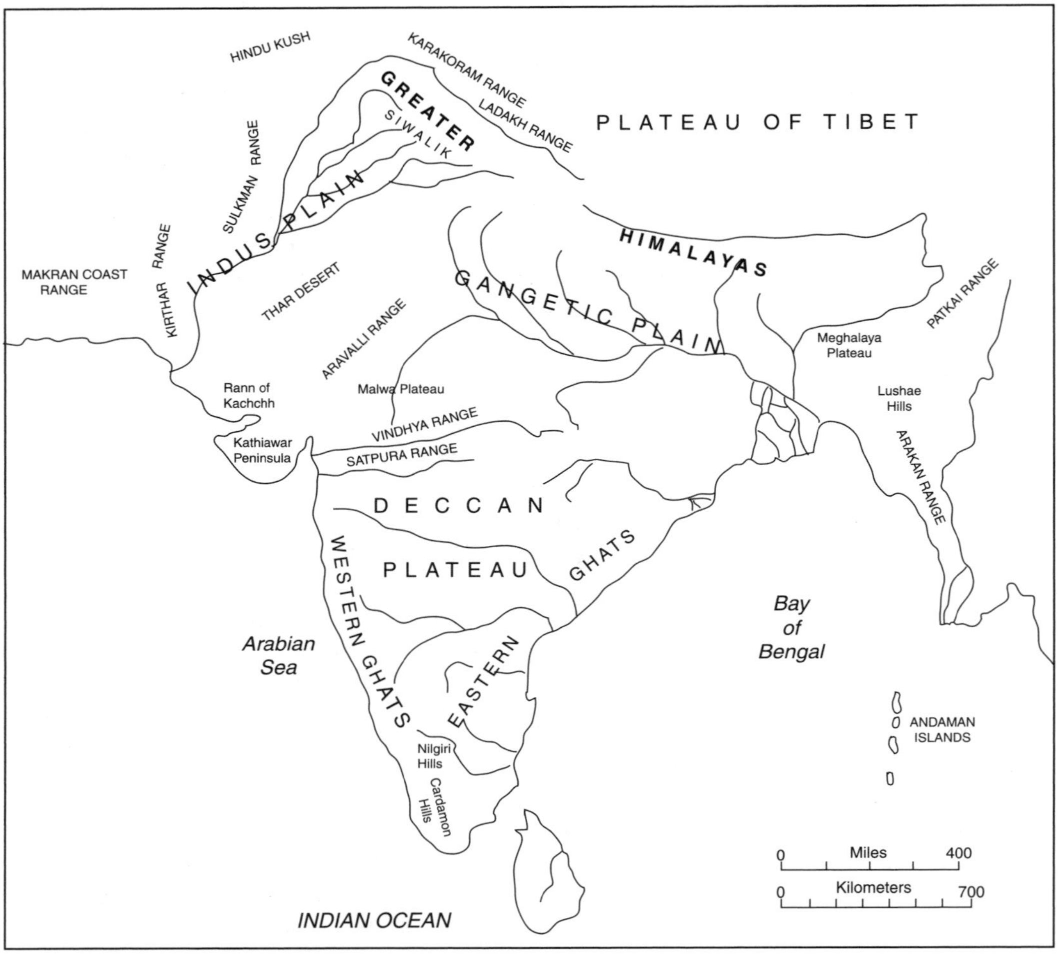

Map 2 – Physical features of South Asia

study of the region, B. H. Farmer (1983), who refers to the same seven countries as Bose and Jalal, underscores the ambiguity of 'South Asia' by mentioning that Burma, until 1935, was a part of the 'Indian Empire' (a reference to British colonial dominion) and thus can be considered a South Asian country (presumably like India). Other scholars have included Afghanistan in their list of the region's countries (see, for instance, Parry and Perkins 1987: 287) as have several government bureaucracies. The Bureau of South Asian Affairs of the Department of State in the United States currently has administrative responsibility for international relations with the following eight nations in the region: Afghanistan, Bangladesh, Bhutan, India, Maldives, Nepal, Pakistan, and Sri Lanka. Moreover, because the study of Tibetan language and religion is part of the South Asia curriculum in doctoral programs at a number of universities, it is safe to say that some academic programs consider that highly contested and semiautonomous region of China to be culturally a significant part of the South Asian region, too.

As these various assessments make clear, the name of the region, as well as where we decide to draw its boundaries, tends to be determined by geopolitical events. Indeed, as K. N. Chaudhuri (1990: 22–23) pointed out in a study of Asia before European contact, world areas such as 'Asia' (more generally) possess little 'natural cohesion.' Moreover, the term is 'essentially Western,' with 'no equivalent word in any Asian language nor such a concept in the domain of geographical knowledge.' In addition, as Jos Gommans (1998: 1) has commented about South Asia as a region, 'closed and fixed frontiers or boundaries are a fairly recent phenomenon' and thus there is naturally some confusion and recurring disagreement about exactly which countries constitute it. The term 'South Asia' appears in the title of this book because it is so widely used, but for the study of religious aspects of the region the terms 'India' and 'Indian' would have served almost equally well.

Dharma in Indic or South Asian religions

Dharma, as mentioned above, is a key term in religious traditions that originate in the Indian Subcontinent. Its root in Sanskrit, the language of the Vedic scriptures and of classical Hinduism, has the sense of 'that which supports or holds together'; while in Pali, the language of early monastic Buddhism, the variant form *dhamma* refers to one of the smallest and most temporary of the many constituent units that together make up the world as it appears to our senses. In Jaina teachings, the term '*dharma*' refers technically to the noncreated medium within which all movement takes place but generally is used much as it is in Hinduism. As Buddhist tradition developed, two meanings of the term '*dharma*' or '*dhamma*' coexisted and complemented one another for Buddhists. The first refers to the changing world of appearances that may beguile and mislead us so that we suppose that suffering (*duhkha*) is our life's deepest potential. The second refers to the body of teaching or doctrine of the Buddha that offers an understanding of things that can make it possible to pass beyond suffering and the world of temporary, fluctuating appearances. The teaching (*dhamma*), the teacher (Buddha), and the community of monks (*saṅgha*) are considered by Buddhists to be the three gems or jewels of their religion. When contemporary Buddhists speak of 'the *Dhamma*' typically they mean the truth as transmitted through the teachings of the Buddha. Similarly, contemporary Sikhs would think of the teachings of Guru Nānak as the core of the Sikh Dharam that is developed in the *Ādi Granth* and through the continuing tradition. For Hindus, reference to *dharma* typically has the underlying meaning of the structural power that holds things together and arranges them into a meaningful cosmos. *Dharma* in this sense is manifested in the order of nature, in the lawful patterns of traditional society, and in the integrity of a person embodying and enacting their traditionally prescribed roles and responsibilities. As a principle of order, *dharma* is complemented by the dynamic principle of *karma* (from the root: *karman*). *Karma* refers to the acts and their consequences that generate discernable patterns in the lives of individuals, families, and societies and in the world at large over time.

In Hindu thinking, *dharma* organizes by differentiating. The *dharma* of various people will differ in correlation with their birth into a particular genetic (gender,

Map 3 – Historical and holy sites of South Asia

family, kin, and caste) endowment, their current age, and their marital status. The *Bhagavad Gītā*, a widely respected Hindu text, repeatedly advises that it is better to live in accordance with your own *dharma*, even if you do that poorly, rather than to live according to another's *dharma*, even if you could that well. Any Hindu who speaks to you seriously about their duty is likely to be speaking about *dharma* and about deep promptings of their conscience or inner nature – and perhaps about the pressures they feel from family and society to face up to their solemn responsibilities, too. *Dharma* is so important that a widely held conviction in South Asia has been that a person should not rely upon their individual tendencies and preferences alone but instead should look to the guidance offered by traditional sources of authority that are transmitted in both oral and written form. In the twentieth century, Mohandas K. Gandhi renewed the power of this idea by bringing out its inherently social and ethical components as resources for nonviolent resolution of conflicts. Running through the great traditions that have come from India, in significantly varying ways that will be made clear in the chapters to follow, is the theme of *dharma* or deep patterns in the nature of things and inner promptings toward the highest possibilities available to human beings.

Traditions of outsiders: the world's gifts to India

Among the great traditions that came to India and then developed a lasting presence in the subcontinent, two that are generally nonproselytizing and nonconverting religions are Zoroastrianism and Judaism. However, the boundaries that set apart followers of each of these traditions are only a little more definite and rigid than the ones that describe the range and extent of South Asia as a region. By and large, the Parsi people who follow the practices of Zoroastrianism and the Jews who follow the way of Torah each recruit new participants into their faith by means of the birth of a child to a mother and into a family already identified with that genetic inheritance and religious tradition. Converts who are assimilated by means of marriage or who are individually instructed, tested, and initiated into membership are relatively few in number but never entirely absent.

Two great traditions from outside the subcontinent that actively recruit by converting or proselytizing individuals and groups are the Christian and the Muslim. Christians arrived early and by the seventeenth and early eighteenth century became allied with European merchants and traders. From the late eighteenth century to the middle of the twentieth, the position of Christian missionaries was further complicated by the transformation of European trading companies into colonizing imperial powers. Even now, a lingering suspicion of foreign missionaries in South Asia continues to be a long-term cost of their association with the colonial empires that previously controlled the region. Similarly, Islam was brought to South Asia not only by Muslim sailors attracted to the spice trade but also by freebooters and foreign armies that came by land across Turkey, Persia, and Afghanistan as well as down from Central Asia. These mixed forms of transmission, like the Christian association with foreign empire, have left an ambivalent legacy in which a genuine appreciation for Muslim faith and culture, and a particular attraction to the tombs and shrines of Muslim saints, is mixed with resentment over centuries of imposed rule and both imagined and real suppression of local patterns and places of worship. Nevertheless, the Muslim population in South Asia forms its largest religious minority, and by sheer numbers alone it could eventually shift the center of gravity of the Muslim world. The relatively new religion of the Bahā'ī does invite converts but does not carry the ambiguous heritage of the older proselytizing traditions that arrived earlier from the Middle East.

The teacher-scholars who are the book's authors

An international group of highly accomplished teachers contributed the chapters, which have been newly written for this book and its student readers. Of the authors of chapters on Indic or indigenous South Asian religions, John Grimes taught at Michigan State University and now teaches at Kodaikanal International School in the hills of South India. He is particularly interested in the philosophical tradition known as Advaita Vedānta and has written several books, including a reliable reference work titled *A Concise Dictionary of Indian Philosophy* (1996). Anne Vallely is the author of *Guardians of the Transcendent: An Ethnography of a Jain Ascetic Community* (2002a) and teaches at the University of Ottawa. Tessa Bartholomeusz completed her chapter shortly before her death and during a distinguished teaching career at Florida State University. An innovator in Buddhist Studies and Women's Studies, she was the author of a book on Theravāda Buddhist nuns titled *Women Under the Bo Tree* (1994) as well as *Buddhist Fundamentalisms and Minority Identities in Sri Lanka* (1998) and *In Defense of Dharma: Just-War Ideology in Buddhist Sri Lanka* (2002). We are privileged to honor her memory and pleased to share her work with you. Pashaura Singh is a professor in the Department of Religious Studies at the University of California, Riverside. He has written a widely discussed study of Sikh scripture titled *The Guru Granth Sahib: Canon, Meaning, and Authority* (2000) and has edited several other books on Sikh history and identity.

The authors of the chapters on religions from the Near East that established an influential and important presence in South Asia are equally distinguished scholars and teachers. T. M. Luhrmann successfully bridges several academic fields as a member of both the Committee on the History of Culture and the Committee on Human Development at the University of Chicago. Her books include *The Good Parsi* (1996). Shalva Weil teaches at The Hebrew University in Jerusalem. She has completed several studies of the Bene Israel and has edited a beautiful volume on *India's Jewish Heritage: Ritual, Arts, and Life-Cycle* (2002b). M. Thomas Thangaraj was born in South India and is a professor in the Candler School of Theology at Emory University in Atlanta. One of his most engaging and creative books has the title *The Crucified Guru: An Experiment in Cross-Cultural Christology* (1994). Peter Gottschalk teaches at Wesleyan University and conducts research in India on the confluence of religious cultures. His book *Beyond Hindu and Muslim: Multiple Identity in Narratives from Village India* (2000) is a landmark study. William Garlington is an independent scholar who has written on proselytizing and the progress of the Bahā'ī faith in the Malwa region in Central India.

The unequal length of the chapters in this book may seem to be unconventional but it is by design. It is intended to reflect the differences in historical depth of presence and in the number of contemporary adherents among the traditions treated by our authors. To allot an equal number of pages to each tradition in order to create a formal balance in the book would be to mislead the reader. All the religious traditions introduced in this book have an intrinsic importance and merit one's respect, but each of them so far has enjoyed a differential degree of influence in South Asia. The design of the book represents this fact by chapter length.

Because the book is an introduction that is intended to serve students in a first course of study of the religions of South Asia and to be understandable to intelligent general readers, the chapters in Parts One and Two are free from long digressions into detailed accounts of currently unresolved arguments among scholar-specialists concerning category formation, prehistory, alternative chronologies of events and epochs, and other heavily theoretical or metatheoretical issues. These are endemic to academic life and of utmost importance, but we believe that they are best appreciated after the student has had an opportunity to master the new vocabulary required for meaningful study of religion in South Asia. Each instructor will have her or his own preferences about how and when to share with students a selection of ongoing problems and alternative perspectives that are debated at scholarly conferences and in academic journals. Authors of the chapters in Parts One and Two each present a 'good to think with' prototype or first model of a tradition, which is suitable for an introductory or survey course, although the book may have a place in intermediate and advanced courses, too. The model versions of the traditions that are introduced in this book are not quite Max Weber's heuristic device of the 'ideal type' but have a similar purpose. They offer a place to begin one's study and a clear image of what one is studying.

Every beginning student and advanced scholar knows, without being told, that first impressions must later be revised on the basis of deeper acquaintance and more mature experience. Near the end of the academic term, or at any point the instructor or student may prefer, the chapter in Part Three is available as a resource for critical discussion at a more advanced level. Its author is Carl Olson who teaches at Allegheny College. He is an award-winning teacher who edited the book *Theory and Method in the Study of Religion: Theoretical and Critical Readings* (2003). Among his many other books are *The Indian Renouncer and Postmodern Poison: A Cross-Cultural Encounter* (1997), *Indian Philosophers and Postmodern Thinkers: Dialogues on the Margins of Culture* (2002), and *The Different Paths of Buddhism: A Narrative-Historical Introduction* (2005).

The coeditors are happy to welcome you to these pages and are confident that the book will reward your careful study. Sushil Mittal teaches at James Madison University, directs its Mahatma Gandhi Center for Global Nonviolence, and is founding editor of the *International Journal of Hindu Studies* (1997–). Gene Thursby teaches at the University of Florida. They shared responsibility for revising this book's chapter on Hindu Dharma (first drafted by John Grimes) and earlier coedited *The Hindu World* (2004), which is another book that brought together new writing by teacher-scholars from several nations.

Recommendations for student readers

If this is your first opportunity to study religions in an academic setting, please be patient with yourself, your instructor, and your classmates. The point of view from which you will be taught may turn out to be unfamiliar and perhaps even surprising to you. Academic study of religion involves learning a lot of facts and an ability to organize data for later retrieval, but it also invites repeated (even if tentative) acts of interpretation and theorizing. Tolerance for diversity is needed for these tasks due to disparate sources of information, the variety of perspectives that can come into play, and the range of unresolved issues that are encountered.

The first challenge when beginning the study of religions is to find workable ways to ground and orient yourself in relation to the long list of new terms that you must learn to use. John Hick, an accomplished British scholar of philosophy of religion, acknowledges this challenging feature of the study of religions:

> Any discussion of religion in its plurality of forms is inevitably beset by problems of terminology. Each tradition has its own vocabulary, expressing its own system of concepts; and whilst these overlap with those of other traditions, so that there are all manner of correspondences, parallels, analogies and structural similarities, yet each set of terms is only fully at home in its own particular linguistic environment. We have very little in the way of a tradition-neutral religious vocabulary.
>
> (2004: 9)

A closely related reason for the need to get grounded and stay oriented while you study is that when religious worlds that are new to you begin to come into clear focus, some features of them are likely to seem intriguing and desirable and others disgusting and repulsive. You may begin to see previously unknown ways to understand and inhabit the world that could seem to you amazingly plausible or absurdly impossible. Either could be upsetting. Hick notes: 'New knowledge and new ideas do, unfortunately, often cause real mental and emotional distress; but this is not a valid reason for rejecting them' (2004: xl). Nor, we might add, is it a valid reason for accepting them.

Finally, there is another level of challenge when engaging in the academic study of religion. It can be summed up in the question of what to do with one's own faith-based positions and personal ethical commitments. Hick addresses that level of challenge, and makes it all the more sharp, when he writes:

> There is no one religion whose adherents stand out as morally and spiritually superior to the rest of the human race. (If anyone claims such a superiority for their own religious community, the onus of proof, or of argument, is clearly upon them.)
>
> (2004: xxvi)

Whether you can and should 'put your own preferences in a box' to be opened only after some period of time, perhaps after the end of the academic term, is a question you ought to ask yourself.

One respected approach to the study of religion does ask its practitioners to become and to remain entirely neutral about what they study. Sometimes called the *phenomenology of religion*, it requires the student and scholar to suspend judgement, to put their own commitments in brackets (called technically the *phenomenological epoché*), in order to engage in unprejudiced study of what may be radically different from their local, familiar, and personally held values.

A more recent approach to academic study of religion, and one that proceeds from an assumption that the requirements of the phenomenology of religion are unsuitable and perhaps impossible, can be labeled for convenience the *critical-theory* or the *postmodernist study of religion.* A root assumption of this kind of approach is that each point of view, preference, and practice inevitably carries with it *political assumptions and implications.* Critical theorists and postmodernists typically express doubt that empathy with the subject under study, which is a second aim of the phenomenology of religion, is any more appropriate than phenomenology's (perhaps impossible) ideal of pure neutrality. Critical theorists claim that every position either openly displays an evident agenda or masks a hidden agenda, and they expect us to ask of ourselves: What is my agenda as I participate in this study? Equally they want us to ask of whatever topic or subject matter is under study: What agenda is at work there? What does it *privilege*, what does it *problematize*, and who or what is likely to *benefit* most from it?

Although this introductory essay can do no more than alert our student readers about these issues, we can recommend two short books that discuss these problems and perspectives in more detail and which are intended for the new student of religions. One is William E. Paden's *Religious Worlds: The Comparative Study of Religion* (1994) and the other is Malory Nye's *Religion: The Basics* (2003). Paden's book may seem more open to a phenomenological approach, while Nye's may seem more compatible with a postmodern way of analyzing religion. In any case, Part Three of this book will provide a further opportunity to become acquainted with some contemporary issues that divide the different approaches to the study of religion.

Remember: *get grounded* and *stay oriented* as you go on this imaginary journey through religious traditions that have developed in South Asia.

Part One

WHAT INDIA HAS GIVEN TO THE WORLD

2. Kṛṣṇa and the ten *avatāras* of Viṣṇu. Courtesy of the artist Nicola Barsaleau.

1

HINDU DHARMA

John Grimes, Sushil Mittal, and Gene Thursby

The tradition defined

What is Hinduism?

There is so much diversity among people who think of themselves as Hindu and such a variety of ways that they have preferred to live their lives that it is impossible to present a 'typical Hindu' who would make it really simple to learn about Hinduism. Instead it is important to take into account many kinds of Hindus and many images. Imagine a red silk *sāṛī* interwoven with gold threads, a homespun cotton *dhotī*, a designer suit and tie; an oval jet-black stone besmeared with crimson powder, a shining gold anthropomorphic image resplendent with precious jewels, a ten-headed goddess waving a bloody sword and riding a tiger; a village woman carrying an earthen pot brimming with water atop her head, a well-to-do New Delhi housewife drawing water into a pink porcelain bathtub, a tribal elder bathing in a river; a young man wearing a cord looped over his left shoulder and draped down his right side, another with divine names permanently inked into his skin, a naked mendicant covered only by ashes and his long matted hair; high castes, low castes, outcastes; beggars, kings, and renunciants; 325 languages expressed in more than 2,000 dialects and 25 scripts. Such diversity, and all of it can have something to do with living as a Hindu. These images may help us to see why definitions of Hindus and Hinduism can seem so baffling. *Hinduism is a complex set of interrelationships among many sorts of people, belief systems, and practices rather than a single uniformly structured, bureaucratically organized, and centrally codified religion.*

A student who is an outsider to Hinduism is likely to think about it on the basis of a Christian or Muslim model of religion. Outsiders seem to have given Hinduism its name, too. But naming by outsiders has been typical of most major religions, including Christianity. (Islam was a term revealed to the Prophet Muḥammad, and so it is an exception.) No Hindu word corresponds exactly to the term 'religion,' and whoever or whatever should be considered responsible for 'inventing Hinduism' (which is how some contemporary or 'postmodern' Western scholars refer to the question of its origin) is a matter of ongoing debate (Haan 2005; Lorenzen 1999). Nevertheless most scholars continue to use the word 'Hinduism' as a general term to denote a constellation of South Asian religious thought and activity that includes an incredible variety of expression and may range from simple beliefs of uneducated folk through elaborate rituals of a priestly intelligentsia to the transcendent meditations of an accomplished mystic. Although many contrasting (in some instances competing, at times even conflicting) forms of belief and practice can be included within the category of Hinduism, in general Hindus suppose that what is essential for one human being in a specific situation and at a particular stage in their development need not be appropriate for another. As a result, the extent of Hindu diversity, complexity, and variety makes a complete and closed capsule definition, including all the features that could be found within the range of things usually considered Hindu, impossible to formulate. Therefore what we call 'Hinduism' in this chapter is an interpretation of the currently available record of the multifaceted ways in which hundreds of millions of human beings in the subcontinent of India, from ancient times to the present, have shaped their lives. In short, Hinduism like Americanism is a term that has been made to carry a variety of different meanings that range from the loftiest ideals to the lowliest forms of behavior. Like Americanism, Hinduism is also linked with a particular geographical place. From ancient times, Hindus made their home in South Asia on the subcontinent of India, and even today Hindus who live elsewhere in the world tend to look to India for models of religious life and for the sources of their spiritual traditions.

Hinduism is not unique, but it is unusual among the world's major religions in having neither an identified founder nor a single defining creed, neither a central authority nor a fixed pantheon, neither a universally accepted scripture nor a seamless system of beliefs. Since neither the Muslim nor Christian model of religion fits it, modern scholars repeatedly comment on the *difference* of Hinduism. Wilfred Cantwell Smith has done so in a way that has been particularly influential: 'Many Christians and many Muslims have come to believe that there is one true Christianity and one true Islam. Hindus, on the other hand, have gloried in diversity. One of their basic and persistent affirmations has been that there are as many aspects of the truth as there are persons to perceive it' (1963: 66). More recently, Heinrich von Stietencron contributed to this line of commentary on what makes Hinduism a different and difficult category to grasp:

> What we call 'Hinduism' is a geographically defined group of distinct but related religions, that originated in the same region, developed under similar socioeconomic and political conditions, incorporated largely the same traditions, influenced each other continuously, and jointly contributed to the Hindu culture. Therefore it is only by distinguishing the various Hindu religions from 'Hinduism' that comparability with other historical religions can be ensured.
>
> (1989: 20)

Organizationally, if not theologically, Hinduism is more similar to Judaism than to either Islam or Christianity. Russell T. McCutcheon has remarked that 'all we seem to have is a host of differing Judaisms all talking *with* each other' (2005: 27; emphasis in original). Academic research has shown again and again, however, that the popular impression that there is a unified, uniform, and unanimous Christian or Muslim religion is mistaken when viewed in light of the evidence of history, the complex variations among the actual lives of Christians or Muslims, and the contemporary discussions about how to interpret the sources of those religions that currently involve their own scholars, spiritual leaders, and scriptural commentaries.

So Hinduism is multifaceted as well as characterized by diversity. It is a category that encompasses religion, philosophy, and interrelated ways of life that form a complete civilization. Leaders in the 'Hindu Renaissance' of the nineteenth and twentieth centuries proposed that Hinduism could serve the world as an example of a universal framework for religious and spiritual pluralism. Yet no concise substantive definition of Hinduism has proven to be wholly satisfactory, in part because the various students of Hinduism, including Hindus themselves, tend to place their emphasis on different aspects of the whole.

Despite its daunting variety, ever since the nineteenth century, influential Hindus have asserted the identity and unity of Hinduism in a successful effort to establish it as a major world religion with the same status as Judaism, Christianity, and Islam. The question that must inevitably be asked is whether any key features in the comprehensive phenomenon known as Hinduism can be identified; and, if so, whether they would be evident only to Hindu 'insiders' or whether non-Hindu 'outsiders' would recognize them, too. In the next section of this chapter we will introduce some characteristic features that we believe will help to organize your study of Hinduism.

As for the origin of the term, the earliest use of 'Hindu' according to the best evidence currently available was in about 500 BCE as the Persian equivalent for the Sanskrit word 'Sindhu.' Sindhu was the ancient Vedic name for a major river but also came to denote the people who lived on or beyond the Sindhu River as well as the region itself. In the fourth century BCE, with the arrival of the army of Alexander (356–323 BCE), the word 'Sindhu' entered Greek as 'Indikoi' and Latin as 'Indus.' The names of India and the Indus River are derived from these words. In the late 1700s British writers began to use the terms 'Hindu' to refer to people in North India and 'Hinduism' to denote the religious beliefs, rituals, cultural values, and social institutions given shape by the high-caste Brāhmaṇs. More recently the term 'Hinduism' has been appropriated by the majority of people in India itself, first as part of an attempt to establish an independent national identity in opposition to the British colonial empire and currently as an expression of religious and cultural self-understanding.

Because Hindu organizational structure does not converge on a single center, interpretation of Hindu scripture is not dominated by one exclusively 'correct' method, and the construction of Hindu religious ideas is not determined by a universally affirmed body of incontrovertible dogma – considerable differences in ideas and practices are generally accepted. Hindus tend to begin their lives with the beliefs they have inherited and then retain them or adopt ones that better fit them. The many manifestations of divinity known to Hindus tend to be considered complementary to one another rather than inevitably in conflict with one another. Moreover, Hindus tend to distinguish themselves from other insiders within Hinduism as well as from non-Hindu outsiders on the basis of practice (orthopraxy) before belief (orthodoxy), and this tendency can diminish the disruptive potential of conceptual and doctrinal differences. Participation in some ritual activities and admission to some religious sites, however, are likely to be limited to specific categories of people on the basis of their heritage, initiation, or religious preparation.

Characteristic features and key terms

Even though the category called Hinduism contains such a diversity of views, beliefs, and practices that it is impossible to present all of them in this chapter, there are a few that may be considered characteristic features.

Authority of the Veda

Perhaps the most generally accepted criterion of Hinduism is the recognition of a large body of ancient literature, originally oral in character (thus known as *śruti*, 'that which is heard'), composed in Sanskrit and known as the Veda or Vedas. The Veda is regarded as sacred text, as revelation, as an absolute authority that reveals unassailable truth. At the same time, however, the Veda's content has long been practically unknown to most Hindus, and it is seldom drawn upon directly for information or advice. It is venerated from a distance and serves as what may be termed 'an authoritative source of Hindu self-understanding.' Anyone who rejects the Veda's authority is called Nāstika (and this includes the Cārvākas [Materialists], Buddhists, and Jainas) and is regarded as unfaithful to the root tradition and thereby heterodox.

Dharma

Dharma is a pivotal concept around which a Hindu's self-understanding revolves. Its meanings and uses exemplify not only what Hinduism is, its identity, but also explain the tradition's tensions, changes, reinterpretations, and diversity. Further, there is an elastic coherence in the term that reflects the elusive yet undeniable coherence of Hinduism itself. There is not one privileged understanding of *dharma* but a complex network of interactions and tensions between different usages. Each use of the term is indebted to, oriented around, and reflects traditional orthodox Brāhmaṇical usage. This brings us back to the necessity of the Veda, for *dharma* is that which can be learned only from the Veda and justified through the Veda.

Traditionally, *dharma* (which can be glossed loosely as 'religion') is what the Veda reveals. The meaning of the term includes such ideas as 'truth,' 'ethics,' 'duty,' 'law,' 'cosmic order,' and 'righteousness.' Literally, *dharma* is 'what holds together,' and thus it is the basis of all order, whether natural, cosmic, social, or moral. It is the power that makes things what they are. This idea contains the implication that what a Hindu does is more important than what a Hindu believes. Thus, by means of ritual (dharmic) actions, Vedic culture sought to create, reinvigorate, nourish, and maintain cosmic order. Eventually, with the development of classical Hinduism, not just specific rituals but every human action was said to contribute to the maintenance of cosmic and social order. *Dharma*, when adhered to, was expected to yield a long, robust life full of happiness and blessings.

A major implication of *dharma* is that the ideal human society is fundamentally hierarchical. Everyone has a place, and things do not just happen, they happen justly. People differ from one another, and these differences are both distinctive and defining. People have different aptitudes, predilections, and abilities. In regard to social position, there are carefully circumscribed castes or classes (*varṇa-dharma*) characterized by particular social functions that generate a horizontal view of society. In addition, there are stages of life (*āśrama-dharma*) that support one's personal development vis-à-vis one's vertical ascent toward liberation from the cycle of births, deaths, and rebirths or *saṃsāra*. This social order is *varṇāśrama-dharma*. There is also *sanātana-dharma* ('eternal religion'), *sva-dharma* ('one's own duty'), *āpad-dharma* ('law in circumstances of calamity'), *yuga-dharma* ('law in the context of a particular epoch or time period'), and *sādhāraṇa-dharma* ('general obligations'). All these various *dharma*s acknowledge and address the fact that humans have different abilities, aptitudes, and responsibilities, and thus *dharma* specifies a variety of ways of being, spiritual paths, and worldviews, each of which is in itself a valid way to foster the eventual fulfillment of an appropriately human religious destiny.

For the ordinary Hindu, the main aims of worldly life require conforming to social and ritual duties and to traditional rules of conduct for one's caste, family, and profession. Such requirements constitute an individual's *dharma*, one's own part in the broader order and fundamental equilibrium in society, nature, and the cosmos. As such, *dharma* involves the ongoing maintenance of the social and cosmic order. Until quite recently it was assumed that *dharma* could be protected or violated only by Hindus because they are subject by birth to its provisions. Those outside the *varṇāśrama-dharma* system, and thus non-Hindu, had neither the obligation nor the right to uphold it. For Hindus, *dharma* is so central that Hindu Dharma is actually a more fitting label for this great tradition than Hinduism. In this chapter the term 'Hinduism' serves as a rough equivalent to Hindu Dharma for the convenience of the reader.

Mokṣa

The assumption that in order for an individual to fulfill his or her destiny it is necessary to preserve, perpetuate, and refine the physical world (uphold *dharma*) and to achieve liberation or an ultimate freedom from bondage (achieve *mokṣa*) is central to Hinduism. Hindu teachings seek to harmonize these two demands. They complete one another yet are in tension with one another. Human beings are governed by physical needs and are social animals who seek to live in harmony with other beings, and yet they are spiritual souls who are destined at some point to transcend all physical and social limitations. A spiritual orientation is a natural consequence of the Hindu worldview, which assumes that the sacred is a given, immanent in the universe. Because of this, every action, person, place, or thing, whether ostensibly secular or sacred, has religious implications. *Dharma* provides a temporal perspective, while *mokṣa* (release or liberation from an otherwise endless cycle of birth, death, and rebirth) provides an eternal solution.

Saṃsāra *and* karma

The tension between *dharma* and *mokṣa* is played out against a background of two important concepts: *karma* and *saṃsāra*. *Karma* literally means 'actions,' and involves the idea that all actions have predictable effects. In a general sense, the idea of *karma* teaches that each person is ultimately responsible for every action he or she performs. Every action produces its necessary result, and every cause produces an effect. 'As one sows so one reaps.' Thus the idea entails that the present condition, character, and peculiar circumstances of a person are the result of his or her past deeds. There are no accidents or coincidences, but *karma* is not a doctrine of fatality or despair. Each action when performed creates a residue, a trace, as well as a dispositional tendency. There is a perfect conservation of the energy of the cosmos. Thus, each action one performs contributes to forming one's character, and even as one is responsible for the person one is, so can one create the person one would like to become.

Saṃsāra is the idea that one's present life is only the most recent in a long chain of lives extending far into the past. *Saṃsāra* is 'the cycle of birth, death, and rebirth' and implies that each individual has lived countless lives, none in his or her current identity or form, all of which have some bearing on the present life. According to this theory, each individual incarnation is but a brief existence in a seemingly endless drama spanning thousands if not millions of lives, both human and nonhuman.

Karma is the factor that determines the condition into which a being is reborn in one form or another. The whole process of reincarnation is called *saṃsāra*. Any earthly rebirth is viewed as cyclic, and all worldly existence is subject to the cycle. *Karma*, acting like a clockwork that always winds itself up while running down, binds individuals to the world and compels them to go through an endless series of (re)births and (re)deaths. *Karma* is indissolubly connected with traditional Hindu views of society and earthly life, and any social interaction results in the mutual exchange of auspicious and inauspicious *karma*. It has given rise to the belief that any misfortune is the effect of *karma*, or one's own deeds, and to the conviction that the course of world history is conditioned by collective *karma*. The idea provides a particularly effective rationale for both the apparent inequalities of life and its seemingly random anomalies.

While the concepts of *karma* and *saṃsāra* seem to provide an attractive explanation for the otherwise undeserved sufferings and unmerited blessings of life, when viewed from the perspective of *mokṣa*, they are regarded as negative or at least insufficient. That is because they bind the individual to an ever-repeating and never-ending cycle of births and deaths, pleasures and pains, and it is only complete transcendence, freedom, or liberation (*mokṣa*) that is a totally sufficient resolution of all the suffering of temporal life.

Paths to liberation

Counterbalancing an individual's temporal social obligations (*dharma*) is his or her eternal destiny or liberation (*mokṣa*). According to a Hindu worldview, the universe, society, and all things within it are temporal, and one day or another will pass away. Thus to seek eternality in the finite is doomed to failure from the start. It is a given in most subtraditions within Hinduism that every individual is, in some sense or other, a part of the divine. That is one's birthright, and all individuals will, by the end of some lifetime sometime, come to experience it. Although exclusive dedication to the search for *mokṣa* has never been the goal of more than a small minority of Hindus, liberation has been a religious ideal that affects all lives. *Mokṣa* determines not only the hierarchical values of Hindu social institutions and religious teachings and practices but also the function of what one must do to find true fulfillment and what one has to realize by direct experience in order to escape from *saṃsāra* and reach spiritual freedom. Worldly life is not finally a cause for regret or resignation. If dharmically lived, it is a preparation for liberation.

Hindus differ in their preferences concerning a suitable way or path to *mokṣa*. Traditionally three paths (*trimārga*) to liberation have been presented as paradigmatical. These are: *karma-mārga* ('path of duties'), the selfless performance of ritual and social obligations; *jñāna-mārga* ('path of knowledge'), the use of meditative nondual wisdom to gain an experiential supraintellectual insight into one's identity with the Absolute; and *bhakti-mārga* ('path of devotion'), devotion to a personal form of God in which the divinity and the devotee remain ever distinct and yet so intimately connected and mutually involved that the distinction may become difficult to discern or remember. These paths are regarded as suited to various types of people, and what is appropriate for one may not be for another. It should be noted that in addition to these three main ways to liberation, there are also many other paths that include yogic, tantric, mantric, ascetic, and synthetic disciplines. In other words, there are as many paths to liberation, strictly speaking, as there are human individuals.

One and many gods

Hindus know innumerable visible and invisible deities. In early Vedic hymns as well as in the classical Hindu pantheon, one meets with the names of countless gods. However we may try to account for this situation – whether we suppose that these gods were originally personifications of natural phenomena, or part of an ancient unphilosophical polytheism, or a sophisticated mystical expression of the One Absolute (and there are many adherents to all these theories) – Hinduism does not insist that everyone must acknowledge any one form of God exclusively. The basic idea, according to some ancient teachings and many contemporary Hindus, is that there is a Supreme Being that may be worshipped in various forms. Early sources for this are in the *Ṛg Veda*, 'The one Being the sages contemplate in many ways' (10.114.5) and 'The one Being the wise call by many names . . .' (1.164.46). That idea seems to be based upon the recognition of the diversity of the human mind as well as the potential for different levels of spiritual development and understanding in each individual.

Most Hindus today worship God as Viṣṇu or Śiva or some form of the Goddess or one of the so-called minor deities. When a devotee chooses to worship one particular form of the divine, the chosen deity is known as an individual's 'favorite or personal god' (*iṣṭadevatā*). This *iṣṭadevatā* becomes the object of the devotee's love and adoration, satisfying his or her spiritual longing.

Brahman-ātman

The concept of God in a particular form (*īśvara, deva*) is a pervasive feature of Hinduism. The ancient Upaniṣads, part of the Veda, revealed a different concept of God as Brahman or the Absolute (which means unqualified or surpassing every description). Brahman can be evoked only indirectly by metaphors and analogies and yet is no different from the inmost self (*ātman*) within each human being and all that lives. This idea has profoundly influenced literature and philosophy worldwide, but if one were to ask most Hindus who or what Brahman is, they would have no clue. Their understanding of God is focused on a particular name and form.

To use figures of speech, there is an unborn, uncreated, eternal, infinite, all-embracing divine principle, which, comprising being and nonbeing, is the sole reality, ultimate cause and foundation, source, and goal of all existence. The ultimate reality is called Brahman and is conceived in both a cosmic (personal) and acosmic (impersonal) mode. Perhaps the most well-known metaphor for Brahman in its acosmic mode, as described in the Upaniṣads, is that it is Existent (*satyam*), Knowledge (*jñānam*), Infinite (*anantam*) or Being (*sat*), Consciousness (*cit*), and it is Bliss (*ānanda*). Further, the transcendental spirit that pervades the cosmos is equated, in some sense or other, with the self within (*ātman/antar-ātman*). This teaching is encapsulated in 'great sayings' (*mahāvākya*) of the Upaniṣads: 'That thou art' (*tat tvam asi*) and 'I am the Absolute' (*aham brahmasmi*). These affirm that every living being has inherent divinity that cannot be destroyed; and as such, though an individual may wander in *saṃsāra* for millions if not billions of incarnations, its destiny is to experience eventually the supreme goal of life. In other words, all life is sacred.

Avidyā *and* māyā

The Upaniṣads teach that ignorance (*avidyā*) is the root cause of suffering and bondage. Each individual 'incarnation of immortality' tends to confuse that which, essentially, he or she is with that which he or she is not and is thus ignorant of true spiritual condition and ultimate destiny. In a sense, it is similar to the Christian concept of 'original sin.' *Māyā* is the concept employed to explain how this mistaken identification of the immortal self with the physical body and mind takes place and also to explain the creation of the universe and everything in it. The Upaniṣads contain two main views regarding *māyā*: first, it is the mysterious, wondrous, bedazzling, deceptive power of God (in which case, the world and its phenomena are considered real), and, second, it is the principle of appearance, the force that brings about the illusory manifestation of the universe. As such, it (as well as all its effects) is considered to be neither real nor nonreal.

History

Before the first millennium CE there is no reliable historiography regarding Hinduism. Chronologies are difficult to establish. With this in mind, one may make a simplified outline of the history of Hinduism in terms of five periods of development that overlap with one another and are not chronologically precise.

First, there is the *Formative Period* that combines the Pre-Vedic Age (the Indus Valley/Harappā civilization flourishing from about 2500 BCE to 1500 BCE) and the age of the Vedic Āryans (2000–800 BCE). Together these hardly constitute a well-documented historical era, but it was a period when the roots of Hinduism were developing. The general themes, if not the precise pattern, were developed there and, to this day, play a major role in Hinduism. In addition to Vedic adherents, the intellectual climate of that time included skeptics, naturalists, determinists, indeterminists, materialists, and nosoul theorists.

The second period is the *Upaniṣadic Age* (*c.* 800 to 400 BCE). The Upaniṣads are generally described as marking the transition from an emphasis on ritualism (*karmakāṇḍa*) to philosophic thought (*jñānakāṇḍa*). Another interpretation is that they were an attempt to recover the lost wisdom of the Vedas by means of meditation and spiritual experience. Using the ancient texts as an authority for their own intuitions, the Upaniṣads seers recovered old truths in new forms, expressing them in a language more intelligible to the age in which they lived. Veda became Vedānta. Although not systematic treatises, the mystical utterances of the Upaniṣads formed the theoretical foundations for much of what was to follow. They contain the great speculative themes regarding the nature of knowledge, God (Brahman), the universe, world-evolution and world-appearance, and the individual (*ātman*) and its destiny.

The third period is the *Classical Age* (400 BCE to CE 600), which includes the composition of the two great epics (*Rāmāyaṇa* and *Mahābhārata*), most of the Purāṇas (compilations of ancient myths, legends, and history) the law books (Dharmaśāstras and Dharmasūtras); the early beginnings of the development of the great devotional traditions of Vaiṣṇavism, Śaivism, and Śāktism; and the condensation of the various philosophical systems (*darśana*) into aphorisms (*sūtra*). Successful heterodox reform movements, Jainism and Buddhism, both arose and developed during this period, which also saw the working out of what are now known as the three traditional paradigmatic expressions of the supreme goal of life: world-affirmation (Vedic), world-negation (Upaniṣadic), and being in the world but not of it (*Bhagavad Gītā*).

The fourth period may be called the *Medieval Age* (CE 600 to 1600) and is characterized by three developments. It saw the flowering of devotion (*bhakti*) to the popular Hindu deities (Viṣṇu, Śiva, and the Devī) corresponding with construction of temples as well as the composition of devotional and poetic literature in Sanskrit and in regional vernacular languages. Second, this was the period of the systematization of Hindu philosophy into six orthodox philosophical schools (*darśana*) with their commentaries and independent treatises that explain, elucidate, and expand upon the original teachings. Third, this period saw the flourishing of the Tantric tradition, one that, though not necessarily opposed to the Vedic tradition, appears as a revelation differing from the Veda in having its own rites and practices.

Lastly, the fifth period, the *Modern Age* (1600 to present), includes the rise and fall of two great conquering empires, the Muslim Mughal and the Christian British, as well as the establishment of India as a nation-state. Hinduism experienced its Renaissance in the nineteenth century, and the twentieth century saw the spread of Hinduism as a major world religion around the globe.

Origins

Scholars generally agree that Hinduism (incorporating its various subtraditions) has grown from two ancient cultural complexes, the Indus Valley civilization (*c.* 2500–1500 BCE) and the Āryan culture (*c.* 1800–1500 BCE). There continues to this day to be a heated controversy concerning the relationship between these two ancient cultures. The received theory, which is still supported by many scholars, maintains that as the ancient, indigenous Indus Valley civilization declined, it was superseded by the Āryan culture that was brought into India by migrating Indo-European people who had originated in or passed through the Caucasus region of Central Asia. The main alternative theory is that the Āryan culture is evidenced in Indus Valley civilization itself and was not introduced into India by migrants from outside the subcontinent.

The issue of Hinduism's origins has far-reaching consequences not only for Indologists but also for archaeologists, linguists, politicians, and modern Hindus; and it is thus fraught with tension. It is no wonder that modern scholars are so interested in, and so passionately divided over, the origins of Hinduism. However, whether the Āryans came from outside India, most scholars agree that Hindu tradition(s) developed from a fusion of ancient elements that incorporated various beliefs and practices of the peoples who resided in India as they interacted and eventually formed what is now called Hinduism.

Indus Valley civilization

The earliest known advanced culture in the subcontinent is the Indus Valley or Harappā civilization, urban-based and flourishing from about 2500 BCE to 1500 BCE (though its roots could reach back into the Neolithic period, 7000–6000 BCE). Mohenjodāro and Harappā are the two best-known of its cities and are among the several sites unearthed by archaeologists. In 1921 John Marshall (1931) began excavations in the Indus River Valley (now in Pakistan) and uncovered planned cities that had sophisticated systems for water delivery and waste removal, residential areas with parallel streets, large grain storehouses, great baths, fire-altars, stone sculptures, what appear to be religious ritual centers, seals and amulets, and a yet to be deciphered script. In a recently excavated citadel mound in Kalibagan, a series of raised brick platforms, fire-altars, and a bathing platform situated next to a well have been uncovered. The entire complex seems to indicate that some sort of religious ritual, complete with purificatory water rites and sacrificial offerings, was performed there.

Excavations have uncovered large numbers of terracotta figurines and steatite seals. Scholars have surmised, due to the large number of them found, that some of the figurines were used in ritual worship. Many of the statuettes appear to be of a mother goddess, and a small number represent a bull, though the bull appears more frequently on the many steatite seals. A few seals represent a seated male figure in what may be called a *yoga*-like posture. He seems to have three faces, and on one seal he is surrounded by animals, including deer, antelope, rhinoceros, elephant, and buffalo. On his head is what may be a hat with two horns, with a plantlike object protruding between them. One interpretation is that this male (god) may have been a prototype of Śiva, the great *yogin* and lord of animals. However, these 'Paśupati' seals do not indubitably have three faces, nor is it certain that the posture is yogic. Several stones that appear to be *liṅga*s (an outward symbol of the formless Reality and a 'mark' of Lord Śiva) have also been unearthed in the excavations, though no direct link to Śiva is evident and some scholars speculate that these may have been pieces used in a board game. In the absence of texts that can be translated, the meaning of the archaeological or material remains tends to be ambiguous.

Many seals seem to illustrate religious and legendary themes, but these cannot be interpreted conclusively. There is evidence, however, of the worship of sacred trees or of the divinities believed to reside in them. Numerous seals depict the theme of a spirit emerging from a Pīpala tree with worshippers standing in front of it with little plants. Though we cannot be certain that this is a direct prototype of what developed in later Hinduism, it is noteworthy that the Pīpala tree continues to play an important role in Hinduism right down to the present day. Further, some seals depict a horned person emerging from the Pīpala tree with a row of seven figures standing in front of it. Again, Hinduism later identifies these seven with both the seven seers (*ṛṣi*) and the seven mothers (*matṛ*).

Many seals depict half-human, half-animal forms. Some depict half-human, half-tiger forms. Others depict half-bull, half-elephant forms. There are also seals showing combinations of lion, ram, elephant, bull, and even unicorn. Still other seals depict a *svāstika* and geometrical designs that resemble the rice-power drawings (*koḷam, raṅgolī*) that continue to be widely used by Hindus.

No building has been discovered at any Indus site that can be positively identified as a temple, but the Great Bath at Mohenjodāro probably was used for ritual purposes, as are the *ghāṭ*s (the steps leading down to a sacred river or temple tank) attached to later Hindu temples. The presence of bathrooms in most of the houses and the remarkable system of covered drains seems to indicate a high value placed on cleanliness and purity.

It is tempting to imagine an unbroken line of connection between the Indus Valley and contemporary Hinduism. However, caution is called for because there is insufficient unequivocal evidence to afford us certainty as to whether excavated remains contain the prototypes of what is significant in later Hinduism. Fire-altars and female figurines, horned deities, Pīpala trees, and *liṅga*s are certainly significant in later Hinduism. However, ritual purity, fertility, and female goddesses are common elements throughout the ancient world, while a steatite-seal image of a figure wrestling with a lion, which has been the object of competing interpretations, might equally be the Hindu god Narasiṃha, or the Hindu goddess Durgā battling with the buffalo-demon, or an image from the Mesopotamian epic of Gilgamesh.

The Indus Valley civilization collapsed rather suddenly around 1500 BCE. There is no consensus on why this happened. Some speculate that it was due primarily to environmental causes such as a great flood that led the Indus River to change its course. Others postulate that it was destroyed by invading Āryans or that an epidemic wiped out the population. Still others contend that its disappearance was a consequence of a combination of these factors.

Āryans

Sometime between about 2000 BCE and 1500 BCE, according to the received viewpoint, Āryans began migrating into the northern plains of India (although some scholars think the migration began as early as 6000 BCE and subsequently continued in several successive waves). Whether it was peaceful or hostile is the subject of much controversy. In either case, some of the migrating tribes stopped in Iran (where they gave their name to the region; 'Iran' etymologically means 'homeland of the Āryans'), while others continued into India where they destroyed (or were a factor in the destruction of) the Indus Valley civilization and became the dominant group. In India the name 'Āryan' took on a social connotation and meant 'noble ones' as distinct from the (non-noble) indigenous people who were subjugated. The migrating Āryans spoke an Indo-European language that developed into Vedic Sanskrit and eventually classical Sanskrit, the primary sacred language of Hinduism. They began to spread over the northern plains of India until they reached the Ganges region (which then became known as the 'Āryan homeland' or *āryāvarta*) and then eventually spread to South India. This is what the received theory supposes.

It is rarely disputed that Indo-Āryan culture has been the dominant culture in India for thousands of years. The disagreement is about where the Āryans originated. Two main theories have been proposed: the Āryan migration theory (which posits that the Indus Valley civilization was destroyed by invading Āryans) and what is sometimes called the cultural transformation theory (which proposes that the Āryan culture is an indigenous development of the Indus Valley civilization whose language was evolving for 8,000 to 10,000 years). Each of these theories is based on evidence derived from archaeology and linguistics. Wherever the Āryans originated, a key to our knowledge of their social structure, their activities, their philosophies, and their religion is found in the Veda.

Vedism and Brāhmaṇism

Āryans in the early Vedic period left few material remains, though they did leave the oral legacy called the Veda or Vedas. The Vedas are the most important surviving record for a diversified and cumulative tradition that most modern scholars say began to solidify somewhere around 1500 BCE. Like the imprecise term 'Hinduism' itself, thought and practices preserved by the Vedas are imprecisely known as 'Vedism' and 'Brāhmaṇism.' The defining mark of this period (1500 BCE to 400 BCE) is the Vedic canon, and its distinctive religious and social theories derived from duty (*dharma*). Vedic society seems to have been structured on the basis of an emerging version of caste (class) and stages of life (*varṇāśrama-dharma*) values. The authority of the Vedic canon lent these social systems legitimacy, persuasiveness, and longevity.

The terms 'Vedism' and 'Brāhmaṇism' are used to distinguish some ancient religious and social practices from alternative Tantric and sectarian forms that are based on a variety of non-Vedic texts. Religious life as reflected in Vedic tradition suggests the image of a journey, of an individual's progress on the path to Truth (*satyam/ṛtam*). Life involves action, both inner and outer sacrifice. The Vedic worldview is based on the belief in an inextricable coordination among nature, the human being, society, ritual, myth, and the divine. Each sphere influences every other sphere. Thus, by means of ritual, humans not only have a part to play in the maintenance of universal order, but they can also influence it, at both personal and cosmic levels.

Vedic texts do not refer to divine images or to permanent buildings designed as temples. Religious life was determined primarily by the interaction of two groups: a priestly group, organized around sacerdotal schools maintained through family and clan lines, and a warrior group, led by kings. The priests served as repositories of sacred lore, ritual technique, wisdom, and mysticism; and the governing warriors served as patrons of the rites and ceremonies of the priests. These two groups, ideally complementary but at times descending into rival interests, crystallized by late Vedic and Brāhmaṇic times into distinct classes: the Brāhmaṇs (priests) and the Kṣatriyas (warriors).

Brāhmaṇism developed from Vedism and, while remaining true to the Vedic worldview, modified and made room for religious and social practices of non-Vedic South Asian traditions. It is known as Brāhmaṇism because of the religious and legal importance it places on the Brāhmaṇ (priestly) class. It takes as sacred truth, in addition to the Veda, various law books (Dharmaśāstras and Dharmasūtras), the two epics (*Rāmāyaṇa* and *Mahābhārata*), and the major Purāṇas. Thus, while both Vedism and Brāhmaṇism accept the Veda as sacred, Brāhmaṇism also includes doctrines that do not specifically derive from the Vedas and therefore is ideologically more inclusive than Vedism. Some of these ideas find expression in various ritual practices such as temple and domestic worship (*pūjā*), in vegetarianism, in devotion, and in other non-Vedic themes that play important parts in later Hindu religious life and thought.

In short, Vedic/Brāhmaṇical tradition has played the role of 'master narrative,' setting the definitions and delineations regarding what is orthodox (or orthoprax) and what is heterodox.

Sectarian Hinduism

Sectarian Hinduism, also known as Medieval Hinduism, began to flourish around CE 600 and continued to flower until approximately CE 1600. It is characterized by devotional movements to locally known deities and the great Hindu deities (Viṣṇu, Śiva, and the Devī), with a corresponding construction of temples, both great and small. This period also saw the composition of poetic devotional literature in Sanskrit and in regional vernacular languages. Furthermore, this was the period of the systematization of Hindu philosophy into the six orthodox philosophical schools. Finally, in this period Hinduism saw the flourishing of Tantric traditions, not altogether opposed to the Vedic tradition but distinguished from it in having separate texts, rites, and practices.

Devotion (*bhakti*) to a God or Goddess in personal form has ancient roots and is a central theme in the *Bhagavad Gītā*, a text whose written version dates to at least 200 BCE. However, it was not until about CE 600 that the devotional revolution exploded onto the scene with the appearance of several South Indian saints who traveled on foot from temple to temple singing the praise of either Viṣṇu or Śiva. The Nāyaṉārs, the sixty-three Śaiva saints, and the Āḻvārs, the twelve Vaiṣṇava saints, inspired a many-sided shift in Hindu religion and culture with their exalted behavior and by expressing their devotion in the South Indian language of Tamil. The Tamil poet-saints were on fire with an intense love of God. It overflowed their hearts and expressed itself in their mystical poetic songs.

The twelve Āḻvārs ('one who has taken a deep plunge into the ocean of divinity') lived during the seventh to ninth centuries. In the *Bhāgavata Purāṇa*, it is said that the devotees of Lord Viṣṇu would appear in South India on the banks of rivers. These eleven men and one woman (Āṇṭāḷ), from high and low castes, spread Viṣṇu's glory through their songs and thus popularized the path of devotion. They addressed their lord in new and novel ways: as a lover, as a king, as a friend, as a brother, as a servant, as a mother, as immanent or easily accessible, and as remote and inaccessible. Their compositions are collected in the *Nālāyiram Divyaprabandham* (The Book of Four Thousand Divine Stanzas). Their ecstatic devotion spread throughout India.

As part of the legacy of the Āḻvārs, five Vaiṣṇava (devotion to Viṣṇu) philosophical traditions (*sampradāya*) emerged that were based on the teachings of five *guru*s: Rāmānuja, Madhva, Vallabha, Nimbārka, and Caitanya. The Vaiṣṇava traditions include the Śrīvaiṣṇavas of Tamil Nadu whose center is the Śriraṅgam temple; the Gauḍīya Vaiṣṇavas of Bengal, Orissa, and Vrndavana; the Viṭhobā devotees in Maharashtra (whose teachings are derived from Maharashtra's great saints, Jñāneśvar, Nāmdev, Tukārām, Samārth Rāmdās, Eknāth, Muktābāī, Janābāī, and so on); the Rāma tradition of Ayodhyā and Janakpur, along with the Rāmānandī Order; and spilling over and beyond the boundaries of Vaiṣṇava devotion is the northern Sant tradition, a loose amalgam of devotional poets who include Mīrābāī, Sūrdās, Kabīr, Nānak, and Tulsīdās. Comparable Śaiva traditions include the Pāśupata, Lākulīśa, Kāpālika, Kashmir Śaiva, Kaula, Śaiva Siddhānta, and Liṅgayata.

Many of the Vaiṣṇava and Śaiva saints traveled extensively on foot in South India, and to some extent in the north, visiting temples and singing the glories of the lord. Thus, not only devotion but also temple worship and pilgrimage began to become an important feature of the emerging Hindu tradition. Devotion to Kṛṣṇa (as the precocious cowherd boy as well as the *pūrna* or full *avatāra*) and to Rāma began to grow. (Over the succeeding centuries, these two have become the best-known and most widely worshipped of Hindu deities on the Indian Subcontinent, throughout Southeast Asia, and in the rest of the world.) Delight in devotional experiences, including uncontrollable joy, fainting, frenzy, trance, tears, chanting in the roadways, and ecstatic dancing, became common. The hierarchical status system correlated with distinctions based on caste and gender was called into question. The underlying assumption of the *bhakti* movement was that, although men and women may have differing inherited and prescribed duties and social positions, all human beings share the inherent duty to love and serve God.

The other major movement that contributed to the rise of the sectarian subtradition was the Tantric movement which arose outside the Vedic/Brāhmaṇical framework. In a broad sense, Tantra refers to a collection of symbols and practices of a ritualistic, sometimes magical, character that are used as means of reaching spiritual liberation or the realization of mundane goals. In a more narrow sense, Tantra denotes various heavily symbolic systems of rituals that are predominantly but not exclusively Śākta (follower of Śakti), propounded by schools and lines of succession of spiritual *guru*s. They teach *sādhana* (self-effort, spiritual discipline, the way) by means of Kuṇḍalinī Yoga and the guided awakening of intense inner experiences.

Tantra is said to be appropriate for the present era in which seekers, trapped within the demeaning conditions of the Dark Age (Kali Yuga), are less able to perform the elaborate rituals of an earlier epoch. Advocates have claimed that Tantric *sādhana* can lead directly to liberation through initiation by a *guru* and instruction in a variety of techniques that employ *mantra*s ('sacred mystic sounds'), *yantra*s ('sacred geometric diagrams'), *mudrā*s ('hand gestures'), and yogic disciplines.

Hindu Tantra as a major sectarian phenomenon disappeared or went underground some 500 years ago except for the Śrī Vidyā tradition which was maintained by Brāhmaṇs and structured to parallel the teachings of the Veda. Most other forms of Tantra fell victim to excessive independent development. Their teachings flouted traditional orthodoxy and orthopraxy; their practioners seemed to think of themselves as if they were a secret spiritual elite that could freely engage in antisocial behavior; and their spiritual methods became too complicated for the common person to comprehend. Tantra seemed to become subversive of widely shared traditions and family values and to hold few direct answers for the ordinary person's daily concerns and aspirations.

On the other hand, Tantra is an aspect of Hinduism that is generally neglected, misrepresented, and disparaged as if it were no more than a medley of magic, superstition, and revolting rituals. Tantric teachings themselves distinguish between a right-handed path (*dakṣiṇācāra*) and a left-handed path (*vāmācāra*). The right-handed path is a discipline open to everyone, regardless of sex, caste, or age and consists primarily in the use of *mantra*s, *yantra*s, and rituals based upon maps of the subtle body. The left-handed path, on the other hand, is open only to certain extraordinary and perhaps heroic-minded individuals. It centers on a ritual in which the initiated adept partakes of five forbidden substances (alcohol, meat, illicit sexual union, parched grain, and fish), thereby transcending the dividing lines between the sacred and the profane, the prescribed and the forbidden, the pure and the impure, with the intent to become free from the bonds of conventional society as well as spiritually liberated.

Cosmos

Deities

In early Vedic hymns as well as in the later Hindu pantheon, one meets with the names and forms of countless gods and goddesses. It may be helpful to remember the Vedic maxim that 'the one Being the wise call by many names.' That would suggest that at the center of the Hindu pantheon is a single God/Goddess or Absolute. Hindus may refer to it (he or she) as the lord *(īśvara* or *bhagvan*), That (*tat*), the One (*tad ekam*), the Absolute (Brahman), or by any one of a number of other names. The One is often identified with one of the great pan-Hindu theistic forms: Viṣṇu, Śiva, or the Devī. Then, on another level, Viṣṇu may be worshipped in one of his *avatāra*s (of which Rāma and Kṛṣṇa are the most popular), or Śiva may be worshipped in one of his many manifestations, and so on. Finally, the pantheon explodes into a burst of names, forms, legends, and manifestations, each of which is a distinctive experience and explanation of how the One is manifest locally, here and now. The point should also be borne in mind that each and every manifestation is the presence, not only individually but also in its entirety, of the One. Though Hindu mythology loves to rank, describe, and thereby delimit the divine, according to a Vedic maxim the supreme truth is simply that God is God.

The Vedic texts do not delineate a single fixed pantheon. Further, the frequently used Vedic term '*deva*' is not a direct and exclusive reference to God as a single ultimate reality but to a divine being or divine power in general. Etymologically, the term implies 'shining, exalted' and refers to everything supernatural: all forms, powers, emotions, meters, melodies, and books, any and everything that requires a supernatural explanation. The gods (*deva*) are usually referred to as 'the thirty-three,' though the *Mahābhārata* (1.1.39) proclaims that there are 33,333 deities, others say to multiply that number a thousandfold. The sage Yājñavalkya (*Bṛhadāraṇyaka Upaniṣad* 3.9.1) replies to the question how many gods there are as '3003; 303; 33; 3; 1,' in connection with the three levels, realms, or worlds – the celestial/heavenly/causal-vastness-spiritual; atmospheric/mid-region/sky/subtle-mental-cosmogonical; terrestrial/earthly/material-physical-external – and depending upon which of the three was their primary location and sphere of activity. The *deva*s are simultaneously physical and psychological forces of nature, personifications of abstract ideas, living realities, and embodiments of a cosmic struggle between forces of order and chaos that plays out both in the universe and within each individual. For instance, Agni, the general term for 'fire,' is not merely the chemical process of oxidation and carbonization of organic matter but simultaneously a *deva*, the manifestation of a transcendent power. Where a mind with a modern scientific bent will see nothing but physical fire, a seer will sense a divine reality.

Among the most well known and most often mentioned of the gods are the following: Indra (to whom about a quarter of all the Ṛg Vedic hymns are addressed), cosmic power, god of the mid-region, strong, powerful, and warlike, whose thunderbolt slays the serpent Vṛta thereby liberating the obstructed waters and the sky; Agni (second most often mentioned and indispensable for the Vedic sacrifice), *deva* of fire, priest of the sacrifice, symbol of the divine will, the outer fire on the sacrificial altar as well as the inner fire of human aspiration, and the mediator between human beings and the gods; Varuṇa, god and guardian of the cosmic principle (*ṛta*), king and ruler of heaven and earth, lord of the vast consciousness, and protector of the truth that resides in the oceans; and Soma (the subject matter of the entire ninth book of the *Ṛg Veda*), god of ritual, the draught of immortality, the great object of priestly interest, and the juice of a plant (no longer known), the extraction and drinking of which formed the center and context of the Vedic ritual. Among other deities mentioned are (in alphabetical order) Aditi (the mother goddess), Aśvins (twin gods associated with healing), Dyaus (heaven), Maruts (the storm gods), Pṛthivī (the earth), Rudra (god of death and destruction), Sarasvatī (goddess of the divine word), Sūrya (the sun god), Uṣas (the dawn), Vāyu (the wind god), and Viṣṇu (the preserver god).

The functions of the Vedic *deva*s declined in significance as the external sacrifice decreased in importance. Vedic teachings were transformed by the appeal of the forest-dwelling sages of the Upaniṣads and may have been eclipsed by forms of popular piety that are evidenced in the Purāṇas. Today, although there have been some noteworthy attempts at Vedic revival, modern cultures generally have lost the ability to enter into the heart of the ancient mystic doctrine, and that has left the Vedic *deva*s largely misunderstood and tends to reduce the ancient tradition to obscurity and the object of ridicule. When the Vedic gods declined in importance, their place was taken by a more abstract ultimate reality (Brahman), on the one hand, and by the great popular theistic deities (Viṣṇu, Śiva, and the Devī), on the other.

In the Upaniṣads, the most characteristic answer to the question 'What is God?' is Brahman. The term 'Brahman,' is untranslatable but identified with the cosmic and acosmic, personal and impersonal, creator, sustainer and inner principle of the universe, and That, the one Absolute. When the One is associated with a generic title, it is designated God (*īśvara*) or lord (*bhagvan*). These titles then led to the development of particular names centering in Hindu subtraditions exclusively devoted to, for instance, Viṣṇu, Śiva, the Devī, and Gaṇeśa.

The emergence of the great theistic deities of classical Hinduism began with the appearance of Nārāyaṇa (Viṣṇu) and Śiva in some of the late Upaniṣads such as the *Śvetāśvatara* and the *Mahānārāyaṇa*. The idea of theism – that there is a personal, supreme, distinct God or Goddess who creates the universe, sustains it, and eventually dissolves it, and who has the power to bestow grace – grew with the epics and finally crystallized in the Purāṇas. The older Vedic deities like Agni, Indra, and Varuṇa and other Vedic *deva*s fell out of favor and were generally ignored except in the performance of Vedic rituals by Brāhmaṇ priests.

Viṣṇu

Viṣṇu (literally 'all-pervading') is worshipped by his followers (Vaiṣṇavas) as the Supreme Brahman, free from any trace of evil, possessing countless auspicious qualities of matchless excellence together with an omnipotent power to accomplish his will, who is the supreme ruler and controller, personal and loving, the material and efficient cause of the world, and the preserver of the universe. Viṣṇu takes five forms: supreme (*parā*), cosmic (*vyūha*), divine incarnations (*vihava* or *avatāra*), inner controller (*antaryāmi*), and in images (*arca*). Viṣṇu is one of the *deva*s in the *Ṛg Veda*, though it contains few references to him. However, as some have observed, just because a deity appears in quantitatively few hymns does not necessarily reflect on its qualitative importance. In the *Brāhmaṇa* section of the Vedas Viṣṇu was called 'the highest of the gods' and was identified with the sacrifice itself. There is also the well-known Vedic myth of his three strides across the universe that later formed the basis of the mythology of his *avatāra* as Vāmana, the dwarf.

> Thrice Viṣṇu paced and set his step uplifted out of the primal dust; three steps he has paced, the Guarding, the Invincible, and from beyond he upholds their laws. Scan the workings of Viṣṇu and see from whence he has manifested their laws. That is his highest pace which is seen ever by the seers like an eye extended in heaven; that the illumined, the awakened kindle into a blaze, even Viṣṇu's step supreme.
>
> (*Ṛg Veda* 1.22.17–21)

In Vaiṣṇava mythology Viṣṇu is irrevocably connected with the *avatāra* doctrine, for it is Viṣṇu who incarnates in the universe to preserve order whenever unrighteousness threatens its existence. The *avatāra* doctrine is distinctively Hindu. Widely accepted, it is the idea of a periodic divine descent to earth in order to vanquish evil and restore righteousness. These divine incarnations are the most popular and thus important part of Viṣṇu's mythology. He has a foremost place in the hearts and imagination of the people, the scriptures, and image worship when it comes to devotion. Among his most commonly listed incarnations (Matsya, the fish; Kūrma, the tortoise; Varāha, the boar; Vāmana, the dwarf; Narasiṃha, the man-lion; Paraśurāma, Rāma with his axe; Rāma in the *Rāmāyaṇa*; Kṛṣṇa in the *Mahābhārata*; Balarāma or Buddha; and Kalkī), Rāma and Kṛṣṇa enjoy particular favor, and an immense body of devotional literature has been created in response to them.

Images of Viṣṇu in temples depict him sitting, usually in the company of his consort Lakṣmī/Śrī; or standing, holding various weapons in his four hands (*śankha*, conch; *cakra*, discus; *gadā*, club; *padma*, lotus), blue in color, and dressed in royal yellow garments; or reclining on the coils of the serpent Ādi Śeṣa, asleep on the cosmic ocean during the period between the periodic annihilation and renewal of the universe. Viṣṇu's vehicle (*vāhana*) is the eagle Garuḍa. His heavenly abode is known as Vaikunṭha. His *mantra* is '*oṃ namo nārāyaṇāya*.' His most common name is Hari, and he is also invoked as Nārāyaṇa, Keśava, and Puruṣottama.

Śiva

Śiva is worshipped by his followers as the great god, the cosmic dancer, the perfect *yogī*, and the primeval *guru*. He is usually depicted in iconography as an ash-besmeared naked ascetic; as a mendicant beggar; as a *yogin*; with a blue neck (from holding in his throat the toxic by-product from the churning of the cosmic ocean, which threatened to destroy humanity); his hair arranged in a coil of matted locks and adorned with the crescent moon and the Ganges or Gaṅgā River (according to legend he brought the Goddess Gaṅgā to earth by allowing her to trickle through his hair, thus breaking her fall); with three eyes, the third eye bestowing inward spiritual vision but also capable of destruction when focused outward; wearing a garland of skulls and a serpent around his neck and carrying in his hands a deerskin, a trident, a small hand drum, or a club; and as the androgynous half-male and half-female, *ardhanarīśvara*. He is one of the complex gods of Hinduism, embodying seemingly contradictory qualities. He is both the cosmic destroyer and the creative lord of the dance, the great ascetic and the symbol of sensuality, and the wrathful avenger and the compassionate lord of souls. He is an embodiment of the polarity that exists within the divine because he reconciles in his person seemingly opposite qualities: terror and compassion, destruction and creation, eternal rest and ceaseless activity. These seeming contradictions make him a most complex and paradoxical figure: mysterious, powerful, aloof, stern and transcending humanity, and yet, at the same time, erotic, husband, benevolent, and loving lord of all creatures.

Śiva's female consort is known under various manifestations as Umā, Satī, Pārvatī, Durgā, and Kālī. The divine couple, together with their sons, the elephant-headed Gaṇeśa and the six-headed Subramaniam (also known as Kārttikeya, Skanda, Murukaṉ), are said to dwell on Mount Kailāsa in the Himālayas. Śiva's vehicle is the bull Nandi. His *mantra* is '*oṃ namah śivayaḥ.*' In temples and shrines, Śiva is worshipped in the form of the *liṅga*, an oval-shaped emblem made of stone, metal, or clay. He is also known as Śambhu, Śaṅkara, Maheśvara, Mahādeva, Mahāyogin, and Īśvara.

The Devī

Not only is the goddess (the Devī) the consort of Viṣṇu or Śiva, but she is also the ultimate power for her devotees (Śāktas), and all the other deities are but her instruments and/or servants. The motherhood of God is considered by Hindus to be the most charming, the most constant, the sweetest of relationships, for the relationship between a mother and her child is unparalleled. No other relationship can compare with it; all other relationships have some sort of restrictions or rules limiting them. As mother's love is constant, so worship of the Devī is easy. The love and protection of the cosmic mother is unbounded.

In the Veda, the goddess is known and worshipped by various names, but none of these manifestations is considered to be all-powerful. As Vāc, she is the word; as Uṣas, she is the dawn; as Pārthivī, she is the earth; as Aditi, she is the mother; and as Sarasvatī, she is flowing inspiration. However, the early Vedic tradition had no one great goddess.

Sometime around the first millennium CE, the full-fledged worship of the great goddess appeared. Since then there has been a tendency to subsume all the many manifestations of the goddess under one great female being. This goddess is most commonly designated as the Devī (goddess) or the Mahādevī (great goddess). Though the various manifestations of the goddess are known individually as benevolent (Ambā, Pārvatī, Sarasvatī, and Lakṣmī), as terror (Kālī), and as terrific and warlike (Durgā), a tendency developed in the medieval period to think of all of them as related beings, as different manifestations of the highest being.

The distinctive character of the goddess is that she is seen as the cosmic mother, as the ultimate power (*śakti*), as the creatrix of the universe, as the compassionate mother who saves human beings, as identified with earth (*prakṛti*), as identified with mysterious power and/or illusion (*māyā*), and as the queen of the universe. Like the male deities, especially Śiva, she embodies both ambiguity and paradox. It is an impossible task to define 'the Hindu goddess' adequately because her diversity defies imagination. She has appeared with innumerable names and forms. She is erotic yet detached; gentle yet heroic; beautiful yet terrific, a wife and lover, benevolent and protectoress, as well as independent, aggressive, malevolent, and the destroyer.

As Śrī Lakṣmī, she is the power of abundance, riches, prosperity, health, and beauty. She is perhaps the most popular goddess in the Hindu pantheon. She is the wife or consort of Viṣṇu, and in this role, she plays the part of the model Hindu wife, obediently serving her husband as lord. In this role, she has incarnated as Sītā, Draupadī, and Rādhā.

As Sarasvatī, she is the goddess of learning and the arts. Dressed in white and riding a swan, she plays a stringed instrument known as the *vīnā* and carries a manuscript and a rosary in her hands.

As Pārvatī, she is Śiva's consort and *śakti*. By herself, she has almost no independent history, and nearly all her mythology is associated with Śiva. Since epic times, when Pārvatī first appeared as a significant deity, she has been identified as a reincarnation of the goddess Satī, Śiva's first wife, who committed suicide because of an insult to her husband. It appears as though the sole purpose of her birth is to lure Śiva into marriage and thus bring the world-denying ascetic into the realm of a worldly householder, complete with a family. Pārvatī, along with Śiva, is the mother of Gaṇeśa and Subramaniam.

As Durgā, the warrior goddess, she is one of the most formidable and popular of the goddesses. She is usually depicted in her iconography as calm and detached, a battle queen, seated on a tiger or a lion, who smiles even as she wields a weapon in each of her ten hands. Her primary function was to kill the buffalo-demon Mahiṣāsura. She was born in a time of cosmic crisis to kill this terrible demon that the male gods had not been able to destroy. Her appeal seems to stem from her world-supportive qualities as well as her independence.

As Kālī, she is the ferocious, destructive aspect of the divine. She has a terrible, frightening appearance. She is jet black and naked, with long disheveled hair. A girdle of severed arms around her waist, a garland of skulls around her neck, children's corpses as earrings, and serpents as bracelets adorn her. Her bright-red tongue protrudes far beyond her blood-besmeared lips. She holds aloft a freshly severed head and a sword in two of her hands while the other two indicate fearlessness and bestow boons. Kālī is usually depicted on a battlefield or in a cremation ground, but devotees call her mother and those who love her understand her to be compassionate and loving.

Devī also manifests as a group of seven ferocious female deities known as the 'seven mothers' (*saptamātṛkā*); as local or regional goddesses in village and family shrines; as aniconic images, such as stones, poles, weapons, and mystical geometric diagrams (*yantra*); as stylized female genitals (*yoni*); and as natural phenomena, such as rivers (Gaṅgā, Sarasvatī, Yamunā, Kāvērī), trees, and mountains.

Other deities

Besides the 'great' deities in Hinduism, there are a number of other deities who are the subject of much devotion. Perhaps the most popular deity in all of Hinduism is the elephant-headed Gaṇeśa. He is known as the remover of obstacles, the lord of beginnings, son of Pārvatī and Śiva. He is found everywhere: in temples, in wayside shrines, in homes, in autorickshaws, and in devotees' hearts. His was a rather late yet dramatic full-blown appearance into the Hindu pantheon, and today no new project or venture begins without propitiating him. His younger brother, Subramaniam, plays a more limited role in the north of India where he is known as Kārttikeya, but in the Tamil region of South India he is considered the Supreme God as Murukaṉ.

In many towns and villages, deities are known by local names. Temples devoted to them are seldom referred to as Viṣṇu or Śiva temples. For instance, the presiding deity of Tirupati temple is known as Veṅkateśvara (lord of the Veṅkata Hill), the presiding deity of Srirangam temple, as Raṅganātha (lord of the stage), and the presiding deity of Madurai temple, as Mīṇākṣī (fish-eyed goddess). Each particular deity has a unique mythology, personality, and history that will identify it with a place. Their stories are told in books known as Sthalapurāṇas, and such local deities play an incredibly important role in Hinduism. If they come to be revered beyond their region, eventually they are likely to be more widely acknowledged as an aspect of one or another of the great pan-Hindu or all-India deities.

Cosmology

Cosmological formulations of the Hindus vary dramatically from myth to myth and from age to age. Most Hindu mythologies agree about the way in which the universe is arranged. However, there are many different but nonexclusive theories about how the universe came to be the way it is. Origin stories include: the universe is the result of a cosmic battle, the unintentional consequence of the action of a god or gods, born from a golden womb, arising out of the waters of chaos, born from the word, and created by Viṣṇu or Śiva or the Devī. There is an oft-told traditional story in which the god Nārāyaṇa (Viṣṇu) floated on the serpent Ananta ('infinite') upon the primeval waters. From his navel grew a lotus from which the creator Brahmā emerged reciting the four Vedas with his four mouths and creating the 'egg of Brahmā' that contains all the worlds.

For theistic philosophies, ones that conceptualize and represent ultimate reality in terms of a particular personal form, an early paradigm that has continuing influence is the hymn depicting the formation of the universe from the dismemberment of the parts of the body of a single cosmic person at the primordial sacrifice (*Puruṣa Sūkta, Ṛg Veda* 10.90): 'The cosmic person has a thousand heads, a thousand eyes and feet. It covers the earth on all sides. . . . When they divided the cosmic person how many portions did they make? His mouth became the priests, both his arms were made into the warrior, his thighs became the merchants, from his feet the workers were born.' For Absolutist (that is, nondual or monist) philosophies a paradigm is the hymn that refers to the divine as That One – *tad ekam* (*Nāsadīya Sūkta, Ṛg Veda* 10.129): 'There was neither nonexistence nor existence then; there was neither the realm of space nor the sky which is beyond. What stirred? Where? . . . Who really knows? . . . The one who looks down on it, in the highest heaven, only he knows, or perhaps he does not know.'

According to a traditional Hindu cosmology popularized in the Purāṇas, the universe has a sacred mountain in its center with seven ever-expanding concentric oceans and continents surrounding it. The islands double in size as one moves from the center outward, and the seven islands are separated from each other by a series of seven oceans, each of which has the width of the island it encircles. In the center of the innermost island, Jambūdvīpa (the Earth), stands the great golden mountain, Mount Meru.

Jambūdvīpa itself is divided into nine regions of which India (Bhārata) lies in its southern area. Bhārata's unique attribute is its designation as a realm (*karmabhūmi*) where actions are subject to the law of *karma*. Because of this attribute, India is the region where liberation or salvation can be achieved.

Above and below the earth, within the great cosmic egg, are further layers or realms. This widely held Hindu worldview divides the universe (as well as the individual) into seven realms (*loka*): physical realm (*bhūrloka*), vital breath realm (*bhuvarloka*), mental realm (*svarloka*), the intellectual realm (*maharloka*), bliss realm (*janarloka*), consciousness realm (*taparloka*), and existence realm (*satyaloka*). There also are seven netherworlds (*tala*): *pātāla*, *mahātala*, *talātala*, *rasātala*, *sutala*, *vitala*, and *atala*. Mount Meru represents the highest realm or true world (*satyaloka*). The entire cosmos is populated by human beings, animals, plants, gods, snakelike beings (*nāga*), celestial nymphs (*apsara*s), heavenly musicians (*gandharva*), and many more types of beings, each of which can be (re)born into any of these realms depending upon their actions (*karma*).

Time

According to Hinduism, time repeats itself in cycles (*kalpa*) of billions of years. The Purāṇas take for granted the endless repetition of cycles of creation and destruction of the universe. There are four ages (*yuga*) in the cycle: a Golden Age (Kṛta or Satya Yuga), which lasts for 1,728,000 human years; a Silver Age (Tretā Yuga), which lasts for 1,296,000 human years; a Bronze Age (Dvāpara Yuga), which lasts for 864,000 human years; and a Dark Age of degeneration (Kali Yuga), which lasts for 432,000 human years. The current Dark Age began with the end of the Mahābhārata war, traditionally dated 3102 BCE. One complete cycle of the four ages is known as a day and a night of the creator Brahmā. Each *kalpa* is approximately 8,649 million earthly years during which time the universe moves from a state of perfection to a progressively more morally degenerate state in which *dharma* gradually declines. The disintegrating world awaits the arrival of the tenth *avatāra*, Kalkī, whose presence will bring to an end this age of darkness and usher in a new Golden Age. A cycle of the four *yuga*s is known as a period of Manu (*manvantara*). After 1,000 *manvantara*s, which make up one day of Brahmā, the universe is destroyed (*pralaya*) by fire or flood and then a subsequent period elapses during one night of Brahmā when the universe is asleep until the process begins again and a new universe is born. This play (*līlā*) cycles repeatedly and so never ends.

Literature

Hindu scriptures comprise some of the most ancient and extensive religious writings in the world. They are both voluminous and varied. In general, Hindu authors divide sacred literature into *śruti* and *smṛti*. *Śruti* (as we have seen, literally 'that which is heard') is a class of Sanskrit texts that are regarded as revelation. It is understood to be the eternal, authorless (*apauruṣeya*) oral authority that was 'seen' by the primeval seers (*ṛṣi*) and that has continued to be transmitted right down to the present from mouth to ear from generation to generation exactly as received. That primary revelation is known as Veda (derived from the Sanskrit root *vid*, 'to know,' meaning 'knowledge' or 'knowledge par excellence,' that is, divine wisdom). Tradition declares that the Vedic revelations were eventually collected and arranged by an ancient seer, the great compiler Kṛṣṇa Dvaipāyana, better known as Vedavyāsa, into the four different collections (*saṃhitā*) of the *Ṛg*, *Sāma*, *Yajur*, and *Atharva*, with each collection being governed by different considerations about their nature and purpose.

Smṛti (literally 'recollection') is a class of texts that are based on human memory and, therefore, tradition. Its role has been to elaborate upon, explain, interpret, and clarify the primary revelation. It is semicanonical and semisacred and appears in numerous versions. This body of auxiliary scriptures includes the two epics (*itihāsa*), the *Rāmāyaṇa* and the *Mahābhārata*, which contains within it what may be the single most influential text in Hinduism, the *Bhagavad Gītā*; the eighteen major and eighteen minor Purāṇas; the Dharmaśāstras and Dharmasūtras (texts relating to law and social conduct); and the Tantras (a collection of practices and symbols of a ritualistic character used as means of reaching spiritual liberation or realizing mundane goals). In practice, the great majority of Hindus acquire their knowledge of religion almost exclusively through *smṛti* texts. In other words, most people do not have direct mystical experiences but base their religious lives on the records of such experiences.

Primary sacred texts: Śruti

Veda or Vedas

Hindus generally assume that ideas and practices that were to develop into what is now known as Hinduism originated in the Veda or Vedas, a body of ancient texts that modern academic scholars tend to believe were compiled into their received form between about 2000 and 400 BCE. Veda is a name that may evoke in the minds of the orthodox an antiquity, mystery, revelation, and wisdom that confers authority par excellence. To the skeptical, however, it may represent a relic from a bygone age whose time has passed but even now entangles and envelops those who associate themselves with it. Strangely, for both those within and without the Vedic tradition, this corpus of primary material is little known and so difficult to access that it defies proficiency. The Vedic source materials themselves cover approximately 3,000 years and, when reduced to writing, consist of many thousands of pages. The language is archaic; the material is vast; the texts are enigmatic; translations into modern languages are few and uneven. It is difficult even for a specialist to attain competence concerning their contents.

For an orthodox Hindu, Veda is the source of every worthy idea or practice that has made an appearance within Hinduism. To the skeptic or the critical scholar, this may seem to be a mere 'tipping of the hat' or a formal gesture of respect without any further commitment, but it is a conviction of the orthodox that true Hinduism derives from the Veda. Even the critical scholar may acknowledge that much of what is most typical of Hindu civilization was prefigured in the Veda; for example, Upaniṣadic insights led to the Vedānta philosophical traditions; Vedic deities, meditation, and prayer led to the devotional traditions; Vedic rituals led to *karma* theories; Vedic accounts of creation led to cosmologies; Vedic religious experiences led to Yoga and Tantra; Vedic social customs led to the Dharmaśāstras and Dharmasūtras; the lives of Vedic sages and kings led to the epics and the Purāṇas; and protests against the Veda led to Jainism and Buddhism.

The term 'Veda' is used to indicate a range of overlapping but different referents. An ancient meaning was a 'direct, inner experience of the truth.' Veda also has been used to designate a body of oral teachings or written texts and can mean 'the entire body of Vedic revelation.' This usage refers not only to the content or subject matter of the verses (*mantra*) but also to the form of expression that they assume. Third, Veda refers to the revealed knowledge that was divided into four collections (*saṃhitā*): *Ṛg*, *Sāma*, *Yajur*, and *Atharva* (along with their respective numerous recensions or *śākhā*) that constitute collections of verses (*ṛc*), chants (*sāman*), sacrificial formulae (*yajus*), and incantations (*atharvan*), respectively. Fourth, Veda was subsequently extended to include not only the four *saṃhitā*s but also the sacrificial manuals attached to the *saṃhitā*s (the Brāhmaṇas), the forest-books that reflect on the inner meaning of the sacrificial rituals (the Āraṇyakas), and the wisdom portions of the Vedas (the Upaniṣads). Fifth, in post-Vedic times, Veda was extended to include the two epics, the *Rāmāyaṇa* and the *Mahābhārata*, which were respectively designated as the 'fifth Veda.' Lastly, Veda has become an encompassing symbol within which potentially all texts, teachings, and spiritual practices can be subsumed.

Modern scholars typically say that the Vedic texts (as defined in the third instance above) point toward a period ranging from approximately 1500 BCE as the time when the earliest Veda began to solidify into the recognizable form we know today. However, scholarly debate over the origins of the Veda is ongoing and so polarized as to be difficult to resolve, with some scholars pushing back the date of the formation of the earliest of the Vedas to around 4500 BCE. Vedic texts themselves contain references to a remote past. In any case, oral transmission must have passed through a long period before the texts assumed their present classification based on families of author-transmitters. Received tradition informs us that the Veda once existed as a single body of divine wisdom. The very word '*saṃhitā*' or 'collection' itself presupposes that there was a time when the various *mantra*s were not 'collected together.' Further, besides collecting the various *mantra*s together in some sort of coherent fashion, great care was taken to devise a mechanical linguistic device by which the sacred teachings could be preserved and passed on to subsequent generations in their pristine purity. For whatever reason, in the course of time it seems to have become necessary to collect and classify the various *mantra*s. Whether the collection was made for the purposes of preserving the Veda, for propagating the Veda, for facilitating rituals, for remembering and honoring the various Vedic *ṛṣi*s who fashioned the *mantra*s, for noting and recording the historical consciousness which was developing as family lineages grew, and/or for homogeneity of subject matter is not the point. Each of these 'reasons' points to the fact that transmission from teacher to disciple, from generation to generation was taking place.

The Vedic texts contain countless themes ranging from the large number of hymns that honor deities and establish ritual sacrificial rules, to myths, parables, prayers, ethical admonitions, music, and so on. A few of the hymns pose speculative, philosophical questions: In the beginning was there being or nonbeing? How did the one become many? Of what does a person consist? What is that which once known, all things are known? Specific concepts, such as *ṛta* and *dharma*, *karma* and *saṃsāra*, *ātman* and Brahman, *prakṛti* (nature) and *māyā* (magical power/illusion), are introduced in the Veda. In general, a spirit of inquiry into 'the one Being' (*ekam sat*) that underlies the diversity of empirical phenomena is found in the Veda.

Exactly what all the hymns and their attendant themes mean, however, is a complicated and controversial subject. The Vedas themselves attest a simultaneous triple meaning to be found in every hymn: the *ādhibhautika* or external ritual worship, the *ādhidaivika* or cosmogonical, giving knowledge of the gods, and the *ādhyātmika* or spiritual, yielding knowledge of the self, of each individual's inner life in its journey from the mortal to the immortal.

Historically, there have been three main attempts to settle the question of the meaning of the Vedas: the prehistorical declarations in the Brāhmaṇas; the medieval attempt by Sāyaṇa; and the widely diverging modern attempts by Western as well as Indian scholarship. The twentieth-century scholar and statesman Sarvepalli Radhakrishnan, like the medieval Sāyaṇa, interpreted the Vedic hymns in terms of primitive prayers to various gods who were but embodiments of natural powers. That naturalistic claim represents the Vedic hymns as simple, naive attempts to interpret the world. Maurice Bloomfield, a modern scholar influenced by ideas of natural and cultural evolution, offered a ritualistic interpretation that posited that the Vedic hymns were primitive descriptions of various methods of sacrifice. Abel Bergaigne attempted to synthesize naturalistic and ritualistic viewpoints by regarding the Vedic hymns as allegories and the gods and goddesses as symbols of social customs and conventions. Other European scholars as well as Ārya Samāj founder Dayānanda Sarasvatī (1824–83) proposed some form of a monotheistic interpretation of the source of the Veda. Brāhmo Samāj founder Ram Mohun Roy (1772–1833) posited a monistic interpretation declaring that the Vedic gods were allegorical representations of the one Absolute or Supreme Being. Dayānanda attempted to reestablish the ancient view that the Vedas are a divinely revealed scripture with one God and all the other gods and goddesses as names for its many qualities and powers. The early twentieth-century activist Balgangadhar Tilak (1856–1920) presented an arctic theory of the Veda tracing the original home of the Vedic Āryans to the Northern Polar Regions. Aurobindo Ghose (1872–1950) presented a mystical interpretation based on his experience with *yoga* that claimed the Vedic hymns were a revelation of India's ancient psychological and spiritual wisdom expressed in a symbolic language that was lost long ago. Georges Dumézil's comparative mythological-sociological approach stressed that the three functions of sovereignty, physical force, and productivity were analogous to the tripartite social organization of Vedic Hinduism. Subhash Kak recently 'decoded' the *Ṛg Veda*. According to him it is in astronomical code and deciphering it reveals a complete map of space and sky as a symbolic altar. He believes that this astronomical paradigm was lost about 3,000 years ago, and with it the key to correct understanding of the *Ṛg Veda* was lost.

The four Vedas

The *Ṛg Veda* is usually said to be the oldest collection of verses. It is divided into ten books (*maṇḍala*) containing 1,028 hymns addressed primarily to various deities and recited by priests during rituals. Books Two through Seven form the core of the collection, with the others appearing to be later additions. They were composed in a variety of meters and by a variety of sages and bardic families. Since they differ in meter, language, and style, it is often thought that they were composed over many hundreds of years. The ten books have been organized into separate collections, each belonging to one of the ancient families of India. The first seven books resemble each other in character and arrangement. They begin with hymns addressed to Agni, and these hymns, with the exception of the tenth *maṇḍala*, are invariably followed by hymns addressed to Indra. Book Nine is entirely devoted to hymns to Soma. According to the *Muktikā Upaniṣad*, there were originally twenty-one *sākhā*s or versions of the *ṛc* verses, belonging to different schools, all but one of which are now lost. The priests of the *Ṛg Veda* are known as *hotṛ* ('invoker'). *Ṛc mantra*s are metrical and meant to be recited aloud for invoking various deities at the time of the fire-sacrifice.

The *Sāma Veda* is a collection of songs (*sāman*), set to fixed melodies, consisting of 1,810 verses, all but seventy-five of which are found in the *Ṛg Veda*. They are meant to be sung by priests known as *udgatṛ* during the fire-sacrifice. According to the *Muktikā Upaniṣad*, there were originally 1,000 *sākhā*s or versions of the *sāman* verses, belonging to different schools, all but three of which are now lost.

The *Yajur Veda* is a collection of sacrificial formulae (*yajus*), set to fixed melodies. The *Yajur Veda*, unlike the *Sāma* that is concerned with just one feature of the *soma* sacrifice, treats the entire sacrificial system. It is concerned with the whole ritual and deals with the duties of the *adhvaryu* priest, the priest responsible for the actual performance of the various sacrificial rites. Eventually, the *adhvaryu* priest became the Brāhmaṇ priest or the one who was entrusted with the supervision of the entire sacrificial ritual in order to counteract by means of expiatory formulae (*prāyaścitta*) any mistakes made by the other priests during the ritual. There are two main recensions of the *Yajur Veda:* the *Kṛṣṇa* ('Black') *Yajur Veda* and the *Śukla* ('White') *Yajur Veda*. Among the Vedas, the *Yajur* has preserved its literature the most fully.

The *Atharva Veda* is the wisdom of the fire-priests (*atharvan*) and a collection of auspicious 'white' magic incantations and terrible 'black' magic curses. It is also known as the *Brahma Veda* either because it consists of the Brāhmaṇas (magically potent formulas), or because it is the special concern of the Brāhmaṇ priest in the Vedic ritual, or possibly as a reaction against being excluded from the other three Vedas (*trayī*) and thus declaring its own greatness by stating that it alone of the Vedas deals with the complete and full Absolute (Brahman).

Brāhmaṇas and Āraṇyakas

The Brāhmaṇa portion of the Veda is comprised of explanatory treatises about 'that fundamental principle or power known as Brahman,' which involves both *mantra*s (sacred words of power) and priests (Brāhmaṇ) who are the repositories of this 'expansive sacred sacrificial power.' Written mostly in prose, these treatises are generally concerned with practical, everyday duties and rules of conduct. They explain the meaning of a given *mantra*, in what ritual it is to be used, how to use it, and what the result of the ritual will be. The Brāhmaṇas connect the sacrificial *mantra* with the sacrificial rite by explaining their direct mutual relation (by reference to the details of the particular ritual), on the one hand, and by explaining their symbolic connection (the sacred significance of the ritual), on the other. The Brāhmaṇa texts often relied on mythology to trace the origins and importance of individual ritual acts, and this is where we find many of Hinduism's ancient legends, cosmogonic myths, and linguistic and etymological explanations. As a class of texts, they deal in a step-by-step, rite-by-rite manner with the whole of the *śrauta* (solemn) ritual. The prose Brāhmaṇas, together with the collected metrical or *mantra* portions, constitute the *śruti* (whence the adjective *śrauta*) or the corpus of the revealed Veda. With the passage of time, the material aspects of Vedic ritual gained prominence and the Brāhmaṇas developed into a separate class or genre characterized by a standardized expository style which eventually solidified into a fixed institutionalization of Vedic ritual. This rigid compartmentalization may have become the impetus for a movement away from ritual toward metaphysics and mystical experiences which expressed itself in the Āraṇyakas and culminated in the Upaniṣads.

The Āraṇyakas (forest-treatises) seem originally to have existed to give mystical, esoteric explanations of secret or dangerous information concerning the fire-sacrifices which transformed it into material for meditation. They are a loosely defined class of texts that vary in their contents and serve as a transitional link between the Brāhmaṇas and the Upaniṣads.

Upaniṣads

The sacrificial worldview of the Vedas eventually gave way to the cryptic mystical intuitions of the Upaniṣadic seers. The Upaniṣads did not reject the early Vedic worldview but reformulated it, moving the emphasis from the external to the internal, from extrovert to introvert, from the object to the subject, from ritual to meditation, from multiplicity to unity. The very name 'Upaniṣad' suggests this, as etymologically it means '(steadfastly) sitting (*sad*) nearby (*upa*)' implying either pupils earnestly sitting around a teacher or an individual sitting near the great inner self (*ātman*).

The Upaniṣads commence an age of systematic inner exploration. What had been implicit in the Vedas became explicit. Emerging out of the Vedas, the Upaniṣads no longer focused centrally on sacrificial rites but rather pursued a direct, immediate, and life-transforming knowledge of God-as-Absolute (Brahman) and self *(ātman*). The Upaniṣads answer the question 'Who is that one Being?' by establishing the equation Brahman is *ātman*. Brahman – that which is greater than the greatest as well as that which bursts forth as the manifest universe, that one Being – is nothing other than *ātman*, identifiable as the innermost self in human beings and in reality the innermost self in all beings. The Upaniṣads mark a major turning point in the development of Vedic-Hindu thought. They place meditation and mystical experience at the heart of the religious quest. They are not concerned merely with an intellectual quest for the self. The quest established by the sages is deeply experiential. Though there are passages of sophisticated philosophical analysis and argument in the Upaniṣads, in the end it is not intellectual conviction but a lived realization that is the aim of Upaniṣadic teaching. Given their focus on lived experience that is based in meditation and on the disclosure of Being that it offers, it should be no surprise that the Upaniṣads were used as a sourcebook and reference point not only by subsequent heterodox dissidents but also by orthodox thinkers.

The Upaniṣads are not the work of a single author nor are they systematic treatises on philosophy. A great deal of their immediate appeal consists in their direct, simple approach to questions about what is real and who is the self, as well as in the fact that most of them are in the form of riddles, debates, or dialogues. They are said to form the concluding portions of the Vedas and so are called the 'Vedānta' (Veda and *anta*; end of Veda). The term is extremely appropriate, and (like most Sanskrit terms) a metaphorical figure is involved. In addition to indicating that the several Upaniṣads each form the concluding part of their respective Veda, the term 'Vedānta' also expresses the idea that the Upaniṣads represent the essence or the goal of the Vedas. The Sanskrit word '*anta*' like the English word 'end' can mean both the 'terminus' and the 'fulfillment' or 'realization.'

It is difficult to determine the original date and the total number of the Upaniṣads. They are not a uniform set or homogeneous group of texts, and they seem to have been composed (or to have attained the relatively fixed form in which we have received them) over several hundreds of years, from about 800 to 300 BCE. Although it is generally said that there are 100 of them, as listed in the *Muktikā Upaniṣad*, more than 200 ancient texts that bear the name 'Upaniṣad' are now known. Many of these, however, appear to be later compositions modeled on the 'classical' Upaniṣadic texts. Orthodox *paṇḍita*s (learned men) regard ten to fourteen of the ancient texts to be original and important. They include the *Bṛhadāraṇyaka, Chāndogya, Taittirīya, Aitareya, Kaṭha, Īśa, Kena, Praśna, Muṇḍaka, Kauṣītaki, Maitrī, Mahānārāyaṇa*, and *Śvetāśvatara*.

One of the greatest Upaniṣadic seers is Yājñavalkya. In the *Bṛhadāraṇyaka Upaniṣad*, he introduces for the first time a number of concepts which will become basic to later Hinduism. He speaks about transmigration, which holds that upon death a person is neither annihilated nor transported to some other world but rather returns to worldly life, to live and die again in some new mortal form. This continuing cycle of birth, death, and rebirth is called *saṃsāra* ('to wander; to circle') in the Upaniṣads. Yājñavalkya then goes on to say that *karma* determines a person's subsequent form of rebirth. In the earlier portions of the Veda *karma* typically refers specifically to sacrificial actions, but Yājñavalkya extended the concept into the moral dimension. Thus, character is determined by action, and as one sows so one reaps – if not within this lifetime then in some future one. Yājñavalkya also foresees an end to the process of births and deaths in *mokṣa*, which is liberation from repeated suffering that one experiences in the ocean of existence.

Another great Upaniṣadic seer is Uddālaka Aruṇi. In the *Chāndogya Upaniṣad*, he is credited with being the transmitter of what are perhaps Upaniṣad's greatest wisdom teachings. Among them are the great sayings (*mahāvākya*): reality is 'one only without a second' (*ekam evādvitīyam*) and 'That [reality] thou art' (*tat tvam asi*). In the search for the hidden ground of being and the true root of one's existence, the essence of all things, Uddālaka was a master par excellence. When teaching his own son he says:

> 'Bring a fig,' says the father. Śvetaketu, the son brings it. 'Divide it. What do you see?' 'Tiny seeds.' 'Divide one of the seeds. What do you see?' 'Nothing.' 'My dear, that subtle essence which you do not perceive, that is the source of this mighty fig tree. That which is so tiny, is the Self of all. This is the truth, this Self, That thou art.' 'Put a handful of salt into a vessel filled with water.' (After the salt has dissolved) 'Bring me the salt.' 'I can't; I can't find it.' 'Sip from this side of the vessel. What do you taste?' 'Salty.' 'Sip from the other side.' 'Salty.' 'Sip from the center.' 'Salty.' 'Throw out the water and come back later.' (He throws it out and when he returns later, the salt is lying there on the ground.) 'You did not see it, but it was always right there. That finest essence. That is the Self. That thou art.'
>
> (*Chāndogya Upaniṣad* 6.13)

There is a tale about ten simpletons that reveals the Upaniṣadic truth of Uddālaka in seven easy steps. Once upon a time ten simpletons set out on a journey. They eventually came to a large, swollen river. The current was strong, and there was no bridge available with which to cross the river. Thus they decided to swim across. When they reached the other side, their leader decided to count their number to determine whether they had all made it safely. His worst fears were confirmed. He counted only nine members present. He asked each of the other simpletons to count, and they reached a similar conclusion: there were only nine of them present, and thus one of them must have drowned. They looked high and low, upstream and downstream, but no trace of the missing person could be found. That could mean only one thing. He had been drowned while crossing the river. They began to weep, and their grief was inconsolable. Soon a wandering pilgrim came by. Wondering why these individuals were weeping, he asked them what the matter was. Their leader related the entire tragic story of how ten of them had started out on a journey and, after crossing the swollen river, only nine of them had remained, with the tenth man drowned, dead, and gone. The pilgrim was a wise person, and a quick glance revealed to him that there were still ten of them present. He guessed how each one of them counted only nine. Obviously every fool had counted all except himself. Thus the pilgrim announced, 'The tenth man is not dead but alive.' The simpletons began to crowd around the wise pilgrim and shout, 'Where is he, where can we find him, please take us to him.' The pilgrim pointed his finger at the leader and said, 'You are the tenth man.' At once the mystery was solved. The tenth man the leader was searching for was none other than himself. The redeeming insight came in a flash: 'I am that missing tenth man!' All sorrow immediately disappeared, and the tears of agony were replaced with waves of bliss.

Every human being is on a journey which is the journey of life. At some stage the individual suddenly becomes aware that someone or something seems to be missing. Each thinks, 'there must be more to life than this.' What or where that something is one does not know. But deep down everyone intuitively has this feeling. (At this point the knowledge that the tenth person/Brahman is one's true self remains obscured. 'I do not know where the tenth man/Brahman is' – ignorance arises.) Thus begins the search to discover if there is someone or something that can bring fulfillment, which can make one's incompleteness, complete. But, at this stage, one does not know who or what it is or if it really exists. (The existence of the tenth person/Brahman is concealed, the tenth person/Brahman seems absent – 'I neither see Brahman nor know if Brahman exists.') Some people give up at this stage and discontinue their search for the ultimate and settle for immediate pains and momentary pleasures. Others begin to notice their sufferings and feelings of incompleteness and become committed to a search for a solution. (One has the feeling that the tenth person is dead. One assumes that one is no more than an ordinary human being subject to birth and death, fear and ignorance, delusion and pain.) A wise person or teacher then enters the scene and reveals that the tenth man/Brahman is living/exists. (This is indirect knowledge.) The wise person further reveals that you are that tenth man. (This is direct knowledge.) This insight into the otherwise obscured but obvious truth immediately destroys the grief and suffering caused by the thought that the tenth man was absent. It destroys the sense of fear, sorrow, and mortality. At the same time, it produces the bliss of the innermost self.

This reality that exists within each and every person is pure consciousness (*cit*), pure awareness (*sat*), the self. The name does not matter. It is what the various names are pointing toward that is of paramount importance. No person can even say that they do not know it. In the very act of denying its existence, one must presuppose it to deny it. No one can say, 'I do not exist.' Who is the I who is saying that they do not exist? Of nothing else in the universe, or beyond the universe, can this be said. That is the uniqueness and specialty of this consciousness, though until it is experienced it might as well be supposed to not exist at all. Nearer than the nearest and yet seemingly farther than the farthest: 'It is only when you search for it, that you lose it. You cannot take hold of it, but then you cannot get rid of it.'

The mark of consciousness is that it always exists and exists by and in itself. It is totally independent, needing neither effort nor support for its existence. To seek it within oneself, all that is necessary is to understand who or what is doing the seeking. One's habitual pattern is to go in search of it as if it were just another object, even if the greatest, grandest object of all. But that is precisely the problem.

Secondary sacred texts: **Smṛti**

Vedāṅgas

Toward the end of the Vedic period (at about the same time as the production of the principal Upaniṣads) and due to the importance of reciting the Vedic hymns in correct sequence with precisely the right pronunciation when performing the rituals, a series of Vedāṅgas (accessories, extensions, or 'limbs' to the Veda) were composed (between about 800–400 BCE). They provided concise technical guidance about subjects that were crucial for proper and timely performance of the Vedic sacrificial rituals. This intense preoccupation with the liturgy gave rise to scholarly disciplines that were part of Vedic learning. These 'limbs' of the Veda are *śikṣā*, which explains the precise and proper pronunciation; *kalpa*, which discusses the correct ways of performing the ritual; *vyākaraṇa*, which is the study of grammar; *nirukta*, which discusses and gives meaning and etymology for rare, difficult, and unusual words (represented by the *Nirukta* of Yāska, *c.* 600 BCE); *chandas*, which specializes in the explanation and practice of verse meters; and *jyotiṣa*, which is a system of astronomy and astrology used to determine the right times for rituals. The Vedāṅgas themselves are not part of the *śruti*, but they are indispensable for those who have to perform Vedic rituals.

Between the *śruti* and *smṛti* texts fall a number of texts of special importance known as the Kalpasūtras. They are a collection of aphorisms dealing with ritual performance. The composition of these texts began around 600 BCE by Brāhmaṇs belonging to the ritual schools (*śākhā*), each of which was attached to a particular recension of one of the four Vedas. A complete Kalpasūtra contains four principal components: a Śrautasūtra, which establishes the rules for performing the more complex rituals of public Vedic sacrifices; a Śulbasūtra, which shows how to make the geometric calculations necessary for the proper construction of the ritual arena; a Gṛhyasūtra, which explains the rules for performing the domestic rites, including the lifecycle rituals (called *saṃskāras*); and a Dharmasūtra, which provides the rules for the conduct of life. By the time these were produced, society probably was becoming ritually stratified into the four classes, each of which had its own duties (*dharma*). The ideal life was constructed through sacraments in the course of numerous ceremonies, performed by the upper classes, which guided the individual from conception to cremation through a series of complex rites.

Dharmasūtra and Dharmaśāstra

Among the texts inspired by the Vedas are the Dharmasūtras, or manuals on *dharma*, which contain rules of conduct as they were practiced in the Vedic schools. Their principal contents address the duties of people at various stages of life or *āśrama*s, dietary regulations, offenses and expiations, and the rights and duties of kings. They also discuss purification rites, funeral ceremonies, forms of hospitality, and daily oblations. Finally they even mention juridical matters. The more important of these texts are the Gautamasūtras, Baudhāyanasūtras, and Āpastambasūtras. The contents of these works were further elaborated in the more systematic Dharmaśāstra, which in turn became the basis of Hindu law. The most famous of these texts is the *Dharmaśāstra* of Manu (*c.* CE 200). It deals with various topics, such as cosmogony, definition of *dharma*, the sacraments, initiation and Vedic study, the eight forms of marriage, hospitality and funerary rites, dietary laws, pollution and purification, rules for women and wives, royal law, eighteen categories of juridical matters, and finally religious matters like donations, rites of reparation, the doctrine of *karma*, the soul, and punishment in hell. Law in the juridical sense is thus completely embedded in religious law and practice. The influence of this text has been enormous, as it provided Hindu society with its practical morality and law and then later served as a lens through which Western 'Orientalists' during the colonial era sought to reconstruct an adequate picture of classical Hinduism.

Itihāsa

The two Hindu epics (*itihāsa*), the *Rāmāyaṇa* (third to sixth centuries BCE) and the *Mahābhārata*, though not primary scripture, are still considered inspired and authoritative. In fact, they play a far more important role in the everyday lives of most Hindus than the Vedas. Children grow up hearing these stories from their parents and grandparents. The heroes of these epics are depicted on television and in the movies. Their names are familiar, and their stories well known. For most Hindus, the phrase 'sacred book' connotes these two epics in particular. These two Sanskrit epics depict the wanderings of prince Rāma in the *Rāmāyaṇa* and the great war of the Bharata clan in the *Mahābhārata*, just as the two classical Greek epics depict the wandering and adventures of a prince banished from his country (Odysseus in the *Odyssey*) and a great war (the *Iliad*).

RĀMĀYAṆA (*THE DEEDS OF RĀMA*)

The story of the life and adventures of Rāma is narrated by Sage Vālmīki who is the traditional author of the epic and thereby India's first poet. The epic has been memorized, recited, and enjoyed by Hindus throughout India for centuries as a source of spiritual uplift and inspiration. It is a sourcebook for *dharma* as depicted through the life of a perfect man. Vaiṣṇavas call it the scripture par excellence for elucidating the doctrine of absolute self-surrender to God (*śaraṇā gati śāstra*).

As the story begins, the sage Vālmīki goes into the forest in search of firewood and *durva*-grass for his daily sacrificial ritual. He looks up into a tree where he sees a pair of love-birds sitting on a branch. Suddenly, the male bird is shot dead by the arrow of a hunter. The female bird lets out a cry of anguish and terror. Words spontaneously well up in the soon-to-be poet's heart, and he utters the now-famous line condemning the terrible crime, 'Since, O hunter, you killed one of this pair of birds, distracted at the height of passion, you shall not live for very long.' He reflects on this utterance. By observing life, especially the tragic and painful side of life, something higher emerges. The tragic cry of the bird when it was separated from its mate by the cruel blow of destiny stirs the poet's heart, and the *Rāmāyaṇa* itself becomes a text of parting and separation. Daśaratha, Sītā, Bharata, and Kauśalyā are all separated from Rāma.

The main story focuses on the young prince Rāma, who is born by a boon given to his father Daśaratha. He has three half-brothers, Lakṣmaṇa, Bharata, and Śatrughna, also born from the same boon. On the eve of Rāma's coronation, Daśaratha exiles Rāma due to a promise he had made to his youngest wife, Kaikeyī, with the result that Rāma is deprived of the kingdom to which he is heir and is sent into the forest with his wife Sītā and his brother Lakṣmaṇa. His father dies of a broken heart and his brother Bharata serves as the kingdom's caretaker while Rāma is in exile. Sītā is abducted from the forest by Rāvaṇa, the demon-king of Laṅkā. While they search for Sītā, the brothers ally themselves with a monkey-king, Sugrīva, whose general, Hanumān, is sent to Sītā in Laṅkā to let her know that her rescue is being arranged. Rāma and his allies then defeat Rāvaṇa, rescue Sītā, and return to the kingdom. When they return, their subjects express doubt that Sītā was able to protect her chastity while abducted. To placate them, Rāma banishes Sītā to a hermitage, where she bears him two sons, Lava and Kuśa, and eventually dies by reentering the earth from which she had been born.

Both Rāma and Sītā have become idealized figures in the Hindu tradition. Rāma is depicted as the perfect male human being and a model of the ideal son, husband, brother, warrior, and ruler. Rāma's reign becomes the prototype of a harmonious and just kingdom. Rāma and Sītā set the ideal of conjugal love; Rāma's relationship to his father is the ideal of filial love; and Rāma and Lakṣmaṇa represent perfect fraternal love. The *Rāmāyaṇa* also identifies Rāma with Viṣṇu (as Viṣṇu's *avatāra*) and so makes him divine as well as human.

There are numerous vernacular versions of the *Rāmāyaṇa*. The most famous of them include Tulsīdās' (CE 1570) Hindi *Rāmcaritmānas* (The Lake of Rāma's Deeds); Kampa<u>n</u>'s (*c.* CE 1100) Tamil *Irāmāvatāram* (The Descent of Lord Rāma); *Adhyātma Rāmāyaṇa*, in which Rāma is no longer merely an *avatāra* but the supreme *parabrahman; Yoga Vasiṣtha Rāmāyaṇa*, a nondualistic philosophical allegory; and *Adbhuta Rāmāyaṇa*, a devotional text that presents Sītā as the *śakti* and more powerful than Rāma. Though details of the story differ in the alternative versions, the story of Rāma and Sītā and their supreme devotee Hanumān has endured. Temples to them are found throughout India, and, according to tradition, as long as the rivers flow on earth and human beings live, so will the story of Rāma and Sītā endure. Most versions of the *Rāmāyaṇa* end with the declaration, 'Whoever hears, sings, recites, or meditates on this story attains the highest state.'

MAHĀBHĀRATA (*THE GREAT WAR OF THE BHARATA TRIBE*)

The *Mahābhārata* is an encyclopedic work, the longest poem in the world, and a veritable treasure house of secular and religious Hindu lore. It contains stories of seers, sages, and divine incarnations; family feuds; beautiful women and dutiful wives; valiant warriors and righteous kings; heinous villains and evil demons; law, morality, and justice; the way to ultimate happiness and liberation.

The *Mahābhārata*, a text of some 100,000 verses attributed to the sage Vyāsa, is the story of a great struggle among the descendants of a king called Bhārata (the modern name of India). The central plot concerns a war between the five sons of Pāṇḍu, known as the Pāṇḍavas (Arjuna, Yudhiṣṭhira, Bhīma, and the twins Nakula and Sahadeva), and the sons of Pāṇḍu's blind-brother Dhṛtarāṣṭra, known as the Kauravas. They are cousins, but the evil Kauravas try to cheat the Pāṇḍavas out of their share of the kingdom and thus war becomes inevitable, a war that eventually leads to the destruction of the entire race, except for one survivor who continues the dynasty. Each of the Pāṇḍavas is the son of a god (Indra, Dharma, Vayu, and the Aśvins, respectively), and the epic is deeply infused with religious implications.

By the time of the *Mahābhārata*, Vedic *dharma* and the way of life that was centered in sacrificial rituals had fallen into neglect and become virtually forgotten. In the *Rāmāyaṇa*, everyone knows what to do and how to do it. The only issue is whether they will. But in the *Mahābhārata*, doubt and uncertainty pervade the text. This is most evident when Arjuna, facing his cousins, uncles, and other relatives on the battlefield as the war is about to begin, becomes filled with doubt and refuses to fight. Kṛṣṇa, the eighth *avatāra* of Viṣṇu, is on the side of the Pāṇḍavas. He is Arjuna's brother-in-law and friend, and, having refused to wield arms in the battle, nevertheless serves as Arjuna's charioteer, a role that is interpreted allegorically. Kṛṣṇa tells Arjuna that he must fight; it is the duty of a warrior to do battle in a righteous cause. One must fight for *dharma* after exhausting all peaceful means. The famous conversation that Arjuna and Kṛṣṇa have on the battlefield before the start of the war is known as the *Bhagavad Gītā*.

The Great War lasts for eighteen days. The Pāṇḍavas, employing both fair and foul means, emerge victorious. However, very few who had entered the war on either side are alive when it ends. After they win the war and after the demise of Kṛṣṇa, the Pāṇḍavas leave the kingdom in the hands of Arjuna's grandson Parīkṣit and depart toward the Himālayas on their way to Indra's heaven. The Great War, according to Hindu tradition, marks the beginning of the current Kali Yuga, the darkening age of strife in which righteousness has given way to unrighteousness, and dissention rules the land.

The Kṛṣṇa of the *Mahābhārata* is primarily a hero, king, friend, and ally of the Pāṇḍavas. Although the epic furnishes some information about Kṛṣṇa, the primary religious sourcebook for him is the *Bhāgavata Purāṇa*. In the *Mahābhārata* not everyone considers Kṛṣṇa to be a divine incarnation of Viṣṇu. Kṛṣṇa helps the Pāṇḍava brothers to obtain their kingdom and when the kingdom is taken from them he helps them to regain it. In the process he emerges as a great teacher who reveals the *Bhagavad Gītā* to Arjuna and subsequently achieves heroic feats with him.

Apart from their influence as Sanskrit texts, the *Rāmāyaṇa* and *Mahābhārata* have made an impact throughout South and Southeast Asia where their stories are repeatedly retold. When these two epics were made into television movies and broadcast throughout India a few years ago, and then rebroadcast for several years, they drew the largest audience in the history of Indian television.

BHAGAVAD GĪTĀ (*THE SONG OF THE LORD*)

The *Bhagavad Gītā* became an extremely influential Hindu religious text from the early modern period to the present even though it is not strictly revelation (*śruti*). It is a brief text, only 700 verses divided into eighteen short chapters, in the form of a reported dialogue. One well-known analogy declares that 'The Upaniṣads are the cow; Arjuna is the calf; Kṛṣṇa is the milkman; and the *Bhagavad Gītā* is the milk.' Another analogy is that 'The Vedas are the cow; the Upaniṣads are the milk; the *Bhagavad Gītā* is the butter.'

The *Bhagavad Gītā* is esteemed for many reasons. Among them, it is part of the *Mahābhārata*; it features two charismatic characters, Arjuna and Kṛṣṇa; the dialogue form gives it dramatic interest; the setting is extremely serious with the future of the country and the fate of righteousness at stake; it has a simple style and a spirit of toleration; at its center is a dilemma for which a solution is provided; and Kṛṣṇa makes several avatāric statements about himself, including the promise that he will incarnate from age to age to protect *dharma* whenever righteousness diminishes and evil arises.

While the opposing armies in the Mahābhārata war are already on the field and prepared to begin battle, Arjuna, the most famous warrior of his day, despairs at the thought of having to kill his kinsmen. He puts down his weapons. Kṛṣṇa, his charioteer, cousin, friend, and adviser, chides Arjuna for his failure to do his duty as a warrior and tells him not to grieve for what is about to happen. His dilemma is that if he fights he will kill his kinsmen and if he does not fight he will disregard his *dharma*, be guilty of cowardice, and allow injustice and unrighteousness to triumph.

Kṛṣṇa teaches Arjuna by describing the soul: it is immortal and so it cannot be killed when the body is killed. The soul neither is born nor dies. It is indestructible and from time to time discards wornout bodies and takes on a new one just as a person will discard old clothes and acquire new ones. 'The truly wise mourn neither for the living nor for the dead. . . . Bodies are known to end, but the soul that is embodied is eternal, indestructible, and immeasurable; therefore, Arjuna, fight the battle. He who thinks this soul a killer and he who thinks it killed, both fail to understand it neither kills nor is killed' (2.11,18–19).

Arjuna's worries at first appear to have merit, but Kṛṣṇa soon reveals that his attraction to 'renunciation' is escapist and motivated by the wish to avoid his worldly responsibilities. He distinguishes between his own people and others, but for a monk all people are the same. His sadness and despondency reveal that he is attached to the things of this world. A monk has a light and happy heart. Finally, Arjuna fails to understand for what he should fight. A warrior serves his king and country, but he fights in a just cause for the sake of *dharma* itself. The cause is just and so Kṛṣṇa admonishes him to go into battle.

Kṛṣṇa teaches Arjuna that even if he does not comprehend the nature of the soul or indestructible inner self, nevertheless he should perform his duty for its own sake. In contrast to the world-affirming orientation of Vedic ritualists and equally in contrast to the world-renouncing ideal of the sages in the Upaniṣads, Kṛṣṇa in the *Bhagavad Gītā* harmonizes the two paths by teaching that in the world action is necessary and unavoidable but that the right relationship to action requires the sacrifice of selfish desire and the renunciation of attachment to the outcome while continuing to act responsibly as determined by one's *dharma*.

> Be intent on action, not on the fruits of action; avoid attraction to results and attachment to inaction. Act, firm in discipline, relinquishing attachment; be impartial to failure and success, this equanimity is called *yoga*. . . . Wise men disciplined by understanding relinquish the fruits born of action; freed from these bonds of rebirth, they reach a place beyond sorrow.
>
> (2.47–48, 51)

Kṛṣṇa continues his teaching by presenting three different ways to release the inner self from the bondage of transmigration. He presents the path of selfless action (*karma-yoga*), the path of devotion (*bhakti-yoga*), and the path of divine wisdom (*jñāna-yoga*). As he does this, Kṛṣṇa also makes statements about himself that are unique to him and open up a new dimension in Hindu theology. The Upaniṣads were reluctant to describe Brahman, but in the *Bhagavad Gītā,* Kṛṣṇa directly reveals himself as the Highest Spirit or Supreme Lord and grants Arjuna a vision of his multiple (and overwhelmingly powerful and awe-inspiring) forms. 'Though myself unborn, undying, the lord of creatures, I fashion nature, which is mine, and I come into being through my own mysterious power (*māyā*). . . . I am the universal father, mother, granter of all, grandfather, object of knowledge, purifier, holy syllable *oṃ*, and the (Vedic) *rik, sāma*, and *yajur*. I am the goal, sustainer, lord, witness, shelter, refuge, friend, source, dissolution, stability, treasure, and unchanging seed' (4.6, 9.17–18). Kṛṣṇa also makes his avatāric promise to humanity that 'Whenever righteousness diminishes and chaos prevails, then I send myself forth, Arjuna. To preserve good, destroy evil, and set the standard for sacred duty, I come into being in age after age' (4.7–8). And he declares that 'Whoever worships me, thinking solely of me, always disciplined, will reach me' (8.8).

The *Bhagavad Gītā* is not a systematic philosophical treatise. It is a classic of spiritual literature, and its influence is enormous. Although it is short and accessible, it has inspired many interpretations and commentaries. Among its several contributions to Hindu tradition are a newfound emphasis on devotion to a personal God who incorporates the Upaniṣadic Brahman, an integration of renunciation with action (a key to living in the world without being of it), the three paths to liberation (which are the foundation for a *dharma*-based Brāhmaṇism, an enlightenment-based asceticism, and a devotion-based theism), and an avatāric doctrine.

By requiring that devotees of God fulfill their *dharma*-based duties ('better one's own duty ill-performed than another's well-performed' [18.47a]), the *Bhagavad Gītā* integrates liberation-oriented ascetic disciplines into the demands of family and responsibilities of daily life. For those who must support a family and work in this world, the *Bhagavad Gītā* gives the promise of final liberation. Kṛṣṇa's teaching that God is present in all beings means that the wise should not see differences between their fellow creatures and should love God in all of them equally. This can motivate a person to promote individual and social welfare. Yet, by emphasizing that each human being has an innate tendency to prefer one or another of the three paths to liberation and also has specific responsibilities based on their birth into a particular caste, the *Bhagavad Gītā* provides support for the differentiating genetic determinisms of the caste system. Thus it is progressive and universalistic while managing to be conservative and particularistic at the same time.

Purāṇas

The Purāṇas (literally 'ancient') are an extensive body of literature concerned with the creation of the universe, containing myths associated with various deities, offering rules for living, recording genealogies and legacies of gods, sages and kings, and providing descriptions of heavens and hells, deities, rituals, pilgrimages to holy places, and the end of the world. They are a compendium of legendary histories of India and the repositories of popular religious lore. Traditionally they are supposed to deal with five topics (*pañcalakṣaṇa*): creation (*sarga*), dissolution (*pratisarga*), lineage (*vaṃśa*), epochs (*manvantara*), and the legends of future lineage (*vaṃśānucarita*), though not all of them actually do so. There are eighteen major Purāṇas, divided into three categories: those which are *sāttvika* and honor Viṣṇu – the *Viṣṇu, Nārada, Bhāgavata, Garuḍa, Padma*, and *Varāha*; those which are *rājas* and honor Brahmā – the *Brahmā, Brahmāṇḍa, Brahmavaivarta, Bhaviṣya, Mārkaṇḍeya*, and *Vāmana*; and those which are *tāmas* and honor Śiva – the *Śiva (Vāyu), Matsya, Kūrma, Liṅga, Śiva, Skanda*, and *Agni*. This system of classification, although often mentioned, does not reveal very much about the nature or contents of these texts. Nor do they deal exclusively with only one deity even though each does have a definite sectarian affiliation.

The Purāṇas contain a wealth of information for understanding the traditions dealing with what are now known as the great Purāṇic deities, Viṣṇu, Śiva, the Devī, Gaṇeśa, Agni, Skanda, and so on. Each text presents a picture of the world and a representation of the beliefs and practices of popular Hinduism from that perspective. The Purāṇas, along with the epics, became the scriptures of the common people. Unlike the Vedas that were restricted to initiated men in the three higher orders, they were available to everybody, including women and members of the lowest order of society. The origin of much of their contents may be non-Brāhmaṇic, but they were accepted and adapted by the Brāhmaṇs, who thus brought new elements into the orthodox religion. Having never been codified, they were passed down as oral traditions with numerous local variations.

The Purāṇas are said to have been composed starting around 300 BCE and continuing until around CE 1000. Hindu tradition ascribes the authorship of the eighteen major Purāṇas to Vyāsa. There are also eighteen related subordinate texts known as Upapurāṇas, though there are variations as to which texts are included within each set of eighteen. There is also another class of Purāṇas known as Sthalapurāṇas, which deal with the legends and lore of a particular place or temple.

Vernacular literature

For a very long time it was considered a sacrilege to write a religious or philosophical work in any language other than Sanskrit, but to be read (rather than heard) by common people, scriptural texts need to be written in a language everyone can read. In the Tamil country of the south, the *Tēvāram* (Garland for the God) and the *Tiruvācakam* (Sacred Utterance) appeared among the Śaiva saints; and the *Nālāyiram Divyaprabandham*, a collection of 4,000 hymns of the *Āḻvārs*, appeared among the Vaiṣṇava saints. Another important Tamil text is Kampaṉ's *Rāmāyaṇam*. In Maharashtra in the west, singer-saints composed hymns and *abhaṅgas*, devotional songs in the Marathi language that express longing of a devotee for God. These include the works of Jñāneśvar (*c.* 1275–96), Nāmdev (*c.* 1270–1350), Tukārām (*c.* 1598–1649), Eknāth (*c.* 1548–1609), and Samārth Rāmdās (*c.* 1608–81). In Karanataka in the upper southwest, the numerous *vacana*s by Basava (*c.* 1106–68) are simple prose poems set to music. There are also twelfth-century compositions by Allamaprabhu and by Mahādēviyakka. In the northern region of India, a number of great religious works were produced in an evolving Hindi language: the nonsectarian devotional song-poems of Kabīr (*c.* 1440–1518); the *Rāmcaritmānas* of Tulsīdās *c.* 1543–1623); Sūrdās' (*c.* 1483–1563) *Sūrsāgar* or 'Ocean of the Poems of Sūr,' a collection of poems on the theme of the childhood of Kṛṣṇa; and Mīrābāī's (*c.* 1503–73) passionate love-songs (*bhajan*) to Kṛṣṇa. In the northeast, there is a rich tradition of devotional works in Bengali, Maithili, and other regional languages that are inspired by the love of Rādhā with Kṛṣṇa (Caṇḍidās, *c.* 1339–99; Vidyāpati, *c.* 1360–1448; and Caitanya, *c.* 1486–1533) as well as works in honor of Kālī (Rāmprasād, *c.* 1718–75).

Main philosophical systems

Although Hindu tradition does not have a term that refers only to philosophy, '*darśana*' is the nearest analogue to 'philosophy' in general and it is used to refer to the main traditional systems of argument, commentary, and analysis. The *darśana*s, more commonly known as the six classical philosophical systems of Nyāya, Vaiśeṣika, Sāṃkhya, Yoga, Mīmāṃsā, and Vedānta, have developed in parallel to one another while engaging in mutual debate and criticism for the past 2,000 years. These systems of thought embody the cumulative reflection of Hindu wisdom through the ages and include epistemology, metaphysics, ethics, social customs, aesthetics, psychology, cosmology, physics, grammar, logic, speculations about language, exegesis of scriptural texts, psychophysical practices, dialectics, and even protests against orthodoxy.

The various Hindu philosophical systems contain such a diversity of views, theories, and subschools that it is difficult to single out characteristics that are common to all of them. In general, however, all of the *darśana*s accept Vedic revelation, begin with spiritual dissatisfaction and culminate in a spiritual orientation, are exegetical in nature, and assume a transcendent reality beyond the physical.

The various philosophical systems did not develop in a purely linear fashion. The major schools started almost simultaneously and developed through mutual criticisms over the centuries. They were based on presystematic Vedic and Upaniṣadic teachings and first were systematized in the form of condensed aphorisms (*sūtra*) or brief threads of thought that expressed the gist of the system by using language in a very concise, telegraphic style. Each *sūtra* was easy to memorize and enabled the founders to express precisely the content of the system taught by their school. However, because the aphorisms are so pithy and abstruse without any additional explanation, they admit of different interpretations. Thus a commentary (*bhāṣya*) literature became the most important exposition of a system. Subcommentaries (*vārttika*) and glosses (*ṭīkā*) were composed to elucidate and interpret both the *sūtra* texts and the commentaries. A third category of philosophical works consists of manuals, independent treatises, dialectical classics, and critiques. They instruct students belonging to their own school and combat criticisms from their opponents. Even though no new *darśana*s were subsequently founded, independent thinking, new innovations, and original insights have continued to develop within the context created by the classical ones. This has motivated Hindu philosophers to find new ways to review and restate traditional positions in response to innovative analyses, interpretations, and critiques down to the present day.

We can call the era when the basic philosophic teachings of most of the various *darśana*s were condensed into aphorisms that precisely expressed the content of the various systems in a technical vocabulary the Aphoristic period (400 BCE to CE 400). But little is known about the founders (*sūtrakāra*) and central commentators (*bhāṣyakāra*) who helped to give shape to the main philosophical systems. Nothing can be said with any precision about their dates and places of birth, identity, or life's activities. The limited information available comprises bits and pieces, speculations, and legends derived from hagiographies or from scant references in other works. Traditionally, the classical philosophers disclaim any originality for themselves and for the doctrines they expound. They understand themselves to be neither more nor less than faithful transmitters of an ancient tradition that preserves a timeless truth so great as to merit repeated refinement and exposition without either needing or allowing any originality or innovation in the modern sense. There is an underlying assumption in Hindu tradition that no individual can claim to have seen truth for the first time, and so an individual can only (re)state, explicate, and defend unchanging truth. The result is an exclusive respect for preserving and expounding upon insights received from the ancients, which are purported to be timeless, rather than a charter to seek new sources of what is true.

The way we are introducing Hindu philosophy as a series of classical schools (seemingly static and complete) owes a considerable debt to the traditional Sanskrit doxographies. It was in the doxographies, the literature that summarizes and classifies the main schools or systems, that the term '*darśana*' gained its meaning as the characteristic term for philosophy. Although the academic community would like a detailed history of Hindu philosophy, sources that would be sufficient to produce such a history have not been found. Therefore we follow the doxographical approach and its classification of Hindu philosophy into six orthodox or 'affirmative' (*āstika*) schools that are linked together in three pairs or allied systems: Nyāya-Vaiśeṣika, Sāṃkhya-Yoga, and Mīmāṃsā-Vedānta.

NYĀYA SCHOOL

Nyāya is famous for its acute analysis of discursive thought. It is a philosophical system consisting of three main parts: a methodology for investigating the nature of things through valid means of knowledge (*pramāṇa*), the art of debate through syllogistic reasoning (logic), and metaphysical knowledge about nature, the soul, salvation, and God. The term 'Nyāya' means 'logical reasoning,' and this school is best known for developing the rules of logic and epistemology in Hindu philosophy. Besides logic, Nyāya is also famous for formulating an elaborate scheme of inference based on syllogism. Gautama (*c.* 400–100 BCE) is the founder of the Nyāya school. He is the author of the *Nyāyasūtra*. Gautama's ideas were later explained, amplified, systematized, and fashioned into a coherent system by Vātsyāyana (*c.* CE 300–400) in his *Nyāyasūtrabhāṣya*.

VAIŚEṢIKA SCHOOL

Vaiśeṣika emphasizes ontology and cooperates closely with its sister philosophical system, Nyāya, on matters of epistemology. Kaṇāda (*c.* 500–300 BCE) is the founder of the Vaiśeṣika school. He is the author of the *Vaiśeṣikasūtra*. Vaiśeṣika's name is derived from '*viceṣa*,' which means 'the characteristics that distinguish a particular thing from all other things.' Thus, the Vaiśeṣika, like its sister system, is a school of pluralistic realism. Its doctrines are based upon the key concept of *viśeṣa*, implying that the world exists independent of a thinking mind and consists of a plurality of reals which are all externally related. The distinguishing doctrine of the Vaiśeṣika school is that nature is atomic. An individual atom is said to be invisible, devoid of qualities, but possessing potentialities that manifest when it combines with others of the same type to form molecules of the elements earth, water, fire, and air. The atoms are eternal and indivisible, and thus creation or re-creation consists in the combination of all the separate atoms into the elements. Praśastapāda (*c.* CE 400) wrote the earliest extant commentary on the *Vaiśeṣikasūtra* known as the *Padārthadharmasaṃgraha*.

SĀṂKHYA SCHOOL

The Sāṃkhya school is said by its expositors to be one of the oldest (if not the oldest) among the schools of systematic Hindu philosophy. They claim that many of its ideas can be found in the *Ṛg Veda* and even more are scattered throughout the Upaniṣads. The supreme sage Kapila, who is said to be the founder of Sāṃkhya, is the author of the *Sāṃkhyasūtra* (*c.* 500 BCE, now lost). The earliest extant authoritative text of the classical Sāṃkhya is the *Sāṃkhyakārikā* of Īśvarakṛṣṇa (*c.* CE 300–400). It is a very influential text and a codification of the Sāṃkhya teachings. It deals with the various patterns of enumeration and sets forth the purpose of teaching, that is, liberation through discrimination between spirit (*puruṣa*) and nature (*prakṛti*). Sāṃkhya's remarkable influence on the development of the other philosophical schools, both orthodox and heterodox, is often noted. In fact, most aspects of Hindu culture – including philosophy, mythology, theology, law, medicine, art, *yoga*, and Tantra – have been influenced by the categories and basic ideas of Sāṃkhya. Some of its teachings such as the three qualities/attributes/constituents (*guṇa*), the dualism of consciousness and materiality (*puruṣa, prakṛti*), and the evolutionary theory of the twenty-four principles (*tattva*) have become an integral part of the Hindu tradition.

The key teaching of Sāṃkhya is that reality is twofold. Spirit is of the nature of pure consciousness – pure, changeless, many, and its mere presence is responsible for the process of evolution. Matter (*prakṛti*) is nonconscious, one, ever-changing, subtle, invisible and therefore must be inferred from its creations. It is composed of the three qualities and is the ultimate cause of the universe though it is causeless itself. Nothing exists apart from these two principles: selves that never are an object and matter that always is an (inferred) object. Selves can discriminate, matter cannot. Spirit has neither birth nor death, is nonactive, and is a patient observer. Matter is active, ever-changing, and undergoes cycles of evolution and absorption. The supreme goal of life, according to Sāṃkhya, is for selves to know by discrimination that the self has nothing to do with matter. Liberation, however, is only phenomenal because the true self is always free. Bondage is only the seeming activity of nature toward one who does not discriminate, that is, who does not observe the distinction between *puruṣa* and *prakṛti*.

Sāṃkhya is also known for its theory of evolution. Primal matter, the principal source from which evolution starts, is one but is said to be a composite of three qualities that are the ultimate building blocks of the universe. Originally these three are invisible and in a state of equilibrium. The three combine and repeatedly recombine due to the proximity of spirit, shifting through various states of mutual preponderance. Material Nature, according to Sāṃkhya, is undergoing continuous transformations. It is the primary matrix out of which all differentiations arise and to which they return. Of nature's three qualities, *sattva* represents luminosity and intelligence; *rajas* is energy and activity that represents the principle of discontinuity and change; and *tamas* is inertia, heavy, coarse, dark, the principle of continuity. When the equilibrium of these three is disturbed, matter evolves in the following order: *prakṛti* → *mahat* or *buddhi* (intelligence) → *ahaṃkāra* (egoism) → *manas* (mind) → *jñānendriya* (sense organs: hearing, touch, sight, taste, and smell) → *karmendriya* (action organs: speech, prehension, movement, excretion, and generation) → *tanmātra* (subtle elements: sound, touch, sight, taste, and smell) → *mahābhūta* (gross elements: ether, air, fire, water, and earth). This emanation scheme may be seen as both an account of cosmic evolution and a logical-transcendental analysis of the various factors involved in experience.

YOGA SCHOOL

The technique of Yoga is ancient and complex. Various yogic spiritual practices are mentioned in several of the major Upaniṣads. Etymologically, the word 'Yoga' derives from the Sanskrit root *yuj*, meaning 'to bind together, to unite.' What is being conjoined? Some say it is the individual self with the transcendental Self; others say it is union with one's chosen deity (*Yogasūtra* 2.44); still others say it is the process of joining the breath, the syllable *oṃ*, and this world in its manifoldness. Yoga has been defined by Vyāsa as 'enstasis' and by Patañjali as the 'cessation of the mind's fluctuations.' In its broadest sense, Yoga is a technique for unifying consciousness as well as the resulting state of union with the object of contemplation, and it can refer to nearly all the spiritual techniques, values, attitudes, and systems of traditional India.

The basic principles of Yoga were first summarized systematically in the *Yogasūtra* of Patañjali (third century BCE). The Yoga system stands in close relation to the Sāṃkhya system, adopting its metaphysics though it adds a twenty-sixth principle (the Supreme Lord, Īśvara) to the Sāṃkhya list of twenty-five. The two systems are complementary. While Sāṃkhya is primarily intellectualistic and emphasizes metaphysical knowledge as the means to liberation, Yoga is voluntaristic and emphasizes the need for extreme self-control as the means to liberation.

The *Yogasūtra* is a short work of 196 aphorisms divided into four chapters. The first chapter, 'Contemplation,' concerns the general nature of Yoga and its techniques. It defines Yoga in its famous second aphorism as 'the cessation of the mind's fluctuations.' It describes the fluctuations, modifications, and modulations of thought that disturb pure consciousness. Then it begins to describe practice and detachment as means by which they may be stilled. A general method to achieve the goal of Yoga is formulated in which the spirit (*puruṣa*) is isolated from nature (*prakṛti*) by means of mind control. The second chapter, 'Spiritual Disciplines,' begins by delineating the afflictions that disturb the mind and answers why one should practice Yoga. It states the external practices of the eightfold yogic path (*aṣṭānga-mārga*) that include the five abstentions (*yama*) of nonviolence, truthfulness, nonstealing, continence, and nonpossession as well as the five observances (*niyama*) of purity, contentment, austerity, study, and surrender to God; the physical postures (*āsana*); breathing techniques (*prāṇāyāma*); and withdrawal from the objects of the sense organs (*pratyāhāra*). The third chapter, 'Supernormal Powers,' delineates the last three limbs of the eightfold Yoga: concentration (*dhāraṇā*), meditation (*dhyāna*), and absorption (*samādhi*). Then it reports the transformative and supernormal effects of yogic practices. The fourth and last chapter, 'The Nature of Liberation,' gives a general exposition of the study and practice of Yoga leading to liberation.

MĪMĀṂSĀ SCHOOL

The Pūrva Mīmāṃsā (First Investigation), also known as Karma Mīmāṃsā (Study of [Ritual] Action), of Jaimini (*c.* 300–200 BCE) concerns itself chiefly with questions about the proper interpretation of Vedic texts. The first four orthodox schools of Nyāya, Vaiśeṣika, Sāṃkhya, and Yoga are orthodox in name only. They are not directly dependent upon the Veda, do not explicitly interpret the Veda, and do not look to the Veda for justification of their doctrines. But Mīmāṃsā is a genuinely Vedic tradition. Its basic assumption is that the scriptural texts are authoritative and faultless and have to be interpreted in order to explain away any apparent absurdities or contradictions. It is a system centered on investigating the nature of Vedic injunctions; its investigation led to the development of principles of scriptural interpretation and to theories of meaning. Jaimini, who composed the *Pūrvamīmāṃsāsūtra*, proposed that Vedic injunctions prescribe actions and that those actions are the means to the attainment of desirable goals including heaven. The earliest extant commentary upon Jaimini's work is the *Pūrvamīmāṃsāsūtrabhāṣya* of Śabara (*c.* CE 200). Prabhākara (*c.* CE 700) and Kumārila Bhaṭṭa (*c.* CE 700) interpreted his commentary, which gave rise to two main schools of interpretation.

Mīmāṃsā's central concern is 'duty' (*dharma*), which is defined as the desired object (*artha*) whose desirability is testified only by the injunctive statements of the Vedas. The *Pūrvamīmāṃsāsūtra* commences with the aim of investigating and ascertaining the nature of religious *dharma*. Religious duty is not a physical entity, so it cannot be known through perception or any of the other means of valid knowledge that presupposes the work of perception. Thus Mīmāṃsā concludes that religious duty is knowable only through the scripture, and the essence of the scripture is injunctions and commandments which tell what ought to be done (*vidhi*) and what ought not to be done (*niṣedha*).

VEDĀNTA SCHOOL

The word 'Vedānta,' as we have seen above, literally means the 'end of the Veda.' Historically, the concluding portions of the Vedas (the Upaniṣads) were known as the Vedānta. By association the philosophical schools that based their thought upon the Upaniṣads are also called Vedānta. Since the Upaniṣads do not provide a consistent system and seemingly propose different views, it became necessary to systematize their teachings. Bādarāyaṇa (*c.* 400 BCE) attempted systematization in the form of short aphorisms called *sūtras*. His work, the *Vedāntasūtra*, is also known as the *Brahmasūtra* because it is an exposition of, and inquiry into, Brahman; as the *Śārīrakasūtra* because it is concerned with the nature and destiny of the embodied soul; as the *Bhikṣusūtra* because those competent to study it are renunciates; and as the *Uttaramīmāṃsāsūtra* because it is an inquiry into the final sections of the Veda. Its first *sūtra* begins, '*athāto brahma-jijñāsā*' (Now, therefore, the inquiry into the real nature of Brahman, the Absolute). Together with the *Dharmasūtra* of Jaimini, which is an inquiry into the duties enjoined by the Vedas, these two investigations (*mīmāṃṣa*) form a systematic inquiry into the content and meaning of the entire Veda, and thus these two *mīmāṃṣa*s are orthodox schools par excellence. Unlike Jaimini, who laid stress on the ritualistic portions of the Vedas and put forth a path of ritual action (*karmakāṇḍa*), Bādarāyaṇa emphasized the philosophical portions, the Upaniṣads, and recommended the path of contemplative wisdom (*jñānakāṇḍa*).

Though Vedānta is frequently referred to as one *darśana*, there are several Vedāntic schools. All of them acknowledge three primary sourcebooks: the Upaniṣads, the *Bhagavad Gītā*, and the *Brahmasūtra*. Together they are known as the triple canon of Vedānta. Broadly speaking, Vedānta may be divided into two main schools with certain particular tendencies: (unqualified) Nondualistic (Advaita) with absolutistic tendencies (with Śaṅkara, *c.* CE 650, as its main proponent) and (qualified) Dualistic (Dvaita) with theistic tendencies (as expounded in Rāmānuja's [*c.* CE 1027–1147] qualified nondualism [Viśiṣṭādvaita] and Madhva's [*c.* 1199–1276] dualism [Dvaita]). Other theistic Vedāntic *bhāṣyakāra*s (commentators) include Bhāskara (eighth century), Nimbārka (eleventh century), Vallabha (*c.* 1479–1531), and Caitanya (*c.* 1486–1533). No commentary on the *Brahmasūtra* survives before Śaṅkara's *bhāṣya* (*c.* CE 650–700).

All the Vedānta schools agree that the central teaching of the Upaniṣads is that Brahman is the ultimate principle underlying the physical universe and the individual souls. The chief difference among the Vedānta schools lies in the manner in which the world and the individual souls can be connected with Brahman. There are certain passages in the Upaniṣads that assert the nondifference of the world and the individual souls from Brahman, and there are others that speak of their difference from Brahman. These apparently contradictory passages have to be reconciled, and the mode of reconciliation adopted by each school represents its basic philosophical position.

According to Advaita Vedānta, the Upaniṣadic texts teaching nondifference are primary and those teaching difference are secondary, intended only to lead to the real teaching of nonduality. Brahman is the only reality, and the universe and the individual soul have no existence apart from Brahman. In an oft-quoted verse, 'Brahman is real, the universe is nonreal, and individuals are not different from Brahman.' Further, Brahman, which is the only reality, is beyond all determination, all attributes. It is only due to ignorance that the attributeless Brahman appears as though endowed with attributes. Thus it follows that Advaita adheres to a doctrine that *karmakāṇḍa* and *jñānakāṇḍa* are independent of each other while Viśiṣṭādvaita argues that they jointly constitute a single work, with Jaimini's coming first and Bādarāyaṇa's coming after it in logical order.

According to the Viśiṣṭādvaita and the Bhedābheda schools, the texts teaching difference and those teaching nondifference are equally important. The universe and the individual souls are therefore different as well as nondifferent from Brahman. In so far as the world and souls are imperfect, they are dependent and different from Brahman, who is perfect and independent. At the same time, they are nondifferent from Brahman in the sense that they form the body and the attributes of Brahman.

According to Dvaita Vedānta, the texts teaching difference convey the real teaching of the Upaniṣads. The universe and the individual souls are absolutely different from Brahman. However, this does not mean that they are independent realities. Brahman is the only independent reality, and the world and the individual souls, while separate from Brahman, are dependent thereon. The Upaniṣadic texts that teach nondifference are intended only to emphasize the independent character of Brahman.

Other philosophies

Kauṭilya's *Arthaśāstra* (*c.* 321–296 BCE) systematized the science of political economy or material prosperity, which is one of the Hindu four goals of life. The work is mainly concerned with human subsistence, wealth, and property. It also covers theories of kingship and realistic statecraft, concepts of the public good, relations among states, and the formation and implementation of policy.

A highly sophisticated philosophy of language developed at least as early as the fifth century BCE with the *Aṣṭadhyāyi* of Pāṇini. The descriptive analytical grammar of Sanskrit in this work, covering the analysis of phonemes, suffixes, sentences, rules of word combination, and the formation of verbal roots, has not yet been surpassed. After Pāṇini's beginnings, full-fledged linguistic philosophies were formulated by the leading thinker of the grammarian school, Bhartṛhari (CE 400), in his *Vākyapadīya*, which analyzed language as a door leading to liberation.

The Śaiva schools are philosophical systems within the religious traditions that worship Śiva as the Supreme Deity. Śaiva theology and philosophy developed primarily outside the Vedic context, relying instead on the Tantras and the Āgamas. There arose a number of Śaiva schools. Among them Vīraśaivism or Liṅgāyatism, which traces its origin to the five great teachers mentioned in the *Svāyaṁbhuvāgama*: Revaṇasiddha, Marulasiddha, Ekorāma, Paṇḍitārādhya, and Viśvārādhya, and to Basava (CE 1106–68), who is the greatest expounder of the system; Śivādvaita of Śrīkaṇṭha (*c.* CE 1200), whose *bhāṣya* on the *Brahmasūtra* identifies Brahman with Paramaśiva; Śaiva Siddhānta, a dualistic school which incorporated Tamil devotion with Kashmir Śaiva nondualism and whose most important philosophers include Appar, Jñānasaṁbandhar, Sundaramūrti, Māṇikkavācakar, Aruṇandi-śivācārya, and Meykaṇḍa (*c.* CE 1200), whose *Śivajñānabodham* is the basic text of the school; and Kashmir Śaivism (also known as Trika, Spanda, and Pratyabhijña), a nondualistic philosophical system attributed to Śiva himself and his *Śivasūtra*. Its most notable exponents include Somānanda (*c.* CE 900–950), Utpala (*c.* CE 925–975), Abhinavagupta (*c.* CE 975–1025), and Kṣemarāja (*c.* CE 1000–1050). It recognizes the entire universe as a manifestation of divine conscious energy and explains how the formless, unmanifest supreme principle, Śiva, manifests as the entire universe.

Tantra

Hindu Tantric literature is extensive, and its sources are many and varied. Like much other Hindu sacred literature, this literature is not yet well catalogued nor thoroughly studied. The texts are usually in verse, vary in length, and cannot be dated before the sixth or seventh century CE. The main body of Tantric texts is in Sanskrit and is known as Āgama ('tradition') as opposed to Veda. The Āgamas are thought of as divinely revealed scriptures that have been handed down from teacher to pupil. The themes of creation, destruction, worship of deities, the repetition of *mantra*s, means of attaining and the attainment of the sixfold desires, forms of meditation, and the four kinds of *yoga* are described in them.

Usually the *āgama*s of the Śaivas are called Āgama; those of the Śāktas, Tantra; and those of the Vaiṣṇavas, Saṃhitā. They are divided into three main branches according to the deity worshipped. *Pāñcarātra* and *Vaikhānasa Āgama*s are Vaiṣṇava scriptures that extol Viṣṇu; *Śaiva Āgama*s extol Śiva; and *Śakta Āgama*s extol the Devī. *Śākta Tantra*s are enumerated as sixty-four and grouped into *dakṣiṇa* and *vāma* or right and left hand. *Vaiṣṇava Tantra*s are said to number 108 (although more than 200 are known) and are grouped into *Vaikhānasa* and *Pāñcarātra*. Those revealed by Sage Vikhanas to his disciples Bhṛgu, Marīci, Atri, and so on are *Vaikhānasa Tantra*s. *Pañcarātra Āgama*s are threefold: *divya* or directly revealed by Lord Nārāyaṇa, *munibhāṣita* or those handed over to the sages such as *Bharadvājasaṃhitā* and *Pārameśvarasaṃhitā*, and *āpta-manujaprokta* or those written by men whose word is trustworthy. *Śaiva Āgamas* are fourfold: *Kāpāla*, *Kālāmukha*, *Pāśupata*, and *Śaiva*. Traditionally twenty-eight *Śaiva Āgama*s are recognized as forming the revealed canon (though hundreds of these scriptures are here and there mentioned).

In theory, the *Śaiva Āgama*s consist of four parts: methods of worship, temple construction, and making images (*kriyā*); philosophical doctrines (*jñāna*); meditative practices (*yoga*); and conduct (*caryā*). However, few of them have survived in that complete form. These are grouped into three divisions: Tantra that teaches rituals, *mantra* that teaches the *yoga* stage of worship, and *upadeśa* that expounds the existence and nature of the three eternal entities – individual souls, modes of bondage, and God (*paśu*, *pāśa*, and *pati*).

The Āgamas typically take the form of a dialogue between Śiva and the Goddess (Pārvatī, Umā) or between Bhagvān and Śrī or Lakṣmī. They contain a collection of practices and symbols that are used as means to reach spiritual liberation, with an emphasis on the authority of the *guru* and initiation. Philosophical doctrines in the Āgamas vary. Some of them teach nonduality, others qualified nonduality, and still others duality. What they share is an attempt to place desire (*kāma*), in every meaning of the word, in the service of liberation.

Ethics and human relations

Varṇa

In Vedic society, as we have observed, *dharma* is one of the most pivotal concepts. Another is *varṇa*. It is introduced in the myth of dismemberment and sacrifice of the cosmic person in the *Puruṣa Sūkta* (*Ṛg Veda* 10.90), which is a myth of origin for the four classes. The highest three of them were known as 'twice-born' because their males underwent Vedic initiation, a rite of passage that gave them access to being full members of a ritual-centered society. The *varṇa* system accepts that people differ from one another and assumes that these differences are reflected in one's aptitudes and predilections. Kṛṣṇa says in the *Bhagavad Gītā*, 'The four castes were created by me according to the division of aptitudes (*guṇa*) and works (*karma*)' (4.13).

A case could be made that the idea behind the four classes (*varṇa-dharma*) is an organic model of social economy in which each of the four classes is like a separate organ with a specific set of functions. The set of functions that is associated with any one class is different from that associated with any of the other three classes, but all are equally necessary for the survival and integrity of the society just as they would be in any organism. Each class is distinguished by its particular contributions, but nevertheless is of equal value to the whole in the way that the lungs, skin, liver, and central nervous system are each important for harmonious and effective functioning of the body. Although the ways that they are structured and how they operate differ, the social body is one.

Some modern Hindus have theorized that castes may have been at first correlated with professions and guilds and then later became hereditary. With the passage of time, perhaps the prestige of the priestly class (Brāhmaṇs) turned the system into a vertical hierarchy. The domain of the priests involves what are considered to be the most important goals in life. Priests are the ones who must be consulted when people are to be married, to be buried, or to have dealings with divine boons and blessings. However, the *dharma* of priests was to protect and preserve the Vedas, to perform rituals, and to teach, free of charge. It was the duty of the warrior class (the Kṣatriyas) to provide simple housing, food, and life's necessities for the priests in return for their service to society. When priests began to perform their duties like merchants (the Vaiśyas) and to charge for their services, according to this devolutionary theory of Hindu social stratification, *dharma* was broken and castes became rigidly arranged into a hierarchical structure with the Brāhmaṇs at the top and the workers (the Śūdras) at the bottom. What once may have been a system of functional interdependence that sustained the harmony of the social whole was transformed into a competitive and divisive force that led to the formation of further subdivisions leading to the multiple castes and subcastes of today. This speculative interpretation of the emergence of increasing caste rigidity has considerable popular support among contemporary Hindus.

Caste as a genetic phenomenon, as an innate status that is inherited and cannot be changed, is not supported in some influential traditional texts. Satyakāma, in the *Chāndogya Upaniṣad*, was accepted as a student by Ṛṣi Gautama not on the basis of caste but on the basis of conduct (because he spoke the truth, which is a trait of a Brāhmaṇ). Yudhiṣṭhira in the *Mahābhārata* says, 'Truth, charity, fortitude, good conduct, gentleness, austerity, and compassion, he in whom these are observed is a Brāhmaṇ; if these marks exist in a Śūdra, then he is a Brāhmaṇ' (3.131.21). Manu said the same.

A distinction is made between 'class' (*varṇa*) and 'caste' (*jāti*). The term '*varṇa*' plays a role in Vedic literature, but the term '*jāti*' does not make its appearance until the Dharmaśāstra literature. In its early use there, it is a synonym of *varṇa*. Later commentators began to make a distinction between the four castes (Brāhmaṇ, Kṣatriya, Vaiśya, and Śūdra) and a multitude of birth groups *(jāti)*. The *jāti*s are complex, with many subdivisions, though their relationship to *varṇa*s remains a controversial subject.

Remember that the word '*dharma*' means 'to uphold, to sustain.' The Hindu caste system as it is represented in the cosmogonic hymn (*Ṛg Veda* 10.90) is an organic structure. The whole is dependent upon the parts fulfilling their duties in a proper manner.

Āśrama

In addition to the four classes (*varṇa*), there are the four stages of life (*āśrama*). These stages emphasize the individual aspects of one's personal development and represent a vertical ascent toward liberation. The stages are the celibate student (*brahmacarya*), householder (*gṛhastha*), hermit (*vānaprastha*), and renunciant (*sannyāsin*). Ideally they are equally divided into four units of twenty-five years each, forming a century of life.

In the first stage of life a young person is to learn the sacred scriptures, acquire the necessary skills to perform ritual functions, acquire discipline, and prepare for a responsible adult life. Celibacy is mandatory during this period, which is to end with marriage. The second stage of life is devoted to production of a family, acquisition of wealth, and repaying one's debts to society, to one's ancestors, and to the gods. A student's *dharma* is to remain celibate and to study rather than to work for a living, and a householder's *dharma* is to lead a conjugal life with a marriage partner and to work in order to support the family. Wealth and pleasure may be acquired, but they should be acquired rightly. There are five main traditional duties of the marriage partners in a twice-born household: *brahma-yajña* (sacrifice to Brahman consisting of studying and teaching the Veda); *deva-yajña* (ritual sacrifices to *devas*); *pitṛ-yajña* (ritual sacrifices to departed ancestors); *bhūta-yajña* (taking care of domestic animals); and *manuṣya-yajña* (feeding guests, the homeless, and the destitute). Most people never go beyond these two stages of life. Remember that both initiation and marriage are sacraments (*saṃskāra*). The third stage of life commences when a person 'saw their hair turn grey and their skin wrinkled and their children's children' (that is, when one's own children have become householders themselves). With the arrival of these events, one is enjoined to give all one's property and wealth to one's children and to retire to the forest, to lead a simple life, and to spend one's time in spiritual pursuits. Finally, the stage of total renunciation is when a person becomes an ascetic, owning nothing, the sky as their roof, the grass as their bed, taking what food as chance may bring, and desiring nothing but one's own liberation and the welfare of all beings. Such a one says 'peace to all' and no longer is concerned about how their body lives or goes. Praise and blame become one, and they move freely from place to place.

The ideal traditional map of the four stages of life is intended to take an individual to the fulfillment of human life by successive steps. As a rule, one should progress through each of the four stages in turn. But in extraordinary cases, some of the steps may be omitted. For instance, Śuka, Vyāsa's son, was born a *sannyāsin*; Śaṅkara, the great reformer of Hinduism (eighth century CE), became a *sannyāsin* from the student stage; and Buddha became a *sannyāsin* from the householder stage.

Puruṣārtha

The *puruṣārtha*s (sometimes referred to as the *caturvarga*) are the four acknowledged aims of human beings. These are mastery of material resources, enjoyment of what is pleasurable and beautiful, responsible performance of one's duties, and the attainment of spiritual realization and release from the limited horizons of human possibilities. The first two goals, *artha* ('what is useful'; wealth) and *kāma* ('what is pleasurable'; desire) represent the economic and the acquisitive values of life. They are means-oriented or instrumental values. Since every object in the universe is impermanent and will pass away one day or other, these two values cannot give permanent results. They are good within their limits, but to expect eternal bliss from temporary objects is a delusion. The third goal, *dharma* (righteousness, duty), is the ethical and moral value. It is a regulative and an integrative value. It is not wrong to pursue strictly instrumental values if one chooses, so long as they are pursued in ways that are compatible with the requirements of *dharma*. What Hinduism asks is that the individual should have their eyes open and be aware of the limited pleasure that such goals can and will produce. Finally, the fourth goal, *mokṣa* (liberation, realization), is said to be the spiritual value. It is an intrinsic and end value. While the first two goals are means to an end (that is, happiness), liberation is the goal itself and not a means to a goal.

Ethics

Hindu ethics do not owe their origin to dogmatic notions of good and evil. The ideas of *dharma, karma*, and *saṃsāra* form the axis around which Hindu ethics revolve. Actions that foster clarity and a greater love for all are 'meritorious,' and actions that foster delusion and selfishness are 'unmeritorious.' Person, place, time, and circumstance all play a part in determining whether a particular action will be conducive to the greater good and will be compatible with traditional guidelines, prescriptions, and prohibitions.

According to Hindu assumptions, desire or an exertion of the will is what impels each and every action. The total of such actions constitute one's conduct and character. Further, such actions may be mental, verbal, or physical. Ideally these three should be aligned. This is technically known as *trikaraṇaśudhi* or 'one in thought, word, and deed.' *Karma* is both 'deed' and the 'results of a deed.' However, *karma* is not fate; it is a perfect conservation of energy. Not only does every action produce its appropriate result, it also leaves behind a subtle trace that shapes one's character. The past can be determined with absolute precision. But the future is uncertain, and character can change (however difficult that may be). A person has the freedom to change their behavior in spite of tendencies to the contrary. The most inclusive context for this is a totally meaningful universe within which there are no accidents, no mistakes, and nothing capricious despite all appearances to the contrary.

Five cardinal virtues found in Hindu scriptures are keys to Hindu ethics. Noninjury (*ahiṃsā*) is the most important of them. In Vedic rituals, animals have been sacrificed; in capital punishment, people have been put to death on orders from their own rulers; and in wars, soldiers and innocent civilians have been killed from earliest times until today. However, the doctrines of *ahiṃsā* and vegetarianism reinforced one another through a common aversion toward killing and eating animals as well as through the importance placed on the cow. Historically, it was primarily the Jainas and the Buddhists who inspired India to vegetarianism. Contrary to popular stereotypes, many Hindus are not vegetarians. Some eat fish, others chicken or lamb, and a few even eat beef. For the most part, Brāhmaṇs (except in Bengal and Kashmir) are vegetarian, although times and dietary practices are changing.

The five cardinal virtues are duties common to all (*sādhārana-dharma*) and should be cultivated by everyone, irrespective of distinctions of caste or stage of life. How these virtues are identified can vary from one scripture to another, and in the sixteenth chapter of the *Bhagavad Gītā* (verses 1–3) one will find a particularly long list that includes fearlessness, purity of thought, steadfastness in knowledge and devotion, charity, self-control, performance of sacrifice, study of the scriptures, austerity, simplicity, nonviolence, truthfulness, freedom from anger, renunciation, tranquility, aversion to faultfinding, compassion for all living beings, freedom from covetousness, gentleness, modesty, steadiness, courage, patience, fortitude, cleanliness, and freedom from malice and conceit. However, all these can be considered variations of the five great cardinal virtues of purity, self-control, detachment, truth, and nonviolence.

Yoga *or* Mārga*: paths to liberation*

Traditionally, Hindu spiritual disciplines (*sādhana*) are divided into three paths or ways (*mārga*): the path of selfless action (*karma*), the path of devotion to God (*bhakti*), and the path of knowledge (*jñāna*). Other paths that are influential but may be less well known include *rāja-yoga* or the path of meditation, *kundalini-yoga* or the path of awakening the coiled inner power, *mantra-yoga* or the path of mystic sounds, *hatha-yoga* or the path of physical postures, and *krīya-yoga* or the path of transmutative actions. Some paths that have become well known more recently are identified with the followers of modern and contemporary spiritual teachers such as Aurobindo's *pūrna-yoga* or all of life as *yoga* and Muktānanda's *siddha-yoga* or perfect path.

In the *Bhagavad Gītā*, Kṛṣṇa describes the three ways to liberation (or, as some say, three aspects of one way). Each of these paths can be considered an independent means to the ultimate goal of life, although the way of knowledge and the way of devotion each typically incorporates the other two ways as prerequisites to their principal path.

Jñāna-yoga

According to the way of knowledge, the path to liberation is in and through knowledge. The question is, 'What is knowledge?' In this context, it is not information. It is not a set of facts about ideas, people, places, or things. Transforming and liberating knowledge is about the immortal soul or inner self. The way of knowledge involves a twofold means, namely, the preliminary auxiliary cause which itself is twofold (remote and proximate means) and the primary direct instrumental means. The remote means (*antaranga sādhana*) consists of the factors that have been prescribed in the scriptural texts as indirectly helpful to prepare for the direct experience of Brahman-Ātman. They include performing rituals, giving gifts, austerity, and doing the duties appropriate to one's class and stage in life. Such activities are purifying and provide a foundation for subtle and profound experience. When the mind is freed from the craving for possessions and the thirst for sense enjoyments, it may then be directed toward higher ends. Selfless actions serve this purpose.

The well-known fourfold requirement (*sādhana catuṣṭaya*) that qualifies an aspirant to pursue the path of knowledge forms the proximate means (*bahiranga sādhana*). The four are discrimination of the eternal from the noneternal; nonattachment to the enjoyment of the fruits of one's actions either in this world or in any other; possession in abundance of the six virtues, namely, calmness, equanimity, turning away from the sense objects, forbearance, concentration, and faith; and an intense longing for liberation. According to tradition, only an individual who meets the fourfold requirement is qualified to study the Upaniṣadic texts under the guidance of a teacher (*guru*) who is learned in scripture and well established in the truth. In this context, a *guru* is defined as a spiritual master who has attained oneness with the divine and without whom a disciple cannot attain liberation.

The proximate path of knowledge (*jñāna*) consists of three steps: hearing (*śravaṇa*), reflection (*manana*), and contemplation (*nididhyāsana*). Hearing means the proper understanding of the meaning of Vedāntic statements. These are of two kinds: intermediary and major texts. The intermediary texts relate to the nature of the world, the nature of the individual, and so on. The major texts impart the supreme knowledge of nonduality. The intermediary texts impart only a secondary or mediate knowledge of the truth. It is from the major or great texts that the direct experience of the plenary reality may be obtained. Even so, unless one is a qualified aspirant, even the hearing of the major texts will not produce the plenary experience due to one's own impediments. Typically these impediments are in the form of long-established false beliefs that could be (and must be) overcome by diligent reflection and contemplation. After the impediments have been removed, there arises the intuitive experience of nonduality or *mokṣa*. This is direct knowledge of the Self. When ignorance is destroyed, self-realization occurs. Kṛṣṇa says to Arjuna, 'Just as fire reduces firewood to ashes, so too does the fire of knowledge reduce all ignorance to ashes' (*Bhagavad Gītā* 4.37).

Bhakti-yoga

The path of love, the way of devotion (*bhakti*) is defined by Ṛṣi Nārada in his *Bhaktisūtras* as an intense love of God. In the *Bhāgavata Purāṇa*, Prahlāda prays to his lord: 'That constant love which the ignorant have for the objects of their senses, let me have that constancy in my love for Thee' (1.20.19). Others, including the great nineteenth-century ecstatic mystic Rāmakṛṣṇa, say the divinely kindled experience of *bhakti* is like 'the continuous flow of lamp oil poured from one container to another' that provides an ever-renewing source of light to illumine all of life. *Bhakti* is an acknowledgement of the generous compassion of God. Kṛṣṇa says, 'Even if an unrighteous person adores me with exclusive devotion, he must be regarded as righteous. . . . My devotee is never lost' (*Bhagavad Gītā* 9.31). Devotion is an emotion (*bhāva*) that is transformed into an essence (*rasa*). It does not stop with mere emotionalism but leads to training of the will and the intellect.

Devotion is built upon the foundations of action (*karma*) and knowledge (*jñāna*). The first requisite is renunciation of the wrong understanding of self that led one into attachment. This will make it possible to perform disinterested actions without the desire to benefit from them. Then disinterested action will help to purify the mind and make it ready for devotion. The second requisite is right knowledge. With such knowledge, one comes to understand oneself to be distinct from matter and its effects and to understand God to be the supreme personality on which one ultimately depends. Then love and devotion grow and reverence toward God increases.

Devotion itself is of two kinds: formal (*prapatti*) and surrender (*śaraṇāgati*). They have been compared to the way of the monkey in which the young will cling to their mother's back through their own efforts and the way of the cat in which the mother cat picks up her young and carries them without any effort on their part. The way of formal devotion is like a ladder leading to heaven. It has four main steps: a clear knowledge of the realms of *karma, jñāna* and *bhakti*; the will to undertake spiritual disciplines in their appropriate sequence; the scriptural qualifications of birth, and so on; and the patience to endure the ills of one's *karma* until it is exhausted. This is a long, gradual path, and it can be expected to be punctuated by challenges and difficulties. Unconditional surrender, on the other hand, preserves the essentials of formal devotion, dispenses with its predisposing conditions, and omits any nonessentials. It is an easier and more direct way to liberation. The prerequisite, however, is a change of heart and an absolute confidence in the saving grace of the lord. The gradual acquisition of merit is not part of this path. The lord is the way and the goal. All that is needed is an act of unreserved self-surrender to divine grace. Kṛṣṇa's promise is, 'Letting go of all duties, take refuge in me alone; I shall deliver you from all unrighteous actions; do not grieve' (*Bhagavad Gītā* 18.66).

According to the Vaiṣṇava tradition, devotion may assume many forms. The role of the devotee in relation to God may be one of servant to master (an influential model is Hanumān to Rāma); friend to friend (Arjuna to Kṛṣṇa); parent to child (Kauśalyā to Rāma, or Yaśodā to Kṛṣṇa); child to parent (Dhruva to Viṣṇu, or Prahlāda to Viṣṇu); wife to husband (Sītā to Rāma); and lover to beloved (Rādhā to Kṛṣṇa). There are also said to be nine forms of devotion (*navavidhā bhakti*): listening to God's glory (*śravaṇa*), singing God's praise (*kīrtana*), contemplating God (*smaraṇa*), worshipping God's feet (*pādasevana*), worshipping God (as in an image) (*arcana*), prostration to God (*vandana*), waiting on God as a servant (*dāsya*), fellowship with God (*sakhya*), and offering oneself totally to God (*ātma-nivedana*).

The soul or inner self (*ātman*) is essentially free and eternal; and it lives, moves, and has its being in Brahman. But somehow it falsely identifies itself with matter and imagines itself to be no more than a mode of matter. Due to the consequences of *karma*, the individual forgets his or her real nature, becomes enticed by matter, and gets caught in the world of birth and death. *Bhakti* changes this self-centeredness into God-centeredness. It turns the mind from material sensuality to an intense spiritual love of God.

Karma-yoga

The way of action (*karma*) is the path of disinterested action or service. *Karma* means work or action, and in general all action binds a person – whether through meritorious acts that produce meritorious results or through unmeritorious acts that produce unmeritorious results. The way of action entails acting in accordance with one's duty without desire for and attachment to the effects or fruits of those actions. Neither praise nor blame, neither reward nor punishment should be one's concern. If one acts selflessly, others benefit and one's character becomes ennobled, too.

Acting with desire, with expectations and swayed by attraction and aversion leads to bondage and unhappiness. Not only are effects produced but also subtle latent traces are left as if a residue, both of which generate more action leading to an endless cycle.

Temporary results can never produce eternal satisfaction. Thus, the way of action seeks to transform all work into worship. Every action needs a motive, and by making worship of God one's motive, all of life becomes an act of worship.

Religious orders and holy persons

While monasticism developed in both Jainism and Buddhism, there have been ascetics in the Hindu tradition as far back as the Vedic period. Many of the Vedic and Upaniṣadic sages were forest-dwellers, and ascetics in Hinduism have been known by various labels: *śramaṇa* (wanderer), *keśin* (long-haired ascetic), *yati* (wandering ascetic), *parivrājaka* (wanderer), *yogī* and *muni* (silent sage), *tapasvi* (performer of austerities), *sādhu* (holy person), *vairāgi* (renunciant), and *sannyāsin* (renunciant). Contemporary scholars disagree as to whether asceticism was a part of the Vedic (householder) tradition or whether it emerged out of reaction to Vedic ritualism. In other words, is there a conflict between the Brāhmaṇ ritualist and the renunciant? How divided and far apart are the householder and the renouncer?

In general, Hindu renunciants wear ochre robes, have shaven heads or long matted hair, and diligently perform spiritual practices for the purpose of liberation. They either live alone on the edges of society, along the banks of rivers or in forests, in mountain caves, or in cremation grounds; or they live in hermitages (*āśrama*) or monasteries (*maṭha*). According to tradition, the great Vedāntic sage, Śaṅkara, founded monasteries in the four corners of India and a renunciate order of monks with ten branches (*daśanāmi*). The ten are associated with different monastic centers: the Jyotiṣpīṭha at Badrinath in the north has the Giri, Sāgara, and Parvata orders; Govardhanapīṭha at Puri in the east has the Āraṇya and Vāna orders; Śāradāpīṭha at Srngeri in the south has the Bhāratī, Purī, and Sarasvatī orders; and Kālikāpīṭha at Dvaraka in the west has the Tīrtha and Āśrama orders.

Roles for women

Within Hinduism, the ideal female is admired and honored; in practice the human female may not be so well treated. Hindu women have been appreciated as wives but shunned as widows. They have been portrayed as goddesses but also persecuted as seductresses who drain the life from a man. Typical roles that are relevant to understanding representation of females in Hindu tradition would include the goddess, wife, widow, lover, consort, courtesan, or prostitute. Females are represented as occupying roles at all levels of reality and relative power: as subservient and dependent or as dominant and independent; as the upholder of tradition or as the innovator and modernizer; and as situated in a matrilineal or a patrilineal family.

During the Vedic Age, women apparently had considerable freedom and many privileges in the spheres of family, civic life, and religion. The high status of at least some women was correlated with the fact that Vedic sacrificial rituals depended on the patronage of married householders who sponsored them. A wife was *ardhānginī*, a partner to her husband in religious rites. Evidence suggests that in early Vedic times, women in the upper classes may have received the sacred thread, studied the Vedas, and participated in the performance of rituals. Women named in the Vedas as sages include Lopāmudrā, Viśvavārā, Ghoṣā, and Indrāṇī. Early women scholars included Kathī, Kālapī, Bahvici, Gārgī Vācaknavī, and Maitreyī. Bişpalā was named as a female warrior.

The end of the Vedic period saw great changes in the status of Hindu women. Brāhmaṇical specialization required longer periods of education and marriage at an earlier age was becoming fashionable, a combination of factors that would have allowed fewer women to participate in Vedic learning. As the extent of Vedic teaching and practice increased, it took longer and longer to memorize it, and women needed that time for bearing and nurturing children. With a growing emphasis on ancestral sacrifices that only males were permitted to perform, the preference for male children increased, and the childbearing function of women was regarded as crucially important for propagating the male line. The transition from ritualism to asceticism evidenced in the Upaniṣads appears to have had an influence on the place of women in society, too.

The classical/medieval period saw the further development of *strī-dharma*, the codes of ideal behavior of Hindu women. During this period, Hindu law books, especially Manu's *Dharmaśāstra* (*Manusmṛti*), defined in detail the roles for women. From then onward the Hindu woman was to focus on her husband; he was to be her most immediate model and avenue of approach to God. Men's religious practices were to be aimed at general prosperity, and women's religious practices were to be aimed at family welfare and domestic prosperity. The *Manusmṛti* prescribed a subservient and dependent status for women. 'By a girl, by a young woman, or even by an aged one, nothing must be done independently, even in her own house. In childhood a female must be subject to her father, in youth to her husband, when her lord is dead, to her sons; a woman must never be independent' (5.148). However, even in the *Manusmṛti* there are both ideological and practical limits to the subservience of women. Manu said that a wife is a physical embodiment of the goddess of good fortune and auspiciousness and that where women are honored the gods will be pleased and where they are not honored no sacred rite will yield rewards. Manu also states that women's property (*strī-dhan*) is for the woman to retain, to use, and to bequeath as she herself may determine.

With the modern age has come an expanding freedom for Hindu women. Foreign influences including the British Rāj and Christian missions, along with internal influences such as India's social reform movements, Mohandas K. Gandhi and Sarojini Naidu sounded a call for changes. *Satī* ('a wife who ascends the funeral pyre of her deceased husband') was legally prohibited, schools for girls were opened, and child marriage was subjected to criticism. Authority for these changes was sought in the Veda. References to child marriage and *satī* were not found there, so they may have been later accretions that found their way into the society. Additional models for advancing the roles of women were found by observing that norms for behavior (*varṇāśrama-dharma* and *sva-dharma*) vary from place to place and situation to situation, and that certain practices do not suit the circumstances of the current dark age of the Kali Yuga.

Institutions and practices

Rituals

The Veda is the earliest and most authoritative surviving source for the practice of sacrificial rituals. It does not require any permanent or immovable place of worship, any lasting images, or written texts. What it does require is one or more qualified priests who have been trained in the proper hymns and procedures. The sacrifice (*homa, yajña*) consists of offering into the sacrificial fire materials such as milk, clarified butter, yogurt, rice, barley, and the *soma* plant. Nowadays various plant materials are substituted because the identity of the ancient *soma* has been lost. It is a Vedic ritual assumption that the essence of what is offered is transported through the fire to the selected *deva*(s).

Two types of Vedic rituals were developed: the solemn public rites (*śrauta*, 'based on the *śruti*') and the domestic rites (*gṛhya*). The *śrauta* rites are the older of the two and require three fires: the householder's fire (*gārhapatya*), round in shape, located in the west, which was mainly used to prepare food for the sacrifice; the fire that would consume most of it (*āhavaniya*), square in shape, located in the east; and a semicircular southern fire (*dakṣiṇāgni*), used to ward off hostile spirits and to receive special offerings to departed ancestors. Between the two main fires was the *vedi*, a ritually insulated grass-lined pit in which oblations and sacrificial utensils were placed to preserve their power when not in use. These rites are complex and complicated and require a number of priestly specialists. The most elaborate of these rituals requires four priests (each a specialist respectively in one of the four Vedas). Other well-known *śrauta* rites include the *aśvamedha*, horse sacrifice; the *agniṣṭoma*, a fairly simple one-day *soma* sacrifice; and the *agnicayana*, a complex rite which lasts for several days. The principal deities involved in the *śrauta* rite are Agni and Soma. Such rites may only be performed by qualified priests and are generally performed for the welfare of the entire world.

The *gṛhya* rites, on the other hand, require only one fire and are performed by a householder for the welfare of his family. The ancient-Vedic householder was expected to maintain a domestic fire into which he made his offerings. Every twice-born Hindu was required to perform this ritual daily. However, with the passage of time, householders began to employ a family priest to perform not only the daily *homa* but also most other domestic rites on behalf of the family. This eventually led to hiring a priest to administer the important lifecycle events or sacraments. These lifecycle events include all the important transitions in life from conception to cremation.

The Hindu sacraments are rites of passage – rituals that mark and make possible an individual's transition from one stage of life to another. These domestic rites are described in the Gṛhyasūtras and/or the Dharmasūtras and the Dharmaśāstras, but not every caste or regional community celebrates every one of them or attaches the same importance to each of them. Rites for females are not discussed in the classical texts. Nevertheless, all the rites of passage are described as 'auspicious' moments, auspicious in the sense that they involve the power to produce good fortune, true happiness.

Rites are divided into daily ritual actions (*nitya-karma*) that are to be performed every day, ritual acts (*naimittika-karma*) made necessary by some special occurrence, and rites for a desired purpose or particular object (*kāmya-karma*). The *saṃskāra*s or sacraments are transitional rites that form and acknowledge the series of identities through which one passes in the course of a lifetime. In undergoing them, a person is rendered ritually pure and is qualified for the next stage in their life. Not only do the sacraments sanctify special moments, they also legitimize and uphold social institutions. Further, it is thought that they purify the individual, and without this ritual purification further action would be ineffective and fruitless. In any case, a man or woman is more likely to experience themselves as renewed and properly prepared for the new part of their life if they have received the sanction and blessings of the elders, sages, and God. The word '*saṃskāra*' means 'perfecting,' thus to 'do well.'

From antiquity there have been differing opinions about the exact number of sacramental rites of passage. The number of *saṃskāra*s listed in the literature varies from thirteen to forty, although four of them are considered most important: birth, initiation, marriage, and death. The birth of a boy, especially the first child, is considered particularly auspicious. By the birth of a son, a father is said to have repaid the debt to his ancestors and to have enabled his forefathers to attain the world of heaven (*svar*). The birth of a daughter is not considered inauspicious, but it does create a greater practical liability in the context of traditional marriage practices in most of the subcontinent where a dowry and other continuing expenses for the parents of daughters must be expected. For a child of either sex, the exact moment of birth is noted because a person's horoscope is cast from it and can be an important factor in arranging a suitable marriage.

The initiation ritual (*upanayana*) for a boy is held at any time between the ages of eight and twenty-four. He is taught the proper way to recite Gāyatri-*mantra* daily. It is addressed to Savitṛ, the sun, and is found in the *Ṛg Veda* (3.62.10): 'We meditate on the brilliance of the Sun; May it inspire our intellect.' At this ceremony, he is also given the sacred thread which is the most obvious external sign that he is among the 'twice-born' and has entered into high-caste society and the student stage of life. The traditional ideal was that initiation would mark the beginning of a long period of Vedic study under the guidance of a teacher (*guru*) during which the student would live in his teacher's house. As a student, it was society's duty to support him. He would receive food from a few households, take it to the *guru*'s wife, and she would apportion and serve it to her husband's students.

The initiation into Vedic learning is for high-caste males. Female initiation, according to Manu, is marriage. The wife serving her husband is equivalent to Vedic study, and housework is equivalent to the fire oblations (*Manusmṛti* 2.67). In some communities, women's puberty rites have been considered an initiatory rite of passage, too. There is some evidence in the Vedas that prior to *c.* 600 BCE females as well as males were initiated with the Gāyatri-*mantra*, were invested with the sacred thread, and studied the Vedas in the house of the *guru*. The epics include accounts of women involved in lighting and tending the sacrificial fire to make ritual offerings to the *deva*s.

Marriage is the next great transition in people's lives. In the Hindu tradition, it is the norm, is expected of all, and inaugurates the householder stage of life in which each individual fulfills the duty to family and society. As a householder it is appropriate to pursue the goals of duty (*dharma*), wealth and worldly success (*artha*), and pleasure (*kāma*). Because of this, it is said that the householder stage is the safest and best fortress from which to engage in the battle of life. According to the *Dharmaśāstra*, a person is born with debts to God, gods, sages, humans, and animals. By performing one's domestic duties, living a righteous life, and having children, the husband along with his wife repays these debts.

Wedding ceremonies vary greatly from region to region throughout India. However, the following practices are usually considered essential. The date is fixed after careful astrological calculation; the bridegroom is conducted to the home of his future parents-in-law, who receive him as an honored guest; at the ceremony, the bridegroom takes the bride by the hand or is linked to her by a cloth, and conducts her around the sacrificial fire; prayers and auspicious *mantra*s are uttered; and seven steps are taken by the bride and groom together to solemnize the irrevocability of their union. Traditionally a marriage is arranged, although traditional Hindu law acknowledges no less than eight forms of marriage: bride given to a priest without dowry, bride given to a priest with dowry, arranged by parents with dowry, arranged by parents, bride buying, seduction, love marriage, and forcible abduction. As you might expect, in the modern era the last few types on the traditional list have been subjected to review, critique, and debate. Traits that are considered when matching a prospective bride and groom typically include same caste and community, compatible horoscope, same area and language, extent of education, age, height, skin color, artistic skills, and socioeconomic status. The matrimonial advertisement pages in modern newspapers, and now on the Internet, generally include references to these categories. The marriage celebration itself is a great social occasion and usually is quite elaborate and expensive.

At life's end is the sacrament of death. The traditional funeral method for most Hindus is cremation. Burial is reserved for small children and others who have not been sufficiently purified by *saṃskāra*s and those who no longer need the ritual fire to be conveyed to the hereafter (such as ascetics, *sannyāsin*, who have renounced all earthly concerns and great sages, *ṛṣi*). Specific features of the rites vary, but typically the eldest son performs the death rituals. With an iron rod, he draws three lines on the ground, saying, 'I draw a line for Yama, the lord of cremation; I draw a line for *kāla*, time, the lord of cremation; I draw a line for *mṛtyu*, death, the lord of cremation.' Some sesame seeds are put into the mouth of the deceased, the body is put on the funeral pyre, and the eldest son then lights it. When the last sacrament has been performed, the individual has made the full transition through the various stages of life and has become a complete or perfected human being, worthy of worship, and thus a source of blessings for all their descendants.

Women's rituals

Many rituals, such as visiting temples, household *pūjā*, pilgrimage, and singing of devotional songs (*bhajan*), are common to both men and women. However, in addition to puberty rites, several rituals are unique to married women with living husbands. Traditionally women would daily light the oil lamps in the house and draw designs (*koḷam, raṅgolī*) on its threshold. Whenever a female visitor leaves the house, the wife offers her auspicious items, such as turmeric, a red powder (*kumkum*), bananas, coconuts, betel nuts, and/or betel leaves. Rites are performed monthly on particular days for the welfare of the husband and/or the entire extended family. There are a number of vows (*vrata*), a type of ritual that is undertaken by women for blessings, long life, or even liberation (*mokṣa*). The *vrata*s require abstaining from certain types of foods, indulgences, or pleasures in order to obtain the blessings of a deity. They are usually performed seasonally or on special occasions. Many women observe *vrata*s as a way of life and routinely observe fasts and other ascetic acts aimed at insuring the safety, happiness, and stability of their households. There are also some *pūjā*s that are unique to women, such as the Kedāra Gaurī-*pūjā*, the Vara Lakṣmī-*pūjā*, and the Sāvitrī-*vrata*. In North India, women perform the *rakṣā-bandhan* ('tying of the amulet'), during which they tie a protective cord around the wrists of their brothers, too.

Temples

In the Indus Valley or Harappā culture, there may have been a few buildings that had been set apart for worship, but the Vedas make no reference to temples or other religious buildings. One of the differences between ancient Vedic tradition and later Hinduism is the institution of permanent temples. Vedic rituals are performed either for the benefit of the patron or the sacrificer (*yajamāna*), usually with the assistance of officiants or Brāhmaṇ priests, or for the prosperity of the entire world. As a rule, the sacrifice takes place outdoors, where a fire-altar is set up only for the duration of the rites, and primary elements – earth, water, air, and space (and their modifications and representatives in the form of natural substances, such as wood, milk, clarified butter, fruits, and so on) – are offered into the sacrificial fire. During the classical period, permanent locations were established, permanent structures were built, and fixed iconic forms were established for the worship of deities. Early surviving stone temples date from the Gupta Empire (*c.* CE 300–500), and there are many large temples in various regional styles by the seventh century. The two main styles of Hindu temple architecture are the northern and the southern. A conical dome, *śikara*, characterizes the northern. The southern has a central shrine that is located in an open courtyard surrounded by a wall with four gates surmounted by a tower (*gopuram*) at each of the four cardinal directions. The *gopurams* are usually shaped in stepped layers with images of deities decorating each level. At a major temple, they may reach more than 200 feet in height.

Hindu India has several large and magnificent city-temple complexes. These include the Jagannātha temple of Puri, Liṅgarāja temple of Bhubaneswar, Konārka temple (also know as the 'Black Pagoda' or Sun temple) in Orissa, Khajurāho temple in Madhya Pradesh, Naṭarāja temple of Cidambaram, Raṅganātha temple of Srirangam, Arunācala temple of Tiruvannamalai, Mīnākṣī temple of Madurai, and Rājarājeśvara temple of Tanjavur. In these temples is installed a presiding *mūrti* (icon/image/idol) of either Śiva, Viṣṇu, or the Devī, typically accompanied by other associated deities.

A temple is the house of God and the place where the deity is both visible and accessible. The architecture of the temple symbolically represents the quest for the divine in ways that contribute to diminishing the distance between the divine and the human. Thus the temple can function as a place of transit. One travels to the temple and moves toward the divine within it by proceeding in a clockwise direction. The interior spaces of a large temple complex are arranged to encourage movement by the devotee from the outside toward the center through a series of enclosures that become increasingly sacred as one comes nearer to the central sanctuary. At the door to the *sanctum sanctorum*, a priest serves as intermediary between the devotee and the deity. The *sanctum* itself may be like a womb or a cave in which one finds mysterious vitality, a divine secret, at its very heart.

A temple should be on a site that has been carefully selected, its structure(s) should be designed and proportioned according to ancient ritual manuals, and it should be prepared for worship by installation of divine images and ritual purification. The temple itself can function like a large sacred geometric diagram (*maṇḍala*) that represents the entire cosmos, the individual human being, and the cosmic *puruṣa* of the Veda. People go to the temple for *darśana*, to be blessed by seeing and being seen by the deity through the ritually consecrated image forms. In a large and traditional temple, the main image resides in the womb-house (*garbhagṛha*) of the temple. One reason the central chamber is called a womb-house is because this is where a spiritual aspirant is 'reborn' and repeatedly renewed. Śiva temples usually have Śiva-*liṅga* as their central image. Viṣṇu temples have images of Viṣṇu or of his incarnations. The Devī temples have images of some form, or else an aniconic form, of the Goddess.

Temple rituals

Priests are trained to perform rituals in temples. Unlike the Vedic *yajña* or fire-sacrifice, a temple ritual (*pūjā*) involves worship directed toward an image. In a temple, the deity is ritually honored as if the worshippers were serving a great king (the Tamil word for temple is *koil*, 'house of the king'). The deity in its image form is awakened in the morning along with his consort; bathed, clothed, and fed; adorned with jewels and garlands of flowers, established in his shrine to give audience to his subjects, and praised and entertained throughout the day; and prepared for sleep at night. Throughout the day, worshippers may have *darśana*, sing devotional songs, offer prayers and gifts, and perform other acts of homage.

Pūjā is usually translated as 'worship.' It may be performed in a home or temple. It is the core ritual of theistic, devotional, or popular Hinduism in which a *mūrti* or a correctly designed and consecrated image becomes the focus for worship and honor of the divine. Thus, the term '*pūjā*' is most often short for *mūrti-pūjā* and typically is used to denote a ritual that centers on an image of the divine, or an aniconic form of a deity, or some other object that is believed to manifest special power or sacredness. *Pūjā* is done to receive the deity's blessings and to develop one's own inner divinity. All large temples and most domestic shrines contain images. They are anthropomorphic representations of deities that are formed in wood or clay, or are carved in stone or cast in bronze, or more rarely are made of precious stones. Frequently seen examples of aniconic images are the *liṅga* for Śiva and *śālagrāma* for Viṣṇu.

A *pūjā* involves three key elements: an offering that is presented to the deity; the auspicious sight (*darśana*) of the deity; and a blessed item of food, a flower, or some similar article that had been offered to the deity (*prasāda*) and then is redistributed to someone who had come to worship and now may take away this tangible blessing from the ritual setting. In addition, three things are usually associated with the worship of a deity: *mūrti* (or *arcā* or *pratimā*), *mantra*, and *yantra*. *Mūrti* is the physical image consecrated for worship. It may be movable or immovable. If immovable, it would be attached to a pedestal and could not be moved once installed. *Mantra* is a set of sacred sounds or words of power. By recalling, contemplating, or uttering *mantra*(s), one invokes the deity associated with it and invests the atmosphere with a divine presence that envelops the devotee and the deity. To be effective, it is widely believed that a *mantra* must be given during initiation by a *sadguru*. Two famous *mantra*s are: '*oṃ namah śivāya*' (I bow to the indwelling auspicious [one]) and '*oṃ namo nārāyaṇaya*' (I bow to the God dwelling in the human). *Yantra*s are sacred geometrical designs in which the deity is said to reside. They are 'instruments' or devices that function as the 'form body' of a deity. They allow the nameless, formless deity to take form, and they allow the infinite personal deity to enter into a delimited ritual sacred space for the purpose of worship. Thus, they are regarded as energetic centers or storehouses of divine power. Not only that, they also serve as an abstract reminder of the presence of the deity. Usually they are geometric designs composed of point, circles, squares, triangles, and rectangles. Typically they are drawn on sand, paper, or wood, or are engraved on metal (gold, silver, copper, or a combination of five metals). Crystal *yantra*s are thought to be the most auspicious and powerful of all *yantra*s.

*Pūjā*s take many alternative forms. A simple worship may consist of an offering of turmeric powder, *kumkum*, flowers, sandalwood paste, incense, and so on. Such a *pūjā* requires neither much ritual knowledge nor much time. More elaborate types of worship consist of an offering accompanied by a specific sequence of activities (*upacāra*), each of them accompanied by the recitation of specified *mantra*s. These types of *pūjā*s may vary from sixteen to 108 offerings or more. Typically the name of a *pūjā* is given according to the number of items that are being offered, for instance, *pañcopacāra pūjā*, five items, and *ṣoḍaśopacāra pūjā*, sixteen items. Among the various types of *pūjā*s, the one with sixteen items or offerings is among the most common. This type of ritual consists of preliminary acts including a declaration (*saṃkalpa*) to perform the worship, as well as rites for the purification of the devotee and the implements used in the *pūjā* and for removal of obstacles to successful completion. Then a series of sixteen main services is offered, beginning with the invocation of the deity. This establishes a relationship between the image, the cosmos, and the individual worshipper. Although the number of services is always counted as sixteen, their kind and sequence vary from source to source. One such list is: invocation, installation of the image, water for washing its feet, water for washing its head, hands, and body, water for the deity to sip, water for bathing the deity, clothing (upper and lower garments), adding the sacred thread, honoring the deity with perfume and flowers or garlands that are offered to the accompaniment of *mantra*s, lighting and wafting incense, lights, offering food, prostrating before the image, greeting and circumambulating the deity, and taking leave of the deity.

Worship or *pūjā* can be understood as the embodying of the deity and the disembodying of the worshipper. In this process, the image plays a crucial role. It provides a fixed, tangible, embodied form by means of which a worshipper may come into contact with an (otherwise inaccessible) greater being and higher level of reality. In other words, in worship the deity 'comes down' to the worshipper who thereby becomes transformed, elevated (at least temporarily), and eventually may be perfected.

At the conclusion of a *pūjā*, grace (*prasāda*), in the form of a consecrated item (such as ash, colored powder, scented water, and/or food), is distributed to the devotee(s). This grace or blessing is the indispensable conclusion to all acts of worship. The *prasāda* is the material symbol of the power and grace of the deity to whom it was offered and with whom it was in close contact. Symbolically, if not materially, the deity has consumed its essence thereby transmuting it and imbuing it with divine power and grace.

To sum up, worship is a series of acts that are intended to respectfully honor a deity. Worship is an opportunity to learn the qualities of devotion, surrender, sacrifice, and obedience. It can train the mind. It can foster patience, generosity, and service. It is an expression of gratitude and devotion that may connect (at least ideally and perhaps at most temporarily) the identity of the worshipper with that of the deity to whom he or she has given a place of honor.

Festivals

Hindus observe many different kinds of festivals; for instance, social festivals (centered in the home), religious festivals (at home and in the temple), literary festivals, and national festivals. Hindu festivals tend to be combinations of ritual observances, processions, music, dance, feasting, feeding the poor, and other activities. Among the several purposes of Hindu festivals are purification to avert malicious influences, strengthening the organization of society, enabling of passage through times of crisis in the lifecycle, and stimulating or resuscitating the vital powers of nature. They are intended to enable individuals, families, and groups to 'rise up' or improve and hence are called '*utsava.*'

Among Hindu festivals (*utsava*), some attract participants at the all-India level and some are regional or local. The principal all-India festivals include Kṛṣṇa's birthday (Janmāṣṭamī); Rāma's birthday (Rāmanavamī); Gaṇeśa's birthday (Gaṇeśa-caturṭhī); and Daśahrā, a ten-day festival to the Goddess, of which the first nine days are known as *navarātri* or the 'nine nights,' and the tenth day as *vijayādaśamī* or 'victory' day. Daśahrā is also known as Durgā-*pūjā*, especially in Bengal; other regions celebrate it as the day Rāma defeated Rāvaṇa. Divālī (Dīpāvalī) is the festival of lights, celebrated everywhere with lamps placed in windows and around doors and floated in rivers, and with exchange of gifts; Mahāśivarātri is the night of Śiva; Holī is the spring festival characterized by exuberance and people splashing each other with red-colored powder and water; and Rakṣā Bandhan is the day when sisters tie colored threads around their brothers' wrists.

Pilgrimages

Pilgrimage to holy rivers and other sacred sites has been a prominent feature of Hinduism since Vedic times and continues to be one of the integrating aspects of Hindu religious life. A pilgrimage is a journey (*yātrā*) to a holy place, a place of 'crossing over' (*tīrtha*) where the ordinary and extraordinary or secular and sacred meet. In one sense, all of India is considered a holy land (*punyabhūmi*) as a place that affords every human being an opportunity to reach liberation. However, from the Himālayas in the north to Kanyakumari in the south and from east to west, particular pilgrimage places dot the landscape. Many of them, including India's seven ancient holy cities (Ayodhyā, Mathurā, Māyā [Hardvār], Kāśī, Kāñcī, Avantikā [Ujjain], and the city of Dvārāvatī [Dvārakā]) and its holy rivers (Gaṅgā, Yamunā, Godāvarī, Sarasvatī, Narmadā, Kāverī, and Sindhu) for many centuries have been held to be sacred. Some of them are considered holy due to an association with legendary or divine individuals of antiquity (Ayodhyā with Rāma; the Mathurā region with Kṛṣṇa); others due to the presence of a deity (Kāśī with Śiva); still others due to the confluence of two or more rivers (Prāyāga [Allahabad]).

Each pilgrimage site has its advocates and supporters who spread the word about its overall superiority and the specific benefits that can result from a visit to it. However, the most acclaimed of all Hindu pilgrimage sites is Vārāṇasī (also known as Kāśī in ancient India, and Banaras in modern India). The reasons for this are many. Vārāṇasī is one of the oldest living cities in the world. For over 2,500 years it has attracted pilgrims and seekers from all over India. It is considered to be the permanent earthly home of Śiva. Legendary figures of antiquity and saints and sages have lived and taught there. Many incredible events from Hindu mythology took place there. It is located on the banks of the holy river Gaṅgā, at a point where the river takes a broad crescent sweep toward the north. There are some seventy bathing *ghāṭ*s along the river, and bathing in the Gaṅgā, a river that fell from heaven to earth through Śiva's matted locks, according to Hindu myth and tradition, grants purity. Great temples grace the city. The famous cremation grounds of Māṇikarnikā-*ghāṭ* and Hariścandra-*ghāṭ* are located along the river there. It is widely believed that by dying within the city, one will gain ultimate and final liberation (*mokṣa*).

Forehead marks

Many Hindus wear a distinctive mark (*tilaka* or *bindī*) on their forehead to indicate their sectarian allegiance. In ancient days, the forehead mark was made of musk (*kastūrī*). When that substance became rare, the mark was made from saffron. More recently, Hindus began to use a red lead power (*sindūr*) or sandalwood paste. These substances are known to have a cooling effect on the body and are believed to help create a cool, calm, and quiet mind. Nowadays the forehead mark is typically made from sandalwood paste, or ash (*vibhūti* or *bhasma*), or a red-colored powder (*kumkum*). A white U- or Y-shaped mark with a red line in the middle indicates that the person is a devotee of Viṣṇu (the U represents the feet of Viṣṇu and the red line represents Lakṣmī); followers of Śiva place three white horizontal marks made of ash; and followers of the Devī usually place a large red dot in the middle of the three. That area of the forehead is known by various names such as the *ajñācakra*, the third eye or the spiritual eye, and is said to be the location of a major nerve center at a subtle (nonphysical) level of the human body. When worn by women, the *tilaka* is a reminder of wedding vows. Its presence does not indicate for certain that the woman already is married, but if she becomes a widow she will no longer put on a *tilaka*. These days the religious significance of the *tilaka* is sometimes neglected or forgotten, and it may be used only for the sake of fashion rather than for religious reasons. One can even see women who are wearing plastic *tilaka*s, available in a wide range of rainbow colors, to match the color of the *sāṛī* they happen to be wearing.

Oṃ

The best-known and most mysterious of all *mantra*s is *oṃ*. It is a sacred syllable that is composed of three letters (a-u-m) in a single sound along with a fourth, silence. The vowels 'a' and 'u' coalesce in Sanskrit to become 'o.' These three letters represent several important triads: three worlds (earth/human, mid-region/nature, and heaven/divine), three deities (Brahmā, Viṣṇu, and Śiva), three Vedas (*Ṛg, Sāma*, and *Yajur*), three elements (fire/Agni, wind/Vāyu, and sun/Sūrya), three twice-born castes (Brāhmaṇ, Kṣatriya, and Vaiśya), and for Vaiṣṇavas, Viṣṇu, Lakṣmī, and their devotee. The *Māṇḍukya Upaniṣad* identifies *oṃ* with the four levels of consciousness: 'a' represents the waking state; 'u' represents the dream state; 'm' represents the deep sleep state; and the fourth (*turīya*) represents the unchanging transcendent state.

> Just as all the leaves of a sprig are held together by its stem, so all words are held together by the sound *oṃ*. The *oṃ* is the entire universe.
>
> (*Chāndogya Upaniṣad* 2.23.3)

> He who knows this *oṃ* and makes this syllable resound, takes refuge in this syllable, in the immortal and fearless sound; having taken refuge he becomes immortal like the Gods.
>
> (*Chāndogya Upaniṣad* 1.4.5)

> *Oṃ* is the bow, the Self is the arrow; Brahman, they say, is the target to be pierced by concentration; thus one becomes united with Brahman as an arrow with the target.
>
> (*Muṇḍaka Upaniṣad* 2.2.4)

> The goal that all the Vedas declare, which all austerities aim at, and that humans desire when they lead a life of continence, I will tell you briefly, it is *oṃ*. This syllable *oṃ* is indeed Brahman. This syllable is the highest. Whosoever knows this syllable obtains all that he desires. This is the best support; this is the highest support. Whosoever knows this support is adored in the world of Brahman.
>
> (*Kaṭha Upaniṣad* 1.2.15–17)

> What was, what is, and what shall be – all this is *oṃ*. Whatever else is beyond the bounds of threefold time, that also is only *oṃ*.
>
> (*Māṇḍukya Upaniṣad* 1)

Oṃ is uttered at the beginning and end of a Hindu prayer, chant, meditation, recitation of a sacred text, and most rituals. With it everything begins and ends. It is not a concept that refers to something else but is itself the Supreme Being in the form of primeval sound.

Modern expressions

Hindu Renaissance

What is generally called the Hindu Renaissance was a nineteenth-century movement to remodel society in ways that were inspired by classical India and Hindu values from an era prior to foreign invasions and the colonial period. British imperial rule, which imagined itself the heir of the Mughal Empire, was even more traumatic because the Christian British, unlike the Muslim Mughals from Central Asia, brought into India powerful new economic, social, political, legal, and educational institutions. The introduction of Western shipping, especially in the cities now known as Kolkata (Calcutta), Mumbai (Bombay), and Chennai (Madras), shifted the balance of India's economy from the heartland to the periphery and from old villages and towns to new coastal cities. An agricultural and caste-based society began to give way to capitalist commerce and currency-based values. British-style education introduced alien ideas about politics, culture, history, and religion. In an attempt to address and question these changes, a number of Hindu social and religious reform movements arose. In time religious reform took on nationalist overtones and gave birth to political organizations. As a result, the modern idea of a unanimous, unitary, and unified religion called 'Hinduism' emerged as a reinterpretation and hybridization of traditional self-understandings that responded effectively to anticolonial nationalist needs and then persisted into the contemporary era in independent India as a religious category that has powerful political overtones. Under the label 'Hinduism' is a combination of the continuation, adaptation, and transformation of earlier and classical cultural patterns.

Brāhmo Samāj

The Brāhmo Samāj (Society of God) was founded in 1828 in Calcutta by Ram Mohun Roy (1772–1833), who is sometimes called the father of modern India. As the social and religious expression of a small but influential group of wealthy and Westernized Indians, the Brāhmo Samāj sought to create a purified form of Hinduism that would be free from all of the following: distinctions based on class or caste identities, child marriage, polytheism, temple rituals involving image worship, lack of education for women, and marginalizing of widows.

Roy was born in western Bengal into an orthodox Brāhmaṇ family, and although he outwardly remained a Hindu, wearing the sacred thread and observing many of the customs of orthodox Brāhmaṇs, the theology he proposed was strikingly non-traditional. He was a modern renaissance individual who was liberal in his social and political views and a radical freethinker in religious matters. He spoke five languages: Bengali, Sanskrit, Arabic, Persian, and English; and he was familiar with the Bible, Unitarianism, Islam, Freemasonry, Deism, and Western social life. He was versed in the Hindu scriptures, too. By applying his critical intellect to religious questions, he came to the conclusion that Hinduism, in its ancient and true form, did not contain all the elements he found distasteful in the religion of his time. He believed that if Hindus would read and understand their ancient scriptures, with reason and conscience as their guide, they would discard the distorted superstitious and illegitimate rituals and questionable social practices that somehow had become associated with Hinduism over the centuries. After his death, Debendranath Tagore (1817–1905), the father of Nobel Prize winning poet Rabindranath Tagore, became the leader of the Brāhmo Samāj. Under his guidance a less rationalist and more mystical doctrine was presented. The third leader of the Brāhmo Samāj, Keshab Chandra Sen (1838–84), admitted women to membership and abolished caste in the Samāj. As his theology became more syncretistic and eclectic, a schism developed, and the more conservative faction remained under the leadership of Debendranath. In 1881 Keshab founded the Church of the New Dispensation for the purpose of establishing the truth of all the great religions in a single institution that he believed would replace them all. Although the Brāhmo Samāj was an elite movement that never attained the status of widespread acceptance as part of the mainstream of Hinduism, it made a major contribution to a process of social and religious reform by drawing attention to the persistence of inhumane practices and the need for education and reform.

Ārya Samāj

At about the time that the Brāhmo Samāj was at its height, Svāmī Dayānanda Sarasvatī (1824–83) founded a very different reform movement in western India. An orthodox Brāhmaṇ from Gujarat, Dayānanda founded the Ārya Samāj (Aryan Society) in 1875. While the Brāhmo Samāj was acknowledging the superiority of Western values, Western science, and Upaniṣadic wisdom, the Ārya Samāj rejected them and instead proposed a 'return to the Veda' in its revival movement.

Dayānanda taught that the Vedas (that is, the four *saṃhitā*s or collections) were eternal, literally true, and universally authoritative. They taught monotheism and morality, not polytheism, image worship, or caste discrimination. Those were not Vedic but Purāṇic and were no more than symptoms of the decline of Vedic society as a result of the destructive *Mahābhārata* war. To improve society what was needed was to go back to the Vedas rather than to accept Western ways of doing things. He admonished Hindus to be proud of their ancient heritage and to reclaim it, not to be ashamed of it as if it were mere superstition as Westerners were declaring. To revive the Golden Age, Dayānanda started Vedic-oriented educational institutions throughout India that did not neglect modern knowledge but contextualized it within the framework of Vedic revelation as he understood it. The purpose of the Ārya Samāj was to unify Hindus by a return to a long-forgotten faith in the Vedas as a complete model for human life. His style was dogmatic and forceful, and it had a major influence in revitalizing the Hindu community in northern India and awakening it to greater self-confidence. His influence continues to be important today through the Ārya Samāj and a family of other social and religious organizations in India.

Rāmakṛṣṇa Mission

Rāmakṛṣṇa (1836–86) was a great revitalizing influence on modern Hindu religion and culture especially through his 'gospel' of the truth of all religions and through his disciple Svāmī Vivekānanda who gained international respect and support for the modern resurgence of Hinduism. Rāmakṛṣṇa was born of poor Brāhmaṇ parents in rural Bengal as Gadadhar Chatterjee and was raised in the Vaiṣṇava-*bhakti* tradition. He received training in all sixty-four Tantric spiritual disciplines from the female wandering renunciant Yogeśvarī and was taught nondual Advaita Vedāntic wisdom by the male renunciant Toṭāpurī. He later became known as the Goddess Kālī's child due to his repeated experience of ecstatic trances and mystic visions of her and of other deities. His followers considered him to be a divine incarnation (*avatāra*) and a supremely realized self (*paramahaṃsa*), a type that has graced the Indian landscape for thousands of years. His continuing influence on the way that Indian spirituality in general and Hinduism in particular is understood may be summarized as 'all religions are true and are but different paths to the One.' This maxim was neither a formal definition nor a mere theory for him but rather a summary of his own personal experience. Rāmakṛṣṇa practiced a number of different Hindu spiritual disciplines that included various forms of *bhakti* and Tantra as well as *jñāna-yoga*. He tried Christian and Muslim ones, too. He had many visionary experiences, and their effect was to confirm for him that he had reached the goal of each tradition and had found that the end of each path was the same.

Crucial to Rāmakṛṣṇa's continuing impact after he left his body (*mahāsamādhi*) in 1886 was the articulation by others of his inclusivist viewpoint, which integrated the diverse and otherwise competing or even conflicting features of Hindu religion. Foremost among his disciples was Svāmī Vivekānanda (b. Narendranath Datta, 1863–1902), a former member of the Brāhmo Samāj. In 1893 Vivekānanda attended, as a Hindu participant, the World Parliament of Religions in Chicago where he presented the idea that Vedānta was the definitive and most representative form of Hinduism and that its central philosophy can permit one to see other religions and types of religious experience as valid in their own right even if all religions and all religious experiences ultimately culminate in an experience of absolute Oneness. Vivekānanda, with his powerful personality and stirring oratory, deeply impressed the audience in Chicago. He lectured in the United States and England for the next four years and then returned to India in 1897 where he founded the Rāmakṛṣṇa Mission, which has been one of the most important educational and service organizations in modern India. The Mission, in addition to its support for education and social service in general, has been particularly active in the field of health care where it puts into practice its teachings of tolerance and recognition of the inner divinity of all.

Theosophical Society

The Theosophical Society is an international modern spiritual movement that has exerted considerable influence in India, especially through its centers in Banaras and in Adyar near Madras (now Chennai). Though not strictly a Hindu tradition, it is based on a form of 'theosophy' in the sense of 'divine wisdom' that had its original inspiration in Western alchemy and occultism and then came to interpret them from an Indo-Tibetan perspective.

The Society was founded in New York City in 1875 by the extraordinary Russian psychic Helena Petrovna Blavatsky (1831–91) in collaboration with Henry Steel Olcott (1832–1907) and William Q. Judge (1851–96). Blavatsky had traveled in Europe, North America, the Middle East, Japan, and India and claimed to have spent seven years studying with Hindu *mahātmā*s – great spiritual teachers, in Tibet. In 1879 she returned to India and founded the world headquarters of the Theosophical Society at Adyar, Madras. Quickly her doctrines took on an Indian character, and she and her followers soon established numerous branches in India and subsequently around the world. Blavatsky's main doctrines appear in her books *Isis Unveiled* and *The Secret Doctrine*.

The Society reached the peak of its influence under its next leader, Annie Besant (b. Wood; 1847–1933), a reform-minded woman who had been born in London of Irish parents. Under her guidance, many Theosophical lodges were founded in Europe and the United States where they helped to acquaint the West with Hindu philosophy although in a rather idiosyncratic form. The Society spread the idea that Vedānta is the definitive form of Hinduism; India is the most spiritual land on the planet; and India has the world's oldest and most universal religious teachings. Besant was well known throughout India for her advocacy of Indian Independence. She proposed that her pupil Jiddu Krishnamurti (1895–1985) was the messianic reincarnation of Buddha, but he himself disavowed that identity in 1928.

Aurobindo

Another modern teacher whose doctrines have had an influence outside India was Aurobindo Ghose (1872–1950), who has been acknowledged as one of the greatest mystic-philosopher-poet-sages of modern India and one of the most representative (and original) of its Neo-Hindu thinkers. His synthetic thought (Integral Yoga) expressed a universal manifestation of the Absolute in a series of grades of reality from matter up to the highest absolute spirit. Aurobindo tried to revive and exemplify the ancient ideal of the Vedic sage for the modern world. His thought was highly innovative; of particular note is his idea of the ascent of consciousness into the 'supramental,' which he presented as a concrete historical task and not merely limited to the inner world of an individual but ultimately involving all humanity and the entire cosmos.

Aurobindo was sent to England as a child and was educated at Cambridge. Upon his return to India at the age of twenty, he became committed to the Indian Independence movement and was jailed for revolutionary activities. While in prison he had a profound religious experience that impelled him to withdraw from politics and settle in the French colony of Pondicherry in South India. There he established an *āśrama* and achieved a reputation as a respected sage. His followers saw him as the first incarnate manifestation of the superbeings whose evolution he prophesied, and apparently he did not discourage that belief. He was a prolific author and wrote, among his many works, *The Life Divine, Sāvitrī*, and *The Secret of the Veda*.

Gandhi and Independence

Mohandas Karamchand Gandhi (1869–1948) was a saint of modern India who made the religion of selfless service and nonviolence his life's mission. He was the most important leader in the Indian Independence movement and appeared to many to be the very quintessence of the Hindu tradition. His austere celibate life, his undeviating allegiance to truth and nonviolence, and his 'fasts unto death' were marks of a life that most Hindus found both appealing and challenging.

He was born into a devout Vaiṣṇava family in Gujarat where he was profoundly affected by Vaiṣṇava devotion and Jaina teachings of nonviolence. While studying law in London, he met Theosophists who introduced him to Edwin Arnold's translation of the *Bhagavad Gītā*, a text that was to form the foundation of his personal philosophy. In London, he also read the Bible and the Qur'ān. Perhaps the most profound impression made upon him during this period was from reading Léo Tolstoy's *The Kingdom of God is Within You*. Henceforth, Gandhi considered Tolstoy to be his *guru*.

After passing the Bar, Gandhi went to South Africa to practice law. He began to simplify his life there and began an active but nonviolent resistance movement that he named 'Satyāgraha' ('Truth-force'). He saw nonviolence as the only appropriate way to express strength that is born of love and truth. In 1915, after successful but incomplete campaigns for equal treatment in South Africa, he returned to India for good.

Gandhi characterized his life as 'experiments with truth.' He would say 'my life is my message,' and first and foremost he lived the vow that one should never deviate from the truth, not even for the sake of a seeming advantage for the country. Truth formed the cornerstone of Gandhi's religion, and one of the preconditions for finding the truth was self-effacement. Gandhi called it, 'making oneself a zero.' The second principle upon which he based his life was nonviolence, and he termed it the only way to truth. Nonviolence, according to Gandhi, is not merely nonkilling; it means an active love so large it includes every living being. Nonviolence is a manifestation of truth in action. The third principle Gandhi advocated was sexual continence, including abstaining from everything designed to stimulate the senses, such as alcohol, tobacco, and drugs.

Thus, Gandhi personalized and modernized the ancient Hindu concepts of truth (*satya*), nonviolence (*ahiṃsā*), and sexual continence (*brahmacarya*). Employing these practices, he sought not only to eradicate untouchability but also to free India from foreign rule. Regarding untouchability, Gandhi renamed the untouchables as *harijan*s, 'people of God.' He gave equal status to the untouchables in his *āśrama*, though he never sought to eradicate caste (as he said, caste was an occupational division of society and not a personal one). Untouchability, on the other hand, was a violation of nonviolence.

The Indian nationalist struggle, of which Gandhi was a leading advocate, resulted in India's independence from the British in 1947. Thus we see in Gandhi a unique mixture of Hinduism and nationalism. He identified Truth with God; nonviolence as truth in action; renunciation, especially celibacy, as a tremendous power for spiritual development; the dignity of manual labor, equality for all; and self-sufficiency. He loved Hinduism, in spite of its many flaws, and lived an exemplary life that shines as a beacon for all.

Modern* Guru*s

The globalization of Hinduism was due initially to Svāmī Vivekānanda's visit to Chicago in 1893 and the subsequent founding of the Rāmakṛṣṇa Mission. Since then many other teachers have followed. The sage of Arunacala, Ramaṇa Maharṣi (1879–1950), spent virtually his entire life at Tiruvannamalai in Tamil Nadu, yet his teachings, which are a pure, experiential form of Advaita Vedānta, have had a significant and still-increasing influence on Westerners. Among the recent and contemporary teachers that he influenced are Paul Brunton, Nisargadatta Maharaj of Bombay, Jean Klein, D. E. Harding, H. L. Poonja (Papiji), and Gangaji.

Paramahaṃsa Yogānanda (1890–1952), unlike Ramaṇa, came to the West and established the Self-Realization Fellowship in the United States, which now has centers around the world. He is the author of the fascinating *Autobiography of a Yogi*, a book that has had a profound influence on an untold number of twentieth-century Western seekers of spiritual wisdom.

During the 1960s, there was a steady flow of Hindu *guru*s to the West, such as Maharishi Mahesh Yogi (b. 1911), the founder of the Transcendental Meditation (TM) movement; the then teenage *guru* Maharaji (b. 1957), the founder of the Divine Light Mission; Bhaktivedanta Prabhupada (1896–1977), who, in 1965, brought the International Society for Krishna Consciousness (ISKCON or the Hare Kṛṣṇa movement) to the West; Svāmī Muktananda (1908–82), the founder of the Siddha Yoga movement; and Bhagvan Shree Rajneesh (1931–80), the controversial Tantric teacher. A number of other *guru*s who have developed large followings in the West include Svāmīs Satchidananda (1914–2002) and Chinmayananda (1916–93), both direct disciples of Svāmī Śivananda of Rishikesh, Gurumayi Cidvilasananda (female successor to Muktananda), and Matajis Amritanandamayi, Sri Ma, and Ānandi Ma. Two other Hindu *guru*s who have had an influence on the West, though they have never left India, include the joy-permeated mother, Anandamayi Ma (1896–1982), and Satya Sai Baba (b. 1926). Sai Baba is easily the most famous of all the Hindu *guru*s with a following in the hundreds of millions around the world. He is famous for his magical powers of producing sacred ash and various objects from his fingertips with a wave of the hand. Besides his magical powers, Sai Baba is well known for his social projects, including the building and running of India's two largest hospitals, the building and running of two universities and thousands of secondary and primary schools, and the providing of water to over 400 villages in Andhra Pradesh. All these services are provided without cost to those who benefit.

Modern technology

The Internet has thousands of sites pertaining to Hinduism. Not only are there websites containing major texts online, but there are also new sites coming online daily that pertain to minor texts, sects, temples, gods, goddesses, *guru*s, festivals, food, matrimony, and on and on. *Pūjā*s and rituals may be performed online to deities in temples in India no matter where one is physically located. Horoscopes are cast and matched by computers. In fact, India has become the world's second leading producer of computer technicians, and the industry is changing the way one can interact with Hinduism.

New technologies now make available recitation of scriptural texts, singing of devotional songs, and the *darśana* of deities and *guru*s in virtually every home or marketplace and at any time of the night or day. What once took place only at specified times in a temple, the home, or *paṭhaśāla* (center of Vedic learning), can now be accessible via computers, CDs, cassettes, televisions, and movie screens. This allows people outside of India to hear and see what once required costly travel. They can also learn in do-it-yourself fashion since there are recordings that guide a practitioner in the proper performance of particular rituals such as the annual changing of one's sacred thread and the annual or monthly ancestral rites.

The new technologies are a mixed blessing. They provide instant access to virtually anyone, but much of this material could be misapprehended without a living teacher to guide one through it. Initiation is a crucial ingredient for most Hindu religious practices. Without it, the power and authority required to perform the rite correctly and effectively may be lacking.

Relations with other religions

Jainism and Buddhism

Hinduism, Jainism, and Buddhism originated in the same milieu. They share many assumptions: existence is sorrowful and requires deliverance, rebirth exists due to *karma*, there is an innate moral law, ignorance is the cause of suffering, everything empirical is impermanent, and spiritual practices are prescribed to remove ignorance. They differ in the status they give to Vedic tradition. Hindus affirm the sacredness and authority of the Veda; Jainas and Buddhists do not and therefore are characterized as 'outside the Veda' and thus heterodox in contrast to Vedic orthodoxy. Jaina and Buddhist monastic institutions were established by members of the warrior class who renounced their position in society in order to attain spiritual realization: Vardhamāna (*c.* 599–527 BCE), known as Mahāvīra, and Siddhārtha Gautama (*c.* 566–486 BCE), known as Buddha. In the face of those heterodox challenges, Brāhmaṇism adapted ancient Vedic institutions and adopted some of the new Jaina and Buddhist ones to transform itself into classical Hinduism while still managing to maintain continuity with Vedic tradition. Various responses to the heterodoxies are evident throughout the range of the major Hindu devotional and philosophical subtraditions.

Buddhism began as a challenge to existing *dharma*. Siddhārtha Gautama, though born a Hindu prince, eventually rejected authority (scriptural, human, and divine), ritual, caste, divine sovereignty and grace, and the soul. All these were either implicit or explicit in Vedic tradition and were to remain in classical Hinduism. As a 'reform' movement, Buddhism admitted persons of any age and caste to practice Buddhism and to enter the monastic life. Early Buddhist emphasis on the monastic order went counter to the Hindu celebration of family life and 'nonrenunciation' as equally important components in the full course of human development which were to be followed by renunciation only in one's elder years. Therefore Hinduism regarded Buddhism as a symptom of cultural degeneration. Hindu opposition took the form of lively debate, ending royal patronage to Buddhist monastic and teaching institutions, and adopting some elements of Buddhist thought and practice – going so far as to name Gautama the Buddha as the ninth incarnation of Viṣṇu. However, his Hindu status is often accompanied by the cautionary qualification that Viṣṇu assumed this particular incarnation in order to mislead and destroy the enemies of the Veda.

Hinduism and Jainism share many social institutions and ritual practices, but there are minor doctrinal differences. In Jainism, the twenty-four *tīrthaṅkaras* or 'path-makers,' of which Mahāvīra was the twenty-fourth, are not regarded as divine incarnations; there is a greater emphasis and dependence upon monasticism; there is a stricter practice of nonviolence (*ahiṃsā*); there are no sacrifices for the deceased; *karma* is a sticky substance that binds the soul; there is no caste system; and there is no belief in God as the creator, sustainer, and moral governor of the universe. However, these differences do not give offense to orthodox Hindus.

Hinduism and Islam

The relationship between Hindus and Muslims has been at times cordial but at times confrontational. History offers examples of an explosive as well as a mutually enriching relationship. Muslim armies invaded India in CE 711, and Muslim rule in most of the subcontinent, except for a few princely states, ended 1,000 years later in 1757. Attitudes and administrative policies of Muslim rulers toward Hindus varied. Some, like Fīrūz Tughluq (r. 1351–88) and Aurangzīb (r. 1658–1707), were anti-Hindu and enforced a poll tax on non-Muslims. Others, like the Bengali Sulṭān Ḥusayn Shāh 'Alā' ad-Dīn (r. 1493–1519) and Akbar (r. 1556–1605), were well disposed toward their Hindu subjects. Where royal courts were Muslim, patronage was likely to be diminished or withdrawn from Hinduism. Some rulers actually had Hindu temples destroyed and replaced by mosques. One well-known and tragic instance was a mosque in North India dating from 1528, the so-called Bābrī Masjid that had been constructed during the reign of Bābur who was the first Mughal emperor. Allegedly it was built on a site where an earlier Hindu temple had marked the birthplace of Lord Rāma, the seventh *avatāra* of Viṣṇu. In 1992 a group of Hindu militants tore the mosque apart in the hope that they would be able to rebuild a temple on the site. In contrast to this competition for space and conflict over place, many great *sant*s (saints) like Kabīr (*c.* 1440–1518) and Śirdī Sāī Bābā (d. 1918) subordinated the differences between the two communities to a higher reality that surpasses the most solemn spiritual pretensions and religious institutions.

Hindu and Muslim beliefs and practices are based on such fundamentally different assumptions that Islam could not be absorbed into Hinduism. Neither could Muslims (currently estimated to be about 15 percent of the population in India and 30 percent in South Asia) make India an Islamic state. Indian Muslims, with few exceptions, are of native descent but in theory have become outcastes with whom dealings by Hindus are restricted by formal rules. Therefore upper-caste Hindus and Muslims ordinarily do not intermarry. The teachings of Islam envision a single community with no place for caste distinctions, but many Indian Muslims do observe them in practice. After centuries of living separately but in close proximity, Hindus and Muslims have found ways to coexist peacefully most of the time, but the Partition of India and creation of Pakistan as a condition of independence from Britain in 1947 has continued to complicate their relationship within India and throughout South Asia.

Hinduism and Sikhism

When proponents of Islam and of Hinduism were struggling for ideological supremacy, Guru Nānak (1469–1539) discovered a third way beyond the polarities of the two dominant traditions. Through disciplined devotional practice of chanting and meditation, a new path to liberation that has affinities with Hinduism was revealed to him. Over time this became what we know today as Sikhism. Hinduism and Sikhism are highly compatible. They differ in a few key doctrines: Sikhs do not believe in divine incarnations; they reject highly elaborate ritualism as well as status determined by caste; and they discourage asceticism and instead uphold the values of married family life.

Hinduism and Christianity

With the ascendancy of the British from about 1757, Hinduism faced two centuries of intense challenge from Christianity. As long ago as the fourth century CE Syrian Christians had inhabited the Malabar Coast of southern India and the Portuguese established communities on the West Coast in the sixteenth century. But these earlier communities had little impact on Hinduism in spite of the presence of missionaries.

Even during the two centuries of British colonial dominance, the greatest effect of Christian presence in India on Hinduism was to motivate change within Hinduism rather than to take large numbers of converts away from it. Christians both invited and provoked Hindus into dialogue with other world religions. Christian critiques of Hindu practices inspired Hindus to develop clearer theories of scriptural authority and better definitions of the ideal society. Beginning in the nineteenth century with the Brāhmo Samāj, and continuing to the present, Neo-Vedāntic forms of Hinduism in particular have been used to explain the seeming 'degenerations' such as 'idol' worship and caste and gender distinctions based on birth.

Perhaps more than any other world religion, Hinduism is frustrating to Christians because Hindus can accept that Jesus was an incarnation of the divine, was specially conceived and born to a virgin, and taught deeply appealing ethical principles in the Sermon on the Mount, but at the same time reject Christian claims to have unique knowledge of God and exclusive possession of the path to salvation. While these claims are dismissed, the good work of missionaries who have made significant contributions to social service is appreciated and respected.

Transmission of the tradition outside of India

Hinduism is now a global phenomenon, and Hindu temples exist throughout the world. Beginning from the fifth century, the Hindu religion and culture became influential in Southeast Asia, including Indonesia, Malaysia, Singapore, Bali, and Java. Brāhmaṇs and merchants, especially Tamilians, established sea trade and then settled there. Local kings modeled themselves on ancient Hindu kings, and the Brāhmaṇ priests performed rituals in the courts of chiefs, who converted to the new religion. The earliest material evidence of Hinduism in Southeast Asia comes from Borneo, where late fourth-century Sanskrit inscriptions testify to the performance of Vedic sacrifices by Brāhmaṇs at the behest of local chiefs. Over time, the civilizations of Southeast Asia developed forms of Hinduism that had distinctive local features. Various manifestations appeared, each adapted to the local culture, but the framework of their religious life was essentially Hindu. Stories from the *Rāmāyaṇa* and the *Mahābhārata* became widely known in Southeast Asia and are still popular there in local versions.

Hinduism has spread to other parts of the world including South and East Africa, the Pacific Islands, South America, the West Indies, North America, Europe, and Australia through a process of migration. This movement took place in two waves. First, during the nineteenth century, empires and nations around the world sought cheap Indian labor. There was also a desire on the part of many Indians to work abroad. Most of these first-wave emigrants were indentured laborers. Then in the 1960s and continuing to this day, a second wave of highly educated urbanites migrated to the major cities of Europe and North America. This second wave comprised professionals, such as doctors, engineers, computer scientists, and university professors.

As the immigrant families prospered in their new world, they felt a need for religious institutions, temples, teachers, and cultural venues to keep alive their tradition in a land that observed no Hindu holidays, had no wandering renunciants, and spoke no Indian languages. Community-inclusive, nonsectarian temples, and pan-Indian cultural centers became a focal point for preserving Hindu tradition. At first, existing buildings were converted to the purpose, but more recently money has been raised to build temples in traditional architectural styles. New temples now exist around the world that duplicate their counterparts in the subcontinent, complete with the proper images, trained priests, appropriate rituals, and familiar educational and cultural activities.

As global Hinduism continues to grow, the greatest challenge it faces is teaching each new generation, wherever it is born and educated, the characteristic elements of traditional culture and values. The tradition is dynamic and continues to redefine itself, as it has for countless eons. In many parts of the world the bonds of the tightly knit

Hindu joint family may seem to be less strong, intercaste and interreligious marriages may become more generally accepted, and women may be taking up new and nontraditional roles. Hindu tradition and the people who observe it in myriad ways have always adapted to changing times and different local circumstances, and nevertheless have found it possible to preserve time-honored forms of life.

Suggested further readings

Basham (1957); Elgood (1999); Fuller (2004); Goodall (1996); Haan (2005); Lipner (1994); Lorenzen (1999); Mittal and Thursby (2004); O'Flaherty (1988); Sweetman

3. A sandstone image of the *tīrthaṅkara* Mahāvīra. Courtesy of John Eskenazi Ltd.

2

JAINA DHARMA

Anne Vallely

The tradition defined

Festooned rickshaws, cars, and garlanded trucks, each blasting its distinctive horn, jostle for space along the busy streets of Mumbai. So too do the people, moving at different speeds on their daily journey: friends, arms linked, saunter at a snail's pace; skinny boys with cups of tea deftly dart through the crowds; businessmen, hollering into cell phones, stride with intent in all directions. In the midst of the flurry, a group of male mendicants wearing simple white robes moves deliberately and briskly through the crowd. The din intuitively keeps its distance, creating a sanctified space around them. They are a striking sight: their serene expressions and purposeful steps distinguish them from the crowd of preoccupied and harried onlookers. Among the monks is a former businessman. At the age of sixty, he gave up his fortune, his belongings, and his family to dedicate himself to the rigorous life of a Jaina mendicant. He will never again possess anything. He will spend the rest of his life wandering from village to village, dependent on others for sustenance, without ever calling any place home. His accomplishments as a businessman were many but are dwarfed before his glorious quest for world-negation. He has attained the highest goal of Jaina tradition. Even unknown passersby call him 'Mahārāja,' honoring him for his courage and spiritual wisdom.

World-renunciation is the dominant religious ideal in Jainism and, though pursued by a tiny minority, plays a central role in Jaina social life and retains a powerful hold on the imagination.

To peer into the world of Jainism is to witness an extraordinary example of human expression. The tradition makes the singular and potentially revolutionary claim that nonviolence (*ahiṃsā*) is the only path to salvation and that violence is the root of all human woes. For Jainas, the concept of nonviolence has considerable reach: it extends beyond the human community to include all living beings, and censures not only physical violence but also harmful speech and injurious thoughts. To define oneself as Jaina is to situate oneself in an animated, vibrant, and distinctive moral universe.

Irrespective of the considerable differences that exist among the Jaina communities worldwide, all emphasize the centrality of the doctrine of *ahiṃsā* in defining their tradition. Whether they are mendicants, who have renounced the social world to pursue a rigorous path of asceticism, or householders busy with such 'worldly' concerns as family and work, Jainas universally share an identity rooted in an ancient ethic of restraint and compassion.

Cosmos and history

Jainism is a tradition that counsels restraint. Like the *śramaṇa*, or world-renouncing, cultures of ancient India (of which it is a celebrated expression), Jaina tradition views the world as a tempest from which the wise withdraw and from which all eventually yearn to escape. The allures of life, with its fascinations and charms as well as its repulsions, are viewed as little more than a ruse that ensnares us in *saṃsāra*.

There were many world-renouncing groups extant in eastern India during the seventh century BCE, the earliest period for which we have historical record of a distinctively Jaina Dharma. The origin of the renouncer traditions is unknown and may be connected, as many Jainas believe, with the indigenous religions of the Indus Valley civilization.

The *śramaṇa* traditions were united in their repudiation of the Brāhmaṇical orthodoxy and its fixation with upholding cosmic and social order (see the chapter on Hinduism in this volume). They rejected the 'florid utterances' and rituals of the Vedic priests as being pointless and wasteful. Rather than seeking to support the social order, they renounced it, viewing it, and worldly life in general, as the fundamental adversary to self-realization.

Mokṣa or liberation was the goal of the various *śramaṇa* traditions, and their analyses of the causes of bondage shared much in common. All held *karma* to be the primary vice through which the soul is trapped and bound to the worldly realm. Understanding worldly life as a scourge – one that is fundamentally hostile to the realization of the true self – was the necessary precondition to achieving freedom from it. But for those who would later come to be known as 'Jainas,' knowledge alone would not be sufficient. *Mokṣa* could never be attained through purely psychological efforts, because, for Jainas, worldly bondage is a real condition requiring bodily exertion to undo. Disentangling oneself from *saṃsāra* requires a physical drawing back from all that it constitutes. The path to *mokṣa* for Jainas necessitates a bodily rigor that distinguishes it from other renouncer traditions. As a consequence, asceticism has always been a central and defining aspect of the Jaina path and remains a powerful and central cultural ideal.

The Jaina ideals of nonviolence and nonattachment are best symbolized by the lives of the twenty-four great mythohistorical ascetic teachers, the Jinas, as well as by the mendicants who emulate their path. The best-known and most beloved of the Jinas is Mahāvīra, an historical figure who lived (according to traditional dating) between 599–527 BCE.

Modern accounts of Jaina history begin with his life. His predecessor, the Jina Pārśva, is believed by Jainas to have lived in the ninth century BCE, and there is some, albeit scant, historical evidence to support this contention. Scriptures tell us that Mahāvīra's parents were followers in Pārśva's lineage. The preceding twenty-two Jinas are beyond historical reach but possess a commanding symbolic reality.

Mahāvīra (an honorific title meaning 'Great Hero') was born 'Vardhamāna Jñātṛputra' into a ruling clan in the northeastern region of India (near present-day Patna). Indifferent to worldly success and pleasures, he yearned only to find the truth of existence. With this aim, he renounced worldly life at the age of thirty to become an itinerant mendicant. In his efforts to distinguish between true happiness (which must be eternal) and the fleeting, ephemeral pleasures associated with the body, he renounced all physical comforts and endured deprivations of every kind.

Without assistance from any human or divine being, Mahāvīra waged war on 'himself,' that is, on his passions and his *karmas*. He taught that our passions are our fiercest foes, represent the only adversary worth fighting, and must be fought on one's own: no one can assist us in destroying our own *karma*. Rejecting the notion of a creator God as well as the idea of grace, Jainas contend that the battle for freedom is a solitary one.

In Jainism, harm to others leads to bondage, but waging war on the self is the only path to salvation. The *Uttaradhyāyana Sūtra* (9.34–36) states: 'Difficult to conquer is oneself; but when that is conquered, everything is conquered.'

Mahāvīra, who was a fearless and heroic combatant, attained his goal of spiritual enlightenment after twelve years, six months and fifteen days on a path of extreme physical austerity. For this, like the great ascetic teachers before him, he is called 'Jina,' meaning conqueror, and from which Jainism derives its name.

Mahāvīra is not understood by Jainas as the founder of Jaina Dharma so much as its restorer. The truths of the tradition are believed to be eternal but in need of rekindling at specified times during the long cycles of time. Jainism shares, with most of the religions of India, a belief in the repetitive waxing and waning of cosmological time. The universe is understood to move through enormous and fixed cycles, for which there are corresponding physical, social, and moral effects. A full cycle takes eons to complete and is divided into two half-cycles, marked by contrasting trends: one of progress (*utsarpiṇī*) and one of decline (*avasarpiṇī*). Each trend (constituting a half-cycle) is subdivided into six phases, marking the advance of decline or progress. We are currently living in the fifth phase of the declining half-cycle, an inauspicious time characterized by increasing natural and social degeneration. The impending sixth phase will be worse still: a time when living creatures will suffer great physical pain and when all decency, as well as the teachings of the Jinas, will disappear.

While the first and last phases of the cycles are opposed, the in-between phases (third and fourth) are marked by ambivalence and are a time of struggle between the righteous and the errant. It is during these liminal phases that the twenty-four great prophetic teachers or Jinas appear, prodding the recalcitrant through their teachings and rekindling faith in the eternal truths through their own lived experiences. Mahāvīra was the twenty-fourth and therefore final, great teacher of our present cycle of time. The devotional, artistic, and scholarly focus he receives from contemporary Jaina communities stems from his closeness to us, chronologically speaking, rather than from the newness of his teachings. Although each of the biographies of the twenty-four Jinas is unique, their teachings are identical, each elucidating the same eternal truths.

The appearance of the twenty-four great prophetic teachers is vital. Without them, truth would be lost to us. All that remains to keep us afloat in these turbulent times of the Kali Yuga (Age of Corruption) are the examples and teachings of these great mythohistorical ascetic prophets. They alone provide us with the hope that escape is possible. For this they are also called *tīrthaṅkara*, a term which means 'bridge maker,' and denotes one who helps to cross the ocean of *saṃsāra*. Jainism is a religion that seeks to preserve and transmit the teachings of the *tīrthaṅkaras*. As such, Jaina ideals are best represented by their life stories as well as by the mendicants whose lives are patterned on them.

From an early age, Jaina children learn the extraordinary tales of the lives of the Jinas, whose biographies extend over many lives, each a moral tale presaging the next.

The children become skilled at making the connections between the Jinas' previous lives and, in so doing, learn the moral law of *karma*. The biographies of the most popular Jinas are highly elaborate and complex, while others include a minimum of detail. But all Jinas share the characteristic qualities of being deeply compassionate, courageous, and self-disciplined. In the final life of each, the Jina-to-be awakens to the true nature of the soul's anguish in *saṃsāra* and embarks on a path to liberate it. In all cases, this means pursuing the path of worldly renunciation. Throughout history, and continuing to the present day, Jainas who become 'awake' to the reality of the soul and its bondage in worldly life regard the ascetic path as the only legitimate one to gain freedom. While most Jainas reject this option for themselves, they accept its logic and honor it as the ultimate path.

Jaina cosmology is a great cosmic drama between sentient beings and the nonsentient matter that ensnares them, played out against a backdrop of time and space (*arūpa-ajīva*). With no conception of a creator God, the *jīva* (soul or sentient being) and *ajīva* (a nonsentient material component that attaches itself to the soul, also called *karma*) are the key and only players in this drama. *Arūpa-ajīva* denotes that which is neither matter nor sentient and primarily refers to space and time but also to the cosmic principles that enable activity and inactivity.

The soul, when animated with passions (*samjvalana*), involuntarily lures karmic matter, which attaches itself to the *jīva*, and obscures its omniscient nature. The bound *karma* distorts the soul and causes further *karma* to be drawn in. Encrusted, the soul is now cast into an endless succession of births and deaths – changing form as a consequence of *karma* but unable to stop the cycle (*saṃsāra*). The human form, like all life forms, is but one 'product' or outcome of this soul–matter association. Freedom is possible but difficult to achieve. The connection between *jīva* and *ajīva* is beginning-less and is sustained by passions (*kasaya*s) – attachment, aversion, greed, and envy. With every ungenerous word or deed or harmful thought, new *karma* is drawn in, adding to the old. *Mokṣa* is a longed-for idyllic state of bliss and omniscience, in which the soul has freed itself from captivity. But this can only be achieved when the inflow of new *karma* is permanently blocked and when the blanket of *karma* that encases and oppresses the soul is scuffed out, layer-by-layer.

Jainas contend that the *jīva* can only be severed from *ajīva* through sustained and rigorous efforts at detachment from worldly life, in other words, through renunciation. Jaina scriptures provide us with detailed analyses of the causes of karmic bondage and of the mechanisms of release. They represent the most fundamental teachings delivered by Mahāvīra over 2,500 years ago. After he attained a state of enlightenment (*kevala-jñāna*), he quickly attracted many disciples who, under his guidance, formed a unified community.

After his death, Mahāvīra's mendicant disciples assumed leadership of the community, which continued to attract followers. However, signs of discord soon appeared, and within two centuries the once cohesive Jaina community had split into two distinct traditions, each with distinctive scriptures and at odds with the other. The precise causes of the sectarian split remain unexplained, but many sources suggest that it was primarily as a consequence of the southward migration by one group of Jainas in the fourth century BCE, in response to a famine in the north. The northern and southern communities then developed in isolation from each other, resulting in inevitable differences. It is claimed that when the southerners eventually returned to the north, they were confronted with a tradition that was alien and intolerable to them. In their absence, recensions of sacred teachings had been made which deviated from the practice of Mahāvīra (Jaini 1979: 5). One very evident example of this was the northern monks' practice of wearing garments. Nudity had been a fundamental expression of nonattachment for Jaina mendicants, which Mahāvīra himself had practiced, and was therefore not open to change. It is surmised that the northerners began to wear simple clothing during the famine; but more importantly, the northerners made the argument that clothing was not an impediment to spiritual progress. The differences between the two groups – and there were others – crystallized over this issue. Tellingly, the names by which the two came to be known reflect the debate's centrality: the group from the south subsequently came to be called Digambara (meaning 'sky clad'), affirming nudity for mendicant males; the group from the north came to be called Śvetāmbara ('white clad').

One of the most interesting differences between the Śvetāmbara and Digambara is over the question of female religiosity, and actually forms one aspect of the larger debate on garments. According to the Digambara, a woman is of inferior religious status to a man because of her flawed physical and emotional nature. As such, she can never achieve *mokṣa*; she would have to be reborn as a male before liberation could occur (Jaini 1991). The Śvetāmbara tradition accepts the arguments on women's 'nature' but does not deny to them the possibility of liberation. This debate forms part of the more general dispute over the requirement of nudity for mendicants. The Digambara claim tautologically that clothing is an obstacle along the path to *mokṣa*, and since women 'must' wear clothing – neither group considers nudity an acceptable practice for women – they are demonstrably inferior. The practical outcome of these theoretical debates is that among the Digambara, women are not permitted to take full monastic vows. Among the Śvetāmbara, by contrast, female mendicancy has a long and even illustrious history. According to the scriptures, since the time of Ṛsabha (Jainism's first Jina of mythic times), nuns have always outnumbered monks by more than two to one. The Jina Mahāvīra is said to have had 36,000 nuns and 14,000 monks as disciples (Dundas 1992: 49).

Although Śvetāmbara and Digambara Jainas disagree over the authenticity and interpretation of scriptures, and most importantly over monastic practice, both hold essentially identical views on the soul, the nature of reality, and the need for renunciation.

Both traditions prospered in the centuries following Mahāvīra's death. Royal support was a central factor in their early successes (as it was with the spread of Buddhism). The mutual disregard of the Brāhmaṇ class, by both local kings and *śramaṇa* groups, led to a natural alliance. Jainas, along with other renouncers, proclaimed the superiority of the Kṣatriya (kingly/warrior caste) over that of the Brāhmaṇs (priestly caste). In the centuries straddling the end of the old and start of the new millennium (300 BCE to CE 400), the *śramaṇa* groups were numerous, organized, and with the allegiances they made with local rulers they constituted a 'parallel civilization' (Jaini 1991: 275) that rivaled the Brāhmaṇical order. The migration patterns of Jainas during the period reflect this sociopolitical reality, in that they are connected with the granting, and subsequent withholding, of kingly favor. By the fifth century CE, in central and southern India, the Digambaras had become an influential cultural force. And the same could be said of the Śvetāmbaras in northern and western India by the seventh century. This period is also marked by a large increase in the number of lay followers, a factor that necessitated the development of scriptures aimed at those on the householder path. The mendicant-scholars' acknowledgement of the lay path as a legitimate (albeit subordinate) one, as well as the high degree of lay participation, contributed to the advance of Jainism during its period of royal support and enabled it to survive when that support was withdrawn.

The golden age of royal support for Jainas came to a close by the eleventh and twelfth centuries, primarily due to the rise of Hindu theism and of Muslim counter-influences. An energetic devotional Hindu movement (*bhakti*) had emerged in South India and by the ninth century CE, with the benefit of royal patronage, it had spread throughout India. From the twelfth century onward, Jainas in the north came increasingly under the dominion of Islam. These factors contributed to a falling out of favor for the Jaina tradition, with its emphasis on asceticism and its denial of a Supreme God.

Jainas began to withdraw, socially and geographically, to the western regions of India, from Rajasthan in the north to Karnataka in the south, where they remain concentrated to this day.

Significantly, long after the end of the *śramaṇa* 'civilization,' when its challenge had become assimilated within Brāhmaṇical orthodoxy, the Jaina Dharma continued to thrive. Buddhism, its closest rival, fared less well in India. It was effectively absorbed within the ecumenical outreach of Hinduism. The Buddha became identified as the ninth *avatāra* of Viṣṇu, and was ensconced within Hinduism's pantheon of deities. It remains a curiosity as to how Jainas, who always have been a tiny minority numerically, have managed to retain their distinctive identity and flourish on the Indian Subcontinent within the dominant Hindu culture.

Sacred life and literature

The sacred literature of the Jainas is held to derive from the Jina Mahāvīra himself. In his omniscient state (*kevalin*) he uttered the sacred sounds that were put to memory by his immediate disciples (called *ganadharas*), and then passed on to subsequent disciples in an oral tradition that continued uninterrupted until the famine of northern India in about 300 BCE.

During this disaster, great numbers of mendicants perished, and with them, the oral tradition. The group that fled south (later known as the Digambara) was smaller in number, and, in the turmoil of famine and flight, they were ill prepared for the arduous task of preserving and transmitting a vast canon. From this point on, the story of the authenticity and preservation of Jaina scriptures becomes a complex and contentious one. The entire Jaina canonical literature, or Āgama, is comprised of three main branches: the Pūrva, the Aṅga, and the Aṅgabahya.

The Pūrvas are concerned with a variety of topics in Jaina metaphysics, cosmology, and philosophy. They constitute the oldest part of the Jaina scriptures, believed to date back to the period of Pārśva, the twenty-third Jina, of the ninth century BCE. The Pūrvas disappeared at the time of the famine but outlines of their content had been memorized and integrated into later works, a commonly used mnemonic device in oral traditions. It is widely assumed that the content of the Pūrvas was incorporated into a body of literature called the Aṅga ('limbs'), which dates from the time of Mahāvīra.

The works of the Aṅga are concerned with a broad range of topics, including mendicant conduct, heretical philosophical schools, doctrine, religious narratives, and laws of *karma*. The final section of the Aṅga, called the *Dṛṣṭivāda*, is believed to have contained the main teachings of the Pūrva. Unfortunately, the *Dṛṣṭivāda* suffered the same fate as the Pūrvas and disappeared from the ranks of the Śvetāmbara Jainas.

Digambara Jainas, despite their exodus, succeeded in retaining portions of the *Dṛṣṭivāda* and put it in writing around the second century CE. This work, called the *Ṣaṭkhaṇḍāgama*, marks the first written scripture of the Jainas. Not long after, a second Digambara work was produced, compiled from the same sources, and called the *Kaṣāyaprābhṛta*. Significantly, the *Ṣaṭkhaṇḍāgama* and *Kaṣāyaprābhṛta* constitute the only canonical works the Digambaras recognize as legitimate. They reject the scriptures retained by the Śvetāmbaras as inauthentic deviations from the original canon (Jaini 1979: 52).

The Aṅgabahya is an ancient subsidiary canon that contains some of the most important Jaina scriptures. Comprising thirty-four texts, it includes dialogues on the nature of the soul, ontology, cosmology, astronomy, the time cycles, accounts of the first Jina of our period (Ṛsabha), monastic discipline, and lectures on a variety of moral themes. Significantly, it also includes a text called the *Prajñapana*, which the Śvetāmbara believe contains the essence of the lost *Dṛṣṭivāda* text and, through it, the lost Pūrvas.

Both the Śvetāmbara and Digambara later produced an enormous postcanonical literature on the basis of the works of their learned *ācārya*s (mendicant-scholars), including works by Jinasena, Hemacandra, Kundakunda, Haribhadra, and Umāsvāti. The writings, called *Anuyoga*s, achieved canonical status within their respective traditions and are today considered to be among the most outstanding works of ancient Indian philosophy.

The work of the *ācārya* Umāsvāti merits special note. His treatise, the *Tattvārthasūtra*, composed in Sanskrit in the second century CE, is the only Jaina text recognized as authoritative by both Śvetāmbara and Digambara Jainas. It effectively integrates the vast canonical teachings to produce a single coherent Jaina philosophy.

Today the tradition of writing commentaries on scriptures and creating new philosophical works remains an important and popular practice among mendicant communities as well as among lay disciples and scholars.

The ascetic ideal

The sacred life of the Jainas, upon which their literature expounds, is unequivocally associated with the ascetic ideal. The 'sacred' in Jainism denotes the transcendent or otherworldly and therefore the sacred path is the one that leads us out of the tangle of worldly existence.

The path to *mokṣa* is an arduous one and successes are achieved only gradually. Jaina scriptures present a view of human life as plotted along a ladder of spiritual progress, called *guṇa-sthāna*s (stages of purity). One's place on the ladder reflects one's level of spirituality and spans the scale from the nadir of ignorance to the zenith of enlightenment. The lighter one's karmic 'load,' the greater the degree of purity and the more advanced along the *guṇa-sthāna*. The lowest state is that of *mithyādṛṣṭi* (the deluded view of reality) where a soul may dwell for countless lives until it acquires *samyag-darśana* (the fourth rung), the correct view of reality. *Samyag-darśana* is not achieved on the basis of study, as this would be completely fruitless for someone in a deluded state. Instead, it is described as arising from a spiritual jolt or an 'awakening' that suddenly enables one to see clearly. Though still very much a spiritual neophyte, one who has attained *samyag-darśana* can now begin the difficult but glorious journey to *mokṣa*.

The *guṇa-sthāna*s are stages of increasing restraint and purification. Lay Jaiṇas, though in the possession of *samyag-darśana*, are assumed to be relatively low down on the ladder (usually on the fourth or fifth rung). Those who possess extraordinary mental and physical control such as the mendicants are assumed to be on higher rungs. The sixth rung (called *sarva-virata*) is attained when one renounces worldly life and accepts the *mahāvrata*s (great vows, indicating absolute restraint). Of course, such a scheme is overdetermined in its support of renunciation, in that the desire to renounce worldly life is itself read as evidence of a higher stage of purity. The absence of such interest is understood to be an indicator of a low spiritual rung.

A philosophy that emphasizes the *mokṣa-mārga* (path of renunciation) as the religious ideal and which considers human life in terms of stages of purification may reinforce a view of lay life as a diluted or weaker form of the mendicant path. While the scriptures (and many scholarly works) suggest such a reading, the actual lived practices of lay Jainas do not bear this out. The overwhelming majority of Jainas throughout history have chosen the path of the 'householder.' Rather than renounce the world, they participate in it unequivocally, actively, and joyfully. In recent years, scholars have been redressing this imbalance in academic interpretive perspective, for instance, by looking at the significant role that 'this-worldly' values such as health, happiness, and wealth have played at all times in Jaina social life (Cort 2001; Laidlaw 1995) as well as by exploring the rich devotional forms of religious expression in Jainism (Kelting 2001). Indeed, one of the most striking features of Jaina tradition is the degree to which the laity is removed from the ascetic ideal it ostensibly esteems. Jainas are well known for their business acumen and, as a community, are highly successful in many this-worldly pursuits.

But there is no need to exaggerate the 'this-worldliness' of the Jainas in response to an earlier overemphasis on Jainism's *śramaṇa* roots. No matter how far removed individual Jainas may be from the mendicant path, in their religious lives they are united in the veneration of the ascetic ideal. Jaina householders do not worship gods in the hope of personal gain nor perform *pūjā*s for worldly success. Instead they venerate ascetics. The beautiful and emotive devotional songs they compose are not sung to a god who can and may respond but to the Jinas who, in their transcendent state, remain aloof. Countless Jaina teaching stories and popular tales narrate the folly of worldly involvement and depict the triumphant hero who is a world-renouncer.

Throughout the long history of the tradition, Jainas have cultivated a nuanced negotiation between worldly involvement and withdrawal. Whatever the connection between the many remarkable 'this-worldly' achievements of the Jainas and their otherworldly ethos, it likely will remain a source of considerable interest.

Institutions and practices

Since the time of Mahāvīra, Jainism has been identified as a *caturvidhasaṅgha* (fourfold community), comprised of monks, nuns, laymen, and laywomen. The success of Jainism as a minority tradition has depended, in large part, on the steady and clearly defined relationship that exists between these groups and especially between those who renounce the world in pursuit of nonviolence and those who remain 'in the world' and support their quest.

Dāna is the institution that sustains the *caturvidhasaṅgha* and is therefore at the very heart of Jaina religious life. It is a simple word that means 'charity' or 'alms' but, through a distinctively Jaina interpretation, becomes the instrument through which the tradition flourishes.

At its most fundamental level, *dāna* is about providing mendicants with food and water since they are not permitted to acquire these essentials on their own. The vow of *ahiṃsā* prohibits them from all activities associated with the growing, the preparation, and exchange of foods. The basics of their vegetarian diet, namely, plants, fruits, and water, all contain life (*jīva*), and for a Jaina mendicant, harming any of these life forms is prohibited. It is only through the piety of householders that the mendicants remain karmically unaffected by the violence inherent in the preparation of food.

The householder chops, cooks, and boils, and, in so doing, renders the food '*ajīva*' (without life). Whatever food the mendicant consumes must be devoid of all life, so that its ingestion will accrue no new *karma*. The householder, who has not renounced the world and is living 'in' society, accepts that a degree of violence is necessary in order to survive. She (it is usually the woman of the home who gives these alms) is happy to provide the mendicants with 'leftover' food (it cannot be made expressly for the mendicants, as this would implicate them in the violence of its preparation).

Dāna is an expression of nonreciprocal unilateral giving. Mendicants do not provide religious instruction 'in exchange' for sustenance; instead, they adamantly deny any exchange takes place since that would implicate them in the worldly life they have renounced. Jonathan Parry succinctly captures the logic of this denial when he writes, 'The reciprocated gift belongs to the profane world; the unreciprocated gift belongs to a quest for salvation from it' (1986: 462).

Dāna, more generally, refers to all forms of religious giving, from the protection that mendicants provide to all living beings (considered its most sublime expression), to the lavish donations given by wealthy families for temple construction. All these result in the accumulation of spiritual merit (*punya*). Without *dāna*, the religious giving of the householders, the monastic institution, and its associated practices could not exist.

Dāna allows the mendicants to pursue their religious practices in a realm removed from the violence and attachment of worldly life. At the time of their initiation, an ascetic-aspirant receives five great vows (*mahāvrata*s). In accepting them, he or she swears to observe nonviolence and to renounce lying, stealing, sexual intercourse, and acquisitiveness or the ownership of possessions.

Each of these vows is all encompassing, and together they are intended to lead to total restraint. For Jainas, both the intention underlying the act (thought, deed, or action) as well as the act itself must be pure. For instance, consuming vegetarian food whilst having harmful thoughts would still result in the accumulation of *pāpa* (bad *karma*). And *pāpa* would be equally accumulated as a result of the unintentional consumption of nonvegetarian food, though of a 'lighter' quantity than if it had been intentionally consumed. Jainism and Buddhism differ on this, with Buddhism giving much importance to the role of intention alone.

The *mahāvrata*s are like an intricate web, limiting worldly involvement and regulating all aspects of one's existence. They leave virtually nothing to chance: they dictate how one sleeps (tranquilly, with little movement), the time one rises (at the auspicious hour of 4 a.m.), what and whether one eats (only vegetarian '*ajīva*' alms, and only if offered), what one wears (simple white cloths for Śvetāmbaras) or does not wear (nudity being a requirement for Digambara ascetics), how one talks (minimally and with restraint), walks (barefoot, carefully with eyes on the ground in front of them), where one walks (from village to village continuously, except for the four months of the rainy season), to where one eliminates one's bodily waste (a place devoid of all *jīva*s).

*Mahāvrata*s are a comprehensive, all-embracing system designed to impede the acquisition of new *karma* (a process called *saṃvara*) and assist in destroying one's existing *karma* (called *nirjarā*). Everything that a mendicant does – from preaching to studying, from fasting to meditation – is with the aim of furthering the processes of *saṃvara* and *nirjarā*.

The religious life of Jaina householders, whose knowledge of and sympathy with the ascetic path was vital for the continued existence of the monastic institution, has obviously always been less constrained. Until the close of the first millennium, it was probably quite variable (Folkert 1993: 12). During that period, a set of scriptures was developed (called *sravakacara*s) addressing the religious life of householders and closely modeled on the mendicant path. They depicted the ideal lay life as one of gradual progress along a path of increasing restraint, delineated in eleven stages (called *pratimā*s), in which the final stage entailed ascetic renunciation.

While some lay Jainas clearly do regulate and interpret their lives according to the *pratimā*s, the vast majority do not. The most popular religious practices are those of devotion, *pūjā* (worship), temple rituals, and pilgrimage – which are Hinduism's most popular forms of religious expression as well. Superficially, there is little to distinguish between Jaina and Hindu popular religion (if we can talk in these generalized terms). But a closer look at lay Jaina religiosity reveals the presence of its *śramaṇa* influences as mediated through forms of religious expression that are more acceptable to householders. Most of the colorful, devotional practices of householders (from home *pūjā*s to faraway pilgrimages) are about celebrating the lives of the Jinas. Intriguingly, the crux of lay Jaina devotional life centers on the worship of heroic ascetics who remain aloof from the cares of the world. The songs and prayers of lay devotees, often expressed in an emotive language of love, do not await response. Instead, they are performed as a type of discipline, with the goal of fostering detachment from worldly life. That reveals the degree to which the renouncer ethos has penetrated the very fabric of Jaina life and is an example of the genius with which Jainism integrates the sober and the joyful, the devotional and ascetic, the otherworldly and the this-worldly.

Ethics

Jaina tradition is known for its ascetic ideal, its astonishingly beautiful architecture, and its philanthropy, among other things. But perhaps it is most renowned for its ethics. An ethical outlook is the very foundation of a worldview, informing every dimension of what we do, bringing into focus that which is deemed worthy of concern, and allowing us to be blind to other realities. For most of the world's religions, ethics are primarily concerned with human-human relations or are understood in terms of relations formed within a human-human-God triangulation. In Jainism, ethics are concerned with the interactions of humans with all living beings; there is virtually no sphere in which humans are free from the obligation of concern. Jaina ethics are distinctive for their rigor, scope, and compassion. Commonly, their essence is captured in the aphorism '*ahiṃsā paramo dharma*' ('nonviolence is the supreme path').

According to Jaina tradition, the universe is infused with countless life forms. Humans are but one of its expressions, along with animals, plants, and elemental forms of life. Each life has a soul, and each soul is inherently luminous, although trapped in karmic matter. Harm to any other life causes us to be burdened with additional *karma* and to sink deeper in the swamp of bondage. Because of this, the world is akin to a moral theater, where every interaction has ethical implications.

The desire to lead a life of nonviolence is the impetus driving the ascetic imperative in Jainism. Padmanabh Jaini explains how Jaina ethics follow from its worldview:

> This awareness of the basic worth of all beings, and of one's kinship with them, generates a feeling of great compassion (*anukampa*) for others. Whereas the compassion felt by an ordinary man is tinged with pity or with attachment to its object, *anukampa* is free of such negative aspects; it develops purely from wisdom, from seeing the substance (*dravya*) that underlies visible modes, and it fills the individual with an unselfish desire to help other souls towards *mokṣa*. If this urge to bring all tormented being out of *saṃsāra* is particularly strong and is cultivated, it may generate those auspicious *karma*s that later confer the status of Tīrthaṃkara upon certain omniscients. When present to a more moderate degree, *anukampa* brings an end to exploitative and destructive behavior, for even the lowest animal is now seen as intrinsically worthwhile and thus inviolable.
>
> universal suffering (1979: 150)

Dedication to the ethical principle of nonviolence derives from Jainism's unique cosmology, which emphasizes the common fate of all living beings. For those who are truly awake to the violence inherent in life, there is little choice but to repudiate it thoroughly. Mendicants acquire tremendous respect because they have renounced the world fully to pursue ethical ideals. In so doing, they have seized upon the opportunity that human birth has given them, refusing to fritter it away as do most humans. A life of mendicancy, and the possibility of *mokṣa*, is only available to humans.

Compassion is not directed so much at the suffering *in* social life but at the suffering *of* social life; it arises from observing worldly life itself. The message of the *tīrthaṅkara*s is that all human beings are capable of conquering the bondage of physical existence and achieving freedom from the cycle of rebirth (Folkert 1993). *Ahiṃsā*, as Jainas formulate it, is not concerned with social roles and obligations, and its teachings are not designed to remedy social ills so much as escape them. It reveals a perception of the world as inherently corrupt and in need of transcendence; it leads to renunciation and motivation to help individuals out of *saṃsāra*. The highest cultural and religious ideals revolve around nonviolence, nonpossession, and nonattachment; and these are embodied in the ascetics.

Jaina ethics are enshrined in the *mahāvratas* – the five 'great vows' that work to 'fence in' or limit worldly entanglement. Nonviolence (*ahiṃsā*) is the first and most fundamental vow. It demands that one avoid violence in thought, speech, and action; and it is believed to be the foundation upon which the remaining four derive. They are truthfulness, nonstealing, sexual restraint, and nonpossession.

Although Jainas treat the human incarnation as a privileged one that should not be squandered, they do not believe that humans possess anything unique that would endow them with an innate superiority. There exist five categories of living beings in the Jaina universe, each corresponding with the number of senses they possess. They are arranged according to the following schema:

Number and type of senses	**Examples of beings**
1. sensed beings, called 'nigodas,' with touch	earth, water, fire, air
2. sensed beings, with touch and taste	worms, leeches, mollusks
3. sensed beings, with touch, taste, smell	all small insects (ants, fleas)
4. sensed beings, with touch, taste, smell, sight	wasps, flies, mosquitoes
5. sensed beings, with touch, taste, smell, sight, hearing	fish, birds, quadrupeds, humans

Source: Umāsvāti (1994: 45).

The greater the number of senses one possesses, the greater is one's ability to understand worldly existence as a state of bondage in need of escape. But an increase in the number of senses does not mean greater moral worth. Consciousness is the inalienable characteristic of every *jīva*, however undeveloped. It is present even in the *nigodas* (the least developed life form); and through progressive development along the *guṇa-sthānas*, they too may culminate in the supreme state of omniscience. Therefore, human distinction from surrounding life forms is a matter of degree, not of kind; and it is established through ethical behavior. Humans alone can be said to be 'ethical.' The designation of 'ethical' or 'unethical' is nonsensical if applied to the behavior of insects, plants, and animals or to those who lack understanding; its employment hinges upon a level of awareness and responsibility that only the human incarnation possesses. In Jainism, ethical practice is the most compelling and potent manifestation of human potential, and asceticism is its highest expression.

It could be argued that Jainas view the meaning of 'the human' in a nonessentialized way that is akin to the ninth-century monk Jinasena's reinterpretation of the priestly class 'Brāhmaṇ' – that is, a status achieved on the basis of ethical conduct as opposed to one ascribed at birth. We become truly human only through moral behavior; in its absence we can claim no special status. Through *ahiṃsā* (restraint, compassion, and nonviolence), human dignity is established in a universe teeming with life.

Relations with other religions

Jaina aptitude for intercultural and interreligious dealings may be among the most important features of the tradition as well as a factor in the survival of a distinctive Jaina identity as a heterodox minority in the context of the potentially overwhelming presence of Hinduism. Padmanabh Jaini, an eminent scholar of Jainism and Buddhism, has argued that the Jaina *ācārya*s recognized early their predicament as a minority that was in need of social interaction with non-Jainas but was vulnerable to assimilation. The leaders had the wisdom to prescribe a middle ground. According to Jaini, this resulted in a practice of 'cautious integration,' the essence of which is captured by the following maxim: 'All worldly practices [those not related to salvation] are valid for the Jainas, as long as there is neither loss of pure insight nor violation of the vratas' (cited in Jaini 1979: 287).

'Cautious integration' involves acceptance of local customs, including language, holidays, dress codes, and cuisine (with the exception of nonvegetarian foods and other prohibited items) as well as the basic framework of the Hindu *saṃskāra*s (lifecycle rituals) such as birth and marriage rites. But perhaps the most conspicuous expression of the practice of cautious integration is seen in the Jaina adoption of the caste system – an ideological construct that runs counter to Jaina teachings. The *ācārya* Jinasena (*c.* ninth century CE) is credited with this adaptation – one that was likely essential for Jainas in order to prosper, given their need for fruitful social integration with the surrounding Hindu populace and the hostility of Brāhmaṇical society toward any deviation from accepted patterns of social behavior (Jaini 1979: 292). Jinasena succeeded by reinterpreting the meaning of the caste system in terms acceptable to Jainism. Pointedly, he maintained that its genesis was a product of social and political expediency and that it was not of divine origin as the Brāhmaṇs claimed. In addition, he redefined 'Brāhmaṇ' to mean an honorable status achieved on the basis of exemplary ethical conduct and not an ascribed status based on one's birth, as was asserted by Hindu orthodoxy.

It has been suggested that the Jaina facility at compromise may be a natural manifestation of its worldview, which rejects dogmatism as a form of ignorance. In particular, much attention has been given to the Jaina philosophical doctrine called *anekāntavāda*, which simply means 'not one-sided.' *Anekāntavāda* states that all truth claims are partial and are unavoidably bound to a particular context; ignorance arises if we mistake partiality for truth. Jainas used the philosophical doctrine tactically to dismiss the rival philosophies of Buddhism and Hindu Vedānta as being *ekānta* or one-sided. Whether or not the motive underpinning the doctrine's use was to draw different viewpoints together or to keep them distinguished, the effect has been to acknowledge a multiplicity of valid perspectives on all matters.

Jainas today continue to explore the potentials of *anekāntavāda* for intercultural harmony and as a tool for world peace. In 2002, for instance, an international conference was convened in Los Angeles at California State Polytechnic University (Pomona) on the value of *anekāntavāda* for the modern world. Throughout their history, Jainas have had to negotiate with practices that deviate from their accepted beliefs, and they have done so in a creative way that has allowed them to maintain the essence and integrity of their own teachings. Jainas now living outside of India – especially in the UK, the US, and Canada – appear to be involved in similar 'negotiations,' fully immersing themselves in their new homelands, embracing the English language, and adopting many of the local cultural customs. Nevertheless, their identity as Jainas remains central and is safeguarded in a variety of ways, paramount among those is the maintenance of their distinctive dietary practices (Vallely 2002b).

Modern expressions and the tradition outside of India

The developments within Jainism in the modern period are too many and varied for a comprehensive examination here. Nevertheless, an overview is possible, highlighting some significant events and possible trends.

The social identity of lay Jainas largely derives from their association with a specific mendicant order: Śvetāmbara Jainas are those householders who support and identify with mendicants wearing white robes; Digambara Jainas are those who support and identify with monks whose asceticism necessitates nudity.

In India, sectarian affiliation plays an important role in determining the boundaries of social engagement (for example, limiting the choices regarding with whom one works, socializes, and marries). As a consequence, the minutiae of Jaina monastic debates have had profound effects on the social organization and identity of lay Jainas. This indeed has been the case since the first split after the death of Mahāvīra. Although the schism between the Śvetāmbara and Digambara was as much a reflection of the different geographic and linguistic regions in which the groups developed as it was an expression of doctrinal dispute, it is not generally understood in these terms. Instead, cultural differences tend to be subsumed within sectarian identity.

Jaina laity, therefore, always has been vulnerable to mendicant rivalries but never passively so. Indeed, it was often educated lay disciples, with a keen knowledge of their scriptures, who would initiate the challenges that led to intermonastic schisms. Ironically, the lofty debates over otherworldly matters are fought and decided on this-worldly terrain. A mendicant who breaks from his order because of a difference of opinion over doctrine or practice needs the support of lay disciples if he (and his challenge) is to survive. The social ramifications of doctrinal disputes can therefore be momentous, leading to the splintering of a previously unified community. Much of Jaina history can be understood in this light.

Jainism experienced a rise in sectarian divisions from the fifteenth century CE onward when it had become well established in the western regions of India and the threat from Hindu and Muslim theism was waning. Many of the reform movements did not survive their leaders but several remain active today. The most important among these are the Sthanakavasis (*c.* fifteenth century) and the Terāpanthis (*c.* eighteenth century), both of which emerged as reform movements from within the Śvetāmbara tradition. The Sthanakavasis rejected the temple and image-worship practices that were ubiquitous at the time, arguing that they were harmful accretions that ran counter to the ideals of nonviolence and nonattachment. They developed their own canon and initiated the practice of wearing mouth-shields, a further expression of *ahiṃsā*, with the aim of not harming living beings in the atmosphere. The Terāpanthis emerged as a reform group from within the Sthanakavasis. They were critical of what they considered to be the mendicants' laxity in ascetic practice and their ignorance of Jaina scriptures. Among the Digambara, a similar reform movement in about the sixteenth century led to the emergence of the Digambara Terāpantha.

Reform and renewal are an integral part of all vibrant religious and cultural traditions. For most of Jainism's long history, they have tended to come from within the mendicant ranks and then extend beyond them, influencing and altering lay religious practice and organization in novel ways.

The twentieth century saw the emergence of visionaries who sought to reinvigorate

the mendicant path and thereby indirectly chal-
c ideal. Raj Candrabhai, Kanji Svami, Ācarya
Citrabanuji are among the most prominent of
rs. With the exception of Raj Candrabhai, a lay
his influence on the thinking of Mohandas
rthodox monks in India who either renounced
e or remained as monks but outside the institu-
Dundas (1992: 232) has suggested that these
ide us with a glimpse of Jainism's future, espe-
here the ideology of the *mokṣa-mārga* has little
modations may be the most recent expressions
gration' that has served Jainism so well in the
the need for total renunciation but, at the same
derpin it.

power to inspire new generations of Jainas
hey were first uttered. Today, especially in the
diaspora, many are energetically interpreting the teachings in decidedly sociocentric
terms that include such things as social activism, animal-rights consciousness, and
environmentalism. Such interpretations are viewed by those who support them *not* as a
departure from the 'authentic' Jaina path but rather as true to the spirit of Mahāvīra.
Indeed, one could argue that it has been a quest to uphold this 'spirit' that has under-
pinned every reform and schism in Jaina tradition since its inception. Mahāvīra's
insights into the human condition, and the sublime ethic of nonviolence that he taught,
makes the path of Jainism a strikingly relevant one in the modern period.

Suggested further readings

Babb (1996); Banks (1992); Caillat and Kumar (1981); Carrithers and Humphrey
(1991); Cort (1990, 2001); Dundas (1992); Folkert (1993); Humphrey and Laidlaw
(1994); Jaini (1979, 1991).

World-negation

280-282
Indian Religions - 89-102,

4. Annual ceremony at which the Prime Minister and President of India honor the memory of Dr B. R. Ambedkar. Courtesy of Ministry of Information and Broadcasting, Government of India.

3

BAUDDHA DHAMMA

Tessa Bartholomeusz

The tradition defined

Like the designation 'South Asia,' the expression 'Buddhist traditions of South Asia' is similarly ambiguous. Buddhism has historical roots that can be traced to the sixth century BCE and to the area near the present-day border between Nepal and northern India. Over many centuries during its formative period, it spread throughout India and into what are now Bangladesh and Myanmar to the northeast, Pakistan to the northwest, Tibet (and through it to Central and East Asia), and to Sri Lanka in the south. Today the Buddhist traditions found in the Southeast Asian nations of Thailand, Cambodia, and Laos share many features with Buddhism as it has survived and revived in Sri Lanka, but in other parts of Southeast, Central, and East Asia the traditions are markedly different from surviving South Asian forms of Buddhism. Although you might expect the term 'South Asian Buddhism' to refer to a single regional variety of religion, there are significant differences among the Buddhism practiced today in the several contemporary nations of South Asia. Some of them retain clear historical links to India; others have stronger ties to Southeast and East Asia. In Sri Lanka, Thailand, Cambodia, Laos, and Myanmar, the dominant Buddhist institutions are identified with Theravāda (the Doctrine of the Elders); in Nepal, Tibet, most of the mountain area that separates South Asia from the main body of the Asian continent, and remaining parts of Southeast Asia, Buddhism has taken the Mahāyāna (Great Vehicle) form.

With the exception of Sri Lanka and Bhutan, Buddhism came close to disappearing as a living religion in most of the region of South Asia long ago. The rise of Muslim majorities in Afghanistan, Pakistan, Bangladesh, and the Maldives in recent centuries, of course, is correlated with the disappearance of Buddhism in those areas. Nevertheless, Pakistan remains an extremely important archaeological site for helping us to understand the early spread of Buddhism along the Silk Road and into other parts of the world. The revival of Buddhism on the Indian Subcontinent is a fairly recent phenomenon that we will describe at the end of the chapter.

The expression 'Indian Buddhism,' which is used to refer to Buddhism as represented in texts that are preserved in the Pali and Sanskrit languages, contains ambiguities, too. In his influential study, *Indian Buddhism* (1970), A. K. Warder assumes that the allegedly original eighteen schools of Buddhism, of which the Theravāda is the only one to survive, represent the 'original' teachings of the Buddha. Though Warder does not define precisely what he means by 'Indian Buddhism,' the first few pages of his study map the terrain of his subject for the reader. For Warder (1970: 3), Indian Buddhism is the Sanskrit and Pali textual tradition, of which the 'canon' of only one of the original eighteen schools, the Theravāda, is 'preserved intact in Ceylon [Sri Lanka], Burma [Myanmar], Cambodia, and Siam [Thailand].' Textual fragments of other schools have been 'preserved in Nepal,' and 'a few scattered texts in Indian languages [are] preserved elsewhere, for instance, in Tibet, in Japan . . . and Central Asia.' Warder includes in his study of Indian Buddhism the writings of the great Indian Buddhist logicians, such as the seventh-century Nāgārjuna, whose philosophy has had little, if any, impact on Buddhism in Sri Lanka, which is the one country considered by Theravādins to have preserved the authoritative early tradition.[1] Instead Nāgārjuna's thought influenced developments in Tibet and China, that is, Mahāyāna Buddhism. The 'Indian Buddhism' defined by Warder is not limited by geography, but then typically South Asian forms of Buddhism in fact do extend beyond the Indian Subcontinent. Put differently, thoughtful analysis of Warder's work reminds us that there are problems associated with using 'Indian Subcontinent' and 'South Asia' to refer to the same area, and neither 'South Asian Buddhist traditions' nor 'Indian Buddhism' are simple and unproblematic labels.

When we use the expression 'South Asian Buddhist traditions' or any of its permutations, therefore, we will pay careful attention to the modern period that is an era in which one-fifth of the world's current population – the 'South Asians' – have been forced to come to terms with living in a multiethnic, polyglot society that is home to all of the world's major religious traditions. Yet, though we are primarily concerned with the modern period, we shall begin with ancient Buddhism in order to help illuminate the trends, patterns, and historical developments that have shaped today's living Buddhist traditions of South Asia. For added clarity we shall choose as our field of study the countries that the South Asian Association for Regional Cooperation (SAARC) established in December 1985 to accelerate the process of economic and social development in the area (Madaan 1997: 634). According to SAARC, South Asia consists of Bangladesh, Bhutan, India, the Maldives, Nepal, Pakistan, and Sri Lanka. But when necessary, we will refer to Buddhist traditions of Myanmar and Thailand. This is because of similarities among the Theravādin Buddhist cultures of the peoples of South and Southeast Asia. Moreover, because Pali is the language of the Theravādin textual tradition that has preserved early teachings that are honored today throughout South Asia, for the sake of consistency we shall use Pali terms but add their Sanskrit counterparts when appropriate. Pali is a liturgical rather than commercial language, specific religious terms of which are known widely by laity and monk alike, and it is chanted in religious rituals throughout the Theravādin cultures of South and Southeast Asia.

In recent years scholars have been reassessing the methods by which Buddhologists (Buddhist and non-Buddhist scholars of Buddhism) arrive at conclusions regarding the nature of ancient Buddhism and its development in India. Earlier there was a tendency to assume that the ancient texts accurately portray the Buddhism of their day, and the Pali and Sanskrit corpus became 'privileged' as a source of information. Gregory Schopen argued, however, that archaeology produces a different and often a conflicting picture of early Buddhism in India. Schopen (1991: 20) proposes that scholarly prejudice in favor of the text represents the persistence of the sixteenth-century Protestant Christian distrust of 'historical human behavior' and its preference for the written word over actual religious practices. Moreover, he warns us that the Buddhist literary corpus, which survives only in very late manuscript traditions, was intended 'to inculcate an ideal' (what its editors, the Buddhist monks, wanted their community to believe and practice) rather than to record what early Buddhist people actually believed and practiced (Schopen 1991: 3). When confronted by archaeology with evidence that ancient Buddhist monks and nuns most certainly possessed private property (a possibility condemned by the textual tradition) Buddhologists have argued that such activity was a symptom of stages in the decline of Buddhism (Schopen 1991: 7–8). Because the texts, particularly the *Vinaya* or monastic code, precluded individuals in the monastic community (*saṅgha*) from owning certain things, including gold and silver, anyone in the community who did so must have been errant or corrupt. However, little evidence is available to confirm that the *Vinaya*'s injunctions were operative in ancient Buddhist societies. On the contrary, there is archaeological evidence that individual monks and nuns were benefactors and patrons. In short, they had private wealth at their disposal, despite an image based on textual ideals that the *saṅgha*'s members were beggars and possessed no personal property. In ancient Sri Lanka there was the same pattern as in India. The Sri Lankan archaeologist S. Paranavitana reported that an inscription found in the course of excavating more than 1,000 cave dwellings that were gifted to the *saṅgha* during the earliest Buddhist period (third century BCE to the first century CE) indicates that at least one donor was a Buddhist monk (cited in Coningham 1995: 231).

If we follow Schopen and resist the temptation to privilege textual materials in our search for understanding how ancient lay and monastic Buddhists actually practiced, we will be in a better position to understand the development of Buddhism and to appreciate its contemporary situation. If we allowed the textual traditions' ideal view to shape our evaluation of modern-day beliefs and practices, we would only be able to see Buddhism-in-decline, even though Buddhism is alive and well in many areas of modern South Asia.

Of course we should continue to explore the content and structure of the Buddhist texts, particularly because they offer the only ancient recorded insights into the life of the one, as tradition tells us, who first delivered the *dhamma* or Buddhist teachings sometime in the sixth century BCE in northern India. The Pali canon was passed down orally within the monastic community and did not get reduced to written form until the first century BCE in Sri Lanka (Collins 1990), which was several centuries after the death of the founder of Buddhism and several thousands of miles from his presumed place of birth at the edge of present-day Nepal, but it gives us an idea of some of the early traditions associated with the life of the founder. His name is Gotama (Sanskrit Gautama), and like a few others before him, he accepted the title of 'Buddha,' the fully awakened one, after he had discovered the truths associated with 'unsatisfactoriness' (*dukkha*) and its remedy. Those truths are embodied in the *dhamma*, and its living representatives are the members of the monastic order, the *saṅgha*. Though tradition testifies that ordinary people can be enlightened, only a Buddha is considered to be 'fully' enlightened: unlike those who attain enlightenment because they learn the *dhamma* after it has been discovered and made available by a Buddha, a Buddha discovers the truth for himself and then teaches it. We shall discuss the (historical) Buddha, the *dhamma*, and the *saṅgha* in later sections of this chapter; yet it is appropriate to point out here that together they make up the 'Three Refuges' (*tiśaraṇa*) or 'Three Jewels' (*triratna*), the 'taking' of which defines a person as a Buddhist layman (*upāsaka*) or laywoman (*upāsikā*).

The *upāsaka* and *upāsikā* usually are familiar with the main teachings of the canon but might be hard-pressed to quote the exact passage when making a point because the Pali canon is voluminous. But regardless of how familiar the members of the laity or the *saṅgha* may be with the texts, and notwithstanding cultural differences between Buddhists in Sri Lanka and Thailand, for example, there are many things upon which most Theravādins would agree. They believe that they are living in the dispensation (*sasana*) of a Buddha, a fully enlightened or awakened being who 'sets the wheel in motion,' as tradition teaches. That means he promulgates the *dhamma*, often represented in Buddhist art by an eight-spoked wheel. According to Theravāda tradition, the dispensation of each Buddha lasts 5,000 years. Theravādins in South and Southeast Asia marked the halfway point with religious celebrations in 1954. In the Theravādin idea of history, time periods (*kalpa*) come into being, pass away, and begin anew. Theravāda Buddhism also expresses its sense of history in the same linear fashion that we in the West take for granted in addition to their cyclical view of time. For instance, the Sri Lankan *Mahāvaṃsa*, a fifth-century noncanonical Pali text that celebrates the Buddhist culture of the island, is also a chronology (*vaṃsa*) of kings who appear in the text consecutively, based on the presumed dates of their reigns. We now turn our attention to the Theravādin Buddhist idea of history and cosmology, much of which was shaped early on by Brāhmaṇical ideas that were mainstream and orthodox at the time when the Buddha 'set the wheel of the *dhamma* in motion.'

Cosmos and history

The idea that the dispensation of each Buddha is to last for 5,000 years is based loosely on a canonical text, the *Cakkavati Sihanada Sutta*. This particular *Sutta* (which means thread; that is, a treatise, discourse, or sermon) begins differently than most. Although the Buddha's sermons are usually preached on the basis of specific questions put forth by one of his followers, in the *Cakkavati Sihanada* the Buddha is asked a question but then delivers a sermon that is unrelated to it. Be that as it may, the *Sutta* is set partly in the past, but for the most part focuses on the future. We can presume that its discussion centers on the *sasana* of Gotama Buddha. A long and dramatic analysis tells us how the world goes through vast cycles. The analysis is followed by a prediction in which moral depravity in this dispensation eventually will result in the shortening of the human life span, so much so that people will live only ten years. Things become so morally bankrupt that people begin murdering each other; fathers kill their children, and children turn on their parents. Even the *dhamma* or teaching of the Buddha is forgotten, another sign of future depravity. Then a righteous king reinstates morality and heralds the new dispensation of a fully enlightened being. At the end of the *Sutta*, we meet that being. He is Metteyya Buddha, whose only other appearance in the Pali canon is in the *Buddhavaṃsa*, about which we shall have more to say below.

Notwithstanding the canonical *Cakkavati Sihanada Sutta* and *Buddhavaṃsa*, each of which provides biographical material regarding fully enlightened beings who 'set the wheel in motion' in different *kalpa*s and who anchor and punctuate Theravādin historical perspective, most of the Pali canonical texts have little to say about cosmology or history. The monks who were editors of the texts were more interested in philosophy than they were in history, including the history of the Buddha, and as a result much about his life remains a mystery. Later traditions will fill in the lacunae, but most of the early and authoritative texts offer no more than fleeting biographical information. In *Ariyapariyesana Sutta*, for instance, we learn from the Buddha himself the events that led to his renunciation: 'While still young, a black-haired young man, endowed with the blessing of youth, in the prime of life, though my mother and father wished otherwise and wept with tearful faces, I shaved off my hair and beard, put on the yellow robe, and went forth from home into homelessness.' In the same *Sutta*, the Buddha discusses the period of his life soon after his renunciation when he learned meditation from some accomplished masters; his enlightenment in what is now Bodh Gayā in India; and his eventual journey to Sārnāth outside the city of Vārāṇasī near the Ganges River where he spoke his first sermon, 'setting in motion the wheel of *dhamma*' (*dhamma-cakka-pavattana*), to five men. Yet, the vast majority of the *Sutta*s provide little else that will help us to understand the life of the Buddha; their main purpose was to present the *dhamma* rather than the biography of the fully enlightened being.

Another canonical text, the *Mahāparinibbānasutta*, offers an account of what the early tradition considered to be the events surrounding the Buddha's death. He passes away at the ripe old age of eighty, surrounded by the people who have become prominent in his monastic order. Though the question as to what happens to a fully enlightened being upon his death remains unanswered in the canon,[2] one possible reading of the silence is that we should assume that when the Buddha died from what appears to have been natural causes (according to the *Mahāparinibbāna*, he ate some bad food), he simply passed away and is no longer accessible. His *dhamma* remains, and its living representatives, the *saṅgha*, have the responsibility to preserve and transmit the teachings. Despite this way of reading the text, Theravāda Buddhist tradition allows relic worship. The preservation of parts of the physical body of Gotama and visits to the sites where they are enshrined provide reassurance to even the most humble follower that the Buddha continues to be present and available to help or at least to inspire them.

According to traditional thinking, it is a great boon to be born in an age such as ours in which the Buddhist teachings are known. Although we are not contemporaries of the historical Buddha, we are living in his *sasana*. During this time the *dhamma* is available through encounters with Buddhists, through university courses, and in all sorts of other venues. Those who will be living at the end of this dispensation will not be so lucky. According to the *Cakkavati Sihanada Sutta*, the *dhamma* will be forgotten. Its salvific methods will no longer be available to enlighten anyone.

They will have to be rediscovered by Metteyya, the next fully enlightened being. Tradition teaches that the one who then will be Metteyya is now passing through a series of preliminary rebirths to develop the virtues that are a prerequisite to enlightenment. According to traditional thought, those of us now living are lucky for another reason: we are human beings. In Theravāda Buddhist cosmology, the human being is the only creature in the entire cosmos, including all its many heavens and hells, that has the ability to attain enlightenment (Pali *nibbāna*, Sanskrit *nirvāṇa*), literally the 'blowing out' of ignorance, hatred, and greed, the *summum bonum* of the religion.

Only human beings living in the dispensation of a Buddha can attain enlightenment and become Arhats – the 'worthy ones' capable of living as enlightened beings in the dispensation of a Buddha. Only humans have the capacity to reason, to discern the nature of the unsatisfactoriness of existence, and the ability to understand its remedy as proposed by the Buddhist teachings. Gods are defined as beings that live out their exceedingly long but temporary lives without experiencing any suffering, and so they lack the motivation to find a way out of suffering. In Buddhist soteriology (understandings of salvation), therefore, the human being is superior to any divine being – at least in potential.

But gods are more powerful than humans when it comes to matters that do not pertain to salvation. Within the temporal realm, divine beings are able to grant boons to the faithful, including help in winning an election, battling a disease, passing an examination, avoiding or getting pregnant. They can also assist by bringing harm to someone else. Deities, like their human followers, can display a range of behavior that goes across the full spectrum from virtue to malevolence. Together with human beings, hell beings, hungry ghosts, and animals, they occupy the world of the five senses – according to the *Abhidhamma* that comprises one of the three main sections of the Pali canon. The other two are the *Sutta* literature and the *Vinaya* or monastic code. The *Abhidhamma* (Sanskrit *Abhidharma*) provides the most systematic account of the Buddhist understanding of the nature of the cosmos, and its complicated imagery is shared by Mahāyāna Buddhism and exerts a worldwide influence in shaping the worldview of contemporary Buddhists (Gethin 1998: 115).

What does the *Abhidhamma* tell us about the cosmos and our relationship to it? It teaches that *saṃsāra* – the cycle of birth, death, and rebirth – includes thirty-one levels of existence into which sentient beings may be born. There are three main subdivisions of this cosmos in thirty-one levels. Going from bottom to top, representing the transition from gross to subtle, they are the World of Five Senses, the World of Pure Form, and the Formless World. At the lower or gross levels of the cosmos is the World of Five Senses, which is the abode of human beings and others with consciousness and five physical senses. At its center is a massive mountain called Meru that is surrounded by concentric rings of mountains and oceans, beyond which lie four continents. One of them, the land where fully enlightened beings come into being and preach the *dhamma*, is identified with India. Below Meru are various hells, temporary places of pain and torture, inhabited by beings whose activities or *kamma* (Sanskrit *karma*) have been unwholesome. On the slopes of the mountain are realms of the deities of the sense-sphere, where rebirth is the result of wholesome *kamma*. In other words, rebirth into any of the thirty-one levels of the cosmos is based upon one's intentional activities.

In the World of Pure Form above Meru are the Pure Abodes where deities reside that are different from the deities in the World of Five Senses. They have consciousness but only two senses (sight and hearing) and are known collectively as the Brahmās. Their experience is more pleasant than that of their counterparts in the World of Five Senses, but they are not the most refined of the divine beings or Brahmās. Those reside in the Formless World and have only consciousness.

This simplified description of Buddhist cosmology, with its imagery of mountains and concentric circles and hierarchies of kinds of beings based on kammic (karmic) activity, may seem a bit strange and difficult to assimilate, but the full details as presented in the Pali canon are far more complicated. The cosmos as represented in the Theravāda texts contains many thousands of world systems, each one of which is stratified by a World of Five Senses, a World of Pure Form, and a Formless World. Human beings who have attained enlightenment, but who require another birth in order to exhaust the momentum or 'residual fruit' of their meritorious *kamma*, will inhabit the five realms of the Pure Abodes in the World of Pure Form.

All others are in transit through the range of the twenty-six realms (the total thirty-one minus the five Pure Abodes that are restricted to the enlightened) and from one to another of the myriad world systems. As they transit from physical place to place, so do they from mental state to state, going through the thirty-one meditative states identified by Buddhist tradition. This is a map of states of consciousness as well as of territories in a cosmos. It intends to encompass all the modes and realms of existence that it is possible for human beings to experience on the basis of their dispositions, tendencies, and voluntary actions.

The meditative states and the realms of existence are temporary. Beings born into one of the hells, for instance, will not remain there forever. Even a hell being will experience some wholesome thoughts, the propensity for which they bring with them from previous lifetimes, thereby preparing them for a birth elsewhere. Yet, the amount of time spent in a hell may seem to be an eternity, and at Buddhist pilgrimage sites throughout South Asia one will find descriptions of various hells so graphic as to be a positive influence on human behavior. In the south of Sri Lanka, for example, pilgrims tour Werahena and Wevurukannala where wall paintings of punishments associated with unwholesome activities are vivid reminders of the potentially severe and long-lasting price of certain kinds of activities – regardless of whether one is in a human or a divine form at the moment.

Cosmology in Theravāda Buddhism reflects a moral hierarchy. Beings that live below us temporarily occupy some hell because they performed unwholesome deeds; beings that live above us in some heaven have performed wholesome *kamma*. (Ironically, however, wholesome activities may have propelled them into a level of existence in which enlightenment is unavailable!) In the hierarchy immediately above humans, according to traditional texts, are the Gods of the Four Kings. Like us they reside in the World of Five Senses (the first, or lowest, of the three main divisions of the cosmos). Gods who reside there, and other deities as well, are subject to death and rebirth. Indeed, everything is in process and so temporary; and each of the gods is said to be performing a role. Just as the role of Darrin on *Bewitched*, the popular television series of the 1960s, was played by both Dick York and Dick Sargeant, the role of the gods is 'played' by different individuals whose kammic legacy secures for them a 'performance' as a deity. In Sri Lanka, the Gods of the Four Kings, or the 'Four Warrant Gods,' are associated with the protection of the island and thus of Buddhism. Each of them will eventually die, allowing another individual to take their place. Moreover, in Sri Lanka there have traditionally been four main gods, but their identity changes over time, except for the god Viṣṇu. The three deities who appear with Viṣṇu are drawn from a list of five, which includes Nātha, Pattini (the only female), Saman, Vibhiṣana, and Katarāgama (Gombrich and Obeyesekere 1988: 30–31). Among these gods, Katarāgama is the most morally ambiguous, for he takes great interest in human affairs and sometimes assists his devotees in achieving unscrupulous goals. But Katarāgama is a god, nonetheless, and presumably so because of his penchant for goodness. Buddhists can call on him and the other deities to aid them in their mundane pursuits; but because the gods as well as the humans are trapped in *saṃsāra*, they cannot help anyone attain enlightenment. There is no concept in any Theravādin culture of South or Southeast Asia of a single almighty deity who can be called upon no matter what the predicament.

Unlike Christian notions of reward and punishment, both of which are meted out by one all-powerful divinity, Theravāda Buddhism does not posit a single divine creator-redeemer that presides over human destiny. As we have seen, gods are like us bound by *saṃsāra* and subject to the same laws of rebirth. Each one of us is the architect of our own future, and our own volitional activity will determine where we shall be reborn. In other words, Theravāda Buddhism places ethical responsibility squarely on the shoulders of individuals who have the option of choosing to perform meritorious activities that have the power to determine not only our happiness in this life but also in many lifetimes to come. We now turn to the Buddhist ethical life.

Ethics and human relations

Theravāda and Mahāyāna Buddhists of South Asia and elsewhere begin their religious ceremonies by paying homage to the Buddha, the *dhamma*, and the *saṅgha*, that is, the Three Refuges. By 'taking refuge,' Buddhists do not surrender to God or to gods. Rather, they accept that the Buddha, the fully awakened one, is the incomparable moral teacher; that his teachings can provide liberation from dissatisfaction and suffering; and that the *saṅgha*, the monastic community, at least in theory strives to attain enlightenment, usually considered too difficult for lay Buddhists. (At present, in the Theravādin world there are no officially sanctioned female members of the *saṅgha*. But there are women, whom we shall call nuns, who are the functional equivalent of monks.) In contemporary Sri Lanka, the *ideal* Buddhist layperson, having made a lifetime commitment to the Three Refuges, engages in the constant practice of virtue – practiced by the Buddha himself in previous lifetimes as we shall see – which includes daily observance of the Five Precepts (*pansil*; for their content, see below). The ethical precepts (*śīla*) are not ends in themselves; rather, they are the steps leading to *samādhi* (concentration, mental purity), a prerequisite of wisdom and necessary if one is to see reality properly, as the Buddha is said to have seen it, that is, to attain *nibbāna*, enlightenment. Though we shall have much more to say about *nibbāna* below, in its most basic definition, it is the ethical state wherein delusion, hatred, and greed – negative mental formations – are extinguished (*nibbāna* as 'blowing out'). In the Theravādin worldview, once one attains *nibbāna*, it is impossible to behave in an unethical fashion. Observation of *śīla*, therefore, prepares the way for enlightenment, theoretically the ultimate aim of every Buddhist. (Yet, it must also be noted that there are characters in the Pali canon who attain enlightenment after long periods of misbehaving but who have the good fortune to have been taught by the Buddha himself. Anguḷimāla, a murderous bandit, is one such Arhat.) Be that as it may, the aspiration of the typical Theravādin Buddhist – whether monk or lay – is finally to attain enlightenment by listening to the *dhamma* preached by Metteyya, the next fully enlightened being. Until such time, one continues to be reborn in different world realms as conditioned by the effects of one's *kamma* or volitional activities.

When one observes the Five Precepts that tradition tells us were expounded by the Buddha in his teachings, one undertakes to meditate upon restraint from injury to creatures, from stealing, from unchastity, from lying, and from the occasion of sloth from liquor. These canonical prescriptions are well known to lay Buddhists, just as the Ten Commandments in the Hebrew Bible are known to Jews and Christians. We would be mistaken to assume, however, that the five moral precepts are the moral equivalent of the biblical commandments. For, in Buddhism, though there is a plethora of deities – and their pantheon differs from context to context – there is no overarching god who adjudicates. Rather, according to the Buddhist worldview – and this is generally true of both the Theravāda and the Mahāyāna – each Buddhist theoretically mediates his or her own morality. This gives special importance to meditation in the way that the moral precepts are observed. When a Theravādin Buddhist proclaims in Pali in the presence of a novice (Pali and Sanskrit *sāmaṇera*), or an ordained monk (Pali *bhikkhu*; Sanskrit *bhikṣu*), 'I meditate upon (*samadiyami*) restraint from injury to creatures,' for instance, the first of the Five Precepts, he or she is not receiving a dictate from above but rather is choosing to live a righteous life. Nonetheless, despite this significant difference between a Jewish or Christian ethical worldview and a Buddhist one, we must keep in mind that, as with all moral systems, they are observed with varying degrees of commitment. In other words, it is important to remember that just as not all Jews and Christians fulfill the ethical vision of their scriptures, Buddhists grapple with the same human moral dilemmas (and with similarly varying degrees of success) as monotheists.

Ideally, the purpose of Theravāda ethical practice is to create a 'middle way' between indulgence and asceticism. As we shall see when we explore the biography of the Buddha, Theravāda Buddhism – in its teachings about the Buddha's life as well as its response to competing religious systems of its day – reveals the content of its thoughts on liberation by alleging that extreme behavior produces only negative mental states. Buddhism thus comes to be known as the Middle Way, particularly because, from the Buddhist point of view, neither the life of indulgent attachment nor complete self-abnegation is constructive in the religious life. Instead one must understand that moderation is the key, and this is true for laity and monastics alike. The middle way between hedonism and asceticism is the principle that informs the 227 rules of the monk's monastic code, the *Vinaya*.

In addition to the Five Precepts of the laity, each of which is geared toward the practice of moral cultivation, the Theravādin Buddhist's ethical worldview is also shaped by the theory that all things are interconnected or the theory of dependent arising (*paṭicca samuppāda*). In the Buddhist view – and this is true of both the Theravāda and the Mahāyāna – no thing exists that is independent. In other words, all things – whether people, gods, trees, automobiles, or fish – come into being contingent upon something else; nothing is preexistent, all things are a series of moments that coalesce and continue to come into being. As such no thing is static, but rather all phenomena, including people, are dynamic and conditioned, a theory that is in clear contradiction to the Brāhmaṇical concept of soul, which is unconditioned. Put differently, no thing has a soul; no thing has an independent self. If one realizes that one has no self, one cannot be selfish. And if one is not selfish, then one is able to act without desire for oneself, directing one's virtuous actions toward the other. Thus, the idea of selflessness (*anatta*), articulated in the theory of dependent arising, is foundational in the Buddhist ethical life.

This is not to suggest that in the Theravādin Buddhist ethical scheme or in Buddhist ontology, people, gods, or other things do not really exist. Rather, they do not exist in the way we think that they do; our ignorance fails to grasp the true nature of reality, that all things are dependent and thus dynamic and in flux. Self and individual, and all such terms that point to a static identity, are conventional terms for realities that are ultimately without essence. The teaching of selflessness is made most explicit in the

Buddhist analysis of the person that, the texts tell us, the Buddha analyzed into five constituents (*khandha*) – namely, body, feelings, perceptions, volitions, and consciousness. Each in turn is not the self, for each is impermanent – for instance, our feelings arise in dependence upon some sort of stimulation, itself contingent upon an event, and so on – and dependent upon something else for its origin. In much the same way, the Buddhist theory of dependent arising allows us to analyze all things for their constituent parts, only to find that each part is dependent upon something else. The classical model for this analysis is found in the early postcanonical *Milindapañho* (Questions of Milinda), purported to be a dialogue between a Buddhist monk (Nāgasena) and a Greek king (Milinda), the latter of whom is portrayed as being interested in Buddhism. When it comes to the king's questions regarding Nāgasena's identity, Nāgasena tells the king that 'no person is to be found,' that 'Nāgasena' is 'an appellation,' 'a conventional usage' (for a being that comes together as a result of causes and conditions). He then draws an analogy with the king's chariot. He asks the king who by now is rather perplexed, whether the chariot can be identified as the pole, the axle, or any of the parts which constitute it. In other words, Nāgasena asks the king whether the chariot's essence can be found in any of its parts or whether the word 'chariot' is just a convenient way of talking about the phenomenon that comes into being as a result of many parts. The king himself then explains that, because of the existence of the parts (that together create the vehicle), the word 'chariot' exists, using the very words Nāgasena employed about his own name. The teaching of this dialogue is that both Nāgasena and the chariot exist, but they exist as a result of conditions, and that neither designation points to an abiding essence, self, or soul (as the Hindus of Nāgasena's day perceived it to be, that is, as independent and immutable).

We have now seen that Buddhist philosophy, which denies the existence of a soul, nevertheless has very clear-cut ideas about morality that are based in large part on the theory of *anatta*.[3] We have also noted that Buddhist ontology includes all phenomena in its critique of the nature of reality, including the deities. In other words, just as people are without souls, but exist nonetheless, each in charge of his or her own ethical life, deities too exist without static selves, some of whom are aligned with virtue, others of whom are morally ambiguous, as we have seen. The Buddha alone is the incomparable moral agent, who, having become fully enlightened, with its attendant extinguishment (*nibbuta*) of delusion, hatred, and greed could only behave with wisdom, loving kindness, and generosity.

Sacred life and literature

Now we are ready to ask a very important question: Who is (or was) the Buddha? Moreover, what does he mean to the pious? In order to answer these questions, we must turn our attention to a variety of contemporary rituals that provide important clues – rituals that we are now prepared to analyze. Thus far, we have seen that any person who goes for refuge to the Buddha, the *dhamma*, and the *saṅgha* – in a ritual that is normally presided over by a *saṅgha* member – is nominally a Buddhist. We have also seen that lay Buddhists are identified by their ethical orientation. Any visitor to a Buddhist temple (*vihāra*) on full-moon days – the most active dates of the religious calendar – witnesses Buddhists clad in white, the color associated with the laity, involved in religious activity, the most important of which is the worship of the

Buddha. At the *vihāra*, the *upāsikā* or *upāsaka* – without the aid of a monk – is able to pay homage to the Buddha by entering a shrine (also referred to as a *vihāra*); in Sri Lanka the shrine is known as the *buduge*, 'image house,' because the edifice contains a statue of him. It is important to note here that the shrine is not comparable to the inner sanctum of Hindu temples, where the deity is said to 'reside.' Rather, there is no inner sanctum in the ordinary Buddhist temple. Indeed, the shrine room is normally open and approachable from all sides and anyone may enter. In other words, and we will use the Sri Lankan experience as our guide, the lay Buddhist – here, neither caste nor gender bars one from this ritual activity – is unmediated (although some women feel that it is inappropriate to approach the altar when menstruating, doubtless in conformity with larger South Asian religious practices, particularly marked in Hinduism). Usually the lay Buddhist will make an offering (at any time of day) to the Buddha, which may include incense or flowers, betel nut, and sometimes sweets and brewed tea. (This same ritual is conducted at domestic shrines, too, a common feature of many homes in Buddhist South Asia.) Moreover, at early evening, as is customary in Buddhist *vihāras*, a cup of tea and some sort of snack is offered to the Buddha by the resident *saṅgha* member or nun.

In our effort to understand who the Buddha is, it is of significance to note that when offerings of food are made to the Buddha in contemporary Sri Lankan Buddhist practice, they are not retrieved and eaten, as is the case with offerings given to deities by Hindus. Devout Hindus are to make offerings to the deities regularly, if not daily then on days of religious significance, and typically believe that the deities partake of the offerings, which have usually been placed on the altars of the gods by temple priests in the morning. In other words, a Hindu ritual specialist mediates this religious activity. Hindus then retrieve the offerings, which are normally some sort of food or sweetmeat. In this ritual transaction, the offered foodstuffs become *prasāda* (Sanskrit: favor, grace, in this case, imparted through leftovers). They are sanctified, thereby attesting to the living presence of the gods. In Sri Lankan Theravāda Buddhism, on the other hand, food offerings made to the Buddha are not eaten. Moreover, other objects, once given to the Buddha by the laity or monks, are not taken away by the devout. Rather, perishables are scattered and consumed by the birds and dogs living in or near the *vihāra*, perhaps suggesting that their function is symbolic. Thai Buddhist food rituals complicate this picture. In Thai Buddhism, which shares Theravādin tradition with Sri Lanka, food left at an altar of the Buddha is retrieved and eaten by the faithful. According to a Sri Lankan monk in America, this particular custom as practiced by Buddhists in Thailand continues to be an enduring feature of Thai ritual life in America as well, thereby providing contrasting ideas about food and its meaning in religious practices of the Theravādin Buddhist diaspora.[4] In Buddhist Sri Lanka, there is no concept comparable to *prasāda* in the daily homage to the Buddha. This food ritual instead suggests that for the Theravādin Buddhist the Buddha is inaccessible – unlike the gods in Hinduism but similar to the *tīrthaṅkara* in Jaina tradition. Indeed, this Buddhist ritual departs from the patterns observed by the majority of South Asians who offer food to numinous presences that in turn may actively involve themselves in human affairs. However, in the Sri Lankan context, there is one exception.

According to Sri Lankan Buddhist tradition, the Sinhala people – the majority population of the island, who are predominately Buddhist – are the custodians of the tooth relic of the Buddha that, since the twelfth century, has legitimated political power. In a daily ritual conducted by high-caste monks, the relic is treated as if it were the living presence of the Buddha, if not a god (Seneviratne 1978). Along the lines of the Hindu treatment of statues of the divinities, the tooth relic of the Buddha is daily awakened, symbolically bathed, and ritually fed. The taboos that accompany each phase of this daily ritual process suggest that, at least in this case, the Buddha is treated as if he were still alive. In typical ritual settings of Sinhala-Buddhist Sri Lanka, caste is no obstacle to worship (although it is also the case that most resident monasteries are organized on the basis of caste). At the Temple of the Tooth in Kandy (the ancient hill capital of Sri Lanka), only monks of the highest rung of the highest caste among the Sinhalas are considered ritually pure enough to come into contact with the relic.

In this context, it is also important to point out the powerful role that relics in general – and not only the tooth relic – have played in the various types of Buddhism, particularly in the Theravādin. Though scholarship until recently (Kevin Trainor's 1997 study is a corrective) has failed to explore the power of relics in Theravādin Buddhism and the ways in which they mediate the Buddha's 'presence,' the textual tradition as well as lived Buddhism testify to a long history of expectation among Buddhists that the Buddha is in some way still accessible, even though he has passed away, presumably for good (a point we shall explore in our discussion of the second refuge). Most Buddhist temples in Sri Lanka lay claim to possession of one of the 'relics' of the Buddha, whether a relic of use (such as an umbrella or begging bowl) or a bodily relic which, though not treated after the fashion of the tooth relic, nevertheless mediates the powerful presence of the Buddha. The Theravādin tradition of relic possession and veneration is indeed ancient: the *Mahāparinibbānasutta* of the Pali canon characterizes the Buddha as being anxious that his bodily relics receive the proper adoration, while fourth- and fifth-century monasteries in India contained chambers in which, it was believed, the Buddha was an abiding presence (Schopen 1990). It is also important to note that Theravāda Buddhist tradition attests to long-standing devotional practices, illustrated in the ancient art of the Gāndhāra region of Pakistan, for instance, which are suggestive of the Buddha's presence long after his demise. As Susan Huntington (1990: 401–408) has argued, despite the assumption that Theravāda Buddhism historically lacks a devotional emphasis, South Asian Buddhist art is witness to a heritage of devotional practices that has emphasized depictions of pilgrimage sites associated with the Buddha's mission. Thus, in South Asian Buddhist art, the treatment of the Buddha's relics – whether bodily relics (for example, the tooth relic in Kandy, the relics entombed in the *thupa*s [Sanskrit *stūpa*; Sinhala *dāgoba*], or reliquaries, which the *Mahāparinibbānasutta* discusses), relics of use (the tree under which he was enlightened, for example, and his robe), or even 'relics' that serve as reminders (statues of the Buddha, for example, and paintings of scenes from his life) – may attest to the Buddha's powerful presence, despite his death. Put differently, in this threefold schema of relics that is recognized by Theravāda Buddhism, it is clear that Buddhists believe that the Buddha can somehow be '(re)presented,' notwithstanding canonical doctrines which lead us to different conclusions, nor the contemporary rituals that assume his inaccessibility.

Thus, despite important differences between Theravādin Buddhism and Hinduism in South Asia that we have highlighted here, and notwithstanding the canon's silence on the issue of the fate of a dead Buddha, the treatment of relics in South Asian forms of Buddhism may suggest that the Buddha is considered to be somehow accessible. Along these lines, it is worth noting that statues of the Buddha that are installed in *vihāra*s in Sri Lanka are consecrated in a fashion similar to the consecration of the images of the Hindu deities. In both cases, the final act is the ceremony in which the eyes of the statue are 'opened,' an act that is attended by various taboos. In both cases, the statue's first gaze falls on a mirror. In the Hindu context, the gaze that is said to come from the newly opened eyes is so powerful that it must fall on a pleasing object, usually a mirror, so that the deity might be pleased at the sight of its own reflection. In the Sri Lanka Buddhist context of the 'eye-opening ceremony' of a statue of the Buddha, the power of the newly opened eye is so tremendous and powerful that the craftsman dares not permit the gaze to fall on him (for Hinduism, see Eck 1985: 7; for Theravāda Buddhism, see Gombrich 1966). In other words, in neither the Hindu nor the Buddhist case would the artisan, whose caste function it is to paint the eyes, allow the statue to cast its glance in his direction. Unless the artisans considered that the statues were now imbued with some sort of awesome power as a result of the ceremony, why would they take such trouble to deflect the statue's gaze? However, it must not be forgotten that, in Sinhala Buddhism, once the statue is consecrated and food is left at the altar, that food is not retrieved by the faithful – it is not considered to be blessed (notwithstanding the Thai tradition). But these sorts of technical questions and ambiguities remain the problem of scholars alone. For, when the lay Sinhala Buddhist recites the Three Refuges as part of a public display of inner piety, usually at the beginning of any ritual occasion, it is doubtful that he or she is considering the theological implications of the First Refuge, but rather the commitment to the moral path propounded by the Buddha and exemplified by him.

On ritual occasions, particularly on the day of the full moon, the lay Buddhist, seated before a *bhikkhu* (draped in saffron, the color associated with mendicancy in many South Asian religious traditions) and under his direction, repeats after the monk (in unison with other Buddhists gathered) the Three Refuges followed by the Five Precepts. Though the entire day is spent at the temple with people coming and going and milling about, many Buddhists, particularly the elderly and women and children, congregate at daybreak to 'take' the refuges. Activities last throughout the day and early evening, punctuated by the midday almsgiving (which must daily commence by noon, according to traditions based on a textual rule) that has been planned by the faithful. In this food ritual, lay Buddhists, usually women, offer savory curries of meat, vegetables, and fruit to the monks, who, according to custom, are seated higher than their donors (as is true of all ritual events as well as casual situations), often times, in a row. Lay Buddhists offer the *saṅgha* alms, from which, the faithful believe, *upāsikā*s and *upāsaka*s receive 'merit' (Pali *puñña*; Sanskrit *punya*), an abstract reward for a concrete transaction, which according to traditional formulations has the power to counteract the (negative) consequences of intentional deeds, or *kamma*, performed in this life and in previous lifetimes. The ritual activities that take place on full-moon days suggest that, from the point of view of the lay Buddhist, the *saṅgha* is the best field of merit (*puññakhetam*), even though the act of giving (to anyone, lay or monastic) is generally considered to be meritorious action.

We are not suggesting that a *vihāra* is the center of activity solely on full-moon days in Buddhist South Asia. Rather, in the villages, in particular, the neighborhood Buddhist temple is the venue not only for religious rituals but serves as the hub of secular activities as well. For not only do lay Buddhists provide the monastics with their daily midday meal – an act that affords an opportunity to gain merit – they also meet friends at the monastic compound, use the library for their studies, and seek the advice of monks; and if the compound is large enough, then the youth engage in athletic activities with fellow Buddhists. Thus, at the temple, where Buddhists gather to pay homage to the Buddha, the first of the Three Refuges, they also engage in assorted activities (secular and religious) with other Buddhists, all of which serves to create a social world in which a Buddhist worldview and ethical system is reinforced. Chances are, moreover, that the lay Buddhists gathered in the *vihāra*s on these ritual occasions are familiar with the traditions and legends associated with the life of the Buddha, many of which they learn, or have learned, in the Sunday school classes – a vestige of the British period in South Asia – that are conducted by monks and nuns (depending on the village and the neighborhood, children are taught either by nuns or monks, that is, by whomever occupies the closest *vihāra*).

The traditional stories that Sri Lankan, or Sinhala, Buddhists grow up hearing about the Buddha are based loosely on canonical and postcanonical stories of the life of the Buddha and are easy to tell. Although the Buddha is never referred to as Siddhattha (Sanskrit Siddhārtha) in the Pali canonical corpus, contemporary Asian Buddhists in all contexts assume that before the Buddha assumed his title, he was known as Siddhattha Gotama (Sanskrit Gautama). The name Siddhattha, like many of the names in the stories associated with the Buddha's life, is significant: it means 'one who has completed his aim.' Siddhattha Gotama's aim was enlightenment, and the story about the enlightenment, as it is told in Sri Lankan Sunday school classes, is widely known throughout Buddhist Asia.

Frank Reynolds' work (1997) on the life of the Buddha is useful in this context for it explores the various lineages of the Buddha that Theravādin Buddhists in the present take for granted. Contemporary Buddhists, as well as the Buddhist authors of the textual traditions (both canonical and postcanonical) have recognized a plurality of fully enlightened beings who teach the *dhamma*, that is, Buddhas, none of whom overlap. The Buddha is one such being, in a series that presumably spans the ages, who discovered truths (associated with enlightenment) unaided by anyone else (god or human).[5] Thus, in terms of categories typically used in Religious Studies, we should refer to the Buddha as a sage, rather than as a prophet, for his knowledge was unmediated. Indeed, tradition itself has taken note of the Buddha's vocation; he is called 'Śākyamuni Buddha' because he is the sage (*muni*) of the Śākya clan (who, tradition claims, were a clan of what is now known as Nepal. People by the name of Śākya are still found there). Though the details of the life of each Buddha are different and though each one has a different name and thus a different identity, the basic life story remains the same: each is said to have discovered the 'Four Noble Truths' (which will be discussed below) and each is said to have seen four sights that triggered the resolve to leave a very comfortable home life to pursue answers to questions related to suffering.

The typical story of a Buddha-life, preserved in the *Mahāpadana Sutta*, is related by the Buddha about the first (in a series of seven) of the fully enlightened beings who teaches the *dhamma* – Vipassi Buddha. Presumably Vipassi Buddha's life has become a model for popular biographies of Gotama Buddha for, in South Asia, Buddhists relate Vipassi's biography as if it is the (historical) Buddha's. In the story of the Buddha's life as it has been passed down to the present and which, as we have seen, is a compilation of various sources, we learn that not only was the Buddha one in a series of fully enlightened beings who have discovered and preached the *dhamma* but also that his own biography spanned many lifetimes. In other words, while he is connected to previous Buddhas, in so far as he, like them, discovers the truth for himself and then teaches it, Gotama Buddha also has another lineage. That lineage connects him to a series of his own previous lives, in which he perfects the virtues necessary for his own enlightenment.

Tradition teaches that he becomes a Bodhisattva (in Theravāda doctrine, a Buddha-to-be) during the career of Dīpaṅkara Buddha, who is reckoned in oral tradition as well as in the canonical *Buddhavaṃsa* and the later *Nidānakathā* as the first fully enlightened being (though the latter text mentions, without commentary, three previous Buddhas, none of whom has a story). In the age in which Dīpaṅkara Buddha appears – in a very distant epoch – one young man by the name of Sumedha (like the name Siddhattha, this name is also significant – it means 'sacrifice'), having come into contact with Dīpaṅkara Buddha after eschewing worldly luxuries and pleasures, vows to become a Buddha in a future lifetime in order to enable others to attain enlightenment. Tradition then follows Sumedha, from his encounters with Dīpaṅkara Buddha, throughout the lives of the fully enlightened beings who follow (he has a relationship with each and every one), down until the birth, enlightenment, and death of Siddhattha, who is known as Gotama Buddha.

In the Theravādin tradition, the future Buddha – the Bodhisattva – at times appears as a human (but never as a female),[6] as an animal (including a lion, a monkey, and a variety of snake), and sometimes as a deity. According to Burmese and Southeast Asian tradition and as assumed by the Theravādin cultures of South Asia, the Bodhisattva perfected the virtues necessary for enlightenment over a series of more than 500 lives. The stories of the previous 'births' of the Buddha, or the Jātaka (birth) tales, are taught to children throughout the Buddhist world, in South Asia and elsewhere. In my own experiences in Sri Lanka and in Nepal, I have on several occasions witnessed children reciting the events of certain of the Jātaka tales; and in America, where many Buddhists of Sri Lankan descent live, Sinhala-Buddhist children seem as familiar with the stories of the Buddha's previous lives as they are in South Asia, as I discovered when I visited the Houston Buddhist Vihāra on a Sunday afternoon in November 2000. In Houston and in Tampa and Los Angeles – and presumably throughout the Sinhala-Buddhist diaspora – children of Sri Lankan immigrants learn Buddhism through the Jātaka tales, each of which extols a certain virtue.[7]

One of the few doctrinal positions that clearly differentiates the Mahāyāna from the Theravāda is the emphasis placed upon the Bodhisattva. Theravāda Buddhists maintain that a Bodhisattva is a Buddha-to-be, and the total number of them is limited by tradition. Siddhattha is a Bodhisattva until he attains enlightenment; and in the Jātakas, which recount legends associated with the Bodhisattvahood of Gotama, we find a more protracted story. Presumably, the being that will be Metteyya, the next Buddha, is now a Bodhisattva, perfecting virtues as he takes rebirth in different forms. Mahāyāna Buddhists, on the other hand, though they recognize that the Buddha was a Bodhisattva until he attained enlightenment, also recognize a plethora of Bodhisattvas, in this case, enlightenment beings, who, rather than attaining *nirvāṇa*, remain in *saṃsāra* to help other beings in their enlightenment quest. Of course, this is what Sumedha did: rather than attaining enlightenment in the dispensation of Dīpaṅkara, he vowed to perfect the virtues needed to lead others to awakening (as a fully enlightened being). Nonetheless, as the two approaches to Buddhism have developed, the Mahāyāna has emphasized the Bodhisattva, who actively works for the benefit of other sentient beings; the Theravāda has emphasized the Arhat, who by example teaches others the way leading out of *saṃsāra*. Arhats moreover are perceived as historical beings, while Bodhisattvas surmount history and geography; they are transcendental beings who, Mahāyāna Buddhist philosophers have argued, are superior to the Arhat. Be that as it may, the Theravāda cultures of South Asia emphasize the stories associated with the Buddha's career as a Bodhisattva, in which he perfected the virtues necessary for full enlightenment.

One of the most well-known Jātaka tales, at least in Sinhala tradition, tells the story of the Bodhisattva in his penultimate life, when he was born as a prince destined to become a king. In this particular tale, the *Vessantara Jātaka* (Cone and Gombrich 1977), the Bodhisattva gives away everything that is his – including his wife and children – in order to perfect the virtue of selfless giving. Until recently in village Sri Lanka, the *Vessantara Jātaka* was chanted by monks upon the death of lay Buddhists, perhaps to prepare the consciousness of the deceased for a better rebirth. It is also probable that the *Vessantara Jātaka* was chanted by monks on these ritual occasions to promote the concept of giving, essential for the continuity of the *saṅgha* which, according to the mandates of the canonical texts and tradition, must rely on the alms of the faithful. Though the tradition is dying out – no one that I know in Sri Lanka at present considers the chanting of the legend of King Vessantara to be an essential feature of funerals – it nevertheless suggests that there is often continuity between the stories associated with the Buddha and with behavior. In other words, the life of the Buddha – whether in his final birth as Siddhattha Gotama or in one of his previous 500 or so lifetimes – serves a didactic purpose. Moral teachings associated with the life of the Buddha, moreover, are reproduced iconically on the walls of Buddhist temples throughout the contemporary Theravādin world and have been the theme of much of the art on the ancient reliquaries or *thupa*s that have been excavated throughout India, Sri Lanka, and the Theravādin cultures of Southeast Asia. In addition, the story of Vessantara continues to take center stage in the grandest merit-making ritual in contemporary Thailand, quite obviously due to its emphasis on the morality of selfless giving (Tambiah 1970: 160–68).

As we have seen, the *Vessantara Jātaka* teaches that the Bodhisattva perfected selfless giving just prior to his final lifetime. According to the traditions (based somewhat on the canonical *Mahāpadana Sutta* but mostly on later renditions of his life, including the *Nidānakathā*, a fifth-century, postcanonical commentary on the Jātaka tales) that lay the foundation for the stories that children grow up hearing, between his lives as Vessantara and as Siddhattha, the Bodhisattva awaited an appropriate time for birth in one of the heavens, *tusita*. There, when the deities (and Buddhists believe in a plethora of deities) tell him that the time is right for the birth of the boy who would become the next fully enlightened being, the Buddha-to-be surveys the world (and this much is true, at least according to the *Sutta*, of the previous Bodhisattvas) and chooses an appropriate family in which to take his final birth. The Bodhisattva, who would be known as Siddhattha (as we have noted, the name is a later tradition), chooses a queen and king in Kapilavatthu (near the India–Nepal border) to be his mother and father.

Māyā, the queen, is portrayed as being very pious. On the full-moon day of a particular Indian summer month, when Queen Māyā is sequestered and thus celibate, she dreams of a white elephant that touches her side (in some iconography on temple walls in South Asia that I have seen, a white elephant actually appears to enter her side). At the same moment, the Bodhisattva becomes incarnate in her womb. Just as in the birth narratives of other exceptional beings in other religious traditions, the birth of Siddhattha sets him apart from ordinary mortals.

As should be clear by now, the events surrounding the final birth (in a series of lifetimes) that leads to the Buddhahood of Gotama is hardly ordinary; the Bodhisattva presides over his own conception. Immediately after the queen has the dream in which the Bodhisattva becomes incarnate in her womb, Māyā and the king tell some Brāhmaṇs about it. They discern that she is pregnant, that the child will be a boy, and that if he adopts a householder's life, he will become a world conqueror (a king). They also tell the soon-to-be-parents that if the child adopts a religious life, he is sure to become a world-renouncer (an ascetic who seeks religious truth). Then, after ten months (the gestation period for all Bodhisattvas), Queen Māyā, while standing, leaning against a tree in the town of Lumbinī (now in Nepal), on the way to her parents' home, gives birth to an extraordinary child – who can walk and talk immediately. After the painless birth, in which the child is received in a net by the gods, Māyā dies within seven days – as is expected of all mothers of Bodhisattvas (for their wombs are too sacred to be occupied by another) – but the baby grows up to be strong and healthy. Those of us interested in comparative analysis cannot fail to notice that the Buddha, not unlike the founders of other religious traditions, begins his life in a remarkable way, which has the effect of marking him and his life as extraordinary from the very beginning.

According to the traditional accounts, soon after the baby was born, the same Brāhmaṇs that foretold the birth of the prince, notice marks on his body that portend the boy's future. According to their reading of the marks – of which there were thirty-two major and eighty minor ones – the boy was a superhuman, indeed. The Brāhmaṇs reiterated that the prince would become either a world-conqueror or a world-renouncer. As the narrative unfolds, we learn that the father of the child, King Suddhodana, eager that his child should inherit his kingdom and thus become a world-conqueror, makes the decision to shield the child from sights that might trigger the child's sensitivity. And it is at this stage in the story that we can begin to empathize with the characters: the very human emotions, which a parent feels for a child, determine the father's actions. In much the same way that a chief executive officer would rather have his child assume the helm of his company, rather than opt to become a wandering hippie (a struggle that played out in many American families in the 1960s), King Suddhodana anxiously encourages the young prince to grow up to be a monarch.

For a short time, all is well in the kingdom. The young prince is given a number of palaces in which to enjoy life, always shielded from the realities of life. Presumably, he never witnesses suffering, old age, death, or any of the problems that regular mortals experience. Moreover, he grows up to be the strongest, brightest, most beautiful man in the kingdom, winning for himself in marriage the beautiful Yaśodharā, whom he marries. But even though he has everything – in addition to a wife, he also has courtesans who please him – Siddhattha is restless. After all, not only is he predisposed to be a world-conqueror, he is also inclined toward being a world-renouncer, to seek religious truths. We are offered glimpses into his religious predisposition when we learn that even as a child, while developing his skills at archery and other physical endeavors, the young Siddhattha meditates (when no one is looking). When he is about twenty-nine years old, and despite the restrictions that his father has imposed, he manipulates his charioteer into taking him outside the walls of the palaces. (The gods, convinced that the time is right for the Bodhisattva to leave the home life in order to attain enlightenment, set the stage for the prince's departure.) In the next sequence of events, the prince sees the so-called Four Holy Sights that in effect precipitate his parting from the kingdom.

On the first journey outside the palaces, he sees an old man. Tradition describes the old man rather graphically, as do contemporary temple paintings. He is stooped over, leaning on a cane; his teeth are decayed and he is bald, with wrinkled, sagging skin. Siddhattha is shocked. He asks his charioteer about the man, the first of the Four Holy Sights. Incredulous – the charioteer cannot believe that Siddhattha is so naive about the realities of time – he nevertheless tells the prince that the prince himself is subject to aging and decay. Dumbfounded and sunk in existential despair, the beautiful and youthful Siddhattha asks to be taken back to the palace. But the Bodhisattva is undaunted. He demands to go on a second journey, during which time he sees the second of the Four Holy Sights – a sick man. The graphic depictions on temple walls – throughout Buddhist South Asia – of the sick man, characterize his ailment as a form of leprosy. In those depictions, blood and pus ooze from the man's boils, while the man himself appears crippled, ragged, and destitute.

Having witnessed the second of the Four Holy Sights, Siddhattha responds in the same way he did to his encounter with the old man: he asks his charioteer about the sight and, upon hearing the answer, is sunk in existential despair, bemoaning his body and its fate. Still undaunted, he demands to be taken on yet another journey beyond the confines of his sequestered existence. On his third visit outside, he is disturbed by the sight of a dead man, known as the third of the Four Holy Sights. Distressed to learn that he too shall die, he returns to the palace, now more convinced than before that even a sequestered life cannot stop one's body from changing, growing old, and dying. Finally he is taken out again. But on the fourth journey, he does not witness old age, disease, or death – each of which is a teaching in impermanence – but rather an ascetic, a wanderer, a seeker of religious truths. Having seen this fourth of the Four Holy Sights, he asks his charioteer why one should want to forsake the world. The charioteer tells Siddhattha about the advantages of giving up the home life. Siddhattha then resolves to do so. He returns to the palace, but his outlook has completely changed. Whereas before he might have been delighted to be serenaded by his courtesans, on the night that he determines to forsake the world they do not move him. In fact, according to the traditional accounts, he falls asleep after being serenaded, waking to find that the women who had been so beautiful during their performance were now sleeping in less than attractive positions. Some of them were snoring; others were muttering in their sleep; and still others were reclining in grotesque postures. Moved by this teaching on the impermanent nature of reality, the Bodhisattva was even more convinced that he must leave home.[8] On that very night which, not incidentally, is the night that his son was born – whom he aptly refers to as a Rāhula or 'fetter' – Siddhattha's Great Departure is completed. Although most men in his Indic culture at the time (and today) would have been thrilled upon learning about the birth of a boy child, Prince Siddhattha considers the baby nothing more than that which has the potential to bind him to the world that he has resolved to abandon. He nevertheless glances at Rāhula and the mother of the child but decides not to wake them, lest his emotions should get the better of him. At twenty-nine, he abandons his wife and child, resolving to return after he has discovered the religious truths that he seeks. The Bodhisattva wanders for six years, learning *yoga* from the great masters and encountering a range of ascetics like himself, some of whom apparently practiced extreme austerities, without success in finding the answers he needed. Then, traditional accounts claim, at the age of thirty-five, he is enlightened under the Bodhi Tree (often rendered the Bo Tree) in Bodh Gayā, India. That enlightenment experience is the foundation of the *dhamma*, the teachings of Buddhism.

As we can see, the story of the Buddha's life that South Asian Buddhist children grow up learning – which includes a biography that spans literally hundreds of births – is a composite that is drawn from a variety of sources. Just as Christian children – who become familiar with the life of the Christ through diverse sources that may at times conflict – are able to recite a typical life of Jesus, Theravādin Buddhist children in South Asia are likewise able to present a typical life of Siddhattha that is derived from a compilation of oral and written traditions (both canonical and postcanonical).

Relations with other religions

Buddhists define themselves as Buddhists by 'going for refuge' to the Buddha, the *dhamma*, and the *saṅgha*. When Buddhists go for refuge to the Buddha, they take comfort in the knowledge that someone – namely, the Buddha – has discovered the truth that can set them free. When one goes for refuge to the *dhamma*, one similarly takes comfort in knowing that the teachings of the Buddha indicate the path whereby one can be set free; and when one goes for refuge to the *saṅgha*, one is comforted by the fact that ordinary mortals have sought, and are seeking, the religious truths propounded in the *dhamma*, and so can anyone.

In doctrinal Theravādin Buddhism, the teachings that comprise the *dhamma* are considered to be the body of the Buddha, now that he is passed away. The *dhamma* is said to incorporate three fundamental teachings, which are also referred to as the 'three marks of existence': all phenomena lack essence (*anatta*, literally 'without soul'); all phenomena are (thus) impermanent (*anicca*); and all phenomena are (therefore) unsatisfactory (*dukkha*). As we have seen, Prince Siddhattha had many experiences in his life that taught him that all things are subject to change. His encounter with the first three of the Four Holy Sights and his experiences with the courtesans, who taught him a powerful lesson of impermanence even though asleep, for instance, were precursors to a theory that was unprecedented in Indian philosophical thought. For, as scholars have pointed out, the period of Indian history that witnessed the rise of Buddhism – commonly referred to as 'the age of transcendence' (eighth to fourth centuries BCE) – also produced philosophical systems that were based on the premise that each human has a soul (*atta*) and that each individual soul is equivalent to the universal soul (Brahman); release from *saṃsāra*, or the realm of rebirth, another 'discovery' of the age of transcendence, required realization of this identity through *yoga* or the harnessing of the mind. But Buddhism challenged the core of this very idea, arguing instead that, in as much as all phenomena are void of soul, all things are therefore subject to change and thus are impermanent. And because most of us journey through *saṃsāra* (here Buddhism assimilates the Hindu idea of rebirth) unaware that reality is void of stasis, ignorantly behaving as if we, and other phenomena, have permanence, only to be constantly disappointed, existence is thus characterized by unsatisfactoriness (*dukkha*). If, on the other hand, we were to see reality clearly, with an enlightened mind, forever lifting the veil of ignorance, we would know that all things are without soul and impermanent.

Dukkha, unsatisfactoriness, one of the three so-called marks of existence, is the first of the Four Noble Truths that are considered to be the core teaching of the Buddhist *dhamma*.[9] Even the life story of the Buddha, with its emphasis upon the luxuries that were afforded him, teaches Buddhists that satisfying the senses is not enough. Siddhattha, upon whom all things were lavished, nonetheless could not find full happiness, due to the realities of old age, disease, and death. In short, even our most wonderful experiences are somehow marred, due to their impermanent nature. And while some things change rapidly, and other things change slowly, all things nonetheless change. The second of the Four Noble Truths is the cause of *dukkha* – namely, thirsting, craving, desire, based on our delusion that things, including ourselves, have permanence. This truth teaches us that we would not have thirst (*taṇhā*) for impermanent phenomena, which leads us to disappointment, if we understood the nature of reality. In other words, we would not be motivated by a falsely posited 'I' or 'mine' or 'me.' Nonetheless, as we have seen, Buddhism does not argue that people do not exist; rather, the claim is made that people and other phenomena do not exist in the way that deluded minds think that they exist. Buddhism, unlike Hinduism, posits 'selfless persons' (Collins 1982) but nonetheless shares the idea with Hinduism that the world of rebirth is unsatisfactory and is to be transcended.

The Third Noble Truth is that the cessation of *dukkha* is possible, otherwise known as *nibbāna*. In other words, there is a way leading toward the cessation of unsatisfactoriness; the path is the Fourth Noble Truth, or the Noble Eightfold Path, which itself has three divisions: wisdom, ethical conduct, and meditation. The cultivation of wisdom includes 'perfect' (*samma*, usually translated as 'right') view and intention; the cultivation of ethical conduct includes perfect speech, action, and livelihood; and the cultivation of meditation includes perfect effort, mindfulness, and concentration. The development of each of the eight is not to be understood as stages in proper spiritual advancement. Rather, each of the eight, or each of the three divisions, is to be cultivated simultaneously, thereby indicating that, in Theravāda Buddhist doctrine, proper behavior is as important as proper insight and mental training. At the same time, it is also the case that, just because one follows the Path, one is not guaranteed the attainment of *nibbāna*. Indeed, there are many instances in the Pali canonical treatises that suggest that characters of questionable ethical disposition attained *nibbāna* without ever having 'trod' the Path (as we have seen, Aṅguḷimāla is one such character). A doctrinal explanation for this may lie in Buddhist ideas about *kamma*, intentional activities, as we have noted, that propel consciousness – itself in flux – through *saṃsāra*. Each individual brings with him or her the fruit of kammic activities (both wholesome and unwholesome) from previous lifetimes which, the logic of the theory of *kamma* suggests, contributes to our abilities to advance spiritually. Put differently, as consciousness, always changing and responding to new environments, is propelled through *saṃsāra*, it carries with it karmic impressions from past experiences that help to determine its future state. In Buddhism, it is consciousness that is reborn from moment to moment and lifetime to lifetime, sometimes allowing for spiritual advancement and sometimes thwarted by negative kammic residue.

When we consider the nature of the Buddhist teachings, including the three marks of existence and the Four Noble Truths, it is important to place them within the context in which they arose in the sixth century BCE. Sociologists of India have long been telling us that the Buddha and his religious movement was not an isolated phenomenon; there were other wanderers (*samaṇa*), who like the Buddha had chosen to 'go forth from home into homelessness,' the traditional formulation for world-renunciation, disavowing society, including marriage, caste obligations, and traditional vocations and professions.

The sixth century BCE, or the end of the Vedic period, during which time the Buddha lived, is a period that underwent a radical transformation. The Vedas, orally transmitted religious treatises that were solely in the care of the Brāhmaṇs, considered to be the highest in the fourfold caste system, were called into question by non-Brāhmaṇs. Very early Vedic assumptions seem to lack the notion of repeated rebirths and to suppose that a human is born and dies only once. By the time of the Buddha, later theories that were correlated with the search for an underlying principle or essence that universally animates all forms of life including human beings, began to circulate. They assume that there is a soul or essence that passes through the life process again and again, taking many different forms as it goes. In the Upaniṣads, which seem to have been transmitted by *samaṇa*s who were challenging the authority of the older Vedic assumptions, it is concluded that the soul of the human, the *ātman*, is equivalent to the essence of the universe, the Brahman. However, the *ātman* is trapped in an endless cycle of birth and death known as *saṃsāra*. Some of the Buddha's contemporaries taught that mortification of the flesh would free the *ātman* from *saṃsāra*; others speculated that meditation upon the equivalence between Brahman and *ātman* would bring final freedom. No matter the method, most of the *samaṇa*s of whom we have a record affirmed the existence of an *ātman* that, by its very nature, is immutable, indivisible, and permanent.

The message of the Buddha was that all phenomena are impermanent, notwithstanding the 'discoveries' of the Upaniṣads. To whom did his message appeal? Texts and archaeology seem to suggest that Buddhism was an urban phenomenon. The Buddhist message seems to have resonated with the new social classes that were produced, in part, as a result of towns that developed from increased agricultural surplus and accumulation of material resources. Just prior to the Buddha's time, the economy shifted from a dispersed agrarian-based system toward a new urbanized base. Some of the city dwellers, freed from the control of the Brāhmaṇ caste, turned their attention toward a new religious message. Inscriptions indicate that the early patrons of Buddhism were householders (*gahapati*), which by the turn of the Common Era had come to mean artisans in guilds and urban merchants (Gombrich 1988: 55–57). As Romila Thapar (1973, 1978: 70–74) has argued, the margin of prosperity made possible by the new economic situation allowed support for maintenance of large groups of renouncers. And it is possible that many of the renouncers themselves, having been displaced by the economic changes and the accompanying anomie, felt that happiness was no longer to be found in society but rather away from it. The Buddha and people like him abandoned conventional society (see Bartholomeusz 2002).

Thapar (1978: 63) has also argued that one of the paradoxes of Indian religious traditions is that the renouncer is a symbol of authority within society, notwithstanding his or her renunciation of it. The typical renouncer is a mendicant who depends on society for sustenance (food, clothing, and shelter). Society in turn depends on the renouncer to point the way toward ultimate liberation. In the Buddhist traditions of South Asia – and this is true of both Theravāda and Mahāyāna communities – renouncers are collectively known as the *saṅgha*, the monastic community which is one of the Three Refuges along with the Buddha and the *dhamma*. In the contemporary Buddhist experience of South Asia, in the Mahāyāna communities of Tibetan Buddhists in exile in India and Nepal and in Buddhist Sri Lanka, the *saṅgha* wields much social, religious, and political influence. In the Tibetan Buddhist diaspora of India and Nepal, the Dalai Lama (who is both a Buddhist monk, and thus a member of the *saṅgha*, and temporal leader of his people) attests to the strong relationship between religion and politics in South Asia. In contemporary Sri Lanka, politicians, prime ministers, and presidents consult Buddhist monks, and it is unlikely that anyone could be successful in politics without the support of the *saṅgha*.

Notwithstanding cultural and doctrinal differences between (Mahāyāna) Tibetan Buddhists and (Theravāda) Sinhala Buddhists, there are many similarities, particularly the situation of nuns. Though there had been a thriving order of nuns, along with an order of monks, in ancient Sri Lanka, the order of nuns ceased to exist there by the twelfth century CE; history is silent about them in all Theravādin cultures by the fourteenth century (see Bartholomeusz 1994). We do not know why the Theravādin order of nuns ceased to exist, though I have reported my research on this question elsewhere (Bartholomeusz 1994). And though at present there are full-fledged nuns (Pali *bhikkhunī*; Sanskrit *bhikṣuṇī*) in Southeast and East Asian Mahāyāna communities, it is likely that the monastic ordination lineage for women was never introduced into Tibet, although no one knows why. Nonetheless, in both Tibetan communities in India and in Nepal, as well as in Theravādin contexts, there are women who practice Buddhism in ways that they believe reflect or revive the order of nuns of the Buddha's day. There have even been movements from time to time since the late nineteenth century to try to reinstate the Theravādin nuns' lineage, but they have not been very successful.[10] Buddhist society does discriminate full-fledged members of the *saṅgha* from those who are not officially ordained – which means that male monastics are more highly regarded and supported than female – but allows women to renounce the world. Hinduism also has space for female world-renouncers, though they have never been supported, nor do large communities of them ever seem to have thrived to the degree that we find in Buddhist South Asia.

The traditional Sri Lankan monastic view of the order of nuns – and this view is shared by traditional monks in Theravādin cultures elsewhere – is that it cannot be revived, given that at present there are no properly ordained Theravādin nuns who could initiate a woman into the *saṅgha*, a requirement of the *Vinaya*. In this catch-22, women who want to become nuns do so without achieving formal status. Though their dress, their vocation, their residence, their practice, and the rules that govern their lives separate them from ordinary laywomen, these women are not officially members of the *saṅgha*; each Theravādin culture, moreover, according them special status that is not however on a par with that of the monks, calls them 'mother.'[11] (It is of interest to note that female ascetics in Hinduism are also commonly referred to as Mātājī – mother, as is the Buddha himself. Although clearly a deeply embedded cultural appellation of honor, the term 'mother' is nonetheless fraught with ambiguities.)

That women, at least according to the traditional (monastic) view, cannot be ordained into the *saṅgha* has not stopped many females of all ages from adopting the lifestyle and vocation of the Buddhist nun; they are technically laywomen, but they symbolize the Buddha's canonical injunction that women like men should be free to 'go forth from home into homelessness.' In contemporary Sri Lanka, females who range in age from five years to eighty have donned the saffron robe of South Asian world-renunciation, presenting themselves as viable counterparts to the *saṅgha*. Both male and female monastics – ordained and lay – act as a 'field of merit,' the giving to which (including alms, such as robes, food, and other requisites), it is believed (in both Mahāyāna and Theravāda Buddhism), yields merit, a metaphysical transaction that helps to offset the fruit of bad *karma/kamma*.

The vocation of the celibate monks and nuns of Buddhist South Asia depends on the individual. Some monks and nuns immerse themselves 'in the world,' providing a range of social services, including politics, while others spend their lives in contemplative isolation, thereby enlivening the traditional idea that Buddhist monastics have one of two 'burdens': books (and putting their teachings into practice) or spiritual insight. This distinction often corresponds with the idea that monastics are either 'town-dwellers' or 'forest-dwellers'; the former assumes that monastics are to remain accessible, while the latter holds that they are to remain aloof from the concerns of the world. In contemporary South Asian Buddhist culture, most monks and nuns carry the burden of books and thus live out their lives in towns and villages rather than caves and remote forests. Nonetheless, many monastics – both male and female – opt to spend short periods in contemplation away from society, which thus suggests that the distinctions between the two burdens are not hard and fast.

It is a considerable irony that the most widely respected efforts to attain world-renunciation tend to have a boomerang effect. The more holy a monastic appears to be, due to his or her separation from society and long periods of concentration and meditation, the more he or she is sought after by society. Because it is such a worthy field of merit from the point of view of Buddhist society, the forest-dwelling monastic is likely to receive alms and gifts beyond the normal requisites, even though he or she has eschewed worldly pleasures to a greater degree than the town-dwelling monk or nun. As a result, even the most diligent contemplative Buddhist monastics become domesticated as a by-product of their mental prowess.

Be that as it may, the requirements of both lay and monastic life are highly valued and intensely guarded by South Asian Buddhist cultures. Monastic life may offer better opportunities for education and diet than lay life in impoverished parts of the region. Put differently, the essential nature of the *saṅgha* as a community that points the way toward liberation and provides opportunities for merit-making activities also ensures that males and females who 'go forth from home into homelessness' in the Buddhist traditions of South Asia are supported, though to varying degrees depending on their gender. The *saṅgha* continues to maintain its authority even in modernized and computerized South Asia, where people of many faiths, ethnicities, languages, and worldviews continue to adjust to their postcolonial and indigenous cultural legacies.

In addition to gender, further factors correlated with birth-determined identities and social status have figured prominently in the history of Buddhism in South Asia. The Indian Subcontinent was the original cultural base from which Buddhist teachings and institutions spread overseas throughout Southeast Asia and from which they were carried overland along traditional trade routes into West, Central, and East Asia. For nearly 2,000 years, Bauddha Dhamma attracted support in India from artisan guilds, urban merchant-princes, and regional royal courts. Sites associated with early Buddhist events, such as the tree at Gayā and the deer park at Sarnāth, drew visitors. Relics of the Buddha became honored, were enshrined at several sites, and served as magnets for lay and monastic pilgrimage traffic. Monks, required by the *Vinaya* or monastic code to remain in one place through the monsoon or rainy season, were able to gather at major monastic educational and retreat centers such as the remarkable one near Patnā at Nālanda. However, by about the thirteenth century CE, the patronage support base for these great Buddhist centers had declined considerably. Worse still there were traveling adventurers and even armies entering India that found those sites easy targets for plunder. Less violent but equally damaging challenges to the Buddhist presence in India came with the arrival of European traders after Vasco da Gama had demonstrated the sea route from Europe and was followed by the French and British. By the middle of the nineteenth century, European traders became colonizers and imperial overlords in South Asia, and Buddhism had all but disappeared from the Indian mainland.

At that low point, a revival of Buddhist institutions began in South Asia. Resources for the revival were found in indigenous self-respect and attracted support from a new class of patrons who were based outside the region. Two important indigenous leaders were Mohottivatte Gunananda, a Buddhist monk in Sri Lanka, who was involved in a famous debate against a Christian missionary in 1873, and the Sri Lankan layman Anagarika Dharmapala, who worked to reintroduce Buddhism in India and founded the Mahā Bodhi Society in 1891. Among prominent outsiders who lent their support to South Asian Buddhists, perhaps the most interesting was Henry Steel Olcott (1832–1907). He was an American who had been a colonel in the Civil War and afterward became closely involved with Helena Petrovna Blavatsky (1831–91) and the establishment of the Theosophical Society in North America, Europe, and South Asia. They visited India and Ceylon (now Sri Lanka) in 1879–80, and Olcott made further visits up to 1883, during which he deeply involved himself with the Buddhist cause and went on public-speaking tours with Mohottivatte Gunananda to promote Buddhism (Prothero 1996).

After India gained independence in 1947, the highly accomplished low-caste leader Bhimrao Ramji Ambedkar (1891–1956) became disillusioned with prospects for the abolition of caste and of all discrimination based on birth, and he converted to Buddhism. Ambedkar was one of India's most remarkable twentieth-century leaders. He came up from humble beginnings in western India, obtained a legal education in London, earned a doctoral degree at Columbia University in New York City, became an expert in constitutional law, and participated in writing the new Constitution of India. During the two decades leading up to independence, he had been a prominent public spokesman for untouchable and low-caste rights and at times was an outspoken opponent of Mohandas Karamchand Gandhi on the question of how to resolve problems of caste-based discrimination (Omvedt 1994). After India attained its freedom, he decided that he must act according to his findings from the many years that he had given to reviewing the world's religions. He found in the teachings of the Buddha, one of the great spiritual leaders of his own country, the most rational and effective basis for universal human equality. In 1950, he addressed a conference of the World

Fellowship of Buddhists in Sri Lanka and in the next few years attended their meetings in Rangoon. He established the Buddhist Society of India (Bhāratīya Bauddha Mahāsabhā) in 1955, and then converted to Buddhism by taking the Three Refuges and the Five Precepts in a large public ceremony held in Nagpur in October 1956. More than 300,000 others in attendance followed his example and became Buddhists at the same time. He continued to travel and lecture on Buddhism after the ceremony but had only a few weeks to live. He died in December 1956 and so he did not have enough time to complete all of the work that was involved in his 'search for a meaningful Buddhism' (Zelliot 2004) to serve as an appropriate vehicle for the long process of humanizing and emancipating people.

In India today, the so-called 'Neo-Buddhism' inspired by Ambedkar continues to be a factor in efforts to improve social and economic mobility for low castes. In general this means it plays a role in politics, and at times the result is intercaste and inter-religious conflict. For instance, low-caste or Dalit Buddhists have become involved in campaigns to reassert Buddhist control over historically significant sites such as Sarnāth and Gayā. These new Buddhist movements also mirror recent Hindu movements to regain control of sites taken by other traditions, such as the Hindu campaign for removal of a Muslim mosque at Ayodhyā. Perhaps inevitably these site-specific forms of religious politics have generated conflicts among various Buddhist groups and have pitted low-caste Neo-Buddhists against Tibetan Buddhists. It should be clear from this that the path to liberation (in its proximate forms as well as in ultimate formlessness) requires the release of many sorts of attachment.

Suggested further readings

Bond (1988); Gombrich (1988); Jondhale and Beltz (2004); Kapstein (2000); Lopez (2004); Reynolds and Carbine (2000); Robinson, Johnson, and Bhikkhu (2005); Williams and Tribe (2000).

Notes

1 Though many scholars have developed this point in their writings, one of the earliest to call this phenomenon to our attention was Bardwell Smith (1978).
2 For the undeclared or unanswered questions, see David Kalupahana (1976: 155–56).
3 Unfortunately for us, Nāgasena does not link the idea of *anatta* to the ethical life, even though the king, prior to receiving Nāgasena's analogy of the chariot, asks Nāgasena whether there is a moral agent if there is no static person to be found.
4 Interview with Bhante Wipulasara, Florida Buddhist Vihara, Tampa, Florida, October 31, 2000. I was there to discuss Sri Lankan Buddhism in America and learned that much of the ritual life of Buddhists in Florida is cooperative: Buddhists from the Thai, Vietnamese, and Sinhala traditions unite during the various important Buddhist religious holidays.
5 Theravādins focus primary attention on a set of Buddhas in which Gotama is the seventh, at least according to the canonical treatise, the *Mahāpadana Sutta*, the 'Treatise of the Great Births'; they also claim a more extended set in which Gotama Buddha, the so-called 'historical' Buddha, is the twenty-fifth in the series. The latter series, based on the canonical text, the *Buddhavaṃsa*, 'Lineage of the Buddhas,' mentions a twenty-sixth, Metteyya; it also includes among the last fully enlightened beings the same list as the *Mahāpadana Sutta*.
6 Frank Reynolds (1997: 29) discusses a fifteenth-century Thai text, the *Jinakalamali*, in which the Buddha is a female in a previous life. But, as far as I know, this tradition is not found in the Sinhala context.

7 A Florida State University Planning Grant has provided funding for my study of Sri Lankan Buddhist monasteries in America.

8 For more on the event of the sleeping women and how they are a lesson in impermanence, see Liz Wilson (1996).

9 For the Pali text of the Four Noble Truths, see *Saṃyutta Nikāya* verses 421–22.

10 One such movement took place in the United States in the 1980s (see Bartholomeusz 1994); and in December 1996, ten Theravādin Sri Lankan *daśa śīla mātā*s (Mothers of the Ten Precepts) were ordained into the *saṅgha* in a ceremony that was presided over by a mixed quorum of Mahāyāna and Theravāda monastics. In as much as there are no properly ordained female monastics in the Theravāda tradition to induct a female into the *saṅgha*, Mahāyāna female *saṅgha* members participated. The ordination took place in Sarnāth, India, where tradition tells us the Buddha preached his first sermon. In March 1998, twenty-two *daśa śīla mātā*s participated in a similar ritual in Sri Lanka; they reside in a *vihāra* in a suburb of the capital, Colombo, and I interviewed them soon after their ordination. It is too early to tell whether the nuns' ordination has changed their status in the eyes of the more traditional monks who represent the *saṅgha*. For more, see the online *Sunday Observer* (Colombo, Sri Lanka), 'Higher Ordination for Buddhist Nuns,' 22 March 1998.

11 In Sri Lanka, they are the *daśa śīla mātā*s; in Thailand, they are the *mai chi*; and in Burma, they are the *thila shin*.

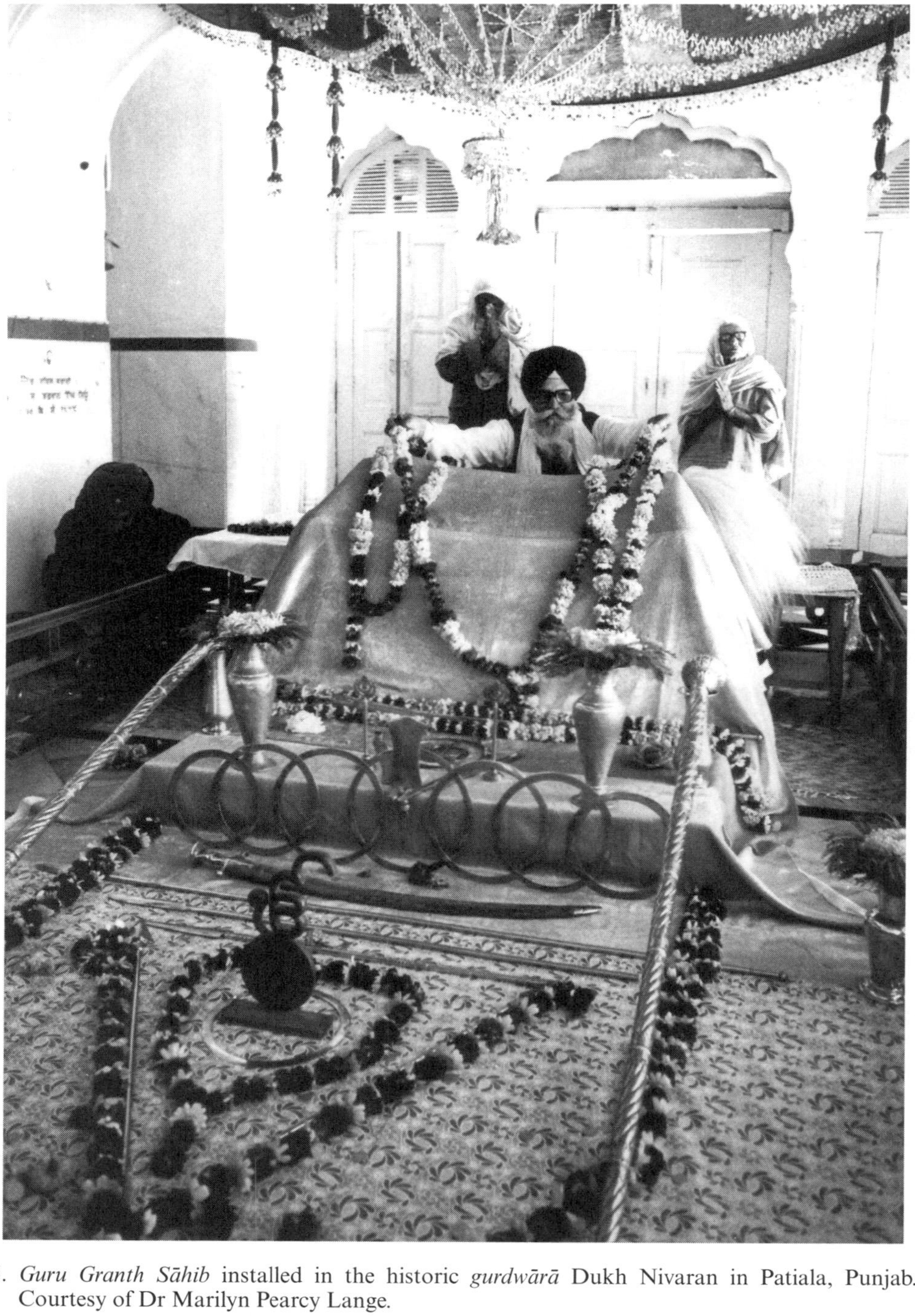

5. *Guru Granth Sāhib* installed in the historic *gurdwārā* Dukh Nivaran in Patiala, Punjab. Courtesy of Dr Marilyn Pearcy Lange.

4

SIKH DHARAM

Pashaura Singh

The tradition defined

Sikh religion originated in the Punjab ('five rivers') region of northwest India five centuries ago. It is a monotheistic faith that stresses the ideal of achieving spiritual liberation within a person's lifetime through meditation on the divine Name. It is also oriented toward action, encouraging the dignity of regular labor as part of spiritual discipline. Family life and social responsibility are important aspects of Sikh teachings. Notably, the Sikh tradition is the youngest of the indigenous religions of India where the Sikhs constitute about 2 percent of India's 1 billion people. What makes Sikhs significant in India is not their numbers but their contribution in the political and economic spheres. The global Sikh population is approximately 23 million; that is more than the worldwide total of Jewish people. About 18 million Sikhs live in the state of Punjab, while the rest have settled in other parts of India and elsewhere, including substantial communities established through successive waves of emigration in Southeast Asia, East Africa, the United Kingdom, and North America. In the last century, about a quarter of a million Sikhs immigrated to the United States of America.

Cosmos and history

Origins of the tradition

The Sikh tradition is rooted in a particular religious experience, piety, and culture and is informed by a unique inner revelation of its founder, Guru Nānak (1469–1539), who declared his independence from the other thought forms of his day. He tried to kindle the fire of autonomy and courage in those who claimed to be his disciples (*sikh*, 'learner'). Notwithstanding the influences he absorbed from his contemporary religious environment, that is, the devotional tradition of the medieval *sant*s (poet-saints) of North India with whom he shared certain similarities and differences, Guru Nānak laid down the foundation of 'true teaching, practice, and community' from the standpoint of his own religious ideals. Among the religious figures of North India, he had a strong sense of mission that compelled him to proclaim his message for the ultimate benefit of his audience and to promote socially responsible living.

Nānak was born to an upper-caste professional Hindu family in the village of Talwaṇḍī, present-day Nankana Sāhib in Pakistan. Much of the material concerning his life comes from hagiographical *janam-sākhī*s (birth narratives). His life may be divided into three distinct phases: his early contemplative years, the enlightenment experience accompanied by extensive travels, and a foundational climax that resulted in the establishment of the first Sikh community in western Punjab. In one of his own hymns he proclaimed, 'I was a minstrel out of work, the Lord assigned me the task of singing the divine Word. He summoned me to his court and bestowed on me the robe of honoring him and singing his praise. On me he bestowed the divine nectar (*amrit*) in a cup, the nectar of his true and holy Name' (*Ādi Granth* p.150). This hymn is intensely autobiographical, explicitly pointing out Guru Nānak's own understanding of his divine mission, and it marked the beginning of his ministry. He was then thirty years of age, had been married to Sulkhanī for more than a decade, and was the father of two young sons, Sri Chand and Lakhmi Dās. He set out on a series of journeys to both Hindu and Muslim places of pilgrimage in India and elsewhere. During his travels he came into contact with the leaders of different religious persuasions and tested the veracity of his own ideas in religious dialogues.

At the end of his travels, in the 1520s, Guru Nānak purchased a piece of land on the right bank of the Rāvī River in West Punjab and founded the village of Kartarpur ('Creator's Abode'; today in Pakistan). There he lived for the rest of his life as the 'Spiritual Guide' of a newly emerging religious community. His attractive personality and teaching won him many disciples who received the message of liberation through religious hymns of unique genius and notable beauty. They began to use these hymns in devotional singing (*kīrtan*) as a part of congregational worship. Indeed, the first Sikh families who gathered around Guru Nānak in the early decades of the sixteenth century at Kartarpur formed the nucleus of a rudimentary organization of the Nānak-Panth, the 'path of Nānak,' the community constituted by the Sikhs who followed Guru Nānak's path of liberation. In his role as what the sociologist Max Weber dubbed an 'ethical prophet,' Guru Nānak called for a decisive break with existing formulations and laid the foundation of a new, rational model of normative behavior based on divine authority. Throughout his writings he conceived of his work as divinely commissioned, and he demanded the obedience of his audience as an ethical duty.

Guru Nānak prescribed the daily routine, along with agricultural activity for sustenance, for the Kartarpur community. He defined the ideal person as a Gurmukh ('one oriented toward the Guru'), who practiced the threefold discipline of 'the divine Name, charity, and purity' (*nām-dān-iśnān*). Indeed, these three features, *nām* (relation with the Divine), *dān* (relation with the society), and *iśnān* (relation with the self) provided a balanced approach for the development of the individual and the society. They corresponded to the cognitive, the communal, and the personal aspects of the evolving Sikh identity. For Guru Nānak the true spiritual life required that 'one should live on what one has earned through hard work and that one should share with others the fruit of one's exertion' (*Ādi Granth* p.1,245). In addition, service (*sevā*), self-respect (*pati*), truthful living (*sach achār*), humility, sweetness of the tongue, and taking only one's rightful share (*haq halāl*) were regarded as highly prized ethical virtues in pursuit of liberation. At Kartarpur, Guru Nānak gave practical expression to the ideals that had matured during the period of his travels, and he combined a life of disciplined devotion with worldly activities set in the context of normal family life. As part of Sikh liturgy, Guru Nānak's *Japjī* (Meditation) was recited in the early hours of the morning and *So Dar* (That Door) and *Ārti* (Adoration) were sung in the evening.

Guru Nānak's spiritual message found expression at Kartarpur through key institutions: the *sangat* ('holy fellowship') where all felt that they belonged to one large spiritual fraternity; the *dharamsala*, the original form of the Sikh place of worship that developed later into the *gurdwārā*; and the establishment of the *laṅgar*, the interdining convention which required people of all castes to sit in status-free lines (*pangat*) to share a common meal. The institution of *laṅgar* promoted the spirit of unity and mutual belonging and struck at a major aspect of caste, thereby advancing the process of defining a distinctive Sikh identity. Finally, Guru Nānak created the institution of the Guru ('Preceptor'), who became the central authority in community life. Before he passed away in 1539, he designated one of his disciples, Lehnā, as his successor by renaming him Angad, meaning 'my own limb.' Thus, a lineage was established, and a legitimate succession was maintained intact from the appointment of Guru Angad (1504–52) to the death of Guru Gobind Siṅgh (1666–1708), the tenth and the last human Guru of the Sikhs.

Successors of Guru Nānak

The early Sikh Gurus followed a policy of both innovation and preservation. The second Guru, Angad, consolidated the nascent Sikh Panth in the face of the challenge offered by Guru Nānak's eldest son, Sri Chand, the founder of the ascetic Udāsī sect. Guru Angad further refined the Gurmukhi script for recording the compilation of the Guru's hymns (*bāṇī*). The original Gurmukhi script was a systematization of the business shorthands (*laṇḍe/mahājanī*) of the type Guru Nānak doubtless used professionally as a young man. This was an emphatic rejection of the superiority of the Devanagri and Arabic scripts (along with Sanskrit and the Arabic and Persian languages) and of the hegemonic authority they represented in the scholarly and religious circles of the time. The use of the Gurmukhi script added an element of demarcation and self-identity to the Sikh tradition. In fact, language became the single most important factor in the preservation of Sikh culture and identity and the cornerstone of the religious distinctiveness that is part and parcel of the Sikh cultural heritage.

A major institutional development took place during the time of the third Guru, Amar Dās (1479–1574), who introduced a variety of innovations to provide greater cohesion and unity to the ever-growing Sikh Panth. These included the establishment of the city of Goindval, the biannual festivals of Dīvālī and Baisākhī that provided an opportunity for the growing community to get together and meet the Guru, a missionary system (*mañjīs*) for attracting new converts, and the preparation of the Goindval *pothī*s, collections of the compositions of the Gurus and some of the medieval poet-saints.

The fourth Guru, Rām Dās (1534–81), founded the city of Rāmdāspur, where he constructed a large pool for the purpose of bathing. The city was named Amritsar, meaning 'the nectar of immortality.' To build an independent economic base, the Guru appointed deputies (*masand*) to collect tithes and other contributions from loyal Sikhs. In addition to a large body of sacred verse, he composed the wedding hymn (*lāvān*) for the solemnization of a Sikh marriage. Indeed, it was Guru Rām Dās who for the first time explicitly responded to the question 'Who is a Sikh?' with the following definition: 'He who calls himself Sikh, a follower of the true Guru, should meditate on the divine Name after rising and bathing and recite *Japjī* from memory, thus driving away all evil deeds and vices. As day unfolds he sings *gurbāṇī* (utterances of the Gurus); sitting or rising he meditates on the divine Name. He who repeats the divine Name with every breath and bite is indeed a true Sikh (*gursikh*) who gives pleasure to the Guru' (*Ādi Granth* pp. 305–306). Thus, the liturgical requirements of the reciting and singing of the sacred word became part of the very definition of being a Sikh. The most significant development was related to the self-image of Sikhs, who perceived themselves as unique and distinct from the other religious communities of North India.

The period of the fifth Guru, Arjan (1563–1606), was marked by a number of far-reaching institutional developments. First, at Amritsar he built the Harimandir, later known as the Golden Temple, which acquired prominence as the central place of Sikh worship. Second, he compiled the first canonical scripture, the *Ādi Granth* (Original Book), in 1604. Third, Guru Arjan established the rule of justice and humility (*halemi rāj*) in the town of Rāmdāspur, where everyone lived in comfort (*Ādi Granth* p. 74). He proclaimed, 'The divine rule prevails in Rāmdāspur due to the grace of the Guru. No tax (*jizyah*) is levied, nor any fine; there is no collector of taxes' (*Ādi Granth* pp. 430, 817). The administration of the town was evidently in the hands of Guru Arjan, although in a certain sense Rāmdāspur was an autonomous town within the context and the framework of the Mughal rule of Emperor Akbar. Fourth, by the end of the sixteenth century the Sikh Panth had developed a strong sense of independent identity, which is evident from Guru Arjan's assertion 'We are neither Hindu nor Musalmān' (*Ādi Granth* p.1,136).

Fifth, dissentions within the ranks of the Sikh Panth became the source of serious conflict. A great number of the Guru's compositions focus on the issue of dealing with the problems created by 'slanderers' (*nindak*), who were rival claimants to the office of the Guruship. The Udāsīs and Bhallās (Guru Amar Dās' eldest son, Bābā Mohan, and his followers) had already established parallel seats of authority and had paved the way for competing views of Sikh identity. The rivalry of these dissenters was heightened when Guru Arjan was designated for the throne of Guru Nānak in preference to the former's eldest brother, Prithī Chand, who even approached the local Mughal administrators to claim the position of his father. At some point Prithī Chand and his followers were branded *miṇā*s ('dissembling rogues').

Finally, the author of *Dabistān-i-Mazāhib* (The School of Religions), a mid-seventeenth-century work in Persian, testifies that the number of Sikhs had rapidly increased during Guru Arjan's period and that 'there were not many cities in the inhabited countries where some Sikhs were not to be found.' In fact, the growing strength of the Sikh movement attracted the unfavorable attention of the ruling authorities because of the reaction of Muslim revivalists of the Naqshbandiyyah Order in Mughal India. There is clear evidence in the compositions of Guru Arjan that a series of complaints were made against him to the functionaries of the Mughal state, giving them an excuse to watch the activities of the Sikhs. The liberal policy of Akbar may have sheltered the Guru and his followers for a time, but in May 1606, within eight months of Akbar's death, Guru Arjan, under torture by the orders of the new emperor, Jahangīr, was executed. The Sikh community perceived his death as the first martyrdom, which became a turning point in the history of the Sikh tradition.

Indeed, a radical reshaping of the Sikh Panth took place after Guru Arjan's martyrdom. The sixth Guru, Hargobind (1595–1644), signaled the formal process when he traditionally donned two swords symbolizing the spiritual (*pīrī*) as well as the temporal (*mīrī*) investiture. He also built the Akāl Takhat (Throne of the Timeless One) facing the Harimandir, which represented the newly assumed role of temporal authority. Under his direct leadership the Sikh Panth took up arms in order to protect itself from Mughal hostility. From the Sikh perspective this new development was not taken at the cost of abandoning the original spiritual base. Rather, it was meant to achieve a balance between temporal and spiritual concerns. A Sikh theologian of the period, Bhāī Gurdās, defended this martial response as 'hedging the orchard of the Sikh faith with the hardy and thorny *kikar* tree.' After four skirmishes with Mughal troops, Guru Hargobind withdrew to the Śivalik Hills, and Kiratpur became the new center of the mainline Sikh tradition. Amritsar fell into the hands of the *miṇās*, who established a parallel line of Guruship with the support of the Mughal authorities.

During the time of the seventh and eighth Gurus, Har Rai (1630–61) and Har Krishan (1656–64), the emphasis on armed conflict with the Mughal authorities receded, but the Gurus held court and kept a regular force of Sikh horsemen. During the period of the ninth Guru, Tegh Bahadur (1621–75), however, the increasing strength of the Sikh movement in rural areas again attracted Mughal attention. Guru Tegh Bahadur's ideas of a just society inspired a spirit of fearlessness among his followers: 'He who holds none in fear, nor is afraid of anyone, Nānak, acknowledge him alone as a man of true wisdom' (*Ādi Granth* p. 1,427). Such ideas posed a direct challenge to the increasingly restrictive policies of the Mughal emperor, Aurangzīb (r. 1658–1707), who had imposed Islamic laws and taxes and ordered the replacement of Hindu temples by mosques. Not surprisingly, Guru Tegh Bahadur was summoned to Delhi by the orders of the emperor, and on his refusal to embrace Islam he was publicly executed in Chāndnī Chowk on November 11, 1675. The Sikhs perceived his death as the second martyrdom, which involved larger issues of human rights and freedom of conscience.

Tradition holds that the Sikhs who were present at the scene of Guru Tegh Bahadur's execution shrank from recognition, concealing their identity for fear they might suffer a similar fate. In order to respond to this new situation, the tenth Guru, Gobind Siṅgh, resolved to impose on his followers an outward form that would make them instantly recognizable. He restructured the Sikh Panth and instituted the Khālsā ('pure'), an order of loyal Sikhs bound by a common identity and discipline. On Baisākhī Day 1699 at Anandpur, Guru Gobind Siṅgh initiated the first 'Cherished Five' (*pañj piare*), who formed the nucleus of the new order of the Khālsā. The five volunteers who responded to the Guru's call for loyalty, and who came from different castes and regions of India, received the initiation through a ceremony that involved sweetened water (*amrit*) stirred with a two-edged sword and sanctified by the recitation of five liturgical prayers.

The inauguration of the Khālsā was the culmination of the canonical period in the development of Sikhism. The most visible symbols of Sikhism known as the five Ks – namely, uncut hair (*keś*), a comb for topknot (*kaṅghā*), a short sword (*kirpan*), a wrist ring (*karā*), and breeches (*kachh*) – are mandatory to the Khālsā. Guru Gobind Siṅgh also closed the Sikh canon by adding a collection of the works of his father, Guru Tegh Bahadur, to the original compilation of the *Ādi Granth*. Before he passed away in 1708, he terminated the line of personal Gurus and installed the *Ādi Granth* as the eternal Guru for Sikhs. Thereafter, the authority of the Guru was invested together in the scripture (*Guru Granth*) and in the corporate community (Guru Panth).

Evolution of the Panth

The historical development of the Sikh Panth took place in response to four main elements. The first of these was the ideology based on religious and cultural innovations of Guru Nānak and his nine successors. This was the principal motivating factor in the evolution of the Sikh Panth.

The second was the rural base of the Punjabi society. Guru Nānak founded the village of Kartarpur to sustain an agricultural-based community. Its location on the bank of the river Rāvī, provides extremely fertile soil for agriculture. Guru Nānak's father, Kālū Bedī, and his father-in-law, Mūlā Chonā, were village revenue officials (*patvārī*) who must have been instrumental in acquiring a parcel of land at Kartarpur. Since the Mughal law recognized Guru Nānak's sons as the rightful owners of their father's properties, Guru Angad had to establish a new Sikh center at Khadur. It confirmed an organizational principle that the communal establishment at Kartarpur could not be considered a unique institution but rather a model that could be cloned and imitated elsewhere. Similarly, Guru Amar Dās founded the city of Goindval. Interestingly, the location of Goindval on the right bank of the Beās River was close to the point where the Mājhā, Mālvā, and Doāba areas converge. This may help account for the spread of the Panth's influence in all three regions of the Punjab. Guru Rām Dās founded the city of Rāmdāspur (Amritsar). During the period of Guru Arjan the founding of the villages of Taran Taran, Sri Hargobindpur, and Kartarpur (Punjab) in the rural areas saw a large number of converts from local Jāṭ peasantry. Further, Guru Tegh Bahadur's influence in the rural areas attracted more Jāṭs from the Mālvā region, and most of them became Khālsā during Guru Gobind Siṅgh's period. It may have been the militant traditions of the Jāṭs that brought the Sikh Panth into increasing conflict with the Mughals, a conflict that shaped the future direction of the Sikh movement.

The third factor was the conflict created within the Sikh community by dissidents, which originally worked to counter and then, paradoxically, to enhance the process of the crystallization of the Sikh tradition. Guru Nānak's son, Sri Chand, was the first dissident who lived a life of celibacy. Although he failed to attract much support from early Sikhs, he created his own sect of Udāsīs (renunciants). This group was closer to the Nātha Yogīs in its beliefs and practices. Similarly, the followers of Mohan (Guru Amar Dās' elder son), Prithī Chand (*miṇā*), Dhir Mal (Guru Har Rai's elder brother, who established his seat at Kartarpur, Jalandhar), and Rām Rai (Guru Har Krishan's elder brother, who established his seat at Dehrā Dūn) posed a challenge to the mainline Sikh tradition. All these dissidents enjoyed Mughal patronage in the form of revenue-free grants (*madad-i-māsh*). Their proestablishment stance triggered the mainline tradition to strengthen its own resources.

Finally, the fourth element was the period of Punjab history from the seventeenth to the eighteenth centuries in which the Sikh Panth evolved in tension with Mughals and Afghans. All four elements combined to produce the mutual interaction between ideology and environment that came to characterize the historical development of Sikhism.

Worldview

The nature of the Ultimate Reality in Sikh doctrine is succinctly expressed in the Mūl Mantar ('seed formula'), the preamble to the Sikh scripture. The basic theological statement reads as follows: 'There is one Supreme Being ('1' *Oankar*), the Eternal Reality, the Creator, without fear and devoid of enmity, immortal, never incarnated, self-existent, known by grace through the Guru. The Eternal One, from the beginning, through all time, present now, the Everlasting Reality' (*Ādi Granth* p. 1). The numeral '1' at the beginning of the original Punjabi text represents the unity of Akāl Purakh (the 'Timeless One,' God), a concept that Guru Nānak interpreted in monotheistic terms. It affirms that Akāl Purakh is one without a second, the source as well as the goal of all that exists. He has 'no relatives, no mother, no father, no wife, no son, no rival who may become a potential contender' (*Ādi Granth* p. 597). The Sikh Gurus were fiercely opposed to any anthropomorphic conceptions of the divine. As the creator and sustainer of the universe, Akāl Purakh lovingly watches over it. As a father figure, he runs the world with justice and destroys evil and supports good (*Ādi Granth* p. 1,028). As a mother figure, the Supreme Being is the source of love and grace and responds to the devotion of her humblest followers. By addressing the One as 'Father, Mother, Friend, and Brother' simultaneously, Guru Arjan stressed that Akāl Purakh is without gender (*Ādi Granth* p. 103). Paradoxically, Akāl Purakh is both transcendent (*nirguṇa*, 'without attributes') and immanent (*saguṇa*, 'with attributes'). Only in personal experience can he be truly known. Despite the stress laid on *nirguṇa* discourse within the Sikh tradition, which directs the devotee to worship a nonincarnate, universal God, in Sikh doctrine God is partially embodied in the divine Name (*nām*) and in the collective Words (*bāṇī*) and the person of the Guru and the saints.

Guru Nānak's cosmology hymn in *Mārū Rāg* addresses the basic questions about the genesis of the universe: 'For endless eons, there was only darkness. Nothing except the divine Order (*hukam*) existed. No day or night, no moon or sun. The Creator alone was absorbed in a primal state of contemplation. . . . When the Creator so willed, creation came into being. . . . The Un-manifested One revealed itself in the creation' (*Ādi Granth* pp. 1,035–36). Guru Nānak maintained that the universe 'comes into being by the divine Order' (*Ādi Granth* p. 1). He further says: 'From the True One came air and from air came water; from water he created the three worlds and infused in every heart his own light' (*Ādi Granth* p. 19). Guru Nānak employed the well-known Indic ideas of creation through five basic elements of air, water, ether, fire, and earth. As the creation of Akāl Purakh, the physical universe is real but subject to constant change. It is a lush green garden (*jagg vaṛī*), where human beings participate in its colorful beauty and fragrance (*Ādi Granth* p. 118). For Guru Nānak the world was divinely inspired. It is a place that provides human beings with an opportunity to perform their duty and achieve union with Akāl Purakh. Thus, actions performed in earthly existence are important because 'all of us carry the fruits of our deeds' (*Ādi Granth* p. 4).

For the Gurus, human life is the most delightful experience that one can have with the gift of a beautiful body (*Ādi Granth* p. 966). It is a 'precious jewel' (*Ādi Granth* p. 156). Indeed, the human being has been called the epitome of creation: 'All other creation is subject to you, [O Man/Woman!], you reign supreme on this earth' (*Ādi Granth* p. 374). Guru Arjan further proclaimed that human life provides an individual with the opportunity to remember the divine Name and ultimately to join with Akāl

Purakh (*Ādi Granth* p.15). But rare are the ones who seek the divine Beloved while participating in worldly actions and delights.

The notions of *karma* (actions) and *saṃsāra* (rebirth or transmigration) are central to all religious traditions originating in India. *Karma* is popularly understood in Indian thought as the principle of cause and effect. This principle of *karma* is logical and inexorable, but *karma* is also understood as a predisposition that safeguards the notion of free choice. In Sikh doctrine, however, the notion of *karma* undergoes a radical change. For the Sikh Gurus, the law of *karma* is not inexorable. In the context of the Guru Nānak's theology, *karma* is subject to the higher principle of the 'divine order' (*hukam*), an 'all-embracing principle' which is the sum total of all divinely instituted laws in the cosmos. The law of *karma* is replaced by Akāl Purakh's *hukam*, which is no longer an impersonal causal phenomenon but falls within the sphere of Akāl Purakh's omnipotence and justice. In fact, the primacy of divine grace over the law of *karma* is always maintained in the Sikh teachings, and divine grace even breaks the chain of adverse *karma*.

Sacred life and literature

Sacred life

The Sikh view of sacred life is intimately linked with the understanding of the nature of *gurmat* ('Guru's view or doctrine') whereby one follows the teachings of the Gurus. Guru Nānak employed the following key terms to describe the nature of divine revelation in its totality: *nām* (divine Name), *śabad* (divine Word), and *guru* (divine Preceptor). The *nām* reflects the manifestation of divine presence everywhere around us and within us, yet the people fail to perceive it due to their *haumai* or self-centeredness. The Punjabi term '*haumai*' ('I, I') signifies the powerful impulse to succumb to personal gratification so that a person is separated from Akāl Purakh and thus continues to suffer within the cycle of rebirth (*saṃsāra*). Akāl Purakh, however, looks graciously upon the suffering of people. He reveals himself through the Guru by uttering the *śabad* (divine Word) that communicates a sufficient understanding of the *nām* (divine Name) to those who are able to 'hear' it. The *śabad* is the actual 'utterance,' and in 'hearing' it a person awakens to the reality of the divine Name, immanent in all that lies around and within.

The institution of the Guru carries spiritual authority in the Sikh tradition. In most of the Indian religious traditions the term 'Guru' stands for a human teacher who communicates divine knowledge and provides his disciples with a cognitive map for liberation. In Sikhism, however, its meaning has evolved in a cluster of doctrines over a period of time. There are four focal points of spiritual authority, each acknowledged within the Sikh tradition as Guru: doctrine of eternal Guru; doctrine of personal Guru; doctrine of Guru Granth; and doctrine of Guru Panth. First, Guru Nānak uses the term 'Guru' in three basic senses: the Guru is Akāl Purakh; the Guru is the voice of Akāl Purakh; and the Guru is the Word, the Truth of Akāl Purakh. To experience the eternal Guru is to experience divine guidance. In Sikh usage, therefore, the Guru is the voice of Akāl Purakh, mystically uttered within human heart, mind, and soul (*man*).

Second, the personal Guru functions as the channel through whom the voice of Akāl Purakh becomes audible. Nānak became the embodiment of the eternal Guru only when he received the divine Word and conveyed it to his disciples. The same spirit manifested itself successively in his successors. In Sikh doctrine, a theory of spiritual succession was advanced in the form of 'the unity of Guruship' in which there was no difference between the founder and the successors. Thus they all represented one and the same light (*jot*) as a single flame ignites a series of torches.

Third, in Sikh usage, the *Ādi Granth* is normally referred to as the *Guru Granth Sāhib*, which implies a confession of faith in the scripture as Guru. As such, the *Guru Granth Sāhib* carries the same status and authority as did the ten personal Gurus from Guru Nānak through Guru Gobind Siṅgh, and therefore, it must be viewed as the source of ultimate authority within the Sikh Panth. In actual practice, it performs the role of Guru in the personal piety and corporate identity of the Sikh community. It has provided a framework for the shaping of the Sikh Panth and has been a decisive factor in shaping a distinctive Sikh identity. The *Ādi Granth* occupies a central position in all Sikh ceremonies, and its oral/aural experience has provided the Sikh tradition with a living presence of the divine Guru. Indeed, the *Guru Granth Sāhib* has given Sikhs a sacred focus for reflection and for discovering the meaning of life. It has functioned as a supratextual source of authority within the Sikh tradition. In a certain sense Sikhs have taken their conception of sacred scripture farther than other people of the Book such as Jews and Muslims.

Finally, the key term Guru Panth is normally employed in two senses: first, the Panth of the Guru, referring to the Sikh community; and second, the Panth as the Guru, referring to the doctrine of Guru Panth. This doctrine fully developed from the earlier idea that 'the Guru is mystically present in the congregation.' At the inauguration of the Khālsā in 1699 Guru Gobind Siṅgh symbolically transferred his authority to the Cherished Five when he received initiation from their hands. Thus the elite corps of the Khālsā has always claimed to speak authoritatively on behalf of the whole Sikh Panth, although at times non-Khālsā Sikhs interpret the doctrine of Guru Panth as conferring authority on a community more broadly defined. As a practical matter, consensus within the Sikh community is achieved by following democratic traditions.

In order to achieve a state of spiritual liberation within one's lifetime one must transcend the unregenerate condition created by the influence of *haumai*. In fact, *haumai* is the source of five evil impulses traditionally known as lust (*kām*), anger (*krodh*), covetousness (*lobh*), attachment to worldly things (*moh*), and pride (*hankār*). Under the influence of *haumai* a person becomes 'self-willed' (*manmukh*), one who is so attached to his passions for worldly pleasures that he forgets the divine Name and wastes his entire life in evil and suffering. This unregenerate condition can be transcended by means of the strictly interior discipline of *nām simaran* or 'remembering the divine Name.' This threefold process ranges from the repetition of a sacred word, usually Vahigurū (Praise to the Eternal Guru), through the devotional singing of hymns with the congregation to sophisticated meditation on the nature of Akāl Purakh. The first and the third levels of this practice relate to private devotions, while the second refers to corporate sense. On the whole the discipline of *nām simaran* is designed to bring a person into harmony with the divine order (*hukam*). The person thus gains the experience of ever-growing wonder (*vismād*) in spiritual life and achieves the ultimate condition of blissful 'equanimity' (*sahaj*) when the spirit ascends to the 'realm of Truth' (*sach khaṇḍ*), the fifth and the last of the spiritual stages, in which the soul finds mystical union with Akāl Purakh.

The primacy of divine grace over personal effort is fundamental to Guru Nānak's theology. There is, however, neither fatalism nor any kind of passive acceptance of a predestined future in his view of life. He proclaimed, 'With your own hands carve out your own destiny' (*Ādi Granth* p.474). Indeed, personal effort in the form of good actions has a place in Guru Nānak's view of life. His idea of 'divine free choice,' on the one hand, and his emphasis on the 'life of activism' based on human freedom, on the other, reflect his ability to hold in tension seemingly opposed elements. Guru Nānak explicitly saw this balancing of opposed tendencies, which avoids rigid predestination theories and yet enables people to see their own 'free' will as a part of Akāl Purakh's will, as allowing Sikhs the opportunity to create their own destinies, a feature stereotypically associated with Sikh enterprise throughout the world. Sikhism thus stresses the dignity of regular labor as an integral part of spiritual discipline. This is summed up in the following triple commandment: engage in honest labor (*kirat karanī*) for a living, adore the divine Name (*nām japan*), and share the fruit of labor with others (*vaṇḍ chhakaṇā*). The formula stresses both the centrality of meditative worship and the necessity of righteous living in the world.

Scriptures and other literature

The *Ādi Granth* is the primary scripture of the Sikhs. It contains the works of the first five and the ninth Sikh Gurus, four bards (Sattā, Balvaṇḍ, Sundar, and Mardānā), eleven Bhaṭṭs (eulogists associated with the Sikh court), and fifteen Bhagats ('devotees' such as Kabīr, Nāmdev, Ravidās, Shaikh Farid, and other medieval poets of *sant, ṣūfī*, and *bhakti* origin). Its standard version contains a total of 1,430 pages, and each copy corresponds exactly in terms of the material printed on individual pages. The text of the *Ādi Granth* is divided into three major sections. The introductory section includes three liturgical prayers. The middle section, which contains the bulk of the material, is divided into thirty-one major *rāg*s or musical patterns. The final section includes an epilogue consisting of miscellaneous works that could not be accommodated in the middle section.

The second sacred collection, the *Dasam Granth* is attributed to the tenth Guru, Gobind Siṅgh, but it must have extended beyond his time to include the writings of others as well. Mani Siṅgh, who died in 1734, compiled the collection early in the eighteenth century. Its modern standard version of 1,428 pages consists of four major types of compositions: devotional texts, autobiographical works, miscellaneous writings, and a collection of mythical narratives and popular anecdotes.

The works of two early Sikhs, Bhāī Gurdās (1551–1637) and Bhāī Nand Lāl Goyā (1633–1715), make up the third category of sacred literature. Along with the sacred compositions of the Gurus, their works are approved in the official manual of the *Sikh Rahit Maryādā* (Sikh Code of Conduct) for singing in the *gurdwārā*s.

The last category of Sikh literature includes three distinct genres: the *janam-sākhī*s (birth narratives), the *rahit-nāmā*s (manuals of code of conduct), and the *gur-bilā*s (splendor of the Guru) literature. The *janam-sākhī*s are hagiographical accounts of Guru Nānak's life, produced by the Sikh community in the seventeenth century. The *rahit-nāmā*s provide rare insight into the evolving nature of the Khālsā code in the eighteenth and nineteenth centuries. The *gur-bilā*s mainly focus on the mighty deeds of two warrior Gurus, Hargobind and particularly Gobind Siṅgh.

Institutions and practices

The Khālsā and the Rahit

From the perspective of ritual studies, three significant issues were linked with the first *amrit* ceremony. First, all who chose to join the order of the Khālsā through the ceremony were understood to have been 'reborn' in the house of the Guru and thus to have assumed a new identity. The male members were given the surname Siṅgh ('lion'), and female members were given the surname Kaur ('princess'), with the intention of creating a parallel system of aristocratic titles in relation to the Rājput hill chiefs of the surrounding areas of Anandpur. Second, the Guru symbolically transferred his spiritual authority to the Cherished Five when he himself received the nectar of the double-edged sword from their hands and thus became a part of the Khālsā Panth and subject to its collective will. In this way he not only paved the way for the termination of a personal Guruship but also abolished the institution of the *masand*s, which was becoming increasingly disruptive. Several of the *masand*s had refused to forward collections to the Guru, creating factionalism in the Sikh Panth. In addition, Guru Gobind Siṅgh removed the threat posed by the competing seats of authority when he declared that the Khālsā should have no dealings with the followers of Prithī Chand (*miṇā*), Dhir Mal, and Rām Rai. Finally, Guru Gobind Siṅgh delivered the nucleus of the Sikh Rahit (Code of Conduct) at the inauguration of the Khālsā. By sanctifying the hair with *amrit*, he made it 'the official seal of the Guru,' and the cutting of bodily hair was thus strictly prohibited. The Guru further imposed a rigorous ban on smoking.

All Sikhs initiated into the order of the Khālsā must observe the Rahit as enunciated by Guru Gobind Siṅgh and subsequently elaborated. The most significant part of the code is the enjoinder to wear five visible symbols of identity, known from their Punjabi names as the five Ks (*pañj kakke*). These are unshorn hair (*keś*), symbolizing spirituality and saintliness; a wooden comb (*kaṅghā*), signifying order and discipline in life; a miniature sword (*kirpan*), symbolizing divine grace, dignity, and courage; a steel 'wrist ring' (*karā*), signifying responsibility and allegiance to the Guru; and a pair of short breeches (*kachh*), symbolizing moral restraint. Among Sikhs the five Ks are outer symbols of the divine Word, implying a direct correlation between *bāṇī* ('divine utterance') and *bāṇā* ('Khālsā dress'). The five Ks, along with a turban for male Sikhs, symbolize that the Khālsā Sikhs, while reciting prayers, are dressed in the word of God. Their minds are thus purified and inspired, and their bodies are girded to do battle with the day's temptations. In addition, Khālsā Sikhs are prohibited from the four cardinal sins (*chār kurahit*): 'cutting the hair, using tobacco, committing adultery, and eating meat that has not come from an animal killed with a single blow.'

Worship, practices, and lifecycle rituals

The daily routine of a devout Sikh begins with the practice of meditation upon the divine Name. This occurs during the *amritvelā*, the 'ambrosial hours' (that is, the last watch of the night, between 3 and 6 a.m.), immediately after rising and bathing. Meditation is followed by the recitation of five liturgical prayers, which include the *Japjī* of Guru Nānak. In most cases the early morning devotion concludes in the presence of the *Guru Granth Sāhib*, in which the whole family gathers to receive the divine command (*vāk lainā* or 'taking God's Word') by reading a passage selected at random. Similarly, a collection of hymns, *Sodar Rahiras* (Supplication at That Door), is prescribed for the evening prayers, and the *Kīrtan Sohila* (Song of Praise) is recited before retiring for the night.

Congregational worship takes place in the *gurdwārā*, where the main focus is upon the *Guru Granth Sāhib*, installed ceremoniously every morning. Worship consists mainly of the singing of scriptural passages set to music, with the accompaniment of instruments. The singing of hymns (*kīrtan*) in a congregational setting is the heart of the Sikh devotional experience. Through such *kīrtan* the devotees attune themselves to vibrate in harmony with the divine Word, which has the power to transform and unify their consciousness. The exposition of the scriptures, known as *kathā* ('homily'), may be delivered at an appropriate time during the service by the *granthī* ('reader') of the *gurdwārā* or by the traditional Sikh scholar (*gyanī*). At the conclusion of the service all who are present join in reciting the *Ardās* ('Petition,' or Sikh Prayer), which invokes divine grace and recalls the rich common heritage of the community. Then follows the reading of the *vāk* (divine command) and the distribution of *karāh prasād* (sanctified food).

The central feature of the key lifecycle rituals is always the *Guru Granth Sāhib*. When a child is to be named, the family takes the baby to the *gurdwārā* and offers *karāh prasād*. After offering thanks and prayers through *Ardās*, the *Guru Granth Sāhib* is opened at random and a name is chosen beginning with the same letter as the first composition on the left-hand page. Thus, the process of *vāk lainā* (divine command) functions to provide the first letter of the chosen name. The underlying principle is that the child derives his or her identity from the Guru's word and begins life as a Sikh. To a boy's name the common surname Siṅgh is added, and to a girl's name Kaur is added at the end of the chosen name. In some cases, however, particularly in North America, people employ caste names (for example, Ahluwalia, Dhaliwal, Grewal, Kalsi, Sawhney, or Sethi) as the last elements of their names, and for them Siṅgh and Kaur become middle names. In addition, the infant is administered sweetened water that is stirred with a sword, and the first five stanzas of Guru Nānak's *Japjī* are recited.

A Sikh wedding, according to the *Ānand* (Bliss) ceremony, also takes place in the presence of the *Guru Granth Sāhib*, and the performance of the actual marriage requires the couple to circumambulate the sacred scripture four times to take four vows. Before the bridegroom and the bride make each round, they listen to a verse of the *Lāvān*, or 'wedding hymn' (*Ādi Granth* pp. 773–74), by the fourth Guru, Rām Dās, as given by a scriptural reader. They bow before the *Guru Granth Sāhib* and then stand up to make their round while professional musicians sing the same verse with the congregation. During the process of their clockwise movements around the scripture, they take the following four vows: to lead an action-oriented life based upon righteousness and never to shun the obligations of family and society; to maintain a bond of reverence and dignity between them; to keep enthusiasm for life alive in the face of adverse circumstances and to remain removed from worldly attachments; and to cultivate a 'balanced approach' (*sahaj*) in life, avoiding all extremes. The pattern of circumambulation in the *Ānand* marriage ceremony is the enactment of the primordial movement of life, in which there is no beginning and no end. Remembering the four marital vows is designed to make the life of the couple blissful.

The key initiation ceremony (*amrit sanskār*) for a Sikh must take place in the presence of the *Guru Granth Sāhib*. There is no fixed age for initiation, which may be done at any time the person is willing to accept the Khālsā discipline. Five Khālsā Sikhs, representing the collectivity of the original Cherished Five, conduct the ceremony. Each recites from memory one of the five liturgical prayers while stirring the sweetened water (*amrit*) with a double-edged sword. The novice then drinks the *amrit* five times so that his body is purified from the influence of five vices; and five times the *amrit* is sprinkled on his eyes to transform his outlook toward life. Finally, the *amrit* is poured on his head five times to sanctify his hair so that he will preserve his natural form and listen to the voice of conscience. Throughout the procedure the Sikh being initiated formally takes the oath each time by repeating the following declaration: '*Vahigurū jī kā khālsā! Vahigurū jī kī fateh!*' (Khālsā belongs to the Wonderful Lord! Victory belongs to the Wonderful Lord!) Thus, a person becomes a Khālsā Sikh through the transforming power of the sacred word. At the conclusion of the ceremony a *vāk* is given and *karāh prasād* is distributed.

Finally, at the time of death, both in the period preceding cremation and in the postcremation rites, hymns from the *Guru Granth Sāhib* are sung. In addition, a reading of the entire scripture takes place at home or in a *gurdwārā*. Within ten days of the conclusion of the reading, a *bhog* ('completion') ceremony is held, at which final prayers are offered in memory of the deceased.

Ethics and human relations

The *Ādi Granth* opens with Guru Nānak's *Japjī* where the fundamental question of seeking the divine Truth is raised as follows: 'How is Truth to be attained, how the veil of falsehood torn aside?' Guru Nānak then responds: 'Nānak, thus it is written: submit to the divine order (*hukam*), walk in its ways' (*Ādi Granth* p.1). Truth obviously is not obtained by intellectual effort or cunning but only by personal commitment. To know truth one must live in it. The seeker of the divine Truth, therefore, must live an ethical life. An immoral person is neither worthy of being called a true seeker nor capable of attaining the spiritual goal of life. Any dichotomy between spiritual development and moral conduct is not approved in Sikh ethics. In this context Guru Nānak explicitly says: 'Truth is the highest virtue, but higher still is truthful living' (*Ādi Granth* p. 62). Indeed, truthful conduct (*sach achār*) is at the heart of Sikh ethics.

The central focus in the Sikh moral scheme is the cultivation of virtues such as wisdom, contentment, justice, humility, truthfulness, temperance, love, forgiveness, charity, purity, and fear of Akāl Purakh. Guru Nānak remarked, 'Sweetness and humility are the essence of all virtues' (*Ādi Granth* p. 470). These virtues not only enrich the personal lives of individuals but also promote socially responsible living. The Gurus laid great stress on the need to earn one's living through honest means. In particular, living by alms or begging is strongly rejected. Through hard work and sharing, Sikh ethics forbid withdrawal from social participation. The Sikh Gurus offered their own vision of the cultivation of egalitarian ideals in social relations. Such ideals are based on the principle of social equality, gender equality, and human brotherhood/sisterhood. Thus, it is not surprising that any kind of discrimination based on caste or gender is expressly rejected in Sikh ethics.

The key element of religious living is to render service (*sevā*) to others in the form of mutual help and voluntary work. The real importance of *sevā* lies in sharing one's resources of 'body, mind, and wealth' (*tan-man-dhan*) with others. This is an expression toward fellow beings of what one feels toward Akāl Purakh. The service must be rendered without the desire for self-glorification, and in addition, self-giving service must be done without setting oneself up as a judge of other people. The Sikh Prayer (*Ardās*) holds in high esteem the quality of 'seeing but not judging' (*anadith karanā*). Social bonds are often damaged beyond redemption when people, irrespective of their own limitations, unconscionably judge others. The Sikh Gurus emphasized the need to destroy this root of social strife and enmity through self-giving service.

Finally, Sikhism is dedicated to human rights and resistance against injustice. It strives to eliminate poverty and to offer voluntary help to the less privileged. Its commitment is to the ideal of universal brotherhood, with an altruistic concern for humanity as a whole (*sarbat da bhala*). In a celebrated passage from the *Akāl Ustat* (Praise of Immortal One), Guru Gobind Siṅgh declared that 'humankind is one and that all people belong to a single humanity' (verse 85). Here it is important to underline the Guru's role as a conciliator who tried to persuade the Mughal emperor Bahādur Shāh to walk the ways of peace. Even though Guru Gobind Siṅgh had to spend the major part of his life fighting battles that were forced upon him by Hindu hill *rājās* and Mughal authorities, a longing for peace and fellowship with both Hindus and Muslims may be seen in the following passage from the *Akāl Ustat*: 'The temple and the mosque are the same, so are the Hindu worship [*pūjā*] and Muslim prayer [*namāz*]. All people are one, it is through error that they appear different. . . . Allāh and Abhekh are the same, the Purāṇa and the Qur'ān are the same. They are all alike, all the creation of the One' (verse 86). The above verses emphatically stress the irenic belief that the differences dividing people are in reality meaningless. In fact, all people are fundamentally the same because they all are the creations of the same Supreme Being. To pursue this ideal, Sikhs conclude their morning and evening prayers with the words 'Says Nānak: may thy Name and glory be ever triumphant, and in thy will, O Lord, may peace and prosperity come to one and all.'

Society: caste and gender issues

Guru Nānak and the succeeding Gurus emphatically proclaimed that the divine Name was the only sure means of liberation for all four castes: the Khatrī, originally the Kṣatriya (warrior), the Brāhmaṇ (priest), the Śūdra (servant/agriculturalist), and the Vaiśya (tradesman). In the works of the Gurus, the Khatrīs were always placed above the Brāhmaṇs in the caste hierarchy while the Śudras were raised above the Vaiśyas. This was an interesting way of breaking the rigidity of the centuries-old caste system. All the Gurus were Khatrīs, which made them a top-ranking mercantile caste in Punjab's urban hierarchy, followed by Arorās (merchants) and Ahlūwālīās (brewers). In the rural caste hierarchy an absolute majority (almost two-thirds) of Sikhs are Jāṭs (peasants), followed by Rāmgaṛhīās (artisans), Rāmdāsīās (cobblers), and Mazhabīs (sweepers). Although Brāhmaṇs are at the apex of the Hindu caste hierarchy, Sikhs place Brāhmaṇs distinctly lower on the caste scale. This is partly because of the strictures the Sikh Gurus laid upon Brāhmaṇ pride and partly because the reorganization of Punjabi rural society conferred dominance on the Jāṭ caste.

Doctrinally, caste has never been one of the defining criteria of Sikh identity. In the Sikh congregation there is no place for any kind of injustice or hurtful discrimination based upon caste identity. In the *gurdwārā* Sikhs eat together in the community kitchen, share the same sanctified food, and worship together. The *Sikh Rahit Maryādā* explicitly states, 'No account should be taken of caste; a Sikh woman should be married only to a Sikh man; and Sikhs should not be married as children.' This is the ideal, however, and in practice most Sikh marriages are arranged between members of the same endogamous caste group. Caste, therefore, still prevails within the Sikh community as a marriage convention. Nevertheless, intercaste marriages take place frequently among urban professionals in India and elsewhere.

The Sikh Gurus addressed the issues of gender within the parameters established by traditional patriarchal structures. In their view an ideal woman plays the role of a good daughter or sister and a good wife and mother within the context of family life. They condemned both women and men alike who did not observe the cultural norms of modesty and honor in their lives. It is in this context that images of the immoral woman and the unregenerate man are frequently encountered in the scriptural texts. There is no tolerance for any kind of premarital or extramarital sexual relationships, and rape in particular is regarded as a violation of women's honor in Punjabi culture. Rape amounts to the loss of family honor, which in turn becomes the loss of one's social standing in the community. The notion of family honor is thus intimately linked to the status of women.

The issue of gender has received a great deal of attention within the Sikh Panth. It is notable that the Sikh Gurus offered a vision of gender equality within the Sikh community and took practical steps to foster respect for womanhood. They were ahead of their times when they championed the cause of equal access for women in spiritual and temporal matters. Guru Nānak raised a strong voice against the position of inferiority assigned to women in society at the time: 'From women born, shaped in the womb, to woman betrothed and wed; we are bound to women by ties of affection, on women man's future depends. If one woman dies he seeks another; with a woman he orders his life. Why then should one speak evil of women, they who give birth to kings?' (*Ādi Granth* p. 473). He sought to bring home the realization that the survival of the human race depended upon women, who were unjustifiably ostracized within society. Guru Amar Dās abolished the customs among women of the veil and of *satī* (self-immolation) and permitted the remarriage of widows. He further appointed women as Sikh missionaries. Indeed, Sikh women were given equal rights with men to conduct prayers and other ceremonies in *gurdwārā*s. In actual practice, however, males dominate most Sikh institutions, and Sikh women continue to live in a patriarchal society based on Punjabi cultural assumptions. In this respect they differ little from their counterparts in other religious communities in India. Although there is a large gap between the ideal and reality, there is clear doctrinal support for the equality of rights for men and women within the Sikh Panth.

Modern expressions

The modern religious and cultural transformation within the Sikh tradition took place during the colonial period on the initiatives of the Siṅgh Sabhā (Society of the Siṅghs). This reform movement began in 1873 at Amritsar. The principal objective of the Siṅgh Sabhā reformers was to reaffirm the distinctiveness of Sikh identity in the face of the twin threats posed by the casual reversion to Hindu practices during Sikh rule and the explicit challenges from actively proselytizing religious movements such as Christian missionaries and the Ārya Samāj. The Tat Khālsā (Pure Khālsā), the dominant wing of the Siṅgh Sabhā movement, succeeded in eradicating all forms of religious diversity by the end of the nineteenth century and established norms of religious orthodoxy and orthopraxy. The reformers were largely successful in making the Khālsā ideal the orthodox form of Sikhism, and they systematized and clarified the Khālsā tradition to make Sikhism consistent and effective for propagation.

Indeed, the Tat Khālsā ideal of Sikh identity, which was forged in the colonial crucible, was both old and new. In addition to the economic and military policy of the British, there were other elements that meshed together to produce a great impact on the emerging Sikh identity. These additional elements in the larger colonial context were new patterns of administration, a new technology, a fresh approach to education, the entry of Christian missionaries, and the modernist perspective based on the scientific paradigm of the Enlightenment. All these factors produced a kind of Neo-Sikhism, characterized by a largely successful set of redefinitions in the context of the notions of modernity and religious identity imposed by the dominant ideology of the colonial power closely associated with Victorian Christianity. As such, modern Sikhism became a well-defined 'system' based on a unified tradition, and the Tat Khālsā understanding of Sikh identity became the norm of orthodoxy.

Among the 23 million Sikhs in the postmodern world, however, only approximately 15 to 20 percent are *amrit-dhārī*s (initiated), those who represent the orthodox form of the Khālsā. A large majority of Sikhs, however, about 70 percent, are *keś-dhārī*s, that is, those who 'retain their hair' and thus maintain a visible identity. These Sikhs follow most of the Khālsā Rahit without having gone through the initiation ceremony. The number of Sikhs who have shorn their hair, and are thus less conspicuous, is quite large in the West in general, and in particular in North America and the United Kingdom. Popularly known as *monā* (clean-shaven) Sikhs, they retain their Khālsā affiliation by using the surnames Siṅgh and Kaur. These Sikhs are also called *ichhā-dhārī*s because they 'desire' to keep their hair but cut it under some compulsion. They are frequently confused with *sahaj-dhārī* (gradualist) Sikhs, those who have never accepted the Khālsā discipline. Although *sahaj-dhārī* Sikhs practice *nām simaran* and follow the teachings of the *Ādi Granth*, they do not observe the Khālsā Rahit and in general do cut their hair. The number of *sahaj-dhārī*s declined during the last few decades of the twentieth century, although they have not disappeared completely from the Sikh Panth. Finally, there are those who violate the Khālsā Rahit and cut their hair after initiation. These lapsed *amrit-dhārī*s, who are known as *patit* or *bikh-dhārī* (apostate) Sikhs, are found largely in the diaspora. There is thus no single way of being a Sikh, and the five categories of Sikhs are not fixed permanently. Punjabi Sikhs frequently move between them according to their situation in life.

Transmission of the tradition outside of India

There are now more than 1 million Sikhs who have settled in foreign lands as a result of successive waves of emigration over the past 100 years. It is not surprising to find the establishment of more than 400 *gurdwārā*s in North America and the United Kingdom alone. The recent years have witnessed among the Sikhs of North America a revived interest in their inherited tradition and identity. This awakened consciousness has produced a flurry of activities in children's education. Sikh parents realize that worship in *gurdwārās* is conducted in Punjabi, which scarcely responds to the needs of children born in North America. At schools these children are being trained to be critical and rational, and they are therefore questioning the meaning of traditional rituals and practices. Traditionally trained *granthīs* and *gyanīs* are unable to answer their queries. Moreover, without adequate knowledge of Punjabi, the language of the *Ādi Granth*, the new generation of Sikhs is in danger of being theologically illiterate.

Moreover, a steady process of assimilation is in progress among second- and third-generation Sikhs. Western culture has added new challenges and obstructions to the Sikh tradition. This situation has created new responses from the Sikh community. Many Sikh parents have started home-based worship in both Punjabi and English in order to meet new challenges from the diaspora situation. They have introduced another innovative feature in the form of Sikh Youth Camps to pass on the Sikh traditions to the children. These camps last one or two weeks. Through them a spiritual environment is created which provides the children with continuous exposure to Sikh values and traditions.

Finally, in the 1970s a group of Caucasian Americans and Canadians converted to the Sikh faith at the inspiration of their Yoga teacher, Harbhajan Singh Khalsa (Yogi Bhajan), who founded the Sikh Dharma movement. These so-called white, or *gorā*, Sikhs, male and female alike, wear white turbans, tunics, and tight trousers. They live and raise families in communal houses, spending long hours in meditation and chanting while performing various postures of Tantric *yoga*. They have thus introduced the Sikh tradition into a new cultural environment. Most Punjabi Sikhs have shown an ambivalent attitude toward these converts. On the one hand, they praise the strict Khālsā-style discipline of the white Sikhs; and on the other hand, they express doubts about the mixing of the Sikh tradition with the ideals of Tantric *yoga*.

Relations with other religions

The ability to accept religious pluralism is a necessary condition of religious tolerance. Religious pluralism requires that people of different faiths be able to live together harmoniously, which provides an opportunity for spiritual self-judgement and growth. It is in this context that Sikhism expresses the ideals of coexistence and mutual understanding. Sikhism emphasizes the principles of tolerance and the acceptance of the diversity of faith and practice. It is thus able to enter freely into fruitful interreligious dialogue with an open attitude. Such an attitude signifies a willingness to learn from other traditions and yet to retain the integrity of one's own tradition. It also involves the preservation of differences with dignity and mutual respect.

The Sikh Gurus were strongly opposed to the claim of any particular tradition to possess the sole religious truth. Indeed, a spirit of accommodation has always been an integral part of the Sikh attitude toward other traditions. The inclusion of the works of the fifteen medieval non-Sikh saints (*bhagat bāṇī*, 'utterances of the Bhagats'), along with the compositions of the Gurus, in the foundational text of the Sikhs provides an example of the kind of catholicity that promotes mutual respect and tolerance. For instance, the Muslim voice of the devotee Shaikh Farid is allowed to express itself on matters of doctrine and practice. This is the ideal that Sikhs frequently stress in interfaith dialogues.

The presence of the *bhagat bāṇī* in the Sikh scripture offers a four-point theory of religious pluralism. First, one must acknowledge at the outset that all religious traditions have gone through a process of self-definition in response to changing historical contexts. Thus, in any dialogue the dignity of the religious identities of the individual participants must be maintained. One must be able to honor a commitment as absolute for oneself while respecting different absolute commitments for others. For this reason the quest for a universal religion and the attempt to place one religious tradition above others must be abandoned. Second, the doctrinal standpoints of different religious traditions must be maintained with mutual respect and dignity. Third, all participants must enter into a dialogue with an open attitude, one that allows not only true understanding of other traditions but also disagreements on crucial doctrinal points. Finally, the 'other' must somehow become one's 'self' in a dialogue, so that the person's life is enriched by the spiritual experience.

The tradition in the study of religions

The first North American conference on Sikh Studies was held in 1976 at the University of California, Berkeley. At that conference it was generally felt that the Sikh tradition was indeed 'the forgotten tradition' in scholarly circles in North America. In particular, Mark Juergensmeyer argued that in the textbooks in world religions the study of Sikhism was either completely ignored or misrepresented. He examined the various reasons for this treatment. He suggested that there are two prejudices in Indian Studies that function against the study of the Sikh tradition. The first prejudice is that against the modern age. Many scholars, following the Orientalist perspective, have been more interested in the classical texts on Indian philosophy rather than a medieval devotional tradition. Since Sikh tradition is relatively modern, it has been completely ignored in Indian Studies. The other prejudice that faces Sikh Studies in Indian literature is the prejudice against regionalism. Sikhism is not only relatively modern but also almost exclusively Punjabi. In his arguments, Juergensmeyer made the case for the utility of Sikhism for the studies of religion.

In the last two decades the study of Sikh tradition has received a great deal of scholarly attention, and there are now five programs of Sikh and Punjab Studies established in North America with the active financial support of the Sikh community. In the West, Sikh Studies is a new field that is slowly gaining the academic respectability that it richly deserves. It provides interesting data to scholars of Religious Studies to address the fundamental question of how Sikhism has become meaningful to 23 million followers around the world. Its doctrines, myths, rituals, practices, and symbols are the channels of the expression of a faith in which one may grow and fulfill one's life. Throughout Sikh history the faith of its adherents has kept them steadfast in the face of adverse circumstances.

Suggested further readings

Cole (1982, 1984); Grewal (1991, 1998); McLeod (1989, 1997, 1999, 2003); Oberoi (1994); H. Singh (1983, 1992–98); N.-G. Singh (1993); N. Singh (1990); P. Singh (2000, 2003); Thursby (1992, 1993).

Part Two

WHAT INDIA HAS RECEIVED FROM THE WORLD

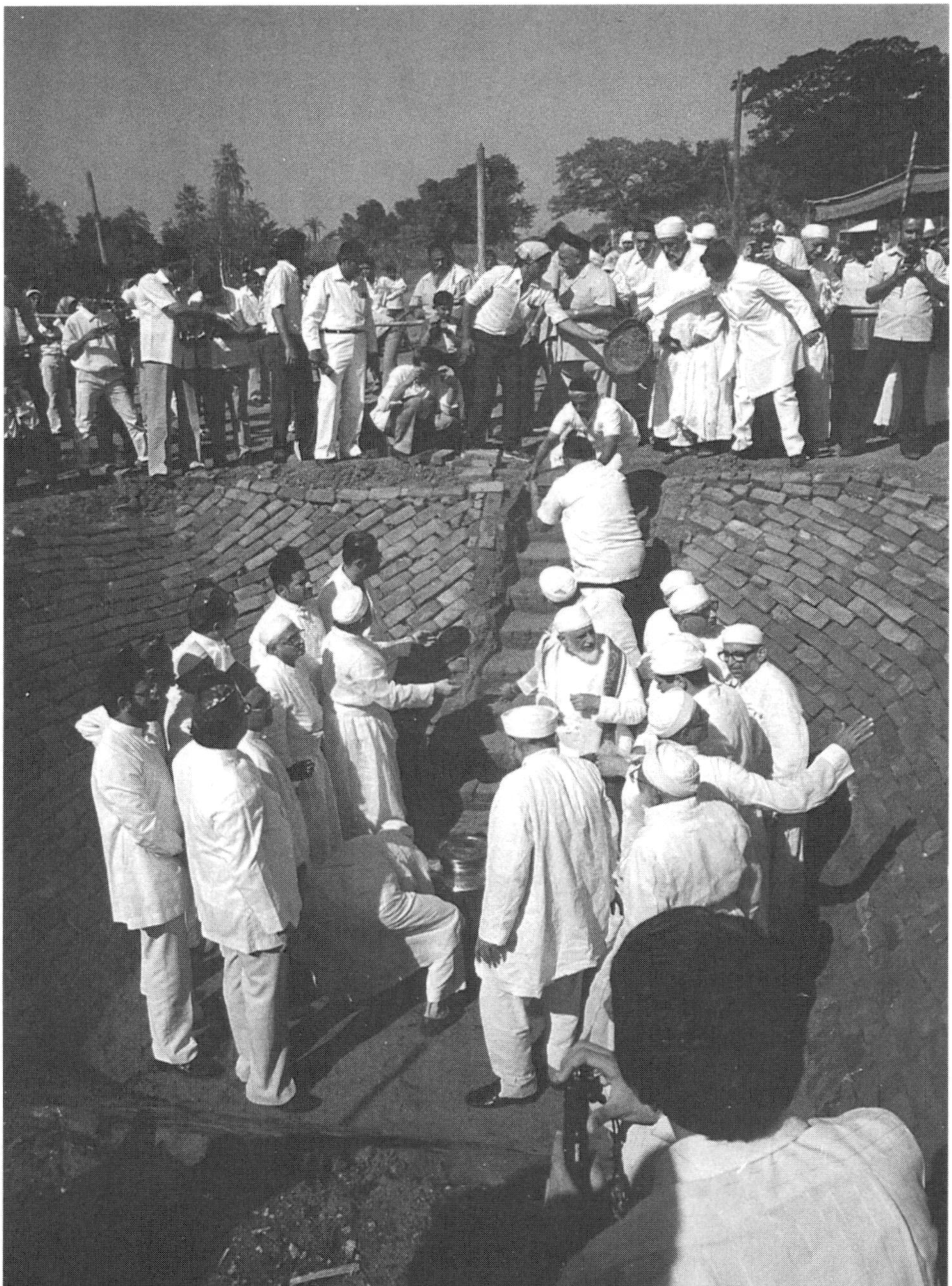

6. Installation of the foundation for a new fire temple at the site of the first Parsi landing in Gujarat. Courtesy of Professor T. M. Luhrmann.

5

INDIAN ZOROASTRIAN TRADITION

T. M. Luhrmann

The tradition defined

Zoroastrianism is an ancient religion based on the teachings of the prophet Zarathustra or (in the Greek) Zoroaster. Its most distinctive elements are the strong dualism inherent in a basically monotheistic theology and the role of fire, which is used to represent divinity and is enshrined in temples as the focus of religious prayer. Originally a Persian spirituality, today there are fewer than 200,000 followers of the Zoroastrian tradition worldwide. The greatest number of them live in India, and the largest concentration of Zoroastrian population can be found in and around Bombay (now Mumbai). There do appear to be modern Zoroastrians in Iran, but recent census figures (which report as many as 25,000 Iranian Zoroastrians) are thought to be misleading, and the only late twentieth-century scholarship of Iranian Zoroastrianism (Boyce 1979; Fischer 1973) describes the remnants of Zoroastrian practice in rural areas. In any event, it is in India that modern Zoroastrianism has had its most recent impact, and acquired a distinctive form, associated with a remarkable group of people, the Parsis, whose history is inseparable from that of Mumbai itself.

Cosmos and history

Zarathustra is thought to have lived in the middle of the second millennium BCE, though there is a good deal of debate about this; the suggested date is based on the similarity of the language in the teachings ascribed to Zarathustra (the *Gāthā*s, which are included in a longer sacred text, the *Avesta*) with the language of the *Ṛg Veda*, which is thought in this analysis to date from around the same period (Boyce 1975, 1979). This dating also makes Zarathustra a rough contemporary of the patriarch Abraham. He seems to have been born into a nomadic people; many passages in the words attributed to him speak of herding cattle. These nomads probably descended from the Indo-Iranian people who had roamed the southern steppes in the fourth millennium BCE. By the third millennium they seem to have separated into two cultures, but even 1,000 years later they shared much in common and the tone and ethos of the two great traditions echo each other across their texts.

The religion that holds Zarathustra's words as its central teaching shares much with its Indo-Iranian past, and Zarathustra may have been a priest in the early Indo-Iranian religion. That religion put fire and water at the center of its practice, as does Zoroastrianism, and its central concept seems to have been *asha* (Vedic Sanskrit *ṛta*, later *dharma*), which remains central in Zoroastrian theology today. To the Indo-Iranians, *asha* was thought to be something akin to natural law, the order of the universe in which the sun rises and the seasons turn in their regular and expected manners. Ritual sacrifice seems to have been thought to strengthen this process and was made daily to both fire and water. Fuel, incense, and animal fat were given to the fire, along with frequent blood sacrifice of an animal, but to the water, the milk, sap, and leaves of a sacred plant were offered. Scholars think that this is the sacred plant mentioned as *soma* in the Vedas and *haoma* in the *Avesta*; it may have been the stimulant *ephedra*. The pre-Zoroastrian texts speak of one wise lord, with two somewhat lesser lords, and an array of abstract personifications of natural elements and human aspirations, like prayer and friendship.

Tradition says that Zarathustra was born laughing and that he left home at twenty to seek the truth. Revelation came to him at thirty, when he stopped at the side of a river and was led into the presence of Ahura Mazda (God) and five other radiant beings. Exactly how he understood these beings is uncertain – the texts that preserve his teachings are obscure. But his teachings are usually taken to carve out a radical difference from the Indo-Iranian tradition by elevating Ahura Mazda, the one wise lord, into a role of singular importance. Ahura Mazda becomes the one uncreated God, existing eternally, who has created all other gods and all that is good. This last point becomes the issue of greatest acrimony in the interpretation of the ancient texts because Zarathustra does speak of two fundamental spirits that are utterly opposed and between whom humans must choose. At least to some extent, Ahura Mazda is a more limited lord than, for example, the Abrahamic deity at the center of Jewish, Christian, and Muslim traditions. But even the God of Hebrew scripture struggles with the presence of other gods. Zarathustra's vision of Ahura Mazda has a radical uniqueness: Ahura Mazda is the source of all good, who creates from himself the other deities mentioned in the Indo-Iranian texts. Far more clearly than in the Abrahamic traditions, Zarathustra sees that the One God cannot remove the misery from human life: 'To all of you the soul of the cow [thought to represent the vision of the good, the human ideal] lamented: "*For whom did ye shape me? Who fashioned me? (For) the cruelty of fury and violence, of bondage and might, holds me in captivity. I have no pastor other than you. . . .*" To him they replied through truth: "*There is no help free of enmity for the cow*" ' (*Yasna* 29.1, 3; Insler 1975: 29; emphasis in original). The text then goes on to explain the presence of two spirits, utterly opposed, between whom the gods did not all choose wisely. 'Since they chose the worse thought, they then rushed into fury, with which they have afflicted the world and mankind' (*Yasna* 30.6; Insler 1975: 33).

It is evident even from these early, obscure texts that Zoroastrianism is a doctrine in which moral issues are very clear and very important. God is good, rational, and knowable; he is truth. He is also purity. Evil is the lie, and all acts which are irrational and hurtful are the acts of evil. A human being is essentially good – this is a striking difference from many other religious traditions – but he or she can choose to be influenced by Ahriman, the evil spirit. The central story of the religion is that the human individual participates in a battle between good and evil in which his or her own freely chosen actions determine the outcome. It is usually accepted that God will ultimately win this cosmic war but only through human initiative.

Zarathustra also seems to have taught that each human being is judged at the end of life. Upon death the soul comes to a bridge over a chasm, the Chinvat Pul, and a woman representing the person's life deeds beckons the soul to cross over. She is either old and ugly or young and beautiful, according to how the soul has acted in the world, and as the soul steps upon the bridge, it either widens to allow passage into the paradise beyond or shrinks to force the soul to fall to hellish depths. And yet regardless of the outcome, at the end of time all souls will be redeemed and the earth will emerge in godly bliss. It is said that Zarathustra was the first to teach the doctrines of an individual judgement, the first to teach of Heaven and Hell, the first to teach of the resurrection of the body and of everlasting life. It is sometimes said that Zoroastrianism is a source from which similar Jewish and Christian teachings are derived (Russell 1987). Then as now, God is represented by fire. He is not fire personified, and contemporary Zoroastrians are quick to point out that they do not worship fire. They use fire to represent God, more or less as the cross represents Jesus. It is not quite clear when the first fire temples were built; Herodotus refers to Persian fire worship, and it may have been that there were very early temples.

Tradition says that for ten years Zarathustra was unable to find any converts among his own people, except for one lone cousin. So he left his people and, after some wandering, came to the court of King Vishtaspa, who accepted his teachings after Zarathustra cured the ruler's beloved horse of illness. While Zoroastrian tradition preserves the story of Vishtaspa, historical records first mention Persian Zoroastrians centuries later, in the ninth century BCE. As described by Herodotus, they were the Medes, who were established in what is today western Iran. They overthrew the Assyrian Empire in 614–612 BCE and extended their dominion over the Persian peoples to the east and southwest. Zoroastrianism seems to have spread quickly during their sixty years of rule.

In 549 BCE the Persian people from the southwest, under Cyrus, an Achaemenian and the current Medean king's son-in-law, overthrew the king and established the first Persian Empire. He went on to conquer Asia Minor and Babylonia (and her subject territories) and also brought eastern Iran under his control. In all likelihood Cyrus and his people were Zoroastrians. The classical historian Herodotus assumed that they were and said of them that 'they do not believe in gods of human form, as the Greeks do. They offer sacrifices to Zeus, going up into the highest mountains and calling the whole circle of the heaven Zeus. They sacrifice, too, to the sun, moon, and earth and to fire, water, and winds. . . . The Persians welcome foreign customs more than any other people' (Herodotus 1.131, 135).

The Persian Empire fell to Alexander in 331 BCE, but a Zoroastrian state emerged again within 100 years, as a Zoroastrian lineage (descending from Arshak or Arsaces) established rule from the border of India to the western boundary of Mesopotamia. In 224 BCE that lineage was overthrown by another, which established the Sassanian dynasty in Iran. It was during Sassanian times that the canonical body of Zoroastrian religious texts was written down for the first time. These texts – the *Avesta*, which included the seventeen hymns attributed to Zarathustra and called the *Gāthā*s – seem to have been transmitted orally until an alphabet was invented for them in this period. Over the next 1,000 years, even past the Islamic conquest, additional religious texts emerged, written in another language (Pahlavi or Middle Persian), that served as commentaries on the original Zoroastrian texts. The theology in these later texts is far crisper than it is in Zarathustra's elliptical verses, and much of the theological debate in modern Parsi circles is in effect an argument about whether the Pahlavi version of the theology is what Zarathustra really meant.

Zoroastrianism arrived in India when some Zoroastrians left their homeland, probably for reasons of religious freedom, and landed on an island off the coast of Gujarat early in the tenth century CE. They then made their way to the mainland and settled in areas still associated with the religion: Sanjan, Navsari, and Surat. A famous tale tells of the local king on the mainland hesitant to accept the newcomers. He presented a cup of milk, full to the brim, to explain that the land was already too densely settled; the Parsi leader added a pinch of sugar without spilling a drop and said that his people would only make the land sweeter. Strict rules about endogamy and the prohibitions on non-Parsi presence in fire temples that continue to be observed in India may date from this period, as such restrictions are not found today in Iran.

Parsis lived quietly in Gujarat for 700 years. When the British arrived, the Parsis began to function in the role of financial mediators and traders. They grew quite wealthy, moved to Bombay, and became the most Westernized 'native' community in India. A 1905 Parsi commentator makes this revealing comment in a book on Indian cricket, which Parsis dominated for many years: 'A Parsi in England feels quite at home. He knows well the history and tradition of its people, and is no stranger to their manners and games. He esteems their sports, liberties and literature. Many a wealthy and educated Parsi now-a-days takes an annual holiday to England, just as a Mahommedan or a Hindu goes to Mecca or Benares' (Patel 1905: 47). Mecca for the Muslims, Benares for the Hindus; a Parsi, J. M. F. Patel suggests without irony, goes on pilgrimage to London. This process of Westernization has had significant implications for the Zoroastrian religion, for while few Parsis converted to Christianity, their ritual-rich religion shifted to a much more secularized vision. Only in recent years, as the community begins to face the prospect of dying out altogether, have Parsis begun to emphasize the satisfactions of ritual practice and the virtues of involvement in the religious life.

Sacred life and literature

As a textual tradition, Zoroastrianism is based on a messy compilation of texts, many of which are missing and few of which have unambiguous translations. The *Avesta* is the oldest collection and the chief source for the spiritual tradition. The texts are composed in two otherwise unrecorded Eastern Iranian languages: the 'Gathic' Avestan, similar to the language of the *Ṛg Veda*, and 'Younger' Avestan. The Gathic Avestan takes its name from the primary texts of the language, the *Gāthā*s, seventeen hymns composed by the prophet and embedded in a longer collection of verses called the *Yasna*, which forms the basis of priestly worship. The *Gāthā*s are both passionate and abstract, with frequent references to the 'soul of the cow' and cattle herding. They are also difficult to interpret. As one scholar remarks, 'Because of their relative brevity and the almost total lack of other earlier or contemporary works of Old Iranian literature, the Gāthās of Zarathustra are truly a text bound with seven seals' (Insler 1975: 1). Other material in the *Avesta* includes hymns to individual deities (the Yashts), a selection of texts addressing purity laws (the *Vendidad*), and a variety of other prayers. A selection of this material has been assembled in a collection called the 'Khordeh Avesta,' which is used by many Parsis as a book of common prayer.

None of these texts was written down before the fifth century CE, and even then many were lost. The earliest extant manuscript now dates from CE 1323. In fact, during the Sassanian period, the *Avesta* was much larger and included a wide range of material: life and legends of the prophet, treatises on cosmogony, books of law, and so forth. All known copies were destroyed in the series of Islamic conquests, although one late Persian book (the *Denkard*) gives a detailed summary of the contents: from this, scholars infer that roughly one quarter of the total remains. It remains, however, because it was the quarter in most constant devotional use, and the texts survived from memory.

In addition, there are a variety of commentaries (*Zand*) that survive, written in Pahlavi. (The *Avesta* with its interpretations is often described as the 'Zend-Avesta.') Among the important texts are the *Bundahishn*, a text on creation whose theology is far clearer than that in the *Gāthās*. Another is referred to as the *Zadspram*, named for the priest thought to be its author, which includes materials on the prophet's life. His life story can also be found in the *Denkard*, which includes a massive amount of other religious material as well. Most of these texts date from the ninth century. There are also writings in other tongues, among them modern Persian and Old Gujarati, which are thought to retranslate older texts but which have not been deeply analyzed by scholars. A collection known as the 'Persian Rivayats' consists of Iranian priests' answers to Parsi priests' questions on ritual and spiritual matters between the fifteenth and eighteenth centuries. There is also a considerable Parsi literature in English and Gujarati that dates from the nineteenth and twentieth centuries.

The central textual challenge around which many community theological debates have been and are organized is the role of dualism and the degree of God's power in the universe. The most famous passage in the *Gāthās* is this: 'Truly there are two primal Spirits, twins, renowned to be in conflict. In thought and word and act they are two, the good and the bad. . . . And when these two Spirits first encountered, they created life and not-life, and that at the end the worst existence shall be for the followers of falsehood (drug), but the best dwelling for those who possess righteousness (asha)' (*Yasna* 30.3; Boyce 1979: 20).

Mary Boyce, a leading Western scholar and translator of Zoroastrian texts, argues that these words indicate that early Zoroastrianism was dualistic. There are two spiritual beings, one good, one bad, utterly opposed to each other and apparently equally powerful. Many of the Pahlavi texts that date from much later are unambiguously dualistic. The ninth-century *Bundahishn*, for example, explains that in the beginning there were both God (Ahura Mazda) and evil (Ahriman), both uncreated, both infinite, with a void between them. God knew that evil must be destroyed but that it could not be destroyed by spirit, being spirit; and so God created the material world as a trap for the evil – in the same manner, says the text, as a gardener sets a trap for the vermin in his garden. By entering the world, evil loses its impregnable spiritual state and becomes something of a parasite, dependent upon the world for its existence. Human beings are created to choose between good and evil in this material world and, by choosing, deprive the evil of substance, and force it to struggle in the futile effort to escape. Death, pain, and suffering have an independent and external cause.

However, many Parsis vehemently disagree with this interpretation (and indeed within the non-Parsi scholarly community there are widely divergent views on what is called the 'continuity thesis' – the thesis that the theology in the *Gāthās* is the same as expressed by the *Bundahishn*). In fact, among contemporary Indian Zoroastrians one can find an array of theological positions. Most Parsis seem to accept the version of

Zoroastrian theology that was articulated during the nineteenth century in response to Protestant missionaries who derided the community's 'dualism' as superstitious and polytheistic. The most famous of these missionaries, John Wilson, gave a much-quoted speech in 1839 upon his conversion of two Parsi boys. In it he denounced 'the monstrous dogma of two eternal principles, which, though not unknown to the ancient Persians, is altogether unreasonable, as inconsistent with the predominance of order, regularity, and goodness in the system of the universe, and altogether impious' (Wilson 1847: 65–66). The written Parsi response was that there is no external evil and there is no other God than Ahura Mazda. The evil spirit is a metaphor that refers to an individual's bad thoughts. As Aspandiarji Framjee wrote in 1841: 'Hormazd [Ahura Mazda] . . . is omniscient and omnipotent. . . . Hormazd is pure; and holy; He is formless, self-existent and eternal. . . . He keeps no partner or companion in His works' (1841: i). A more modern writer asserted in a 1979 pamphlet entitled *What a Parsee Should Know*: 'There is no Dualism in our religion in the proper sense. . . . In course of time, it was forgotten that the Evil Spirit was the creation of Ahura-Mazda Himself and it was raised almost to the level of a rival of Ahura-Mazda' (Vimadalal 1967: 64–65). It is a typical point of view today that the so-called Dualism merely denotes the tendency in the modern mind to deviate from the path of righteousness.

In this modern version of Parsi Zoroastrianism, the central text is understood to be the *Gāthās*; Zoroastrianism is understood to be an ethical system compatible with science; and ritual practice becomes attenuated to the vanishing point. By the turn of the nineteenth into the twentieth century, many Parsis had begun to argue that ceremonies are distractions from the real religion, which is the rational, ideal union of scientific secularism and spirituality. As a 1918 essay on 'the advancement of religion' put it: 'We now turn to the highest stage of religious culture. The mental caliber of the people of this stage [in which she includes modern Parsis] does not require the props of religious rites and ceremonies for the maintenance of religious sentiment, but is strong enough to presume that sentiment without this aid' (Engineer 1918: 10). Probably as a consequence of this emphasis on science and rationality, the ritual practice and textual understanding in much of the contemporary community has become quite limited. A visitor to the community may well be struck by the large number of Parsis who report dissatisfaction with their own knowledge of the faith, and who find their own religiosity anemic. Many Parsis as a result have become more engaged with Hindu or Hinduized spiritualities or with other faiths such as Christian Science.

Institutions and practices

Like many ancient religions, Zoroastrianism is primarily a purity religion (see Choksy 1989; Modi 1885). The extensive ritual practice prescribed by the religion is premised on the need to remove badness or evil by washing, removing, flicking away, and making sacred. Orthodox rules around purity are among the most stringent in all religious practice. Traditional rules governing menstruation, for example, forbid the woman from touching anything not made of iron. She may not sleep in the house as usual but on an iron cot in a special room for the purpose and often outside of the main living area; she may not wear her common clothes; she may not touch anything except through iron implements; and she must take a ritual bath upon completion of her menses. Few follow these restrictions so strictly these days, but those who are orthodox will sleep in a separate bed and often have separate clothes for the duration. And Parsis are perhaps most widely known for the rituals in which they dispose of the dead without defiling earth, water, or fire. Corpses are left exposed to the air to allow them to be eaten by vultures. The buildings where they are left awaiting this fate are called 'Towers of Silence' (*dokhma*). Intense arguments surround the practice, some within the Bombay community praising the ecological wisdom of the method and others condemning it as barbaric.

The basic ritual act in the religion involves wearing the *sudreh* and *kusti*, the sacred shirt and thread, with which both male and female children are invested somewhere around the age of seven in an elaborate and expensive ceremony (the *navjote*). These items are regarded as basic indications of Zoroastrian identity and attempts to find out how observant someone is will begin by questioning whether they wear the *sudreh-kusti* and, then, whether they perform their *kusti* prayers. These are prayers that are supposed to be said upon awakening (although there can be some variations on the normal procedure), before meals, after excreting, and before any other prayers (for thanksgiving, worship, requests for intervention, and so forth: books of prayers and sacred verses suitable for prayers may be easily purchased). The *kusti* prayers involve the recitation of Avestan and Pahlavi verses while untying the *kusti* thread wrapped around the waist, using it to shake off or drive away impurity (or evil), and retying it. As one unties the *kusti*, one says: 'Protect us from the foe, O Mazda and Spenta Armaitai! Begone, daevi Drug! Begone the one of the Daeva-origin, begone the one of Daeva-shaping, begone the one of Daeva-begetting! Begone, O Drug, crawl away, O Drug, disappear, O Drug! In the north you shall disappear. You shall not destroy the material world of Asha!' (trans. in Boyce 1984: 58).

All Zoroastrian prayers are spoken in the ancient tongues; this presents a considerable challenge for the modern community, as very few individuals actually learn to understand the prayers they memorize. A 1987 dissertation sampled 200 Parsis enrolled as college students in two Bombay colleges. Ninety percent of them said that they wore their *sudreh-kusti* all the time, and 89 percent said their *kusti* prayers at least once a day. A full 70 percent said that they have 'no understanding at all' of what they prayed (Taraporewalla 1987). There is a widespread perception in the community that the level of understanding of the religion and interest in following its edicts is declining among the young, although the trend may have reversed in recent years.

Those who consider themselves observant (probably calling themselves 'orthodox') may perform a variety of other practices. They may say obligatory prayers, covering their heads and softly reciting the ancient verses in a singsong voice for an hour or more. They may carry incense around the house, reciting one of the standard prayers (the Ashem Vohu) after the house is swept and clean. They may rise in the morning, bow to the sun, and rub their hands over their face when the sun has touched it. On festive occasions, they may offer milk baths (such as for a child's birthday) and prepare a festive tray, with an oil lamp, red vermilion powder, betel nuts and leaves, almonds, turmeric sticks, and other items, which is presented to the recipient as he or she stands on a small wooden platform, facing east. And there are many other rituals, chosen to bless a new house, to express joy, to commemorate the dead, and to protect during a journey. But Zoroastrianism is fundamentally a solitary religion. There are occasional public rituals, for lifecycle events (the *kusti* ceremony or *navjote*) or even just thanksgiving (the *jashan*), where white-clothed priests sing the prayers in lowered monotones, and there is a sacred well in the city of Mumbai, close to a frenetic commuter rail station, where people gather to pray. But they pray alone.

Ideally, the good Zoroastrian visits a fire temple once a day. These temples (*agiaries*) are the primary institutions of the religion and are considered the seat of religious power. In contemporary Mumbai there are forty-four fire temples, each with an ever-burning fire fed on sandalwood by white-frocked priests. Some of these are highly sacred, in temples designated Atash Behrams (there are only eight Atash Behrams in India, and each is a place where an ancient fire from earliest Zoroastrianism has been kept burning continuously or to which a flame from such a fire has been transferred): these fires have been consecrated from fire taken from sixteen sources (lightning being one) and purified ninety-one times. Others are less so, but in all, the maintenance of purity is what gives the fires their sacred quality. Each fire sits inside a special area which may be entered only by the priests, and the priests themselves acquire their role only through elaborate ceremonies designed to remove the dross of the everyday. They too must be purified before they enter the temple. While in the temple, lay Parsis typically pray (again by themselves) and offer sandalwood by purchasing it from a vendor and giving it to the priest to burn on the fire.

In addition to the fire temples in Mumbai, there are fire temples throughout India in places settled by Parsis. Among the most important are those fire temples established in the earliest places of Parsi settlement in Gujarat, with the holiest being the fire temple in Udwada, a little town on the coast.

Ethics and human relations

The central concept in Zoroastrian spirituality is *asha*. Variously translated as truth, righteousness, or natural law, it can also be understood as purity: the absence of the lie, which is evil or *druj* (also transliterated as *drug*). I. J. S. Taraporewalla, a much-admired priest and translator of the *Gāthās*, asks: 'And what then is this *asha*? Scholars translate it variously as "Purity," or "Righteousness" or "Truth," but it is far more than any of these words in their *ordinary sense*. It is the Eternal Truth, the One Reality' (1965: 21; emphasis in original). Most devotions end with the Ashem Vohu, an Avestan prayer embedded in the *Yasna*. In translation it reads: 'Asha is good, it is best. According to wish it is, according to wish it shall be for us. Asha belongs to Asha Vahista' (Boyce 1984: 57).

By the end of the nineteenth century in India, this emphasis on *asha* had become entrenched in community imagination and practice as an absolute prohibition against lying. The general resonance of the word 'truth' in the contemporary community would be hard to overestimate; it carries the penumbra of meanings that *asha* does. What is good is true, and what is true is good. Parsis pride themselves on their truthfulness and not infrequently contrast their honesty with the dishonesty of non-Parsis. Indeed, the community has an admirable reputation for honesty in modern India. This commitment to honesty had clear business advantages during the colonial period, and at least by the late nineteenth and early twentieth centuries, the concept of truth took on this aspect of business reliability for the Parsis. The business heroes of the eighteenth and nineteenth centuries are presented as gaining commercial credit through their uprightness and truthfulness; contemporary Parsis describe their truthfulness as a commercial asset. Parsis often tell the story that all the banks in Bombay used to employ Parsis as bank tellers because 'in earlier days' Parsis always spoke the truth. These days, many Parsis will say, the importance of truth both within the community and without has declined.

The community is also famous for its charity. Charity has always been a religious virtue of the community, commended in the holy texts. But during the colonial period, charitable activity became the primary indicator not only of religious goodness but also of political and economic power, the means through which a secularized, progressive, Westernized Parsi achieved recognition. Much of earlier Bombay was built with charitable Parsi funds, the more so as the British colonial government began to confer knighthood on those who were outstandingly benevolent. Between 1820 and 1940 the Parsis built over 160 fire temples; in the same period they erected over 40 *dharamśāla*s (rest houses, used to house the poor) and *bāg*s (low-income housing), and donated funds to 350 schools, libraries, educational centers, hospitals, clinics, and wards. Parsis in general provided funds in such amounts that Parsi charities reported annual incomes of well over 1 million rupees during the first forty years of the twentieth century (Hinnells 1996; Lala 1981, 1984).

Modern expressions

The two most interesting modern expressions of Zoroastrianism can be said to be responses to the somewhat dry, highly rationalized form of the religion that emerged as the dominant spirituality from the colonial encounter. The first is an esoteric version of Zoroastrianism produced in the late nineteenth century as a result of theosophy's attempt to win followers in India (see Luhrmann 2002). This is Ilm-e-kshnoom, an extremely intricate interpretation of rituals and texts. It holds that the words of the *Gāthā*s themselves have a magical, divine power when spoken, and that those words have hidden meanings understood only by those with higher knowledge. Followers of Ilm-e-kshnoom also emphasize the *Gāthā*s among the Zoroastrian texts but are much more ritualistically inclined than most Parsis. They tend to be what others would call orthodox, meaning that they follow the extensive purity rules which are meant to govern the pious Zoroastrian's life and that they practice a wide variety of the rituals associated with maintaining purity and godliness.

The Bombay Theosophical Society was founded in 1879 and immediately proved attractive to Zoroastrians. Fifty percent of its original members were Parsi. Theosophy was a Western occult religious philosophy that was rich in magical symbolism, but it presented itself as a scientific and pragmatic approach to nature. 'TRUTH,' its founder proclaims in her magnum opus, 'high-seated upon its rock of adamant, is alone eternal and supreme. We believe in no Magic which transcends the scope and capacity of the human mind' (Blavatsky 1960, 1: v). As it happened, those close examinations of the facts led to the theosophical recognition that all religions were based on Eastern religions because Theosophists were able to contact great souls ('*mahātmās*') who existed on other spiritual 'planes.' The teachings they delivered enabled Theosophists to peer beyond the veil of mere human philosophy into the real. That reality was fundamentally Hindu (at least, Hinduism, as understood in Theosophy, contained the closest representation of the true facts of the spiritual world) and included reincarnation, spiritualism, mesmeric magnetism, and a range of techniques for contacting and manipulating spiritual matter.

And, in fact, Zarathustra was the source of it all. 'The secret doctrines of the Magi, of the pre-Vedic Buddhists, of the hierophants of the Egyptian Thoth or Hermes, and of the adepts of whatever age and nationality, including the Chaldean kabalists and the Jewish *nazars*, were *identical* from the beginning' (Blavatsky 1960, 2: 142; emphasis in original). Blavatsky goes on to say that Zarathustra was really the first, or one of the first, names of these powers and that 'all these gods, whether of the Zoroastrians or of the Veda, are but so many personated *occult powers* of nature' (Blavatsky 1960, 2: 143; emphasis in original). In 1882 Henry S. Olcott gave a lecture in Bombay in which he argued that Zoroastrianism was more true, more real, than the mystifications of other upstart religions (such as Christianity) and could be said to contain the deepest truths of all religions. Some 1,500 listeners, most of them Parsi, received him with prolonged cheering. Colonial-era Bombay was not the only place, nor Parsis the only group, from which Theosophy gained adherents. For some time, the date of Olcott's arrival in Sri Lanka was even celebrated as 'Olcott Day.' But Theosophy had different kinds of impacts in different settings. In Sri Lanka, Olcott's influence seems to have led to the revival of a more restrained, inwardly directed Buddhism. (Gombrich and Obeyesekere 1988 describe the Buddhism he helped to produce as Protestant Buddhism.) The Zoroastrianism Olcott encountered, however, was the child of late nineteenth-century rationalization. It had already been Protestantized (at least, that is one description of the faith that emerged from the colonial encounter; see Luhrmann 2002), and the result was somewhat sterile. Theosophy encouraged an occult, symbolic reading of the *Gāthā*s and yet described that approach as scientific.

In 1914 a deeply respected priest, M. N. Dhalla, educated in the Western scholarly approach to religion at Columbia University in New York City, published his magisterial understanding of the faith. *Zoroastrian Theology* argued that the Zoroastrian religion was a wonderful philosophy encumbered by unnecessary and superstitious rituals. Three years later Phiroze Masani replied with *Zoroastrianism Ancient and Modern*, a ringing denunciation of Dhalla's 'cruel and obnoxious ideas.' His is a colorful book – one chapter subtitle, for instance, reads 'Bosh about animal-slaughter from foreign writers' – and in it Masani introduced Ilm-e-kshnoom. Students of this esoteric Zoroastrianism resist the association with Theosophy, but Kshnoom is ideologically quite similar to Theosophy and followed directly in its wake. The teachings of Kshnoom were said to have come from great master souls, hidden in caves and on mountaintops behind a spiritual magnetic veil, and protected from death by its energies. Those souls revealed themselves to a shy Parsi boy, who then reluctantly shared their wisdom with others.

Kshnoom holds that Zarathustra was not a man (as Dhalla had suggested) but an angel who came down to earth in human form. The words he spoke, then, have a magical character, and Kshnoomist Zoroastrians believe that when they speak those words properly, their vibrations will change the world. Kshnoom also teaches that certain words in the *Avesta* have hidden meanings, accessible only to those with esoteric knowledge. So Kshnoomist lectures are elaborate textual interpretations. The lecturer will take a prayer, or a portion of a sacred text, and explain its hidden significance. The style has the same arcane flavor as typical of Kabbalistic interpretation. For example, Masani disputes Dhalla's claim, made on the basis of analysis of variations in linguistic style within the ancient texts, that the only portion of the *Avesta* that should be attributed to Zarathustra is the *Gāthā*s:

> Perhaps the writer of the book [Dhalla] may go further and say that the word 'Yazata' is also not to be found in the Gathas and that therefore all the Yazatas are of a later growth. But the former use of 'Vispe' meaning 'all' and the superlative degree 'Mazishtem' meaning 'the greatest' with Srosh suggest a latent force of the word 'Yazata' which the adjectives 'Vispe' and 'Mazishtem' must qualify, and we find the forms Yazai and Yazemnaongho in the Gathas formed from the same verb Yaz from which the noun Yazata is derived.
>
> (Masani 1917: 36)

This is heady stuff for those who previously found their religion bland. It seems to promise higher knowledge and deeper insight. Masani goes on to explain that all the *Avesta* is inspired, that all of its rituals are necessary and practically effective (except for the animal sacrifice, which he abhors; real Zoroastrians, he explains, are vegetarian, a view of Zoroastrianism unique to Kshnoom), and that true Zoroastrian priests have magical powers exceeding those of a *yogī*. It is also scientifically true that: 'The fight of Zoroaster with the Daevas is not an allegorical story, but a scientific fact based on the most abstruse laws of vibration, colour and magnetic electricity' (Masani 1917: 395).

Among Parsis, Kshnoom evokes some of the same response that the occult does in the West. Those not drawn to it sometimes deride it as lowbrow and unscholarly. Also, lectures on Kshnoom are often given in Gujarati (practitioners say that Gujarati has a more powerful vibration than English), and, as a result, many Parsis find lectures difficult to follow (in a recent survey, 44 percent of the elders and 52 percent of the youth said that they thought only in English [Writer 1993: 253]). Yet Kshnoom is the intellectual home for many of the more politically powerful orthodox members of the community. Kshnoomists founded and now run the Council of Vigilant Parsis, a politically effective vehicle for orthodox reform that can initiate meetings attended by hundreds. And many, many Parsis read Kshnoomist material, even if they do not attend the lectures and even if they feel embarrassed about some of the Kshnoomist claims. Above all, Kshnoom advocates the full practice of Zoroastrian rituals, including the menstruation prohibitions, as spiritually meaningful as well as practically effective. That message is compelling for those who are drawn to religious practice but who do not understand the tradition in which they were raised.

The desire to reach out to Zoroastrians who want more from their religion but feel ignorant also inspired a second and possibly more powerful (because more proselytizing) theological innovation. This is an orthodox movement that has emerged under the leadership of a man who studied with Mary Boyce and who returned to Bombay during a time of community unease. He started a revitalization movement, directed at Parsi youth, which promised to take the community back to its roots and to teach it the 'true' Zoroastrian religion. Khojeste Mistree led a series of lectures and discussions in the late 1970s that were received in the community as if, many people said, he were a rock star. He spoke about why the religion was personally meaningful and explained the prayers and rituals. Hundreds and hundreds of people attended the lectures. Mistree became famous, and he and his students formed a religious institution called Zoroastrian Studies. His teachings are widely used within the community and abroad. Yet while widely known, they are also controversial.

Zoroastrian Studies was not simply a new way to teach the theology with which most Parsis grew up and knew vaguely. Instead, Zoroastrian Studies taught a theology founded on the Boyce continuity thesis that argues that the dualism obvious in the later Pahlavi texts reinstates the theology of the *Gāthā*s and that all Zoroastrian religious texts must be regarded as spiritually salient. Mistree believed passionately that this theology was not only the original Zoroastrian theology but also the most sensible religious theology available, and that Zoroastrianism was unique in solving the puzzle of human pain with logic and wisdom:

> If good and evil do come from the same source, why would Zarathushtra so emphatically have declared their different sources and irreconcilable natures? Can a perfect, all-good Being (God) remain perfect, if part of the nature of that Being is deemed to be evil? In Zarathushtra's mind the answer was clearly 'NO!' . . . The great strength of Zoroastrian doctrine lies in the fact that the agency which perpetrates excess or deficiency by way of poverty, chaos, disease and eventually death, is not that which is ordained by God but that which is perpetrated by the antagonistic spirit of evil.
>
> (Mistree 1982: 50)

The claim that Zoroastrianism was special, and that what was special about it was its theology, was deeply appealing even to those who could not quite accept it. 'He would explain the *sudreh-kusti*,' one Parsi remarked, 'and why you should wear it, and you might accept the idea of the *sudreh-kusti* keeping away evil and not quite accept evil as he saw it and still be excited by his teaching.'

Mistree saw his task as not just explaining the religion but also helping Parsis to recreate themselves as a community. He called his teaching text *Zoroastrianism: An Ethnic Perspective* and presented it as a tool to help Zoroastrians learn about themselves. He began his teaching in a period in which there were legitimate fears that the community might disappear altogether. By the time he began to teach, one in five Parsis was over sixty-five, and figures suggested that 20 percent of the community never married and that of those who did marry, one in six marriages was an intermarriage. (When a Parsi female marries a non-Parsi, her children are not accepted as Parsi.) Given the absolute refusal to accept conversion, the community was at serious risk. Mistree hoped to inspire people to save the community by teaching them what was worth saving. The route he chose was orthodoxy, but it was orthodoxy recognizably different from Kshnoom. It did share similarities: Mistree encouraged a far stricter use of ritual than most Parsi practices, as Kshnoomists do, and, like them, he opposed intermarriage and conversion. But, unlike them, he explicitly opposed the Protestantized dualism common in the community, in which the evil principle is subordinated to the good, not equal (or nearly equal) to it, and he did so with the tools of Western scholarship. Far more than the Kshnoomists, he emphasized that Zoroastrianism was different from Hinduism and Christianity (and, by implication, from Islam). He explained that Parsis should not believe in reincarnation because it was a Hindu concept and that they should not believe in the absolute omnipotence of God because it was a Christian concept. And he explicitly presented his theology and practice as a means to revitalize a community he saw as at risk of assimilating out of recognition. It is this emphasis on antiassimilation, intended for people too comfortable with themselves rather than the dispossessed, that makes this orthodoxy seem more like other new orthodoxies among successful diaspora groups (for example, American Jews) and less like communal revivalism common in South Asia.

Perhaps the most interesting feature of Zoroastrian Studies is that it teaches an orthodox Zoroastrianism which is unlike any other Zoroastrianism and, for that matter, unlike religion as experienced by most South Asians. This is because it has been shaped by the needs that gave rise to it, and those needs are deeply modern and specific to a community which fears its own extinction through dissolution into the larger society in which its members are embedded.

The new orthodox Zoroastrianism has the following characteristics. First it has a theological focus, far more so than a religion whose members do not need to rediscover it afresh. Unlike many religious practitioners, those who go through training in Zoroastrian Studies gain a significant appreciation for their own religious texts. They do not simply learn to do the rituals and prayers; they learn about the religion by reading the religious texts and talking about them with each other. Even those who come through the training remark privately that they do not care about the theology by saying that they do not care about '*Bundahishn* this' and 'Pahlavi that' – naming the specific sources they have studied in class. Mistree held classes for his own inner circle, often consisting of text-based theological discussions.

Second, the focus of the teaching is not to convey knowledge for its own sake but to invest the texts, their theology, and their rituals with personal significance. This is done in a deliberate, self-conscious, and intimate manner. After teaching on a theological text, Mistree would often lead a guided meditation on the text, so that students would have their own experience of Zoroastrian imagery. When people told me why they found the Zoroastrian Studies approach so appealing, they cast their story in terms of the personal relevance of its theology. One woman, for example, told me that she had been raised in an orthodox family, and she had followed the rigid laws governing menstruation and purity for many years. But when she was nineteen, her mother died. She said that she fought with God, telling him that he could not take her mother away; and yet he did, and for her it was terribly difficult to come to terms with a God who was supposed to be your protector, whom she had obeyed so earnestly, and who had then betrayed her. When she went to one of Mistree's classes, she was beside herself with excitement. 'I remember clearly the scene that evening, [my son] as a small child on the sofa, as if someone had come in with a new discovery, although all the time it had been there. It was such a relief to know, looking at the dirt and sickness, that God was not responsible.'

Third, this inner experience of the religion as personally meaningful is considered in these classes to be more important than the actual knowledge of the texts or the practice of the ritual. After all, you will only be motivated to follow the religion (and to marry a Parsi) if its rules become emotionally salient to you. Nonetheless it is a striking shift, for the texts and practice of this ancient religion scarcely mention a personal relationship to divinity. Zoroastrian Studies is more interested in getting Parsis to feel committed to their ethnicity than it is in producing orthodoxy: the orthodoxy is a means to an end, and not the reverse. Mistree travels widely and has lectured in many communities where intermarriage is inevitable (a Parsi child may be the only Parsi in his town, for example). There he has urged people to accept a 'two model, one community set up,' so that progressive and orthodox can accept each other and tolerate each other's strategies for preserving the faith and its people. The goal of the many tapes, books, and classes that Zoroastrian Studies produces is to 'catch' people before they leave the faith and to keep them attached to it as best it can.

Fourth, there is an explicit recognition on the part of Zoroastrian Studies that while being born Parsi just happens, being Zoroastrian is a conscious choice. This is not to say that members of Zoroastrian Studies seriously fear that many Parsis will convert out of Zoroastrianism. They know, however, that many Parsis find other faiths more gripping because they know so little about their own. They believe that the job of an organization like Zoroastrian Studies is to make the religion seem different from other religions and more desirable to those born Parsi. And they were the first to see this need so plainly. So Zoroastrian Studies makes Zoroastrianism fun. It organizes field trips with a group of youths and makes sure there is time to party. It printed a children's book on Zoroastrianism with bright, cheery pictures. Out of necessity, the group sees itself as selling something to people who must be persuaded that they want to buy. Their job is to reach out to those previously uncommitted to the faith and to draw them in. The religion they teach may be ancient, but the manner in which they teach it is very modern.

Transmission of the tradition outside of India

Parsi Zoroastrianism has spread widely across the globe, particularly after Indian Independence, when some worried that the Parsi role in non-British India would be much reduced. There are over 10,000 Parsis in North America and over 5,000 in Britain, and there are Parsi communities in Australia, Hong Kong, East Africa, and in many other places.

While Parsis tend to concentrate in particular cities in a country (for example, London, Toronto, Houston, Chicago, and Los Angeles), individual families can be found in many settings. Even the Parsi concentrations are not numerous enough to enable Parsis to socialize with the same exclusivity that they might in Mumbai. As a result, the Zoroastrian experience in these settings is quite different from in Mumbai. There is often no fire temple, no *dokhma*, and no opportunity for the large festival gatherings that mark the Zoroastrian year. Instead, Parsis organize large semiprofessional gatherings called 'congresses,' which in North America meet on an annual basis. They also have organizations that set dates for community dinners and get-togethers. At the 1994 North American Zoroastrian Conference one woman said: 'When you come to this country, there is a common pattern. First you shun all community events. You think of them as boring and unsophisticated. And then after so many people have asked you about Zoroastrianism, and you feel embarrassed but also curious, after you have come to terms with being different, you begin to attend the dinners and congresses and parties, and they do not seem silly but comfortable. And you begin to learn from the congresses how to verbalize what it is to be Zoroastrian.'

In these settings so removed from Mumbai, Parsis have to confront the fact that each has a different sense of what it is to be Parsi. In the congresses, for instance, there are 'youth' groups where young men and women literally sit in a circle and discuss their experience of Zoroastrianism. They discover that it is different for each – a human phenomenon, but one rarely confronted in so explicit a manner. They also confront the inevitability of changes in the tradition. In Houston, it is not possible to demand that your child marry a Parsi. You might go to great effort to introduce your children to other Parsi young adults, and even to send them together on skiing trips and rafting adventures, but if an American-raised Parsi child is the only Parsi in his or her high school or college class, the chance that he or she will marry a Parsi is small. So the dilemmas that seem great conundrums in Mumbai disappear, and the question becomes how to retain any sense of being Zoroastrian at all. Here Mistree's teachings become important, and the style he has adopted has also been adopted by other approaches to the faith. Parsis have constructed teaching texts and take-home study courses to instruct people in their religion, and in North America they have become much more tolerant of spouses from outside who marry into the community, learn about the religion, and may even convert. They also have come to accept the *navjote*s (initiation ceremonies) of those children born of one Parsi parent and one non-Parsi parent.

In North America, these adaptations are made more complicated (or easier, depending on one's perspective) by the fact that Parsis are not the only Zoroastrians. There are in North America many Iranians of Zoroastrian descent who arrived around the time of the fall of the Shāh of Iran. As it happens, some of these Zoroastrians have been quite wealthy and have funded the building of fire temples and community centers. But Iranian Zoroastrianism has a different ethos from Parsi Zoroastrianism. It is less exclusive: there are far fewer restrictions on intermarriage, conversion, and the presence of non-Zoroastrians in fire temples. Iranian Zoroastrians often speak Farsi, and not English, as their first language, and their English is often poor. The tensions between the two communities have been at times considerable, and some community organizations have split along ethnic lines.

Relations with other religions

It has been argued that postexilic Judaism owes much to Zoroastrians through Jewish appreciation for Cyrus, who freed them, and that Judaic concepts of Heaven, Hell, and even of a messiah can be attributed to their enthusiasm for Cyrus' ideas (Boyce 1979). Some even argue, as we saw above, that because Zarathustra was the first to teach the doctrines of an individual judgement, the first to teach of Heaven and Hell, the first to teach of the resurrection of the body and of everlasting life, Zoroastrianism is the source of those concepts in Judaism, Christianity, and Islam (Russell 1987).

In turn, Islam has been the source of most of the trouble Zoroastrianism has had as a religion. Tolerated and harassed at different stages by Muslim Persians, the religion has survived in Iran until the present day but in very small numbers. There are no known historical records that unambiguously demonstrate that the Parsi migration to India was because of religious persecution, but it is commonly assumed that people were motivated to leave Persia in numbers to preserve their right to practice their faith.

Meanwhile, in contemporary India there seems to be relatively little anti-Parsi feeling from Hindus and Muslims. This may be the consequence, at least in part, of the remarkable charitable activity of the community. They built hospitals and schools and other institutional resources that they shared with members of all religions. It is true that when the Prince of Wales went to Bombay in 1921, Indian nationalists boycotted his arrival, Parsis came out to greet him, and urban riots in the wake of the visit left fifty-three people dead. But in general there seems to have been little tension over the last century between Parsi and other religious communities.

The tradition in the study of religions

In the nineteenth century the study of Zoroastrianism was used in the critique of evolutionary arguments that suggested a purely human origin to the belief in God. The discovery of a monotheistic religion that was demonstrably ancient suggested to some Englishmen that religion could not have followed the evolutionary development postulated by anthropologists and thus could not be explained as a psychological phenomenon. As one stated: '(The Gâthâs) present truths of the highest moral and spiritual significance, in a form which constantly reminds us of the Pentateuch and the Prophets. . . . They are absolutely irreconcilable with the theory which regards all spiritual and soul-elevating religions as evolved by a natural process from a primitive naturalistic polytheism: they support the view, which alone supplies a true, rational, and adequate account of the movements of human thought, according to which religious beliefs were first set in motion by communications from God' (Cook 1884: iv, cited in Bilimoria and Alpaivala 1898: 79–80). The early German translations of the texts did indeed have a Christian feel, and some Western scholars of the nineteenth century went so far as to say that Zoroastrianism was the earliest monotheism. Many argued that Zoroastrianism was ethically superior to other faiths (see the collection gathered in Bilimoria and Alpaivala 1898). Meanwhile, in popular elite European culture, Zarathustra became a figure associated with mystic wisdom. The nineteenth-century classicist and philosopher Friedrich Nietzsche borrowed the name of Zarathustra because of its aura, as did Theosophy and other Western esoteric movements.

More recently, academic scholarship has struggled with the attempt to understand the difficult texts and the relationship between the Pahlavi and Avestan materials. The scholarship is deep but limited to a small handful of people who have sufficient knowledge of the languages to engage with the texts. Important scholars include Mary Boyce, Jamsheed K. Choksy, Ilya Gersevitch, John R. Hinnells, Helmut Humbach, Stanley Insler, James R. Russell, and R. C. Zaehner.

Suggested further readings

Boyce (1979); Choksy (1989); Desai (2001); Luhrmann (1996); Mistry (2002a, b); Zaehner (1961).

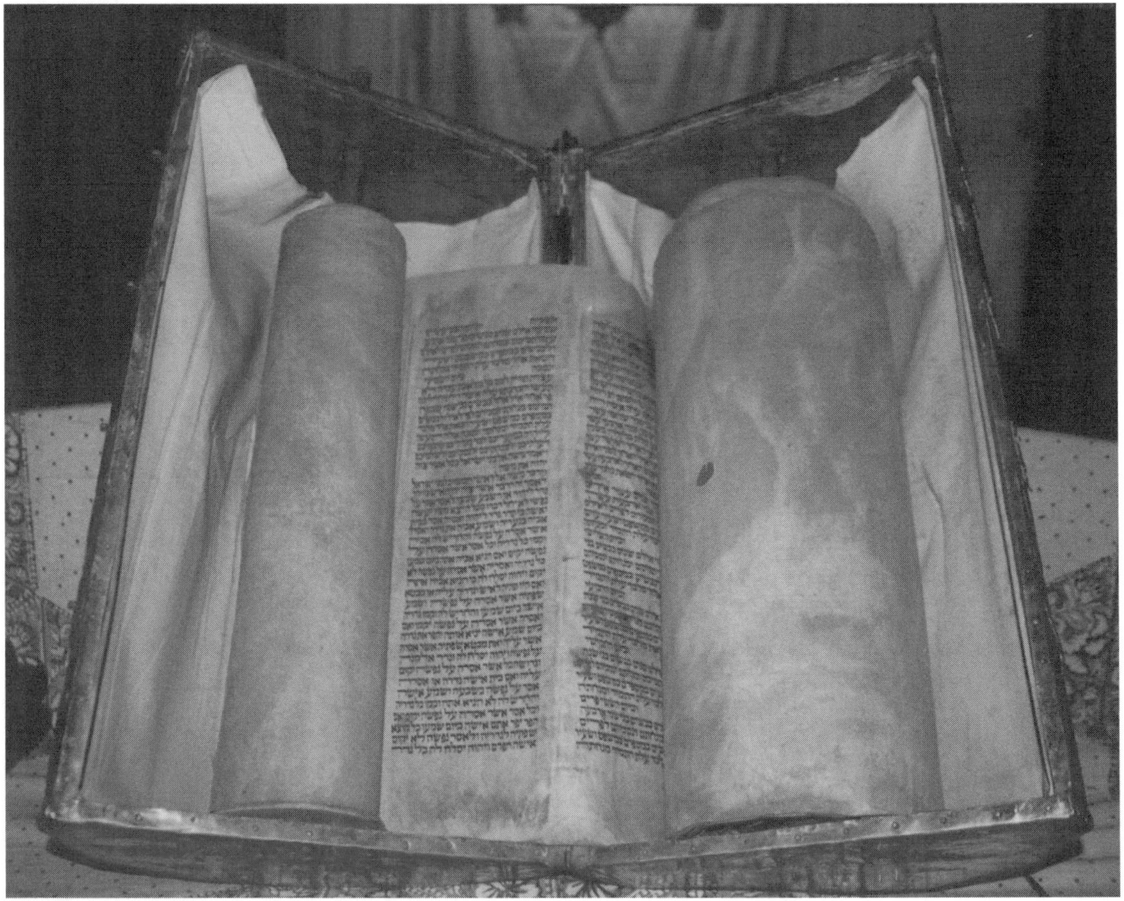

7. Torah scroll in the Bene Israel synagogue at Alibag, south of Mumbai. Courtesy of Professor Shalva Weil.

6

INDIAN JUDAIC TRADITION

Shalva Weil

The tradition defined

Judaism is a universal monotheistic religion with a belief in a transcendent creator of the world. Its fundamental orientation is practical and this-worldly with no official body of dogma. However, it possesses an orthodox system of codification, based on the Pentateuch and the books of the Prophets and the Hagiographa (the Writings) and embodied in the rabbinical traditions of Judaism. It thus rests on the Written Law and the authority of the Oral Law, notably the Talmud, and its codifications. These laws such as *kashrut* (dietary laws) are designed to elevate the Jew and distinguish him or her from animals as well as to define his or her religion vis-à-vis peoples from other religions.

Judaism places emphasis on the observance of the commandments, between Man and God and between Man and Man. The religion is organized around Jewish liturgy, the festivals, and the rituals that mark the lifecycle. Jewish themes span the creation of the universe, God's covenant with the patriarchs (Abraham, Isaac, and Jacob), the liberation from bondage in Egypt, the revelation at Mount Sinai, Israel as a homeland, and the future Redemption in the messianic age. Judaism also incorporates more mystical traditions, as exemplified by Hasidic and kabbalistic practices, which are not necessarily accepted by the mainstream.

Judaism has never been a significant religious force in South Asia, and there has never been more than a miniscule number of Jews there. Judaism, a monotheistic and iconoclastic religion, has even appeared to be in opposition to the dominant religion of Hinduism with its emphases on polytheism and iconocentrism, although in recent years similarities have been expounded. Judaism is practiced in a community with a minimum of ten men, namely, a *minyan* (quorum), and does not encourage individual, otherworldly expressions of spirituality. In the Orthodox and the Conservative traditions, a person is Jewish matrilineally, religion being defined by the mother. In the Reform and the Liberal branches of Judaism, a person can be Jewish patrilineally, too. A person can become Jewish through conversion, but Judaism is a nonproselyte religion and does not encourage converts.

Ancient South Asian Jewish communities have been found only in India, where three minutely different Jewish communities flourished. At their peak in 1947, these Jewish communities numbered 23,000 souls (Reissner 1950), although their contribution to India was outstanding in the academic, literary, and military fields (Roland 2002). Today, no more than 5,000 Jewish members of all three communities remain, while larger Indian Jewish diasporas flourish abroad. In addition, some groups, primarily in the states of Mizoram and Manipur in northeast India and in Tiddim in Burma, are claiming that they are descendants of the 'Lost Israelites.' From the nineteenth century on, tiny Jewish communities functioned in Burma, Singapore, Malaya, China, Thailand, and elsewhere. Established by Jews of Iraqi origin, these latter communities were frequented in the second half of the twentieth century by Jews who found a temporary haven there after the Holocaust as well as occasionally by Jewish and Israeli businessmen and transients.

Cosmos and history

Judaism is based on the study and interpretation of texts and praxis within Jewish communities. As far as we know, Jewish communities per se were not established in South Asia until relatively late (although Judaism may have reached the Malabar Coast in the first century), but there is evidence of Jewish contact with local inhabitants in South Asia long before. Linguistic evidence confirms the possibility of early commercial connections between Israel and South Asia from the time of the Bible, where in the book of Kings, the ships of King Solomon (*c.* tenth century BCE) transported cargo with *kofim* (Hebrew: apes), *tukim* (peacocks), and *almag* (sandalwood). These words of Dravidian origin (*almag* is said to be *valgum*) found in the Hebrew Bible confirm the possibility that early traders brought back items of South Indian origin to build the Temple. There is no evidence that the Jewish traders or King Solomon's henchmen set up Jewish communities.

Travelers' tales in the Talmud mention trade with India (Hoddu) and include specific Indian commodities, such as ginger and iron, but, although they refer to Hindus and Jews, they make no reference to Indian Jews. In the book of Esther, the kingdom of King Ahaseuerus stretched from Hoddu to Kush, which is usually said to be Nubia or Ethiopia.

From the ninth century CE, Jewish merchants known as Raadanites traded from the Middle East to South Asia and back. Documents discovered in the Cairo Genizah describe trade in spices, pharmaceuticals, textiles, metals, gold, silver, and silks from the eleventh to the thirteenth centuries between Arabic-speaking Jews and Hindu partners. However, the evidence does not indicate that Judaism was disseminated.

In the seventeenth century Jewish merchant centers were established in Madras, Calicut, and other places. In addition, an independent Jewish traveler, Hazrat Saeed Sarmad, carried on trade between Armenia, Persia, and India and practiced Judaism until he renounced a materialistic life to become a Hindu ascetic or *sādhu*. Aurangzīb, the Mughal emperor of India, executed Sarmad in 1659 (Ezekiel 1966).

During the nineteenth century, Jewish emissaries traveled to Asia from Palestine and other Jewish centers to make contact with Jews in far-flung places, often in the belief that the scattered Jews were members of the legendary ten lost tribes. According to the Bible, the tribes of the Kingdom of Israel were conquered by the Assyrian kings from 725 BCE on and were exiled to 'Halah, Habor, the cities of Medes, and the river Gozan.' There has been speculation over the years that the tribes wandered to the Hindu Kush and India and possibly further afield and that the river Gozan mentioned in the Bible may in fact be the Ganges.

Three established communities of Jews practiced Judaism as a religion in South

Asia: the Bene Israel, the Cochin Jews, and the Baghdadis. All three communities operated in India. Before Partition, the Bene Israel had synagogues in Karachi (today Pakistan), Aden, and Rangoon, Burma. The Baghdadis established Jewish communities wherever they handled their commerce in Burma, Singapore, Malaya, Hong Kong, China, Thailand, and elsewhere.

According to the Bene Israel tradition, the ancestors of their community were members of the lost tribes of Israel who had stayed in the Kingdom of Israel. They set sail around the year 175 BCE from Israel to escape persecution by enemy conquerors. Their ship capsized off the coast of Konkan, south of present-day Mumbai. The survivors lost all their possessions, including their holy books. Welcomed by the local Hindus, the Jews took up the occupation of pressing vegetable oil. They were called Shanwār Telīs ('Saturday Oilmen') because they refrained from work on Saturday in accordance with the dictates of the Jewish religion. They remembered the Jewish prayer 'Hear O Israel!' declaring monotheism; they observed some of the Jewish holidays and fasts; and they circumcised their sons as commanded by the Jewish religion. However, they did not know the Oral Law, had no rabbis, and were isolated from the practices and customs of mainstream Jewry.

From the eighteenth century on the Bene Israel began a lengthy process of bringing their practices in line with other Jewish communities in the world. This process was aided by their contact with the British in India, the resulting move to Bombay and other cities, and access to the English language and higher education. The ultimate outcome of their identification with world Jewry was the gradual emigration of the majority of the Bene Israel community to the Jewish state in Israel during the last half of the twentieth century.

The Jewish settlement of the Cochin Jews on the Malabar Coast is ancient. One theory holds that they arrived with King Solomon's merchants, as mentioned above, although there is no corroboration that a community was actually established. Another account, repeated in South Indian legends, claims they arrived in the first century CE, when Saint Thomas (d. CE 53), the disciple of Jesus, supposedly brought Christianity to India. Records noting that the ruler Bhāskāra Ravi Varman (CE 962–1020) granted seventy-two privileges to the leader of the Jews, Joseph Rabban, document the Jewish settlement in Kerala. In 1344 the Jews moved from Cranganore to Cochin.

During the Portuguese period and after Vasco da Gama (*c.* 1460–1524) led an expedition via the Cape of Good Hope to India in 1497–98, some Jewish traders from Europe and elsewhere settled in Cochin to become part of the Paradesī (Malayalam: foreigner's) Jewish community, whose synagogue was established in 1568. One member of that community, who rose to prominence under Dutch rule, was Ezekiel Rahabi (1694–1771); he acted as the principal merchant for the Dutch in Cochin and signed his memoranda in Hebrew. The Paradesī synagogue celebrated its quarter centenary in the presence of Prime Minister Indira Gandhi in 1968.

The Malabari Jews, who claim original settlement in the area, lived in five major settlements – Cochin, Ernakulam, Chendamanglam, Mala, and Parur – where they established seven synagogues and led a full Jewish community life. After the establishment of the State of Israel in 1948, most of the Jews from Cochin, motivated by Zionism, immigrated as a community to Israel in 1954.

From the eighteenth century on, Jews from Baghdad and other cities in Iraq shifted their enterprises to India and other South Asian centers. One of the founders of the

Bombay community was Joseph Semah, who arrived in India in 1730 from Surat; another was Shalom Cohen, a merchant who settled in Calcutta in 1798. Other Jews, who established thriving businesses in the East, as far afield as Singapore, Hong Kong, and Shanghai, as well as magnificent Jewish community structures, followed the Jewish merchants, who escaped deteriorating conditions in Iraq. The 'Baghdadis,' as they became known, kept up family and trade ties with other members of their community throughout South Asia. One of the most prolific families was the Sassoon family, who arrived in Bombay in 1832. After the withdrawal from India of the British, with whom the Baghdadi Jews had associated as non-native Indians, many of them decided to emigrate to England and other English-speaking countries and a few to Israel.

Sacred life and literature

Sacred life among Jews is all-encompassing, covering both lifecycle events and the rhythm of the festivals. All three groups of Indian Jews adhere to the monotheistic nature of Judaism and observe the major festivals and commandments. Some of the sacred life of the Indian Jews is unique, however, influenced by Hindu and Muslim practices. This is particularly the case with the Bene Israel of Maharashtra, who led an integrated life in Indian society, distinguished from their neighbors only by their belief and practice of the Jewish religion. Even among the Cochin Jews and the Baghdadis, Indian Judaism developed special traits, such as partaking of Indian delicacies on particular festivals or the observance of specific wedding or burial customs, which reflect the influence of local customs.

The most important Jewish festivals for the Bene Israel are Rosh Hashana (New Year), Yom Kippur (Day of Atonement), Simhat Torah (Rejoicing of the Torah), and Pessach (Passover). On Rosh Hashana the whole community appears in its finery in synagogue, and between Rosh Hashana and Yom Kippur it is customary to visit friends and family. The day after Yom Kippur is known as Shila San or 'Festival of Stale Things,' a festival not observed by members of other Jewish communities, when Bene Israel members visit relatives, offering them *gharrie*s, a type of doughnut made of rice and wheat flour, yeast, and overripe cooked scrapings of cucumber fried in oil.

On Yom Kippur, known as 'The Festival of the Closing of the Doors,' members of the Bene Israel community, dressed exclusively in white, arrive in synagogue before dawn so as to avoid contact with other (polluting) people on the way (Weil 1994).

On Simhat Torah, the Bene Israel celebrate by dancing merrily in the synagogue; they auction off all the *aliyoth* (literally 'going up' to the Torah), as well as the four species used in ritual worship on the festival of Tabernacles (of which Simhat Torah is a culmination), and the right to pull down the fruits hanging in the synagogue *sukka* (tabernacle).

On Pessach, Bene Israel make *matzot*, the traditional unleavened bread eaten by Jews on this festival, from rice rather than wheat. Some whitewash their houses and tin all their copper pots.

In addition, the Bene Israel observe particular folk customs, such as hair-shaving ceremonies for babies, pilgrimages, and special ways of celebrating the festivals, often adapted from local customs. An unusual feature of Bene Israel religious worship is the intensive belief in the popular Jewish prophet Eliyahoo Hannabi (the prophet Elijah), reminiscent of saint worship in Hinduism and Islam, although also known in Judaism. Elijah is invoked on all auspicious occasions, including circumcisions and purification after childbirth. Whereas Jews in other Jewish communities in the world believe that Elijah ascended to heaven from a site somewhere near present-day Haifa in Israel, the Bene Israel fervently believe that he departed on his chariot from a village called Khandalla in the Konkan. Bene Israel go on pilgrimage to the site, where they point out the footprints of Elijah's horses. There, they make wishes for the redemption of vows or pray for thanksgiving (Weil 2002a).

Lifecycle rituals also include some unique elements. For example, the evening before the marriage ceremony, the *mehaṁdī* (henna) ceremony takes place simultaneously in the houses of the bride and groom, who wear flowers tied round their heads, and have henna daubed ritually on their forefingers. A dish called *melida* is prepared, composed of rice flour and sugar covered with fruit and decorated with a rose in the center, while frankincense is burned by the side. The *melida* is blessed and distributed, and the prophet Elijah is invoked.

Among the Cochin Jews, the rituals of the annual cycle, as well as the lifecycle, are imbued with sacred vitality. During Rosh Hashana, the men wear white shirts, sometimes with a pale-colored design, and the women wear long white *luṅgīs*; fresh skullcaps for men and new kerchiefs for women and girls are prepared. After prayers on Rosh Hashana, blessings over the fruits and vegetables follow Kiddush, the sanctification of the wine. The practice of this custom is more elaborate than in other Jewish communities around the world. On the eve of Yom Kippur, between the last meal and the beginning of prayers at the synagogue, all family members ask forgiveness from each other, as is customary in many Jewish communities; then children go to the elder members of the extended family, bend to the ground with both hands to touch the latter's bare feet and kiss their fingertips (a distinctly Indian custom) as the elders put their hands on the children's heads and bless them.

On the festival of Succot (Tabernacles), the community erects a booth (Hebrew *sukka*; Malayalam *paṇḍāl*) in the synagogue grounds, which is a temporary structure, covered with palm leaves, commemorating the temporary shelters in which the Israelites lived during their forty-year sojourn in the Sinai Desert. In the Cochin Jewish community, every family covers the *paṇḍāl* with plaited coconut palms and decorates it with leaves, flowers, fruits, and jasmine garlands. On Simhat Torah, a temporary ark, *manara* (Malayalam), is constructed in front of the *heichal* (Hebrew), the ark, of the synagogue, and the Torah scrolls, with silver or gold metal cases, are displayed in it. During the morning and afternoon prayers, there are seven circumambulations around the downstairs pulpit while young men carry the Torah scrolls. The liturgy, texts, and melodies are performed in local Shingli style to the accompaniment of singing, handclapping, and dancing, with everyone partaking of alcoholic drinks and refreshments. (Shingli is a language and performance style originating in Southern India. Its exact place of origin is unknown. While it may be associated with Sri Lanka, it is generally believed to be from Cranganore, now Kodungalloor, in the state of Kerala.) According to Cochin custom, the most recently married bridegroom should read the beginning of the new cycle of the Torah, since symbolically every Jew should be 'wedded' to the Torah.

The cleaning of the house for Pessach and the preparation of special unleavened foods and handmade *matzot* keeps Jewish families busy for months before the festival. Forty-nine days, ritually counted every night, link the festivals of Pessach and Shavuot (Pentecost), the day on which the Jews received the Torah from God on Mount Sinai. On this day, the special Cochin Shingli liturgy is recited, in addition to the prayers in the traditional prayer book. At the synagogue, adults shower the children with sweets and tiny Indian baked sweet balls called *chukunda*.

Among the many unique Jewish customs of the Cochin Jews, outstanding is the wedding ceremony, when the groom himself recites the benedictions. In other Jewish communities, the rabbi or guests recite these blessings. Under the *chupa* (bridal canopy), he holds a gold chalice containing wine in which the wedding ring, tied to a loop made with seven strings, is immersed. He himself states that he is betrothed to his bride according to the laws of Moses and Israel. He drinks from the cup, which he gives to his bride, and places the ring on the index finger of her right hand, with the words 'Behold, thou art consecrated to me.' A young boy then reads the *ketuba* (marriage contract), according to Shingli custom (Hallegua 2002).

Among the Baghdadi Jews, sacred life was influenced by Muslim practice in Iraq as well as new customs adopted in India. A number of rituals were devised for the protection of the mother and child around birth, including wearing charms and hanging amulets at the baby's bedside. Nutmeg, garlic, a small blue bead, and God's name might be pinned onto the baby in order to safeguard him or her. Sometimes, when an elderly person died, a piece of the shroud was used to make a garment for the newborn child, to ensure that he or she live a long life. On the fifth night after birth, the baby was held in the arms of a female relative and an ornamental *pañjā* (hand) was daubed in saffron on the wall of the room to keep evil spirits away. In India, the children tossed a large sheet on which sweets, chocolates, peanuts, sunflower seeds, dried dates, popcorn, and roasted chickpeas were placed and shouted *shasha* as they shook the sheet. They then put the sweets and seeds into little bags and distributed them to the offspring of family and friends. A party used to be held the night before the circumcision at which *mezammerim* (singers) sang Hebrew and Arabic songs, learned men read out portions of the kabbalistic book, the *Zohar*, and a musician played a harmonium while guests were entertained at a dinner party. At the circumcision ceremony, at home or in the synagogue, the godmother, *takhdumai*, carried the baby boy into the room and handed him over to the godfather, *sandak*, who then took a seat on Elijah's chair with the baby on his lap. While the women were shouting 'Kilililee, kilililee,' the *mohel* (ritual circumciser) performed the operation (Cooper and Cooper 2002).

In the past marriages were arranged. Once the girl's family had accepted the proposal from the boy's father, the contract was formalized, and the engagement was known as *bāt pakkā*, a Hindi designation, indicating that negotiations had been completed. The groom's family gave the bride a small gift of jewelry such as gold bangles. Some time after the *bāt pakkā*, the marriage was held in the synagogue. Prior to the wedding, a henna party for the bride known as the *khadbah*, a word of Arabic origin, was held. On the morning after the wedding, the bride's mother sent a tray of sweetmeats, including *badām jalakī* (almond rings), to her daughter and son-in-law. During the rest of the week, the bride's family hosted the *sheva brachot* (Hebrew: seven blessings). On the Saturday after the wedding, the bride's mother gave a party for the women celebrating the consummation of the marriage and her daughter's initiation as a woman.

The sacred literature of South Asian Jews is based on the Bible, the books of the Prophets, and the Writings. Portions of these books are recited in the sacred language Hebrew every week in synagogues around the world. The Bene Israel, who constituted the largest Jewish group in South Asia, were ignorant of the Oral Law and the interpretations on the Bible developed by other Jewish communities and only became aware of them relatively late in history. Nevertheless, they read out the Portion of the Week in Hebrew and recited prayers in Hebrew in the synagogue. Primarily the Christian missionaries translated the Bible and some other holy books for them in the nineteenth century into vernacular languages such as Marathi. Ironically, missionary activity resulted in a rapprochement of the Bene Israel to Judaism and not to Christianity. The missionaries reinforced the Bene Israel's Jewish identity by establishing schools for the Bene Israel children, educating them in the English language, and translating the Jewish Prayer book and other religious works from Hebrew into Marathi. This encouraged the Bene Israel to translate their holy books into Marathi. In 1846 an illustrated Passover Haggada telling the story of the exodus of the Children of Israel from Egypt appeared in Marathi.

In Cochin the Jews, who were in touch with Portuguese and Dutch Jewry, pray from the standard Jewish Sefardi (Spanish and Portuguese) prayer book used by Sefardi communities all over the world. (The Ashkenazi Jews who originated in Germany and Europe have their own prayer book, which is similar but contains some variations.) In addition, they knew the Oral Law and the interpretations on the texts, but they never produced their own rabbis. They also recited special prayer songs, composed in Shingli. The identities of most of the composers, as well as the exact dates of authorship, are unknown, but the musical heritage is preserved by all the different communities of Cochin Jews.

The Baghdadi Jews had a strong tradition of scholarship from Iraq, which produced many of the world's greatest rabbis and *halachic* (Jewish legal) decisions. They ordered their lives around Jewish legal response and produced many books of Jewish interest. In particular, they delved into Jewish mysticism and read the *Zohar*, a kabbalistic text, on ritual occasions. In Calcutta and in Bombay, the Baghdadi Jews operated several presses, both translating holy texts into Hebrew and publishing original works. Many of these were written in Judeo-Arabic, the Baghdadi Jews' dialect.

Oral tradition bolstered the written word in keeping alive the sacred life of India's Jews. Between the Bene Israel, the *kīrtana* (Sanskrit: literally 'poet,' 'seer') is just one form of communication, along with ballads, folk songs, and short songs, which served as an educational tool repeating refrains from the Bible. The *kīrtana* was aimed at simple people and had a popularist character. The Bene Israel probably adopted it some time at the end of the eighteenth century. During the nineteenth century, it gained in popularity and consisted of the presentation of biblical stories composed in Marathi verse, the vernacular of the Bene Israel, and sung to Hindi tunes by the *kīrtanakāra* (lead singer of the *kīrtana*), usually with musical accompaniment. By the end of the nineteenth century, a special Bene Israel *kīrtana* group had formed in Bombay. Associated with this group was Benjamin Samson Ashtamkar, still remembered today by Bene Israel as the greatest *kīrtanakāra*, who composed many biblical and apocryphal *kīrtana*s.

Cochin Jewish Malayalam folk songs, traditionally sung by Jewish women in Kerala, cover biblical, wedding, historical, and ritual themes (Weil 1982). In the Song of

Everayi, the narrator tells of one Ephraim the Mudaliyar, accompanied by Rabbi Abraham the Dutch, who began his sojourn to Cochin in Jerusalem, stopping in Egypt and Yemen and ending up in Paloor Bay in Kerala with a carpenter who constructed the synagogue. The Malayalam song apparently reiterates the route the ancient Israelites took to Cochin (Jussay 1982). Today the Cochin Malayali women's tradition is being revived in Israel in an international project (see Johnson 2002).

Institutions and practices

The heart of any Jewish collectivity is the Jewish community and communal institutions. The South Asian Jewish communities are no exception. In 1796 the first Bene Israel synagogue, Shaar Harahamim (the Gate of Mercy) was consecrated at Mandvi in Bombay by Commandant Samaji Hasaji Divekar as a thanksgiving for his escape from death while a prisoner of Ṭipū Sulṭān during the Second Anglo-Mysore War. In 1843 some Bene Israel broke away from that synagogue to establish the city's second synagogue, the Shaarei Ratson (Gates of Desire), also known as the New Synagogue. More than thirty synagogues and prayer halls have since been built in India.

As a result of the opportunities offered to the Bene Israel by the British in the army and the railways, at the end of the nineteenth century, Bene Israel families began to immigrate to other centers as far as Burma and Aden. Groups of Bene Israel lived in the hill-stations along the railway lines; a large community was settled in Karachi. In 1856 the Bene Israel began settling in Poona, and the Baghdadi Jews and the Bene Israel concentrated in neighborhoods like Rasta Peth and the adjoining Nana Peth. The lane in which the Succoth Shelemo (Tabernacle of Solomon) synagogue was erected in 1921 is called Israel Alley. In 1934 another Bene Israel synagogue was built in Ahmedabad. In 1956 the Judah Hyam Prayer Hall was opened in New Delhi to cater for the needs of Jews in the capital city. Today only a few of these are able to maintain a regular *minyan* (quorum) on the Sabbath, and in the villages outside Mumbai several beautiful synagogues rarely open for prayers during the year. All synagogues in India, except the Jewish Religious Union, which was affiliated with the British Liberal Union, follow the Orthodox tradition, despite their overt affiliation to different synagogue movements outside India. The Jewish Religious Union was founded in Bombay in 1925 by Jerusha Jhirad, a Bene Israel gynecologist, who in 1966 received the distinguished Padma Shri award for outstanding services in the field of social welfare. In the 1950s this synagogue commissioned Liberal rabbis from abroad to minister to the congregation. The Bene Israel themselves never produced a rabbi of their own in India, although individuals versed both in Sefardi and Bene Israel liturgy acted as *hazzanim* (cantors) in the synagogues. Recently, an Israeli-trained Bene Israel rabbi has served in Mumbai.

A variety of sports clubs, Zionist organizations, and charitable and credit associations operated in Bombay, Poona, and other centers over the years. The Stree Mandel, which was established in 1913 as a women's organization, is still active today. In 1875 'The Bene Israel Benevolent Society for Promoting Education' established the 'Israelite School,' an English-language primary school that developed into a high school in 1892. In the 1930s the school became known as the Elly Kadoorie School after its Baghdadi benefactor and taught its pupils, most of whom were Jewish, Hebrew as well as English and Marathi. Today the school has become a Marathi-language school in which fewer than twenty of the 1,200 pupils are Jewish. The Israelite School Old Students' Union, which later became known as the Maccabean Fellowship, was established in 1917. The Jacob Sassoon Free School's pupils were in the past nearly all Jewish. The Bombay ORT school for boys was established in 1962, and the school for girls in 1970. The ORT schools provide technical and vocational training for Bene Israel students, many of whom immigrated to Israel with a basic knowledge of Hebrew.

The Bene Israel in India today represent a vibrant, if small, community. Owing to large-scale emigration, communal activity has declined, and Bene Israel newspapers and periodicals, once prolific, are now published infrequently. Notwithstanding, consolidation has taken place between the different Indian Jewish communities; in 1979 the Council of Indian Jewry was established to represent the interests of all Indian Jews. Due to lack of numbers, members of the Bene Israel and Baghdadi communities and Jews of other origins are forced to cooperate in order to maintain communal institutions. In 2004, the Mumbai Jewish community baked communal *matzot* together and distributed them to all members.

The Cochin Jews are organized in eight communities or *yogam*, each around its own synagogue, which acts as a social control device that determines the fate of its members. In extreme cases, where social taboos are ignored, the congregation can excommunicate a member. One of the earliest records of the division in the community was recorded in 1344, when some of the Jews from Cranganore moved to Cochin, three years after the port of Cranganore was silted up and Cochin was founded. The divisions between the Paradesī Jews and the other Malabaris are well documented (Segal 1967). In addition to synagogue services, many social activities are organized around the synagogue compound. In particular, Zionist meetings are held with emissaries who arrived from Palestine before and after the establishment of the State of Israel.

Baghdadi Jewish institutional life was founded in Calcutta by the first settlers and enhanced by members of the Sassoon and Elias dynasties. In 1832 the prince of the Exilarch, David Sassoon (1792–1864), while fleeing with his family from the persecutions of the Daud Pasha of Baghdad, arrived in Bombay. He established the Magen David synagogue in 1861. Jacob Sassoon constructed the magnificent Knesseth Eliyahoo synagogue in 1884. In addition, the Sassoon families donated to hospitals, schools, libraries, and more. In Calcutta, the Baghdadis constructed as many as eight synagogues with more than 100 Torah scrolls in the city. In the summer, in the heyday before Partition, they set up home-away-from-home with sports clubs, Jewish scouts, and prayer meetings in Darjeeling, the mountain resort famous for aromatic tea, and in the winter, in Madhapur, a railway-junction town frequented by Anglo-Indians.

Ethics and human relations

India has been the model host country for different communities of Jews, who have never suffered from anti-Semitism at the hands of their fellow countrymen (except during a brief period in South India under the Portuguese).

Since the Indian Jews were so well integrated into society and not persecuted, they developed caste-like traits, defining their place in society. They were thus influenced in their external relations with Hindus, Muslims, and Christians, and they were affected internally. Thus, the Bene Israel, although 'out-of-caste,' were, as we have seen, incorporated in the villages as Shanwār Telīs or 'Saturday Oilmen,' and many rose during the nineteenth and twentieth centuries in the hierarchy to 'clerk caste' or middle class. Internally, they were divided into subcategories, reminiscent of subcastes, made up of 'White' and 'Black' Jews, designated *gorā* or *kālā*. Traditionally, these two groups never intermarried and never interdined, although the distinctions have all but faded in recent years. The Cochin Jews, similarly, appear to have been influenced by the hierarchical system of society. They are divided into 'White' or 'Paradesī' Jews non-indigenous to Kerala, and Malabari 'Black' Jews who claim that they were the original inhabitants. Members of the two minute groups have never intermarried; they were organized in separate communities with their own synagogues, and in the past, interaction was restricted in different spheres between them. In addition, the Paradesī Jews had manumitted slaves known as *meshurarim*, with whom they did not intermarry and who did not have rights to go up and read from the Torah. The struggle against this state of affairs began with A. B. Salem, a lawyer, who became the leader of the *meshurarim* and fought for equal rights for this group. Today these divisions have disappeared, and members of the Paradesī community have married with the *meshurarim*, particularly after the transplantation of the majority of the community to Israel.

The Baghdadi Jews, in their turn, mixed with the British Rāj and, as non-Indians, were accepted in their clubs and social circles. Baghdadi Jews would not pray in the synagogues of the Bene Israel, whom they did not regard as full Jews, possibly imitating the caste-like divisions in Indian society. Again, declining numbers have changed this situation, and today there are no Baghdadi Jews left to run the synagogue services in Mumbai so a Bene Israel *hazan* (cantor) is employed.

Since Jewish doctrine emphasizes, 'Jews are responsible for one another,' they build strong communities in which the synagogue is the center. The mutual responsibility of Jews for one another extends to charity and justice. For example, the Home for Destitutes and Orphans, which today caters for a handful of elderly people, was established in its present form in Bombay in 1934. The home had its precursor in the 'Bene Israel Benevolent Society' of 1853, one of the earliest Bene Israel voluntary organizations of which we have a record. Beyond the Jewish community, Jews also believe that they should contribute on a humanitarian basis to others less fortunate than themselves. The Bene Israel and Cochin Jewish communities extended charity and education to their members and were well respected in larger society.

The Baghdadi Jews, who included among their ranks wealthy dynasties such as the Sassoons, not only established strong Jewish communities in Bombay, Calcutta, Rangoon, and other cities in South Asia but also looked after poorer Jews and contributed to the wider society. In Mumbai, by way of example, David Sassoon established the David Sassoon Mechanics Institute, the David Sassoon Library and Reading Room, the David Sassoon Industrial and Reformatory Institution, the Clock Tower at the Victoria Gardens (now the Veermata Jijimata Udyan), and the Statue of the Prince Consort at the Victoria and Albert Museum (now the Bhau Daji Lad Museum). In the 1860s David Sassoon contributed to an old-age home for the destitute, the David Sassoon Infirm Asylum Niwara, and to the Sassoon Hospital in Pune, which was completed after his death in 1867. Today the Sassoon Hospital is the largest district hospital for Pune District, incorporating in its compound the Sir Jacob Sassoon European Hospital, opened in 1909, and the Rachel Sassoon Hospital. In Mumbai, David Sassoon's son Albert contributed toward the Elphinstone Technical High

School, which was also called the Sassoon Building; Sir Jacob Sassoon built the Sir Jacob Sassoon High School (1903) at Byculla, which many Bene Israel children attended; Sir Jacob was also the largest single donor toward the famous Mumbai monument, the Gateway of India, constructed in 1924; and his brother Edward Elias (1853–1924) invested in the E. E. E. Sassoon High School (Lentin 2002).

Special mention must be made of the way the Jewish communities and Indian society at large received refugees from the Holocaust and offered them a haven (see Bhatti and Voigt 1999).

Today, despite their low numbers, the Jews of South Asia are remembered for the just treatment meted out to other Jews and their contribution to others, which can still be viewed in surviving institutions in several cities.

Modern expressions

The Indo-Judaic tradition in South Asia has largely come in line with the form of Judaism practiced in Israel and in other Jewish communities. Synagogue attendance is dwindling in India as intermarriage with members of other religions is rising; there are fewer and fewer who know how to lead a prayer service, and synagogues are neglected or being closed. More Bene Israel are concentrating in Thane, a suburb of Mumbai, and a few other pockets of religious life, where regular prayers continue unabated.

Today's Jews of India can be divided into two subgroups: those who stay because of their overriding attachment to India, and those who will emigrate to Israel and reunite with their families and the majority of their community. The former group includes Indian nationalists, non-Zionists, and those who are too old to envisage emigration. The latter group includes Zionists who see the eventual future of the Indian Jewish community in Israel, in spite of hundreds of years of harmonic coexistence with the non-Jewish population of India. There are many visits between the two countries, as Indian Jews and young Israeli backpackers go back and forth to India and other popular destinations among post-army youth. Despite the relatively large numbers of Israeli and Jewish travelers visiting different locations in South Asia, to the best of my knowledge, no new Jewish communities have been established in South Asia. However, the Lubavitcher Hasidic movement (Chabad) holds an annual communal *seder* (meal at which the exodus from Egypt is recounted) at Passover for Israeli and Jewish backpackers in Kathmandu, Nepal.

Over the past fifty years, small groups in different parts of India have identified with Jews, although none of them is accepted officially as Jewish unless they convert to Judaism in cooperation with recognized Jewish religious authorities. The most prominent group, collectively known as the Shinlung, claims descent from the Ten Lost Tribes. This group, composed of Kukī and other tribes from Mizoram and Manipur states with an offshoot in Tiddim in Burma, has adopted some Judaic practices since the 1960s. These people, who today call themselves the 'Children of Menasseh,' have set up Jewish prayer halls and observe certain Jewish customs. Over 700 from Manipur and Mizoram have immigrated to Israel and converted to Orthodox Judaism there. Groups claiming to descend from the Ten Lost Tribes also have emerged in Andhra Pradesh and other regions of India.

Transmission of the tradition outside of India

The Indo-Judaic religious tradition has survived in diasporic communities of Indian Jews primarily in Israel. In 1947 the British pulled out of India, and the following year, the State of Israel was declared. Today, due to natural increase, over 50,000 Bene Israel reside in Israel; almost the entire community of Cochin Jews lives in Israel, where they number some 7,000; and some 1,000 Baghdadi Jews are also found in Israel. As we saw above, the Baghdadi Jews identified with their British rulers, so when the British Rāj disintegrated in Asia, most Baghdadis preferred to emigrate to England, Australia, and North America, where they created new diasporic communities. Many Baghdadi Jews write with nostalgia of their previous homes in India and, tracing their family histories over decades and continents, describe the new environment they created in other countries (see, for example, Silliman 2001).

The process of emigration and the adaptation of the Bene Israel in their new homeland in Israel entailed many changes in religious life. At first, the Bene Israel were not accepted as 'full Jews' in Israel, and they were only recognized as such after a two-year struggle with demonstrations and strikes in 1962–64. Their nonacceptance by other Jews is still a bitter memory today. In Israel, the Bene Israel adapted some of their traditions and took on others. For example, it is no longer possible to visit the Elijah site in Konkan, so Bene Israel visit Mount Carmel. They have also adopted many items from the Oral Law, which they did not know in the past. However, a surprising number of Indian traditions live on, such as the prewedding *mehaṁdī* ceremony and the *melida*. The younger generation of Indians define themselves as Israelis and tend to classify themselves as 'secular' or 'religious' Israelis, but the majority say they are 'traditional.'

In Israel, the Bene Israel organize as a community, spinning family and ethnic ties tighter and tighter. While there is increasing marriage with other Jews in Israel, the vast majority are still endogamous, that is, contracted within the ethnic community. Marriage is sometimes negotiated across national borders; social relationships and political orientations are conducted irrespective of territorial blocks. The educated elite communicates with kin and friends through the Internet. For the less educated, the video reformulates the cultural traditions of the Indian diaspora and 'markets' India over the screen. Bene Israel in Israel read and write in Marathi newspapers like *Mai Bolli*; telephones speed up the ever-present communication. Every year, along with regular young Israeli backpackers, hundreds of Bene Israel go to India in organized groups to pray in the synagogues there and buy the latest Indian fashion and jewelry. These 'Indian' tourists to India return with suitcases stuffed with spices, gold, silks, and scarves, as well as letters and gifts for friends and relatives who could not make the journey. They then 'return' to their Israeli homeland with tangible pieces of their previous 'homeland,' India. In addition, they keep up ties between Israel and other smaller Bene Israel 'diasporas' in the United Kingdom, Canada, United States, and Australia.

The Cochin Jews live primarily in agricultural settlements in Israel, and while there is no wider Cochin Jewish 'diaspora,' Cochin Jews also move between Israel and India, particularly in the last decade. In Israel, where there are Cochin Jewish synagogues, such as the synagogue at the *moshav* (agricultural settlement) called Nevatim, Cochin Jews pray according to Shingli rites and enact their religious ceremonies according to

Cochin custom, but they are also influenced by general Israeli trends; many are exogamous marrying Jews of other ethnic origins. At Nevatim, there is a Cochin Jewish heritage museum, and at the Israel Museum in Jerusalem, there is a reconstructed Cochin Jewish synagogue imported from Cochin itself.

Relations with other religions

Judaism is an endogamous religion, and it is prohibited to marry members of other religions (unless they convert, which is not encouraged). Since Hindus (and members of other religions in India) were unable to marry people of other castes, this arrangement was convenient, and intermarriage with non-Jews was practically unknown in the past. Today, with the liberalization and globalization in India, intermarriage is occurring more frequently in urban centers such as Mumbai, although it is still frowned upon by the Jewish community and is certainly not the norm.

Hinduism and Judaism have elements in common as orthopraxies that have developed complicated systems of law, purity codes, and dietary restrictions that serve to define the religioethnic boundaries of the community. Nevertheless, unique customs adapted from Hindu practices characterize the Judaism of the Indian Jews, including the prewedding henna ceremony among the Bene Israel, the rites of and belief in the prophet Elijah, and the festival of Shila San on the day after Yom Kippur, when the souls of the ancestors departed and alms were given to the poor. According to some authorities, Cochin Jews isolated themselves from the non-Jewish world during the eight days of Passover, imitating the Brāhmaṇs' asceticism in Hinduism by reasserting their purity, nonpollution, and high-caste status in Indian Kerala culture. Added to other high-caste behaviors of endogamy and dietary restrictions and using a sacred language, Hebrew, Cochin Jews maintained their distinct identity while adopting some Hindu royal and ascetic symbols into their Jewish tradition (Katz and Goldberg 1993).

In Kerala, Cochin Jews also shared common characteristics with the more numerous Christians by virtue of their minority status vis-à-vis the Hindus. Two basic patterns of interrelationship between Christians and Jews in India can be discerned: the symmetrical pattern, whereby there is an equal and corresponding relationship between members of the two religions; and the asymmetrical pattern, whereby an unequal distribution pertains (Weil 1982). In the case of the Cochin Jews and the Canaanite Christians who are South Indian Christians tracing descent from Thomas of Cana, the symmetrical pattern dominates. Both groups share a common local tradition, customs, folk tales and songs, and lifestyle.

The asymmetrical pattern is based upon unequal access to resources between Christianity and Judaism stemming from the fact that Christianity is intrinsically an active missionizing religion, which attempts to bring Jews and members of other religions to the Christian fold. During the nineteenth century, American and British missionaries worked among the Bene Israel and the Cochin Jews but had remarkably few successes among either group, despite the fact that the missionaries translated holy texts into the vernacular and set up Christian schools for village Bene Israel.

Today a kind of 'New Age' spirituality mixing elements in Judaism, and particularly kabbalism, with Hinduism and Buddhism is popular among Israeli travelers to South

Asia. They visit *āśrama*s in India, Tibet, and Nepal and delve into mysticism, which is all part of what Rodger Kamenetz (1994) called 'the "Ju-Bu" phenomenon.' During the past decade, there have been several Jewish-Buddhist meetings held in the presence of the Dalai Lama in Dharmasala, in Jerusalem, and elsewhere.

The tradition in the study of religions

Indo-Judaic Studies have been slow to develop, but this state of affairs is gradually changing as the field is beginning to receive legitimation and to make its mark on the academic map internationally. The expansion of the field can really be attributed to the last decade. It may be related to the influence of what Y. Sheleg (2000) calls the 'new spirituals,' who incorporate elements of Hindu practice such as meditation with Jewish practice and learning. It can also be attributed to the establishment of Israeli diplomatic relations with India in 1992 and to the informal meetings and lectures organized by voluntary organizations such as the Israel–India Cultural Association, the official friendship organization between the two countries founded in Israel in 1992.

Indians, as well as Israelis and diasporic Jews, have entered the scholarly arena of Indo-Judaic Studies. C. R. Das (1996) edited a special issue of *Eastern Anthropologist* on Indian Jews; Margaret Abrahams published an article on the Indian Jews in Israel (1995); and a few graduate students, including S. Sreekala (1995), completed dissertations on Indian Jews in Israel. The Israeli journal *Pe'amim* published new research in Hebrew on Indian Jews and Indian Jewish texts, and the Ben-Zvi Institute hosted several seminars on the subject. In 1995 the American Academy of Religion set up its Comparative Studies in Hinduisms and Judaisms Consultation, and in 1997 its Hinduisms and Judaisms Group. The academic discipline received a boost with the publication of Hananya Goodman's edited volume, *Between Jerusalem and Benares: Comparative Studies in Judaism and Hinduism* (1994), a pioneering effort, which brought together a group of scholars to investigate what Goodman calls the 'resonances' between the great Judaic and Hindu traditions. Similarly, the publication of Barbara Holdrege's monumental *Veda and Torah* (1996), which provided equal space and importance to Hinduism and Judaism alike, was a milestone. Holdrege succeeded in imparting the contextuality and textuality of both religions, and instead of characterizing the Hindu and Jewish traditions as opposite ends of the spectrum of the world's religions, she argued that the Brāhmaṇical and rabbinic traditions were both 'embodied communities.' Both religions study texts that codified their norms in the form of scriptural canons; both represent ethnocultural systems concerned with peoplehood, identity, and tradition, particularly as it is transmitted through family, ethnicity, and culture; and both represent religions of orthopraxy with complex legal systems and laws about purity and impurity.

The publication of the *Journal of Indo-Judaic Studies* began in 1998 and has consistently published interesting and important articles on comparative religion, Indian Jews, history of commerce between the Middle East and India, India and the Holocaust, and more. Books and journal articles on South Asian Jews, including information on the newly emerging groups who want to affiliate with Judaism (Parfitt 2002), continue to be published at a steady pace (for example, Daniel and Johnson 1995; Roland 2002; Weil 2003). The publication of the volume *India's Jewish Heritage: Ritual, Art and Life-cycle* (Weil 2002b) attracted great attention and is already in its second edition. In

2002 an international conference was held at Oxford University entitled 'A Perspective from the Margins: The State of the Art of Indo-Judaic Studies' at which some twenty scholars from three continents convened to discuss issues related to the emerging Indo-Judaic Studies arena.

Suggested further readings

Ezra (1986); Goodman (1994); Isenberg (1988); Katz (2000); Narayanan (1972); Roland (1989); Silliman (2001); Weil (1996).

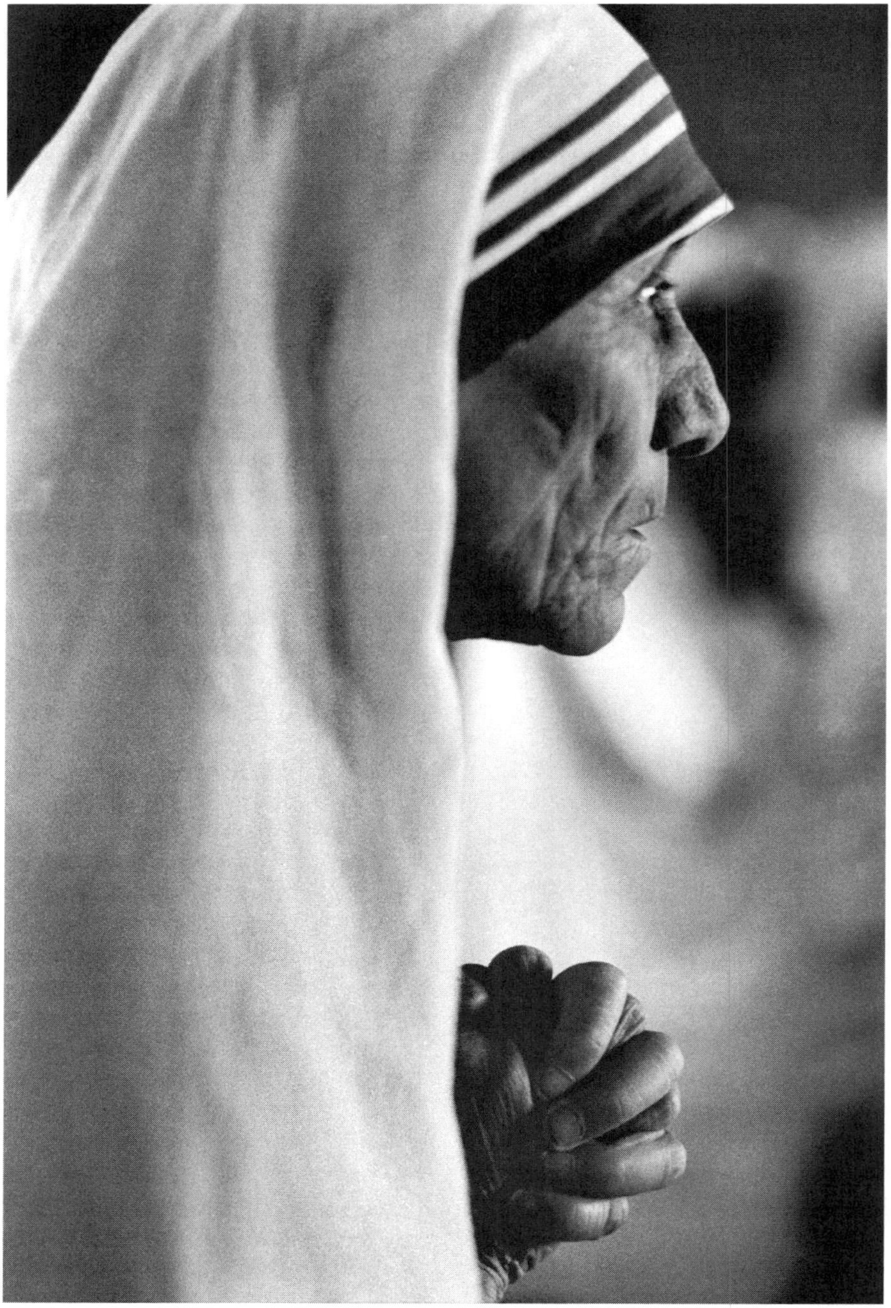

8. Mother Teresa of the Missionaries of Charity. Reproduced by permission of Magnum Photos and photographer Raghu Rai.

7

INDIAN CHRISTIAN TRADITION

M. Thomas Thangaraj

The tradition defined

Christianity had its beginnings in the Middle East during the first century of the Common Era in and through the life, ministry, and teachings of Jesus of Nazareth. Jesus was indicted as a criminal and crucified. His disciples claimed that he was resurrected from the dead on the third day and had shown himself to several of them. They began to proclaim his resurrection as good news in and around Jerusalem, and, traveling from Jerusalem to different parts of the Greco-Roman world of their day, they established Christian communities that included both Jews and Gentiles. It is believed that Saint Thomas, one of the disciples of Jesus, traveled to India and established churches in India during that very first century. Although not all historians agree on the veracity of this claim, there is even today a Christian tradition in India that traces its beginnings to the arrival of Thomas in South India. It is certain, however, that Christianity was a part of the religious landscape of India from the fourth century onward, if not before.

According to the 2001 census, approximately 3 percent of the population of India is Christian. Some statisticians include those Indians who are called 'crypto-Christians' due to their secret admiration for and devotion to Christ without membership in a Christian church and thus put the number of Christians closer to 5 percent of the population. There has not been any significant increase in the number of Christians in India during the twentieth century, though there were mass conversions to Christianity in earlier centuries. Christians in India belong to all the three major ecclesial traditions, namely, Eastern Orthodox, Roman Catholic, and Protestant. The Indian Orthodox Church, Orthodox Syrian Church of the East, Armenian Apostolic Church, Chaldean Syrian Church, and a few other smaller Orthodox groups carry on the Eastern Orthodox tradition. These churches are mostly based in the southern state of Kerala. Roman Catholics comprise nearly half of the Christian population in India. They are spread throughout India. Protestants are divided into nearly 1,000 denominations. Some of these denominations had their beginnings in Europe or North America, while others are indigenous churches established either by individual charismatic leaders or by groups of local Christians. The Church of South India, a union of former Anglicans, Presbyterians, Methodists, and Congregationalists, has a membership of around 3 million. The Church of North India, a similar union of major Protestant churches, is 1.5 million strong.

Christians are not evenly distributed in the Indian landscape. 'The states of Kerala,

Tamilnadu and Andhra Pradesh together account for more than 60% of India's Christians' (Barrett *et al.* 2001: 363). There is also a concentration of Christians in the northeastern part of India – in the states of Nagaland, Meghalaya, and Mizoram. The Christian population is significantly smaller in the northcentral and western parts of India.

Indian Christianity derives its multiplicity and variety not only from its denominational differences but also from the regional and linguistic peculiarities. Christianity as it is practiced in Nagaland in the northeast is significantly different from that in Tamilnadu in the south because of the differences in local culture and language. These differences are manifested in worship patterns, liturgical practices, and church architecture, and in the observation of individual rituals, rites of passage, and family ceremonies such as weddings and funerals. Thus any description of Christian tradition in India will be dependent on the region, language, denomination, and social groupings.

Cosmos and history

As already mentioned, there is a strong historical tradition claiming that Saint Thomas, the disciple of Jesus, came to India during the first century and established churches. The most recent historical scholarship supports this view and maintains that 'The age-old consciousness of the community of St Thomas Christians – that their origin as Christians is from the mission of St Thomas the Apostle in India – stands sufficiently justified' (Mundadan 1989: 64). There is also a tradition, less historically justifiable, that there was a community of Christians on the western coast due to the evangelistic efforts of Bartholomew. The Christian community that claims its connection to the work of Saint Thomas had a lively connection with the East Syrian or Persian Christians. For all practical purposes it was a Syrian Orthodox church. Its membership included both Persians and local inhabitants. During the Middle Ages, a Latin mission was established in Quilon, but it did not last for long. These Latin Christians had good relations with the Saint Thomas Christians, and various visitors during this period noted their existence, often referring to them as 'Nestorians.'

The arrival of the Portuguese opened a new page in the history of Christianity in India. In 1498 Vasco da Gama reached India via the Cape of Good Hope in Africa and thus established a route to India from Europe that enabled trade between India and Portugal. The Portuguese kings were interested, in addition to trade, in the spread of Christianity in India. Their zeal for the spread of Christianity led to their securing ecclesiastical rights in the lands conquered or to be conquered in Africa and Asia. This is known as the Portuguese 'padroado' or the right of patronage (Thekkedath 1982: 5). Goa, a town on the western coast of India, was made a bishopric, and Franciscans and Dominicans carried on the mission. The initial history of the encounter between Portuguese and Syrian Christians was one of friendly relations. Soon the Portuguese had established their churches and bishoprics firmly on the western coast of India. It was at this time that King John III of Portugal appealed to the Pope to send missionaries to India. So Francis Xavier (1506–52), a Jesuit priest, was sent to India as a missionary. Xavier was able to convert to Christianity a large number of people belonging to the fisher caste, primarily on the eastern coast of India. He was able to build the Roman Church in India on firm ground with an increasing membership.

The initial friendly relations between Syrian Christianity and Western Catholicism were to be marred by differences in beliefs, practices, and especially ecclesial governance. While Syrian Christians continued to recognize the patriarch of the East, Portuguese Catholics demanded allegiance to the Pope in Rome. There were also differences among them with regard to the number of sacraments, the manner of giving communion, and priestly celibacy. These differences led to hostility, and finally at the Synod of Diamper by Roman Catholics, held in 1599, a permanent divide between Syrian Christians and Western Catholics was created. The Synod declared a clear renunciation of the power of the patriarch and the beliefs and practices of the Syrian Church. The struggle between these two groups of Christians went on until 1653, when the majority of Syrians rebelled unsuccessfully against the Roman authority and Portuguese hierarchy. Some of those who revolted resumed Roman obedience, while a minority persisted as an Eastern Orthodox tradition.

The Roman Catholic missions flourished in the centuries that followed. Akbar (1556–1605) the Mughal emperor became interested in Christianity and welcomed Jesuits in his court. He also hoped for a new religion, called Tawhīd-i-Ilāhī (Divine Unity), combining elements from the existing three religions: Hinduism, Islam, and Christianity. The Jesuits withdrew from the court once such a new religion was envisaged. Another notable missionary among the Jesuits was Roberto De Nobili. De Nobili came to Madurai, South India, in 1606 and began his work among the higher-caste groups in and around that city. He separated himself from the existing Catholic mission, adopted the lifestyle of a Hindu monk, mastered Sanskrit and Tamil, and was able to attract several high-caste Hindus to the Christian faith. De Nobili had a vision of generating a Christian faith that was rooted in the local Hindu cultural ethos and practices, including the caste system. He published several works in Tamil and wrote hymns both in Tamil and Telugu. Although De Nobili's work was successful in the initial stages, he came into conflict with the Roman authorities with regard to his views on inculturation and his evangelistic methods. Another notable Jesuit missionary was Constant Joseph Beschi who published both poetic and prose works in Tamil during the period 1711–42. These were missionaries who attempted to free Christianity in India from what might be called the 'reproach of foreignness.'

The Protestant mission in India began with the arrival of two German missionaries, Bartholomew Ziegenbalg and Henry Pluetschau, who were sent by King Frederick IV of Denmark. They arrived in the coastal town of Tranquebar (Tharangampadi), south of Madras on July 9, 1706. They proceeded to learn Portuguese and Tamil, since these were the two languages that were dominant at that time in South India. Ziegenbalg had a keen mind to grasp the languages of India and began translating the Bible into Tamil. He was able to establish congregations in and around Tranquebar and thus began the Protestant expansion in India. He was to be followed by several missionaries from the West, who represented the various denominational and national missionary societies. The establishment of various Protestant mission societies in the West (such as the Society for the Propagation of the Gospel, and the Church Missionary Society [both of the Church of England]; the Baptist Missionary Society; the London Missionary Society; and others) led to the arrival of many more Western Protestant missionaries in India. Thus Protestant Christianity grew in India, with several denominational and national linkages with the West. One of the leading figures in the Protestant missionary activity of the nineteenth century was William Carey, who established the Serampore Mission near Calcutta and promoted the cause of Christianity in many ways. He was involved in translating the Bible into several Indian languages, founding the first institution of higher learning in India (Serampore College), and working with the Hindu reformers and the British rulers to ban the practice of *satī*.

While the Protestant expansion was taking place in India, the Roman Catholic tradition experienced its own parallel expansion. In addition to establishing parishes and dioceses in India, the Roman Catholic Church was heavily involved in founding and maintaining educational institutions around the country. Various religious orders were involved in medical, technical, and other differing forms of service.

The further history of Syrian Christianity in India is marked by the development of a schism that led to the formation in 1887 of the Mar Thoma Church. The Church Missionary Society's missionaries were invited by the Metropolitan Mar Dionysios II, who held an office that was presumed to derive its authority from the missionary apostle St Thomas, to teach in their seminaries and bring about a revival in the Syrian Church. Their involvement in the life of the Syrian Church led to the formation of a reformed party by a group of Syrian Christians under the leadership of Abraham Malpan. They ultimately left the Syrian Church and formed the Mar Thoma Church.

One of the remarkable features in the history of Christianity in India is the movement toward unity among mainline Protestants in the twentieth century. It began with a call in 1919 by a few church leaders, who met in the town of Tranquebar and issued what is now called the Tranquebar Manifesto. Conversations toward unity continued from then on between the Anglican, Methodist, Presbyterian, and Congregationalist churches in South India, ultimately leading to the formation of the Church of South India, an organic union of all four denominational traditions, on September 27, 1947. Similar conversations took place between Protestant churches in North India, which led to the formation of the Church of North India in 1970. There are continuing conversations even today among the three churches – Church of South India, Church of North India, and Mar Thoma Church – toward a conciliar formation of a church of India. The Lutherans, Baptists, American Methodists, and others remain as churches in their own right. The attempts to broaden the unity among Protestants have not led to further mergers, though there is a spirit of ecumenical collaboration. Ecumenical cooperation is seen clearly in the work of the National Christian Council of India, which came into being in 1912 under the name National Missionary Council of India. The goals of the National Christian Council are to assist the various churches in their missionary vocation, to coordinate the activities of the regional councils, and to help form Christian opinion on matters of national and social interest through consultation among churches (Firth 1976: 235).

Since Vatican II, the Roman Catholic churches in India have been working together with Protestant churches in matters of common concern. When the Eastern Orthodox churches joined the World Council of Churches in 1961 during its assembly in New Delhi, an intentional collaboration between Protestants and Eastern Orthodox Christians in India gained importance.

Sacred life and literature

The sacred life of Indian Christians is guided by several elements, chief of which is corporate worship. Here again, a variety of expressions abound. The Eastern Orthodox churches formed their liturgical practices in the Syrian tradition, with Syriac as their liturgical language. This was to be followed later by the use of Latin rites among some Syrian Christians and the use of the local language Malayalam. The Divine Liturgy (liturgy used during the celebration of the Eucharist) takes precedence in the life of Orthodox Christians in India.

The Roman Catholic churches initially adopted the Latin liturgical traditions and in their contacts with the Syrian Christians developed Syrian rites as well. However, Vatican II brought a significant change in the worship life of the Roman Catholic churches in India. These changes included the use of vernacular languages for liturgy, the employment of local musical traditions, and the adoption of Indian architectural patterns in the building of churches. There have been genuine attempts to present Christian worship through local cultural idiom.

Protestants brought the worship patterns of the varying Western Protestant denominations. These were adapted to the local settings through a limited incorporation of local language, cultural practices, and music. However, there remained a domination of Western liturgical elements in Protestant worship. Over the centuries, the Protestants themselves have gone through a liturgical renewal and now adopt local religiocultural practices for Christian worship. The formation of the Church of South India in 1947 led to a process of forming Christian worship in an ecumenical mode that is inclusive of the various Protestant traditions. *The Book of Common Worship*, published in 1963, is the outcome of such an attempt. The most recent attempt at a truly Indian liturgy is exemplified in the alternate version of Eucharist liturgy published in 1985. It encourages people to conduct the service in as authentic an Indian style as possible. The liturgy is organized around five stages: Entry (*praveśa*), Awakening (*prabodha*), Recalling and Offering (*smaraṇa-samarpaṇa*), Sharing in the Body and Blood of Christ (*darśana*), and Blessing (*preṣaṇa*). The language of the liturgy is guided by concerns of both inculturation and the liberation of the oppressed.

Apart from the Eastern Orthodox, Roman Catholic, and mainline Protestant churches, Pentecostal and nondenominational churches have had their own modes and methods of inculturation of Christian worship. For example, Pentecostal churches were among the first to exploit the emerging light music tradition of India (a mixture of Western and Indian musical traditions) for their worship and piety.

What is common to these Christian churches is the conscious and intentional attempt to develop and practice the worship of the Christian community in local linguistic and cultural forms.

The sacred life of Indian Christians is also shaped by home-based religious practices. Indian Christians have adapted several of the Hindu rites of passage into their own religious life. These practices vary according to region and denominational affiliation. Christian weddings take on several local cultural practices that are Hindu in origin. Indigenous elements are more conspicuously present in worship settings outside the church building. The prayer meetings held in homes, lyrical or musical preaching performed on festive occasions, prayer services at homes related to rites of passage, such as puberty, marriages and funerals, and other such home-based worship services bear clear marks of indigenous elements and influence. In addition to Christmas and Easter, most Christian congregations celebrate Church Anniversary Festival, which commemorates the building of the church in that place, and Harvest Festival in which people bring their farm products to offer to the church as a mark of their gratitude and thanksgiving to God. These are occasions for much more celebrative worship services.

The form and nature of these worship services differ from region to region and according to earlier denominational links. Although there have been attempts, especially in theological seminaries, to celebrate Hindu festivals, most Christians tend to see these as beyond the appropriate boundaries of Christian life and witness.

There are several major community events that shape the sacred life of Indian Christians. The Mar Thoma Church has conducted an annual revival meeting since 1895, called Maramon Convention, in which thousands of Mar Thoma Christians and others gather for several days of preaching, prayer, and celebration. The Syrian Orthodox churches have their own celebrations and events. The celebration of the sainthood of Saint George is one such (see Dempsey 2001). The Roman Catholic churches have adapted the Hindu festival processions for their own festivals. The Hindu practice of pulling the temple chariot along the streets of the town on festive occasions has been adapted by Roman Catholic churches for festivals connected with local Roman Catholic shrines. Protestants, on the other hand, have tended to avoid any appearance of close similarities to Hindu festivals but rather have celebrated the church anniversaries, Christmas, and Easter with a few elements that have Hindu cultural roots, for example, the wearing of new clothes for Christmas.

One way to describe the sacred life of Indian Christians is through the category of difference. In forming their sacred life Indian Christians seek to be distinct from their Hindu and Muslim neighbors. Therefore, the use of Western music, Gothic and Roman church architecture, and other such Western Christian practices functions to highlight their difference from their Hindu neighbors. At the same time, Indian Christians are keen to locate their sacred life squarely in the cultural ethos of India and therefore see themselves as different from Western Christians, whether Roman Catholic or Protestant.

As far as sacred literature is concerned, the Bible has occupied a central place in the religious life of Indian Christians since the arrival of Protestant missionaries from the West. The Eastern Orthodox traditions within India did not pay attention to the translation of the Bible into local languages. Therefore the sacred text for the Orthodox is the liturgical practices rather than a written document such as the Bible. A Malayalam translation of the Bible was available to the Eastern Orthodox Christians only through the work of the Protestant missionaries in the nineteenth century. The Roman Catholic missions in India were slow to engage in the translation of the Bible into local languages, yet they produced other Christian literature in local languages right from the beginning of their mission. As early as 1616, Thomas Stephens, a Roman Catholic missionary who worked among the Konkani people, published a magnificent Marathi poem of 10,962 verses on biblical history to take the place of the Hindu Purāṇas (Neill 1984: 241). Other Roman Catholic missionaries wrote extensively in local languages in both poetry and prose yet were hesitant to translate the Bible into local languages. Some even actively opposed the Protestant translations of the Bible. For example, Abbé J. A. Dubois (1977: 65–68) objected that the translations offered by the Protestant missionary societies were of a very low literary quality and that the Bible was not easily comprehensible or appealing to Hindus if it was simply translated and given to them.

The translation of the Bible into the local languages of India was a high priority in the activity of the Protestant missionaries. The first Protestant missionary, Bartholomew Ziegenbalg, as we have seen, translated the New Testament into Tamil within five years of his arrival in India. William Carey extended the work of Bible translation to include translations into most of the languages of India. As Robin Boyd writes, 'He [Carey] and his colleagues eventually set up at Serampore what might almost be called a Bible factory with different linguistic departments, and succeeded in translating the Bible, in whole or part, into more than thirty languages' (1979: 15–16).

The relationship between the Bible and the Hindu scriptures has been a matter of debate throughout the history of Christianity in India. The early Protestant missionaries while translating the Bible named it as the Veda or Vedāgama (a combination of Veda and Āgama, the two major scriptural corpora in Hinduism). Robert De Nobili had referred to it as the fifth Veda, relating the Bible to the legend that the fifth Veda of the Hindus was lost in antiquity. One of the more creative attempts at relating the Hindu scriptures to the Bible was made by P. Chenchiah, a twentieth-century Christian lay theologian, when he suggested that Indian Christians might accept the Hindu scriptures as their Old Testament instead of the Hebrew Bible. He argued that one could read the Hindu scriptures in light of Christ, in the same way that Jesus' early Jewish disciples read their own Hebrew scriptures (Boyd 1979: 158). Most Christians in India do not accept this view, though many would see the Hindu scriptures as a preparation for the arrival of the Bible in India.

Sacred literature other than the Bible abounds in the history of Christianity in India. Indian Christians have been prolific in the writing of hymns, epic poems, apologetic writings, and theological treatises, both in English and in vernacular languages. These writings were heavily influenced by Hindu ways of thinking, imaging, and articulating. Some of the well-known hymn writers are H. A. Krishna Pillai, Subba Rao, Vedanayagam Sastri, Narayan Vaman Tilak, and Brahmabandhav Upadhyaya. These poets reflected *bhakti* (devotion) sentiments similar to those found in Hindu *bhakti* literature. A significant body of Christian literature, theological and devotional, also exists in the English language. These writings were produced primarily in the late nineteenth and twentieth centuries. The list of such writers includes Svāmī Abhisiktananda, A. J. Appasamy, K. M. Banerjea, V. Chakkarai, P. Chenchiah, Raimundo Panikkar, Manilal C. Parekh, M. M. Thomas, and Brahmabandhav Upadhyaya. While such treatises are available, the sacred life of Indian Christians, especially in rural settings, is shaped primarily by church worship and home-based religious practices.

Institutions and practices

Christianity came to India with its institutional character already developed. The Syrian Orthodox Church inherited the ecclesial structure of the Eastern churches with its patriarch in Syria. The Roman Catholic Church carried with it the Roman and Papal structures into Indian church life. Although there were conflicts between the Syrian Christians and Roman Catholics over understandings of ecclesial and institutional governance, Roman Catholics maintained their linkage with the Roman institutional structure. The Protestants, in their denominational multiplicity, also imposed their modes of institutional structure and governance on their own denominational churches in India. While some of the major Protestant churches, such as the Church of South India, the Church of North India, the Methodist Church in India, and most Indian Lutheran churches, operate with the tradition of having bishops as the presiding officers of their churches, others function with the autonomy of congregations over issues of governance. The institutional character of the Christian churches in India has been a contrast and a challenge to the ordering of Hindu religious life, which is independent of clearly defined institutional structure.

The life of the Christian churches in India is also guided by another set of institutions related to the ecclesial structure. These are schools, colleges, hospitals, and social service agencies organized and maintained by Christian churches. The early part of the nineteenth century saw the founding of several colleges throughout India due to the work of missionaries, chief of which were Alexander Duff in Calcutta, John Wilson in Bombay, whose work led to the establishment of Wilson College, John Anderson in Madras, who founded the Madras Christian College, and Stephen Hyslop in Nagpur. While these colleges were admitting only male students, there were separate colleges founded for women as well, notable among them the Women's Christian College in Madras, Isabella Thoburn College in Lucknow, and Lady Doak College in Madurai. Roman Catholic missions were also involved in the founding of several colleges and schools throughout India. Notable among them are Loyola College in Madras, St Xavier's College in Bombay, and St Xavier's College in Calcutta. It should be noted that hundreds of elementary, middle, and high schools were founded throughout India by the Christian churches in India. There were varying perceptions about the relationship between these educational institutions and the evangelistic task of the churches. Some missionaries like Alexander Duff saw the educational project as a potential way to convert Hindus to the Christian faith, although in reality Hindus who were educated in Christian schools and colleges did not necessarily abandon the Hindu religion to turn to the Christian faith (Firth 1976: 182–85). Others saw the educational mission simply as a duty of love and care. Even today, the Christian communities in India are heavily invested in this form of educational service. In addition, there is an increasing interest in offering nonformal education to the poor in hopes of raising their sociopolitical consciousness to initiate change and liberation.

Organized medical missions are a phenomenon of the nineteenth- and twentieth-century missionary activity in India. The American Board of Commissioners for Foreign Missions sent John Scudder, the first of many medical missionaries, to Madras in 1836 (Firth 1976: 205). More medical missionaries followed, and hospitals and medical and nursing schools began to appear throughout India. Some of the well-known schools are the Christian Medical College in Vellore and the North India School of Medicine for Christian Women in Ludhiana, Punjab. The Christian Medical Association of India is currently an organization that functions as a clearing house for all Christian medical institutions and medical personnel.

One of the unique features of Indian Christianity is the establishment of Ashram (Sanskrit *āśrama*), patterned after the Hindu ascetic and monastic traditions. Ashrams were places where the residents practiced regular and intense spiritual discipline, followed a simple lifestyle, and adopted Hindu cultural and religious patterns in worship, prayer, and architecture. The twentieth century saw the emergence of several Ashrams, both Protestant and Roman Catholic. Two doctors in South India, Dr Jesudason and Dr Forrester-Paton, founded the Christukula Ashram in Tamilnadu in 1921. In the same year, Anglican missionary J. C. Winslow established an Ashram at Pune that was later renamed as Christa Prema Seva Sangh in 1934 (Neill 1970: 144). There were other Ashrams associated with the work of people such as Stanley Jones, an American Methodist missionary, and Bishop Peckenham Walsh of the Anglican Church in India.

The Roman Catholics had their own share of Ashrams as well. Notable among Roman Catholic Ashrams is the Saccidananda Ashram, near Trichy in Tamilnadu, established by the work of Jules Monchanin in 1950. Bede Griffiths succeeded him. Bold experiments in Hindu-Christian spirituality were attempted and continue to be maintained even today.

Ethics and human relations

Indian Christians have needed to discover and negotiate Christian ethical values and understandings of human relations in a context where Hindu ethos and communal values prevail. Hindu ethics are dominated by the concept of *dharma*, meaning justice, order, duty, and religion. *Dharma* entails two aspects, namely, *varṇa-dharma* and *āśrama-dharma* (see chapter 1 for a full discussion). The former is the recognition of one's duty in light of one's position in caste hierarchy, and the latter is the discovery of one's duty in relation to one's stage of life. Indian Christians had to negotiate their view of ethics and human relations around this ethical framework. The Eastern Orthodox Church in India accommodated itself easily into the caste structure of Hindu society. 'Syrian Christians have been for centuries encapsulated within caste society, regarded by Hindus as a caste, occupying a recognized (and high) place within the caste hierarchy . . . and seem[s] to have been quite content to accept and operate the caste system without any egalitarian protest' (Forrester 1980: 14). The joining of low-caste groups to the Syrian Church in the nineteenth century jolted this comfortable positioning of Syrian Christians within the caste hierarchy. Syrian Christians have since encountered great difficulty in accepting the low-caste Christians as their equals within the church (Forrester 1980: 110–14).

The Roman Catholic Church has its own share in the problem of the practice of caste within the church. A Roman Catholic missionary success was the conversion of fisherfolk on the southern tip of India. The fisherfolk belonged on the lower rungs of the caste ladder, and thus the Roman Catholic Church was a church of the low caste. Missionaries like Robert De Nobili, on the other hand, attempted to win converts from the upper caste by the adoption of Hindu rituals and practices. He believed that one need not renounce caste by becoming a Christian (Forrester 1980: 15). In the midst of all these missionary experiments, the Roman Catholic tradition in India regarded caste as a civil institution and adopted a policy of accommodation. Though the caste system is verbally condemned as contrary to Christian faith, there is an accommodation of it in the organization of the church and in the individual lives of Roman Catholics.

Protestant missions did not have a unified view of the role of caste distinctions within Christian community. For example, the Lutherans were more accommodating than Anglican missionaries. The only success in the Protestant missionary battle against caste is the practice of Eucharistic participation without caste considerations. Ecclesial governance, family relations, and individual Christian behavior are still governed by caste considerations in most Protestant churches. Since a majority of Christians practice endogamy, caste distinctions continue to be perpetuated within the churches.

Modern expressions

Three distinct movements are shaping modern expressions of Christianity in India. The first is the movement called inculturation. It attempts to express the Christian faith in and through local cultural and religious idioms and practices. This has been prominently noticed in the Ashrams founded by various Christian leaders and communities. In addition, inculturation is at work in the current intentional liturgical renewal that aims to express Christian worship practices through Indian cultural forms. The Roman Catholic churches in India have been on the forefront of this renewal since Vatican II. For example, the National Biblical Catechetical and Liturgical Centre in Bangalore exemplifies such bold attempts. A renewed interest in Indian classical, folk, and popular music is present in most churches. Since Indian Independence in 1947, Christian communities have been consciously engaging in removing the appearance of 'foreignness' in Indian Christianity and creating an Indian Christian existence that is shaped and influenced primarily by Indian cultural ethos.

The second is the Christian Dalit movement. It has grown over the last thirty years. As noted earlier, the majority of Christians belong to the lowest castes in the caste system. Among them, a significantly large proportion belong to the so-called 'untouchables,' who were named by Mohandas Karamchand Gandhi as *harijan*, meaning 'people of God.' In the Constitution of India, they are referred to as 'Scheduled Castes,' for the purposes of affirmative action. In recent times, the scheduled castes have claimed the name Dalit for themselves. The word 'Dalit' means 'oppressed' or 'crushed.' Dalit Christians have faced two major challenges.

First, despite converting to Christianity, their status within the Christian churches had not changed significantly. Ecclesial power remained largely in the hands of non-Dalits among Christians. Today, Dalit Christians have made noticeable progress in the sharing of power within the churches' hierarchies. For example, many of the current bishops of the Church of South India belong to the Dalit community. Moreover, theological thinking and ecclesial practice within churches had been historically controlled and shaped by the ethos of Christians other than Dalits. Therefore, a concerted effort is afoot within churches to develop Dalit theologies and ecclesial practices. In their theological task, Dalit Christians have discovered an agenda that 'includes interacting theologically with the little theological traditions of Dalit Christians, with other theological traditions within the Indian Church, and with Dalits who do not share their Christian convictions' (Webster 1992: 218). Some of the leading figures in the development of Dalit theology are Sathianathan Clarke, V. Devasahayam, James Massey, Arvind Nirmal, and M. E. Prabhakar.

The second challenge for Dalit Christians is the claiming of the compensatory discrimination available to Dalits within the Constitution of India. The Constitution, while affirming the equality of all citizens before law irrespective of caste, class, race, religion, or place of birth, offers to the states the right to make special provisions for the upliftment of scheduled castes and scheduled tribes. Dalits who became Christian were not included in this provision, on the grounds that Dalits no longer belonged to the caste system once they accepted Christianity as their religion. Currently, the Dalit Christians, with the support of other Christians, are asking the government to address this particular disparity.

In meeting these two challenges, Dalits have made considerable progress. As John Webster notes,

> The most significant development during this period of Dalit Christian history has not been the emergence of a new Dalit Christian elite. . . . Instead this period has witnessed the emergence of Dalit Christians from the obscurity in both Church and society. . . . Even without political reservations, Dalit Christians have become increasingly active both in the wider Dalit movement and in their own particular movement for equal justice. In this process some of the barriers dividing Christians from other Dalits have been removed and there are signs of the two coming closer together in a shared struggle for equality.
> (1992: 176–77)

The third movement within modern Indian Christianity is the rise of indigenous churches in India. Of course, the Eastern Orthodox churches are indigenous in that they were dependent right from the beginning on Indian financial resources. The Mar Thoma Church, too, is truly indigenous without any links to traditions outside of India. Protestant churches, however, depended heavily on Western Christian traditions and support. So the founding of indigenous churches began as early as the nineteenth century among Protestants. 'One remarkable Hindu believer in Christ at Madras was O. Kandaswamy Chetti, founder of the Fellowship of the Followers of Jesus, who openly confessed his faith in Christ as the only Saviour but declined baptism' (Hedlund 1999: 31). Arumainayagam Sattampillai of south Tamilnadu founded the Indian Church of the Only Savior (popularly known as the Hindu-Christian community) in 1857 in protest against Western missionary domination (Thangaraj 1971). Roger Hedlund (1999: 32) mentions a few others such as the Indian Pentecostal Church of God, founded by K. E. Abraham around 1930. Some of the contemporary examples of indigenous churches include the Apostolic Christian Assembly, founded by Pastor G. Sundaram, the movement around K. Subba Rao in Andhra Pradesh, the New Life Fellowship in Bombay, Agape Fellowship churches in the state of Punjab, and the Isupanthi movement in North Gujarat (Hedlund 1999: 33–36).

Transmission of the tradition outside of India

Indian Christians who migrated to other nations, especially in the Arabian Peninsula, Europe, and North America, have established Indian Christian congregations in those places. Since Indian Christians speak a wide variety of languages, the diaspora communities have gathered as language-based Christian congregations outside India. Few studies have yet been undertaken to describe and understand the nature of Indian Christianity within the diaspora communities. A major work on this subject is *Christian Pluralism in the United States: The Indian Immigrant Experience* (1996) by Raymond Williams. There are Indian Christian congregations in most of the major cities in the United States, such as Atlanta, Boston, Houston, and New York. These cities have several Indian Christian congregations, and each is organized around either a common language or a common ecclesial tradition. For example, 'An India Catholic Association of America was informally organized in 1979 and then incorporated in 1980. The single organization served Indians of all three rites [Syro-Malabar, Syro-Malankara, and Latin] until 1982, when the Malankara Catholic Church was founded and the other groups began to meet separately' (Williams 1996: 144). All the three traditions have established parishes throughout the United States. Protestants from India have their own churches according to their particular ecclesial traditions. The Church of South India bishops authorized extraterritorial parishes in 1975 and have at times supported those parishes with ministerial personnel. Other church groups from India, such as Brethren, Pentecostals, and others, have established their own parishes in the United States. Similar patterns of Indian Christian parishes are occurring in Britain, Canada, and several of the Arab nations. In the United States, Eastern Orthodox Christians from India are more highly organized than either Roman Catholics or Protestants from India. In 1979 the Malankara Orthodox Diocese of North America and Europe was established. In 1988 the Mar Thoma Diocese of North America was established. Other Orthodox churches in India have organized missions and dioceses for their members who have immigrated to other countries in the West.

One of the problems that immigrant Indian Christians face outside of India is the practice of their peculiarly Indian Christian faith in a culture other than that which has sustained their own Christian existence. Therefore, Indian Christians face the double challenge of keeping their Christian faith and their Indian cultural ethos together in a foreign land. New immigrants play an important role in maintaining the Indian and Christian sides together in the life of Indian Christians abroad.

Relations with other religions

The relations between Indian Christianity and other religious traditions within India take different forms depending on the denomination, region, and caste. As mentioned earlier, the Eastern Orthodox tradition in India accommodated itself into the prevailing Hindu social ethos such that it did not experience any major conflict with the religious communities around. Such friendly relations were extended not only to Hindus and Muslims but also to a small Jewish community in the state of Kerala. During the precolonial period, the relationship between Syrian Christians and Hindus was one of mutual appreciation and help. For example, 'At least one Hindu temple regularly lent out its temple elephants to Syrian worshippers for use in their festival processions' (Bayly 1989: 253).

The Roman Catholics and Protestants have maintained, over all, mutual respect and friendship with people of other religions over the last five centuries. In the field of social reforms and changes, Hindus and Christians have worked together. For example, the work of Hindu reformers like Ram Mohun Roy and Mohandas Gandhi has drawn on Christian resources and support. Hindus and Muslims have generally been appreciative of the humanitarian service of Christians throughout India. However, a majority of Protestants in India have maintained an attitude of condescension and condemnation toward their neighbors of other religions. They have been informed by a certain missionary view that looked upon Hindus and Muslims simply as people to be converted to Christianity. Such a view is accompanied by considering Hindu religion as idolatrous, superstitious, and even demonic. Such religious attitudes have not fully isolated Indian Christians from their neighbors. One would find, here and there, in the history of Christianity in India, instances of either Hindus or Muslims persecuting Christian converts. But these were rare and sporadic. The Hindu view of the multiplicity of paths to God had a built-in tolerance that accommodated the new religion within its own worldview. As Hugald Grafe puts it, 'The relation between the two religions during the 20th century is characterized by a breaking apart of the religious-communal and the purely religious aspects: On the one hand communal clashes between Hindu and Christian groups, on the other hand a spirit of disdainful or benevolent toleration or cautious dialogue' (1990: 165–66).

After independence, the provisions of the Constitution of India have guided relations between Christianity and other religions. The followers of every religion in India are guaranteed the right to practice, profess, and propagate their religion. It is the Indian Christians who have made the most use of the provision given in the Constitution to engage in evangelistic activity. Such an engagement is looked upon with suspicion by a minority of Hindus. It is often represented as Christians' attempt to 'proselytize' through fraudulent and coercive means. Recent years have seen a few cases of attacks on individual Christians, their communities, and their churches, especially in the northern part of India. Certain states within the nation have attempted to pass regulations and laws to control the proselytizing activity of Christians. 'Freedom of Religion' bills have been passed in several states, the Supreme Court of India has annulled some of them, but the question of 'conversion' continues to be a bone of contention in India.

There are also intentional attempts by Indian Christians to promote dialogue between Christianity and other religions in India. The Christian Ashrams often function as places of dialogue at the level of mystical religious experience. The Church of South India and the Church of North India have their own programs of dialogue. The Roman Catholic churches in India have promoted friendly and dialogical relations with Hindus through their varied organizations and institutions. The Roman Catholic and Protestant seminaries in India have been pioneers in the promotion of dialogical relations between Christians and others. For example, the Tamilnadu Theological Seminary has had an ongoing program of dialogue since 1972. The future of Indian Christians' relationship with Hindus and Muslims in India rests upon how the people of India succeed in maintaining freedom of religion and the possibilities for dialogue and mutual enrichment.

The tradition in the study of religions

Indian Christianity has been the subject of study almost exclusively among church historians and missiologists for a long time in the West. Although Indian Christianity has contributed greatly to the study of religions through the work of several missionary scholars, historians of religion have not paid much attention to the phenomenon of Indian Christianity. For example, Bartholomew Ziegenbalg, the first Protestant missionary to India, studied the Hindu tradition with care and published an important work titled *The Genealogy of the South Indian Gods*. Other missionary scholars engaged in the translation of Hindu scriptures and other Indian literature enabled Western scholars of religion to understand religious traditions of India. G. U. Pope's translation of *Tiruvācakam* (Sacred Utterance), a Tamil Śaiva devotional literature, illustrates this as well.

European missionaries began the tradition of studying Indian Christianity as a separate religious phenomenon in India. C. G. Diehl's *Church and Shrine: Intermingling*

Patterns of Culture in the Life of Some Christian Groups in South India (1965), the research on village Christians in Andhra Pradesh conducted by P. Y. Luke and John B. Carman titled *Village Christians and Hindu Culture: Study of a Rural Church in Andhra Pradesh, South India* (1968), Bror Tiliander's *Christian and Hindu Terminology: A Study in Their Mutual Relations with Special Reference to the Tamil Area* (1974) are supreme examples of such work by missionaries.

In recent times, there has been a growing interest among historians of religions in engaging Indian Christianity as a religious phenomenon in its own right and not just an extension of the Western missionary enterprise. The Church History Association of India has been influenced by the discipline of history of religions in such a way that extensive discussions were held on the importance of choosing the phrase 'History of Christianity in India' over against 'Indian Church History.' More and more scholars in the West, in India, and elsewhere are turning their attention to Indian Christianity. In the last ten years several books have been published studying Indian Christianity from historical, ethnographic, and sociological angles. These works include Bent Smidt Hansen's *Dependency and Identity: Problems of Cultural Encounter as a Consequence of the Danish Mission in South India Between the Two World Wars* (1998), Susan Bayly's *Saints, Goddesses, and Kings: Muslims and Christians in South Indian Society, 1700–1900* (1989), D. Dennis Hudson's *Protestant Origins in India: Tamil Evangelical Christians in India, 1706–1835* (2000), and Corinne G. Dempsey's *Kerala Christian Sainthood: Collisions of Culture and Worldview in South India* (2001).

Suggested further readings

Boyd (1979); Dempsey (2001); Devasahayam (1997); Firth (1976); Forrester (1980); Grafe (1990); Hedlund (1999); Mundadan (1989); Hudson (2000); Neill (1984, 1985); Raj and Dempsey (2002); Thekkedath (1982); Webster (1992); Williams (1996).

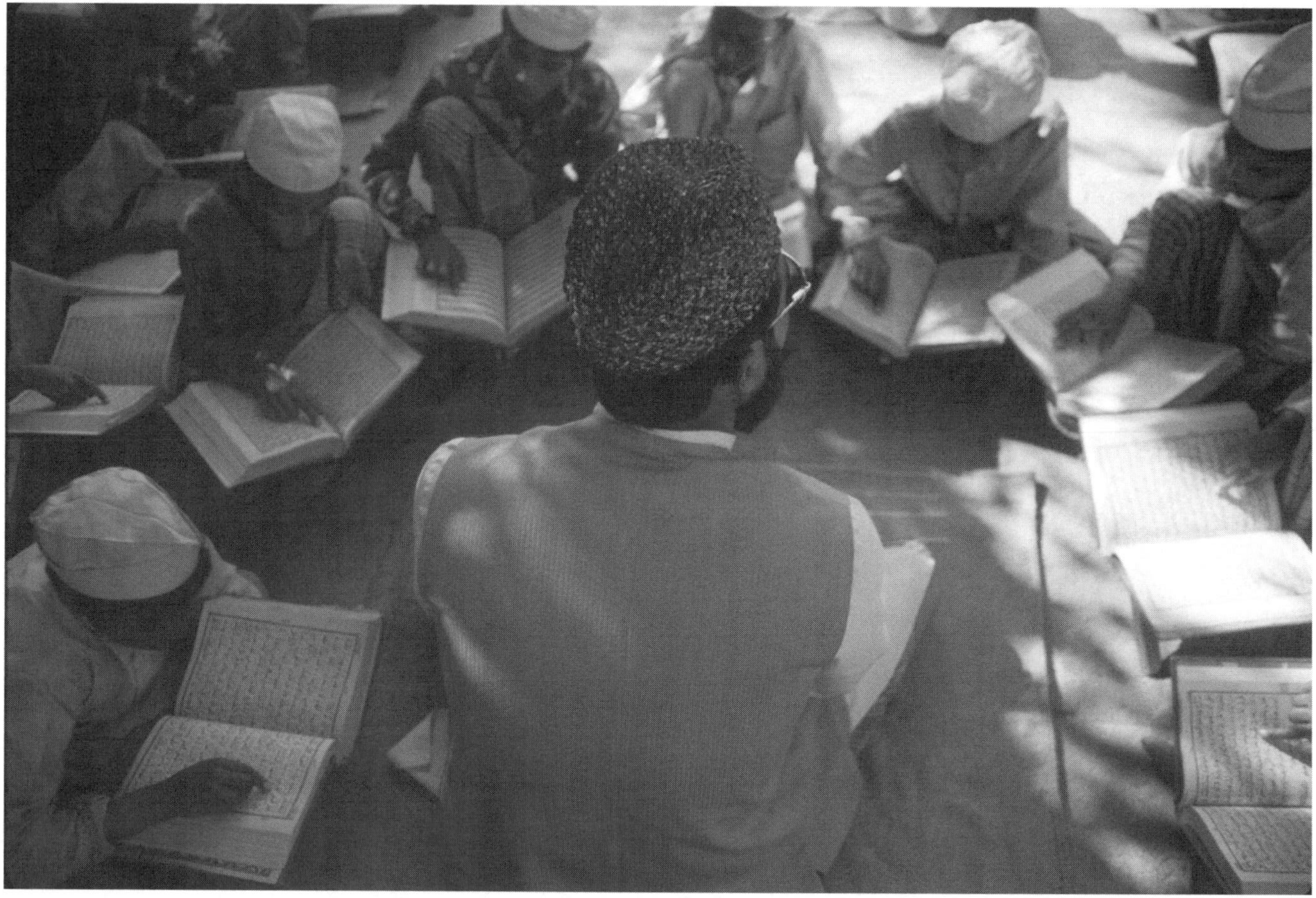

9. Training in Qur'ān recitation at a *madrasah* in northern India. Courtesy of Professor Peter Gottschalk.

8

INDIAN MUSLIM TRADITION

Peter Gottschalk

The tradition defined

Islam is an unusual religious tradition in that it had a term for itself from the very beginning of its historical origins. In the Qur'ān, the most revered source of understanding for Muslims about Islam, it is written 'The religion before Allāh is Islam' (3.19). 'Islam' means literally 'submission.' The Qur'ān mentions this term repeatedly and uses it in juxtaposition with other religions. Not only does the Qur'ān name this religion but also those who adhere to it. 'O Lord!,' Qur'ān 2.128 exhorts, 'make us Muslims, bowing to Thy (Will).' Muslims, then, are those who submit themselves to God. This submission is demonstrated through the utterance of the *shahādah*, 'There is no god but God' (*lā ilāha illa'Llāh*) and 'Muḥammad is the Messenger of God' (*Muḥammadun rasūl Allāh*). Beyond this, Muslims differ in their understanding of what is necessary to live in submission.

Of course, it is misleading to base a description of Islam entirely on a 1,400-year old Arabic text – a focus that would emphasize uniformity and conformity rather than diversity and multiplicity – for an understanding of a tradition vibrant among 140 million Indian Muslims today. Instead of focusing on singularities, it is more useful to think in terms of 'Muslim traditions' and 'Islamic worlds': the plurality of 'traditions' and 'worlds' reflects the multiplicity of cultural expressions that self-consciously define themselves using the shared terms 'Muslim' and/or 'Islamic.' In other words, despite the astounding diversity among the myriad Muslims in India and more than 1 billion Muslims in the world, they all lay claim to a common name for an identity (Muslim) and a way of life (Islam).

Because of this, and in spite of the myriad opinions about what constitutes Islam and what defines a Muslim, the overwhelming majority of them will refer to the Qur'ān as an unassailable authority in their answers. Since the beginning of Islam this text has featured prominently in the variety of Muslim self-perceptions. Not only did Muslims define themselves as such and name their religion as Islam from their earliest days as a community, but the Qur'ān also exhibited its own 'self-understanding' of its own role. In the beginning of the book's second chapter, it is written, 'This is the Book; in it is guidance sure, without doubt, to those who fear Allāh' (2). Most Muslims understand that this book has no rival because it is God's words to humanity as directly revealed to the Prophet Muḥammad and perfectly preserved by the Muslim community (*ummah*).

'Islam' and 'Muslim' represent categories of religion and human community, respectively. As such, they are implicitly defined in relation to other religions and human communities. The categories found in the Qur'ān reflect the seventh-century social environment in which the text took form. These include 'people of the Book,' 'believers,' and 'unbelievers.' Before engaging these categories, however, we must clearly distinguish between the terms 'Islam' and 'Muslim' because, although they are closely associated, they are not interchangeable. 'Islam' refers to a specific *dīn* ('way of life') among the many that humans practice. 'Muslim' denotes those who identify themselves in some way with this specific *dīn*. In English-language sources, 'Islamic' and 'Muslim' connote somewhat different meanings. This chapter will use 'Islamic' to denote objects and phenomena directly associated with the *dīn* of Islam while 'Muslim' will describe any cultural connection to those who identify themselves as such.

The 'people of the Book' (*ahl al-kitāb*) are mentioned in the verse (*āyāt*) following the first Qur'ānic citation above: 'Nor did the people of the Book dissent therefrom except through envy of each other' (3.19). Although Muslims understand that the Qur'ān has no rival because of the perfection of its preservation, it had predecessors. Muslims believe that three revelations in book form preceded the revelation of the Qur'ān: the Psalms, the Torah, and the Gospel. Because Jews and Christians are communities fashioned around these texts – which Muslims consider to have been revealed as the Qur'ān was – Muslims include them among the 'people of the Book.'[1] However, Jews and Christians differ from Muslims because they failed to maintain their God-entrusted texts and allowed corruptions that misled each community. Therefore, Muslims often define themselves as both among the people of the Book and apart because their careful tending to the Qur'ān has allowed them to live lives most closely hewing to the way of submission God intended.

More generally, the Qur'ān distinguishes between 'believers' and 'unbelievers.' One Qur'ānic passage reads, 'It is He Who has created you; and of you are some that are unbelievers and some that are believers: and Allāh sees well all that ye do' (64.2). This demonstrates well that Muslims have tended not to define themselves entirely in terms of belief but in terms of action as well, which their omniscient deity observes. The categories this passage uses of 'unbelievers' and 'believers' would suggest that what separates Muslims from others is acceptance of a specific belief. Certainly the *shahādah* mentioned earlier represents the essence of Muslim beliefs, and it is for this reason that it is often listed as the first of the 'five pillars of Islam.' Yet most Muslims expect, as the passage implies, that belief necessarily entails specific behaviors and practices. It comes as no surprise, therefore, that the other four pillars (prayer, alms, fasting, and pilgrimage) involve action. Moreover, each of these actions involves a relationship between the individual and both God and other Muslims. Through these shared practices, each of which has its social dimension, Muslims weave a tapestry of interaction meant to ideally culminate in a single, undivided *ummah*. This term can be used for any society, but Muslims primarily use it in reference to their *ummah*, the Muslim *ummah*. As a united *ummah*, Muslims ideally pray together, share their wealth with the less fortunate, fast at the same time, and join millions of others in Makkah for the pilgrimage. Although Muslims practice and believe in a great variety of ways, few use terms like 'sect' or 'division' to describe these differences, especially because the Qur'ān warns against divisiveness (30.31–32).

The singularity of the Islamic *ummah*, like most other dimensions of Islamic life, was best evidenced in Muḥammad's life. As the messenger who delivered the perfect revelation of the Qur'ān and the leader of the first Islamic society, Muḥammad continues to represent the exemplar of being Muslim and living Islam. Muslims often take the accounts of his interactions with the polytheists, Jews, and Christians who inhabited late sixth- and early seventh-century Arabia as the best demonstration of how Islam defines itself. Born and bred in Makkah (Mecca, in contemporary Saudi Arabia), Muḥammad early in his life is understood to have distinguished himself by the integrity of his character. When he shared the revelations that first came to him in CE 610, the predominantly polytheist Makkans became increasingly incensed with the implications Muḥammad's monotheistic claims would have for their own beliefs and the lucrative visits of the surrounding Arabs who annually journeyed to the shrines of their gods and goddesses in Makkah. Many of the earliest chapters of the Qur'ān sharply condemned the practices of worshipping multiple deities instead of Allāh (literally 'the One') who would be understood as an omniscient, omnipotent, and singular deity responsible for creating everything. And so Muḥammad and the earliest Muslims distinguished themselves as monotheists from the polytheists around them.

However, Muslims also soon had to distinguish themselves from the other monotheists in the region: Jews and Christians. Not surprisingly, many in these groups resisted the claims made by Muslims about the priority of their revelation. For instance, Qur'ān 3.65 reflects some of this debate when it asks, 'People of the Book! Why dispute about Abraham, when the Law and the Gospel were not revealed till after him? Have you no understanding?' Qur'ān 3.67 answers the situation, 'Abraham was not a Jew nor yet a Christian; but he was true in faith and bowed his will to God's [which is Islam], and he joined not gods but God.' Along with warnings against the claims made by the first two groups, the Qur'ān contains ample verses promoting the collegiality of Jews, Christians, and Muslims.

Within a few generations after the Prophet's death,[2] certain Muslims began to identify, assess, and compile accounts (*ḥadīth*) of Muḥammad's conversations, perspectives, appearance, and behavior (termed his *sunnah*) into collections. These again demonstrate the point that being Muslim ideally connotes more than a set of beliefs but a way of being in relationship with God and humans and that it involves more than a group of ritual practitioners but a way of forming society. Through these core perspectives, Muslims define some of their various cultural traditions as Islamic and, in some spheres of their lives, distinguish themselves from those around them.

The tradition in the study of religions

Among all religions examined in Western studies of religions, it can be argued that the study of Islam has been the most problematic because of social encounters characterized by cultural misunderstandings, religious competition, and political conflict between Europe (and later the United States) and Muslim-majority countries. It must be remembered that nothing like current academic studies of religions has existed in most cultures. As it developed in the West, it derived from a tradition of Christian apologetics and polemics that contrasted Christianity with non-Christian practices and beliefs so as to justify the first against the latter. Only in 1877 did the secular study of religions separate itself from theological studies in European universities. For this reason, this chapter, more necessarily than those dealing with other Indian traditions, must begin with an exploration of the history and nature of those studies in order to challenge certain understandings deeply embedded among many non-Muslim Western readers. It is important to recognize the roots of Christian and European antagonism to Islam and Muslims.

Western antipathy to Islam and Muslims

Evidence abounds from Islam's origins of a competition between Islam and Christianity. In the Qur'ān, a comparison of Muslim belief with that of Christians (as well as Jews and polytheists) serves to differentiate 'the straight path' from those who have deviated. Claims that Christians allowed the Bible to be corrupted and that they misidentified Jesus as the son of God rather than the prophet he was, serve as a critique warning Muslims to avoid the 'mistakes' that characterize Christian belief. Other passages suggest that Christians and Jews responded negatively to these claims. For instance, *āyāt* 4.20 laments, 'Those to whom we have given the Book know this as they know their own sons. Those who have lost their own souls refuse to believe.' This competition between some Jews, Christians, and Muslims in parts of Arabia would soon be overshadowed by larger political contests that characterized the first 100 years that followed the Prophet's death.

Following the death of Muḥammad, an incredible seventh-century expansion of Arab Muslim political control across the Middle East and North Africa and into both the Iberian Peninsula and southern Europe challenged Christian politics and theology. It meant that the Byzantine Empire – ruled from Constantinople (present-day Istanbul) and based on an Eastern Orthodox ideology – lost control not only over the Christian-dominated southern Mediterranean lands but also Jerusalem, cherished site of Christ's resurrection. Worse, although forced conversions occasionally followed these conquests, many residents in these lands voluntarily converted to Islam even though Jews and Christians enjoyed special *dhimmī* status as 'people of the Book.' (In fact many Jews and non-Byzantine Christians welcomed Muslim rule because it alleviated them of the occasional persecution they suffered under Constantinople's Orthodox-informed chauvinism.) These losses dealt more than an economic and political blow to Europe's Christian leaders; they also challenged expectations of Christianity's inherent superiority and inevitable expansion. Not surprising then, Christian Europeans (Orthodox and Roman Catholic) portrayed Muslims as a malignant, violent threat whose success must be due to Satan's support for their heretical beliefs. Although this particular image has all but disappeared in the Western study of Islam, a portrayal remains prevalent of Muslims as intolerant zealots who offer the conquered 'infidel' the choice between conversion and death. This depiction may owe more to European Christian self-perceptions than anything else.

It was, for instance, the papal-approved series of crusades that, from the eleventh to the fourteenth centuries, united Western Europe under a devotedly Christian mission to militarily return Jerusalem to Christian control and resulted in the slaughter of Jewish and Muslim communities in Europe, Anatolia, and the Middle East. Later, Ferdinand and Isabella combined their forces under the banner of a Christian Reconquista that destroyed a centuries-old culture of Jewish-Muslim-Christian interaction and drove most Muslims and Jews off the Iberian Peninsula with the offer of conversion, deportation, or death beginning in 1492. Contemporary conflicts with European nations and the United States regarding political and commercial interests in the

Middle East have not offered many avenues for altering Western perceptions. It is emblematic of the persistent focus on militant Muslims and enduring images of violent Islam that much existing scholarship traces the origins of Muslims in India to the conquests of the Turko-Persian rulers of the eleventh century (who, although Muslim, invaded South Asia in the cause of looting and expansion – not Islam). However, Muslims first appeared in South Asia at the time of Muḥammad when Arab traders, long present on the western shores of the subcontinent and on the isle of Sri Lanka, began to convert to the faith.

Contemporary scholarship on Indian Muslims

Challenges to these assumptions have been retarded by two unfortunate tendencies in much English-language scholarship. First, Islam has generally been equated with Middle Eastern Studies, which, reflecting Western geopolitical interests, has often been dominated by political studies. Until the mid-1970s, scholarship paid little attention to Islam even in the Middle East where it was perceived to have little play on the political landscape. This changed drastically in 1979 with twin events. The first was the success of the 'Islamic Revolution' that displaced the US-supported Shāh of Iran with a theocratic democracy, and the second event was the Soviet Union's invasion of Afghanistan. This brutal incursion would be successfully defeated by the decade-long efforts of Afghans who identified themselves as warriors of Islam (*mujāhidīn*). The second tendency derives from the Arab-centric perspective of English-language scholars (despite the fact that fewer than 20 percent of Muslims are Arab and that Pakistan, India, and Bangladesh have the highest Muslim populations outside Indonesia) that causes Islam to appear as a foreign encroachment on 'indigenous' Indian cultures. Many surveys of 'Indian religions' omit Islam because the subcontinent does not represent the origination point of the religion, even though few surveys of European or American religions would omit Christianity or Judaism for the same reasons. Moreover, Western biases regarding Islam's zealotry and examples of Muslim intolerance toward the non-Muslim (Hindu) majority of South Asia have stirred antipathy among religion scholars of the region, who then view Muslims as primarily a force inimical to the communities they study.

Thus it has been common to depict Muslims as somehow a society apart among other religions in South Asia. Indeed Westerners have long portrayed Muslims throughout the world with the presumption that they practice a deliberate separatism from those among whom they live. This is evident even in the terms utilized by religion scholars. Although Western authors seldom apply the term 'Christiandom' as a collective epithet for their own Christian-influenced cultures, 'the Islamic world' remains a common phrase that implies a world that willfully stands apart. So, for instance, scholarship seldom refers to the British in India as 'Christian' (though most were) while it by default identifies Indians by religious identity. The implication is that the British primarily act as members of a nation while Indians basically behave as members of a religion.

More recent scholarship has demonstrated, however, how South Asian cultures cannot be defined by categories of religion alone and how interrelated faith and practice, let alone daily life, have been. Although residents of large urban areas may differentiate themselves into neighborhoods characterized by religion, it is important to understand that social division also involves caste, class, and regional characteristics. Even so, a Hindu family in Banaras that seeks to marry their daughter will necessarily have to work with specific Muslim communities: one that will rent the wedding carriage to carry her and another to make the silk *sāṛīs* she will wear. This demonstrates how indeed Muslims dominate some aspects of Indian society, how these sectors are characterized not by Muslims alone but by *birādarī* (kinship groups) as well, and how daily interactions commonly require mutual interaction among these groups.

Fortunately, in the last few decades a wide-scale reevaluation has been unfolding in scholarship that has recognized that the presumption of a radical separation of Muslims from non-Muslims is simplistic, if not dangerous. Enriching their portrayals of historical and modern Indian Muslim lives, increasing numbers of scholars have turned from a paradigm of incessant conflict toward a more nuanced view of coexistence and interaction. Key to this effort, many now realize, is an attempt to transcend the ready descriptors 'Hindu' and 'Muslim' that have for too long been the primary means of identifying any specific individual, community, or attribute thereof. In part this has become possible through new historic research that has looked beyond the rhetoric of an ideal Islamic order and demonstrated the integrated nature of Muslim royal courts. Ethnographic research, meanwhile, has begun to focus on the lived interactions between contemporary Muslims and those with whom they live.

Cosmos and history

The life of Muḥammad and the early ummah

For many Muslims, the history of Islam begins with the original humans, Ādam (Adam) and his wife Ḥawwā' (Eve), who first submitted to Allāh (however imperfectly). From an academic standpoint, however, the history of Islam began with those who would, historically, first identify themselves as 'Muslim' and accept Muḥammad's claim regarding the revelation of the Qur'ān. Because of Muḥammad's role in receiving the revelation and communicating it to humanity, his life has taken on the greatest prominence for most Muslims. The Qur'ān, *sīrah* (biographies), and *ḥadīth* (accounts) have represented the most valuable sources about that life for Muslims. However, these sources have often been supplemented by popular legends about Muḥammad that have been developed from interpretations of Qur'ānic passages. The account below draws from all of these sources and reflects a general narrative of the Prophet's life that many Muslims would recognize even if they might dispute some details.

Muḥammad's early life negotiated a series of pitfalls. Born in perhaps CE 570, he was soon orphaned. Thereafter, he was raised by, first, his grandfather ʿAbd al-Muṭṭalim and, then, uncle Abū Ṭālib in Makkah and soon found his way, like so many urban Arabs of his time, into the life of a merchant. Islamic legends describe some of his travels with caravans to parts of West Asia. When the wealthy merchant Khadījah proposed marriage to him, he accepted, and they began a twenty-five year life together. Not uncommonly, Muḥammad would climb the rocky hillside of Mount Ḥirā' outside of Makkah in order to spend time alone in prayer and meditation. At a time when most Arabs recognized a multitude of deities and worshipped them in iconic form, Muḥammad stood among the few monotheists, known as *ḥanīf*s, who, though not Jewish or Christian, believed in a single god. During one of those prayer sessions, the angel Gabriel (Arabic: Jibrīl) appeared to him and commanded 'Iqra'!' (Recite!). 'I cannot read,' Muḥammad replied. The angel persisted, and then, according to a commonly held understanding, he recited *sūrāh* 96, the first revealed chapter of the Qur'ān (which means 'recitation'). When Muḥammad returned to Makkah, he shared the revelation with Khadījah who accepted what he said, thus becoming the first Muslim to embrace what had been given to Muḥammad. ʿAlī ibn Abī Ṭālib, his cousin and son-in-law, and Abū Bakr, his father-in-law, soon followed. Thus, according to Islamic dating, the *jāhiliyyah* ('time of ignorance') ended, and a new epoch had begun.

As Muḥammad began to share the revelations publicly, they attracted many Makkans with their message that stressed charity to others as Allāh's will. Accession to this will inform Allāh's ultimate judgment on each individual's life that would condition his or her existence after death. The Arabs of the time would have been largely unfamiliar with these themes of monotheism, judgment, and an afterlife unless they had contact with some of the Jewish and Christian communities that existed on the Arabian Peninsula. For most of the residents of Makkah, the message that Muḥammad brought contrasted directly with their polytheistic understandings and their beliefs that death extinguished life entirely without anything to follow. The power of this omniscient, omnipotent, and singular god had no parallel among the many deities worshipped at the time. The notion of a deity's judgment also contrasted with a notion that an inescapable fate ruled one's life and that justice existed solely in the hands of one's tribe. If someone injured a member of the tribe, the tribe exacted a punishment on someone – anyone – from the other tribe. The Qur'ān's concept of individual responsibility clashed with this notion of corporate culpability.

So it should not have come as any surprise that as the nascent Muslim movement attracted numbers, it also attracted resistance due to the divergence in belief and practice. Undoubtedly, this sentiment was only compounded by the threat the growing Muslim community soon posed to Makkah's commercial interests. For three months each year, the tribes declared a cessation from the predatory raiding by which many sustained themselves. These months of peace allowed for the unmolested passage of tribes to Makkah where images of their 360 deities were housed in the Kaʿbah, a building shaped like a towering cube. This pilgrimage provided an important source of income for many of Makkah's merchants and other business people. The strength of Islam's monotheism was matched only by its antagonism to worshipped images. Although Abū Ṭālib's support of Muḥammad brought the protection of their tribe, the Quraysh, as both the numbers of Muslims and the impact of their ideology grew, resistance arose even within the tribe itself. Soon some of Muḥammad's own tribesmen would be plotting to assassinate him. Meanwhile oppression mounted for less prominent Muslims as well. One Makkan tortured his slave, an Abyssinian by the name of Bilāl, while demanding that he renounce his new faith in Islam. Abū Ṭālib eventually ransomed him and released him as a free Muslim. Yet the implications became increasingly threatening for many Makkans. Even the mighty Hamzah, the renowned and recently converted warrior and another uncle of Muḥammad, could protect Muḥammad for only so long. Vicious oppression drove Muslims from their homes and into desert encampments. The personal toll these attacks brought to Muḥammad is reflected in the many Qur'ānic verses that offer him succor in the face of his travails. For instance, *āyāt* 50.39 cajoles, 'So bear with patience what they say and sing the praises of your Lord before the rising of the sun and its setting.' The pressure on

Muḥammad was soon magnified by the deaths of, first, his beloved and supportive wife Khadījah (*c.* 618) and, then, his protector and kinsman Abū Ṭālib (*c.* 619).

Relief came when a delegation from the neighboring city of Yathrib asked Muḥammad to act as an arbitrator for conflicts between the tribes of the city. He agreed on the conditions that the other Muslims would be allowed to settle there and that all the citizens of Yathrib, except for the four Jewish tribes, agree to convert to Islam. With this agreement in hand, Muḥammad authorized the first gradual emigration of Muslims to Yathrib, which would ever after be known as Madinah ('the city'). Muḥammad left last with Abū Bakr, and they too came safely to Madinah but only through the miracle, according to popular belief, of a spider's quickly spun web that hid their presence in a cave from Makkan pursuers.

That the Islamic calendar begins with the *hijra* or migration from Makkah to Madinah (that year is counted as 1 AH or 'after *hijra*') signals the salience of this event in the minds of most Muslims. After all, Madinah represents the first Muslim society in which the followers of Islam no longer existed as a despised outsider group but as a self-supporting society. The revelations shifted in accordance with the new conditions of Muslims. The themes changed from exhortations to monotheism and warnings of judgement to discourse on issues regarding the ordering of society and the compassion of Allāh. The Madinian-revealed verses included general proscriptions and prescriptions about drinking, eating, divorce, and warfare. Primary among those themes were topics of social justice. Perhaps it is for this reason that Islam appealed first to the lower status and less privileged, even before the *hijra* (Denny 1994: 66). Qur'ānic revelation exhorted the maintenance of widows and support of orphans as well as rules for just dealings regarding transactions. In one of its most potent passages, the Qur'ān condemns the practice of female infanticide so common in this patriarchal culture. In this prolonged description of the final judgment day, the juxtaposition with the awesome events of cosmic upheaval underlines the significance of the voice of the forsaken child: 'When the sun is folded up, the stars turn dim and scatter, the mountains made to move, the ten-month pregnant female camels are abandoned, the wild beasts stampede on the run, when the oceans surge and swell, when the souls are reunited (with the bodies) and the little girl buried alive is asked for what crime she was put to death' (81.1–9). The Arabic for 'compassion,' *al-Raḥīm*, stands as one of the most prevalent names for Allāh, featuring prominently in the *bismi'llāh* prayer that is commonly recited at the initiation of any new endeavor. Muḥammad frequently manifested this quality in his role of the *ummah*'s leader, even in combat.

Muḥammad, previously a prophet heading a small band of followers, became the leader of this society, responsible for coping with problems of law, security, and the economy. Despite the hospitality of the Madinians, the Anṣār (the supporters), life for the displaced Makkans, the Muhājirūn (the emigrants), did not come easily as the Madinian economy could not simply expand to accommodate the new population. So some of the Muslims turned to the common tradition of raiding caravans. Their effectiveness excited the anger of Makkan merchants who sent military expeditions to defend their trade routes and attack Madinah itself. Most of these failed however, and the Muslims' successes seemed to strengthen their resolve that with Allāh's help anything, even the capture of Makkah, seemed possible. Meanwhile, through deft diplomacy, which included marrying into a number of tribes following the death of Khadījah, Muḥammad effectively built a remarkable coalition of Bedouin tribes that increased the pressure on Makkah. Finally, the Makkan leaders capitulated, and the Muslims reentered Makkah with little bloodshed. Muḥammad led Muslims into the Kaʿbah that was cleansed immediately of the images it contained and rededicated to the One God.

Muḥammad returned to Madinah for his final two years of life. The revelations continued and were recorded conscientiously even as more Arabian tribes joined his coalition and became Muslim. In CE 632 he died having completed a final pilgrimage to Makkah. His close companion ʿUmar ibn al-Khaṭṭāb, approaching a crowd gathered to hear about their dead leader, declared: 'O men, if anyone worships Muhammad, Muhammad is dead: if anyone worships God, God is alive, immortal' (Isḥāq 1987: 683). In this way, Muḥammad's final act in life served as yet another testament to the beliefs he promoted.

This story of Muḥammad, from the perspective of most Muslims, represents a central narrative of understanding what Islam is and how to be a Muslim. Muḥammad, indeed, was never anything more than a man, and the narrative provides its own warning about what happens when the shape of humans becomes mistaken for the presence of Allāh. Nevertheless, Allāh chose Muḥammad as the final prophet who would both communicate the most perfect text and, as the person most intimate with it, act as its most important interpreter. For this reason, many Muslims, informed about the Prophet's personal perspectives, behavior, and appearance through the Ḥadīth, model themselves on his example physically and in their mannerisms. They demonstrate their respect for him when they say or write the equivalent of 'peace be upon him' (PBUH) when they pronounce or write his name. Yet, most Muslims would take the mistaken Western term for them as 'Muhammadans' with chagrin because their commitment is to Allāh, as the proclamation of faith makes clear, 'There is no god but God, and Muḥammad is the Messenger of God.'

Although only a man, Muḥammad was witness to miracles beyond the revelation of the Qur'ān. Perhaps one of the most famous involved his Night Journey (*al-isrā'*) and Ascension (*al-miʿrāj*). As implied in the Qur'ān (17.1) and reported in the Ḥadīth literature, a winged horse summoned Muḥammad one night for a journey from Makkah to 'the far mosque' which later traditions would understand as Jerusalem. Astride this creature, known as Burāq, Muḥammad flew to the top of what is now known as the Temple Mount, the then abandoned plateau on which the Jewish temple had stood centuries earlier. From there, after leading the preceding prophets in prayer, he ascended a ladder to Paradise in the company of Jibrīl. At each level of this multilayered Paradise, he met earlier prophets until, on the penultimate level, he encountered Mūsā (Moses), the first of Allāh's *rāsul* (literally 'messenger') who prepared him for his meeting with the One God and had him petition Allāh to decrease to five, instead of the originally commanded fifty, daily prayers. Upon his return from Paradise and return flight on Burāq, the regular practice of daily prayers is understood to have begun.

Cosmic history

Despite the significant historical and cultural diversity in their understandings, most Muslims believe that it is this Paradise that the righteous will encounter on the Day of Judgment (*Yawn ad-Dīn*). Preceding this event, according to Shīʿa and some Sunnī theology, a *mahdī* ('divinely guided leader') will return to guide the faithful after all moral order in the world has decayed entirely. Then a *dajjāl* ('deceiver') will arise in an attempt to lead believers astray, only to be destroyed by the *mahdī* and a returned Jesus (Smith and Haddad 1981: 66–70). Final judgment follows. As part of the Islamic emphasis on individual responsibility and culpability, the Qur'ān warns of this Reckoning – a day when all humans will be resurrected and face Allāh, one at a time, to have their deeds judged. Those whose good deeds outweigh their bad enjoy an eternal Paradise; those who do not, face one of the seven levels of the inferno. (Dante would later fashion the topography of his *Divine Comedy* after this model.) And, so, history culminates (and ends) with this event – a history that involves the consistent effort on the part of Allāh to mercifully guide humanity despite their repetitive failures to accede to his guidelines. The repeated revelation of Allāh's Book despite earlier failures to keep it free of corruption provides one example of that mercy while the finality of the Qur'ānic revelation and Muḥammad's prophethood reflects Allāh's expectations, reinforced by the inevitability of judgment, that Muslims will maintain Islam.

Muḥammad represents the end of a succession of prophets (*anbiyā'*) who testified to Allāh's 'signs.' These prophets did not act as predictors of the future as the common English usage would suggest but rather as individuals who warned about the mistakes the society around them was making. Ādam represented the first prophet and others are Nūḥ (Noah), Sulaymān (Solomon), and Ayyūb (Job). Four prophets ranked on a level of higher regard because they brought books that Allāh intended to help humanity live in the way Allāh prescribed. These four, known as *rusul*, are Mūsā (Moses) who brought the Torah, Dā'ūd (David) who brought the Psalms, 'Īsā (Jesus) with the Gospel, and Muḥammad with the Qur'ān. This list makes clear that Muslims understand Judaism and Christianity to be the predecessors mentioned in the previous section – the 'people of the Book.' No prophets, however, would follow Muḥammad – another mark of his uniqueness. So when the early *ummah* lost Muḥammad, they lost their religious leader as well as their social and military leader.

After Muḥammad

The inertia behind the growth of Islam, however, could not be stopped by Muḥammad's death. After an initial period of uncertainty regarding the leadership of the *ummah* and the fidelity of previously converted tribes, Muslim Arabs exploded out of Arabia, inspired by the ideology of Islam and likely propelled by population pressures. Within 100 years, Muslim armies conquered lands from the Iberian Peninsula to the periphery of India, which they knew as al-Hind. Just as the unity of this empire would soon be rent by divergent interests and regional forces, so the singularity of the *ummah* that has remained an important ideal of Muslims today began to be threatened by differences in groups with the death of the charismatic Muḥammad, who had previously provided uncontested leadership.

Upon his death, dissent arose as to who would succeed Muḥammad as leader of the *ummah*. Since Muslims understood that no one could replace Muḥammad, a deputy (caliph) would be declared. But how would that person be chosen? Most believed that the Arab tradition of choosing the first among equals from the tribal heads would suffice. One group, however, argued that the leadership should be a matter of familial descent and looked to 'Alī, his cousin and son-in-law and father of his two grandsons. In contrast with the majority, who came to be known as Sunnī ('of the custom'), this protesting group came to be known as Shīʿa ('the party [of ʿAlī]'). The Shīʿa represent the largest non-Sunnī community among Muslims. Although the *ummah* overruled the Shīʿa in its first three choices of caliphs (Abū Bakr, ʿUmar ibn al-Khaṭṭāb, and ʿUthmān ibn ʿAffān), ʿAlī became the fourth caliph. In the power struggle that followed ʿAlī's death in 660, his first son, Ḥasan, soon withdrew his bid for leadership, while his second son, Ḥusayn, was slain in a tragic battle by his political contenders while on his way to meet partisans who encouraged him to seek the leadership. This battle, which occurred at Karbalāʾ in what is today Iraq, followed an heroic stand by Ḥusayn and his entourage (including family members) as they faced starvation, dehydration, and overwhelming military force. Ḥusayn's death continues to be commemorated today by Shīʿa and some Sunnī on Muḥarram (the 'sacred month'). But the Shīʿa did not alone challenge the direction that many of the *ummah* sought to take, although no other group would remain such an identifiably discernable community.

Islam in premodern South Asia

Islam arrived in India long before any Muslim armies did. Some of the Arab traders who had established homes on the coasts of Sri Lanka and southern India converted to Islam in the course of their commerce with the residents of the Arabian Peninsula. In CE 711, a Muslim Arab army reached Baluchistan and Sindh in the south of today's Pakistan. This represented the last gasp and eastern-most extent of the century-long military expansion that followed Muḥammad's death. The wealth and strength of regional rulers blunted the edge of the incursion and brought it to a halt. For the next 300 years, the states ruled by Muslims from Spain to Sindh demonstrated increasing cultural divergence from the Arab patterns that first informed Islam as regional cultures influenced the émigré Arabs, and their newborn religion, through a process of gradual inculturation. When Muslim-dominated states began to pressure Indian territories in the eleventh century, they did so as part of neither a singular social body, nor unified political system, nor continuous religious expansion, but rather as something quite different.

Ethnically Turkish and Persian groups in Central Asia vied with one another for control over territory and wealth. As some of these succeeded in consolidating their power bases and could afford to look beyond the regions of their direct control, India became a tempting opportunity. Contrary to the frequent perception today of the subcontinent as an economically impoverished place, al-Hind had long held the reputation as a fabulously wealthy land. And so Maḥmūd of Ghazna (a city in Afghanistan) began a series of raids into the upper plains of the Indus and Ganges Valleys in quest of loot at the turn of the eleventh century. His soldiers targeted whatever sites promised the most treasure, and these were Hindu royal palaces and temples and Hindu and Buddhist monasteries. That these men identified themselves as Muslim seems incidental because Islamic ideology no more justified their attacks than Hindu or Buddhist ideology motivated their opponents' defense. Maḥmūd's raids were followed by the efforts of some Turko-Persians to expand the extent of their rule beyond the Hindu Kush mountains that separate Afghanistan from South Asia. Ultimately, a series of dynasties established themselves in the northern Indus Valley in the city of Lahore and in the northern Gangetic Valley in and around the city of Delhi.

These states more obviously relied on Islam as an ideology of state, including the justification of rule. They, therefore, destroyed temples associated with the political entities that preceded them and founded mosques, sometimes atop the temple ruins, as expressions of their new rule. This has long been contrived as a wholesale assault on Hinduism: the natural result of an endemic fanatical religious bigotry. But such was seldom the case. The difference became most apparent with the arrival of the Mughals, a displaced Turko-Mongolian family that claimed descent from the Mongols Jenghiz Khān and Timur – hence the name bequeathed to them by others: Mughal (their name for themselves was Gurkani) (Thackston 2002: xlvi). Each capital city that the Mughals at one time or another used eventually developed a large mosque opposite a massive fortress that housed the royal residence. Although few of the Mughal emperors followed a particularly strict Islamic lifestyle or aggressively promoted Islam, the Mughal state premised its authority to rule on the claim that it manifested the sovereignty of Allāh. This legitimation via a deity paralleled earlier, non-Muslim forms in India so that non-Muslims recognized the form and accommodated themselves in such a way as to be able to serve the state. Inversely, many Muslims accommodated themselves to serve states based on Hindu-legitimation schemes, as demonstrated through the life of one member of the contemporary military elite.

In sixteenth-century South India, ʿAin al-Mulk Gīlāni, a Muslim by name, served the Muslim Bahmānī Sulṭān, the Hindu Vijayanagara king, and the Muslim Bījāpūr Sulṭān without exercising any apparent preference nor experiencing any obvious discrimination. Rather, like other members of a military elite whose services royal courts sought enthusiastically, ʿAin al-Mulk adapted himself to the ritual language and procedures of each newly adopted employer. ʿAin al-Mulk's service to Vijayanagara would have required some fluency in the Telegu, Kannada, and/or Sanskrit languages, while in Bījāpūr he would have relied on Dakhni, Persian, and/or Arabic. Premodern rulers defined their courtiers primarily according to their loyalty, not religious identity (Wagoner 2003).

Just as Muslim Arab culture transformed as it moved into new social environments, so did the Turkish and Persianate Muslim cultures that Central Asians introduced, including their forms of Islam. The three most prominent agents in this transformation were the royal court, the army camp, and 'Ṣūfīs.'

As just mentioned, Islam played a legitimating role in the rule of many Muslims before Independence in 1947, and so those who participated in the court required familiarity with an Islamic vocabulary used in the language and ritual of rule. This no more required the adoption of Islam as a personal set of practices and beliefs than did participation in Hindu courts with their reliance on Sanskrit and particular forms of patronage. However, becoming a Muslim may have been perceived to offer enough advantage to warrant formal conversion. Besides these courtiers who circulated through Hindu and Muslim court life, rulers too typically negotiated a variety of religious traditions in efforts to maintain their position. Because rulers had domain over territories that included people with a range of religious affiliations, most patronized a variety of religious institutions and specialists. Although their non-Muslim subjects may have recognized the form of Islamic ritual as legitimating the rule, they did so with the expectation that the ruler would protect all the various forms of religious order among the population under his dominion. Thus the same Muslim rulers who had destroyed temples that manifested the legitimation of their political rivals patronized yet other temples (as well as Brāhmaṇs) in their effort to demonstrate their role of protecting the *dharma* (that is, the Hindu moral order), as Hindus expected of whomever ruled them. This required familiarity of the *sulṭāns* and emperors with the cultures of their subjects. Mughal emperors famously sponsored translations of Sanskrit epics, such as the *Rāmāyaṇa* and the *Mahābhārata*, in Persian texts adorned with meticulously painted miniatures that drew on a wealth of ethnographic details regarding contemporary non-Muslim dress, practices, and food.

The Turkish-speaking soldiers who served these courts lived a life quite apart from their superiors. Their encampments involved intimate interaction with local residents in *bāẓārs* and the like. As a measure of these interactions, a new language arose called Urdu that literally means 'the camp.' This language merged Persian and Arabic with the local vernacular to provide a means of everyday communication. Although Urdu would develop over the next several centuries as a means of both crafting refined poetry and being eloquent in a status-conscious society, it undoubtedly served as an interlinguistic bridge, a vehicle of mutual experience that facilitated the increased familiarity of the general population with Islamic practices and ideals.

Finally, Ṣūfīs – or at least those later identified as such – served to both transmit Islamic paradigms to the broader population and translate them into local understandings. Many of these men (although some women are found among them) associated with *ṭarīqah*s ('brotherhood'), which defined themselves according to the spiritual lineage of teachers. However, others did not. Although the *ṭarīqah*s would commonly claim Muḥammad as the originator of a chain (*silsilah*) of spiritual teaching, the actual origins of Islamic mysticism cannot be easily discerned. The famous eleventh-century Ṣūfī of Lahore, Abū-l-Ḥasan ʿAlī al-Hujwīrī, quotes a much earlier Ṣūfī when he wrote, 'Today Sufism is a name without a reality, but formerly it was a reality without a name' (1990: 14). Hujwīrī's sanguine statement reflects both the ill-defined origins of Sufism and the contempt that many Muslims have for those who claim to be contemporary mystics.

Nevertheless, currently in Bihar, Jharkand, and West Bengal, Ṣūfīs hold a revered place in the social memory of many communities as founders of villages and towns and the peaceful impulse to conversion for residents. Local residents explain that Ṣūfīs settled deliberately in rural locations so as to develop '*junglī*' (uncultivated) areas and teach Islamic lessons to locals. Richard Eaton (1993) has argued persuasively that these stories derive from sixteenth- and seventeenth-century hagiographic traditions that have been reinforced by the Protestant-informed worldview of Western scholars. Whoever these land developers were, they apparently learned the vernacular languages of the region and translated Islamic perspectives into linguistic and conceptual idioms that were locally understandable and to which some indigenous perspectives slowly conformed. Whether they understood themselves as such, those popularly identified today as Ṣūfīs played a critical role in the expansion of the *ummah* in South Asia, as demonstrated in the popular narrative of a Ṣūfī enshrined in rural India.

In Chainpur, a village in the north Indian state of Bihar, a Ṣūfī tomb stands at the edge of the dried-mud covered brick houses that crowd away from the precious, dark-colored farmland. A gathering assembles during the annual celebration of the entombed Aṣṭa Awliyā'. A few men who join the festivities answer the questions of someone new to the area about the Ṣūfī. 'He was a *walī* ("a favorite of God"),' Ahmed Khan explains. 'Seven hundred years ago . . . when he came here, people were uncivilized. They did not know about *dharma, mazhab* ['religion']. . . . He was born in Makkah.' When asked why Aṣṭa Awliyā' came to this area, another man replies, 'To spread Islam,' to which Ahmed adds, 'It was jungle then. There was only jungle.' Asked to explain the changes the Ṣūfī brought, Ahmed explains that the local people believed in him strongly and so they built his tomb. A third person adds, 'For the people of [the village], Aṣṭa Awliyā' is a special *guru*.' Although all three men identified themselves as Muslim, their answers reflect the composite culture of many parts of India as they use terms (*dharma* and *guru*) that derive from Sanskrit-based religious cultures.

Complex cultural contexts such as this prove difficult to describe, reliant as we are on the concept of 'religions' which include the mutually exclusive categories of 'Islam,' 'Hinduism,' and 'Buddhism.' Although it may be true that on the level of certain elites (such as the *'ulamā'*, Brāhmaṇ scholars, and monks) a rigid orthopraxy ('proper practice') or orthodoxy ('proper thought') could be imagined and maintained, among most South Asians no such jealous allegiance led to a firm refusal to engage in practices or beliefs defined as non-Islamic or non-Hindu. Such expectations reflect the Protestant origins of the Western study of religions with defined confessions of belief that prompted inclusion or exclusion based on a strict set of beliefs. Although some Muslims assiduously distinguished Muslims from *kāfir*s (non-believers), for many during the era of the Delhi Sultanate and Mughal rule religion did not provide an exclusive community of belief so much as a range of options for devotion to a deity or saints, for remedy from malaise, and for discernment of the future. Non-Muslims frequented Ṣūfī shrines, and Muslims, the *samādhi* (tomb) of non-Muslim *sant*s (saints). Meanwhile, elites often patronized temples, tombs, mosques, and other religious institutions without regard to their own religious identity. As a result, many ideas and practices that we may be tempted to describe as 'Islamic' could be found among non-Muslims, while styles of poetry, fashions of literature, and styles of artistic representation derived from non-Muslim sources influenced developing expressions of regional Muslim religiosity.

One of the best demonstrations of this is the *bhakti* movement. Undoubtedly influenced by Islamic monotheism and mysticism, *bhakti* poets wrote and sang their devotion to a god or goddess, portraying themselves as the friend, child, or even lover of the deity. The fifteenth-century poet Kabīr represents an unusual *bhakti* because of his unrelenting criticism of orthoprax practices among both Hindus and Muslims. However, this unique approach also demonstrates the fusion of devotional elements from both traditions into a vision very difficult to categorize. The blunt blandishments he administers to members of various traditions demonstrate both the existence of Hindu and Muslim identities in his day and a popular movement's willingness to deride the significance of such identities relative to devotion to God. So writes Kabīr (1986: 50–51; *śabda* 30):

> Brother, where did your two gods come from?
> Tell me, who made you mad?
> Ram, Allah, Keshav, Karim, Hari, Hazrat –
> so many names.
> So many ornaments, all one gold,
> it has no double nature.

For conversation we make two –
this *namāz*, that *pujā*,
this Mahadev, that Muhammed,
this Brahmā, that Adam,
this a Hindu, that a Turk,
but all belong to earth.
Vedas, Korans, all those books,
those Mullas and those Brahmins –
so many names, so many names,
but the pots are all one clay.
Kabir says, nobody can find Ram,
both sides are lost in schisms.
One slaughters goats, one slaughters cows,
they squander their birth in isms.

Kabīr's carefully calibrated and balanced poetry uniformly criticizes Hindu and 'Turk' (a common description of Muslims harkening to the Turkish cultural and linguistic identity of much of the invading Central Asian armies). His singsong litany of practices (*namāz* and *pūjā*), figures (Mahādeva and Muḥammad), texts (Vedas and Qur'āns), and specialists (Mullās and Brāhmaṇs) rattle the sanctity they might hold for the audience in provocative challenge to focus on Rām (Kabīr's ubiquitous and nonsectarian name for the One God) instead of trappings of devotion external to the relationship with God.

'Islam,' therefore, refers to a set of practices and beliefs that, considered together, represent a sort of ideal. Muslims may have, at times, recourse to this ideal but more often negotiated a complex landscape of religious opportunity and commitments that varied tremendously among South Asia's myriad cultures. Some practices such as the formal prayer or *namāz* were likely to have been exclusive to Muslims. Shrine visitation would not have been, though, and neither would Muslim participation in holidays such as Holī and Dīvālī. Much of this changed, however, in the modern period.

Islam in modern South Asia

Since the beginning of the period of British rule, a set of impulses for far more exclusive notions of Islam and Muslim identity has arisen. The causes of this are multiple, and since a later section will provide more details on specific movements, only a few prominent historical influences will be briefly considered here.

British imperialism

Although they competed for business with several other European companies, the British East India Company would achieve goals unimaginable in 1600 when it received a royal charter to trade in South Asia. By 1757 the Company had taken the place of a regional ruler as Bengal's tax collector in the service of the Mughal emperor. A century later, they had effectively executed such successful political and military strategies that they held a great many more territories by direct or indirect rule. But in 1857, a rebellion (described by the British as the Mutiny and by Indian nationalists as the First War of Independence) swept across North India. In their effort to find a cause to explain this bloody uprising against the supposedly munificent rule of the 'British Rāj,' the British fell back on long-held European images of fanatical Muslims inspired by Islamic rage. Although those who had rebelled had been encouraged by some Muslim leaders and enlisted the support of the powerless Mughal heir, more Hindus than Muslims participated in the violence. Nevertheless, the British apportioned blame overwhelmingly to Muslims (associated as they were with the previous political order) and convinced themselves that Muslims could no longer be trusted (Robb 2002: 146–47).

The British government gave increasing preference to Hindus and Sikhs in a political system that severed the interreligious patronage exchanges existing in the pre-British period while polarizing indigenous identities overwhelmingly along religious lines. Hindus and Muslims increasingly identified themselves primarily as such in part to fit within imperial systems (such as the law courts) that provided segregated systems for different 'religious communities.' As observed earlier, premodern South Asians certainly identified themselves and one another according to religious association, but governmental and legal systems did not define them specifically as such. In response to their declining fortunes, many Muslims pined nostalgically for the Mughal past while others promoted Islamic revival and reform that often relied on sharp differentiation between Muslims and their Hindu and Sikh neighbors and (predominantly) Christian overlords.

Representational democracy

The British often justified their rule and exploitation of South Asia because Indians had yet to learn the art of what the British envisioned as enlightened self-government. Many South Asians rose to the challenge motivated by the tantalizing goal of self-rule, the attractive ideals of democracy, and/or political ambition and adapted themselves to the evolving form of government. In this new system, political parties economized their effort to attract votes by identifying and appealing to blocs of voters. Influenced by British classifications of the population (especially informed by the decadal censuses), South Asian politicians often appealed to the supposed interests of religious groups. The success of the Indian National Congress party in the 1930s, for instance, to stump for restrictions on the slaughter of cows (bovine being revered by most Hindus and consumed by many Muslims) was an attempt to define an issue attractive to Hindus at the expense of Muslims who felt increasingly targeted and alienated.

Communication and transportation technology

The tremendous technological advances that brought increasingly rapid improvements in the efficiency of communication and transportation and an accompanying decline in costs meant that far-flung members of the *ummah* could communicate with and encounter one another far more easily than ever before. These technologies existed in a symbiotic relationship with European imperialism that both succeeded because of its technical superiority and expanded its reach through a worldwide infrastructure made possible through that same success. For instance, each foreign harbor secured by European coal-fired warships (superior technology in the nineteenth century) meant the possibility of a new coaling station from which naval power, and commercial shipping, could be projected yet further. But not only Europeans enjoyed the faster, cheaper, and safer passage steamships provided. Whereas fewer than 300,000 Muslims performed the pilgrimage or *ḥajj* to Makkah in 1965 (Bukhari 2002), today, benefiting from consumer air travel, more than 2 million participate. Among Indians, at least 10,000 participated in the *ḥajj* annually in the 1880s (Pearson 1996: 54) while more than 100,000 travel today. This means that more Indian Muslims encounter increasing numbers of Muslims from around the world, accelerating the spread of perspectives and ideologies. Even as more Muslims increasingly encounter the diversity among Muslims, movements seeking to unify Muslims become increasingly successful. This has been particularly true in South Asia with, for instance, Mawlānā Mawdūdī whose works find interested audiences worldwide.

The culmination of these dynamics crested fatefully with Partition. Faced with the imminent departure of the British and the successful rise of Hindu-themed politics of the Indian National Congress, a group of Muslim politicians in the Muslim League gradually decided that only the threat of Muslims demanding a separate Muslim nation would safeguard the interests of Muslims. When this strategy failed, they considered the actual creation of such a state their best option. They intended Pakistan, as they called the state, to be a haven for Muslims and Muslim culture with a secular government, not a theocratically Islamic one. Although many South Asian Muslims disagreed that there was any need for the creation of this state, the Muslim League successfully brokered a deal with the British and used both the threat and action of violence to finally gain the agreement of the Indian National Congress.

Waves of violence rolled across the northern parts of South Asia preceding and following the celebration of India's and Pakistan's Independence at midnight on August 14/15, 1947 as whole populations of Hindus, Muslims, and Sikhs moved toward their adopted homelands. Although most Muslims preferred to remain where they lived already, the severity of the violence caused more violence, and so many moved to avoid the worsening local situation. Hindu and Sikh emigrants to India shared horrific stories of slaughter, assault, and plunder, reaffirming depictions common in the minds of many British of Muslims as intolerant barbarians even as non-Muslims visited these same horrors on Muslims. The perpetual conflict between India and Pakistan – usually characterized by political tension and low-scale military exchanges but erupting in full-scale war three times since Independence – has made Muslims in India self-conscious of their patriotism. Not infrequently, their allegiance to India has been challenged with a suspicion that their sympathies – whether during open combat or cricket matches – lie with Pakistan. This contributes to a sense among many that to be Muslim is to be a marginalized Indian.

Contributing to a rise in this suspicion about Muslims has been the ascent of the Hindutva movement. Drawing on the worldview of various nineteenth-century thinkers and using specific premodern heroes as symbols, Hindutva proponents consider India to be essentially a Hindu nation. Hindu, for them, represents less a religious identity and more a cultural identity that anyone who considers himself or herself Indian must embrace. The movement, most forcefully manifest in the Saṅgh Parivār (Family of Organizations) led by the Rāṣṭriya Svayamsevak Sangh (RSS or Society of National Volunteers), depicts Muslims as perpetual foreigners (since they descend from outside invaders) or lost brethren forcibly converted from Hinduism. The destruction of the then unused Bābrī Masjid in 1992 most poignantly illustrated this perspective. Charging that the original Mughal emperor, Bābar, had demolished a temple commemorating the site of the god Rāma's birthplace and erected a mosque in its stead, members of the Rāṣṭriya Svayamsevak Sangh stormed the controversial site and demolished the 400-year-old mosque. When Muslims protested, riots ensued with thousands murdered, most of them Muslims. A chilling effect swept through many Indian Muslims even as the political party of the Saṅgh, the Bhāratīya Janatā Party (BJP or Indian People's Party) surged to national power despite these tragic events. Another round of violence was sparked in Gujarat in 2002 when a group of Muslims burned Hindutva activists alive in the train carriage from which they had initiated verbal assaults. Once again, Hindu mobs used their superior numbers to overwhelm not only the few aggressors but also then to attack innocent Muslims wherever they could find them across the state. Officials estimate that perhaps 2,000 died and 100,000 were displaced in the riots, most of them Muslim.

Among the outcomes of these events, individual Muslims have had their identity more poignantly defined as 'Muslim' despite the multiple social worlds in which most engage. Every individual person lives in communion with a number of different groups (for example, family, neighborhood, work-related, nation, sports teams) and so encounters the world with multiple identities. The identity that comes to the fore depends on the social context in which the individual finds himself or herself. However, the increasing polarization of communal politics in India decreases the identities shared between Hindus and Muslims. Although many Muslims remember playing Holī or celebrating Dīvālī with their neighbors or fellow workers, today more consider these to be 'Hindu activities' that Muslims must exclude themselves from in accordance with a more rigidly defined identity of 'Muslim.' Nevertheless, many Muslims share overlapping lives with their neighbors and other Indians.

Sacred life and literature

Muslims have often emphasized that Islam involves not only a relationship between the individual and Allāh but relationships with other humans as well. Social justice features prominently in those relationships and shall be considered in the section 'Ethics and human relations.' Moreover, the social dimension of Islamic prescriptions for life is prominent in the practices that compose the ideal sacred life. Once again, most Muslims first turn to the Qur'ān and then to the Ḥadīth for the basis of this ideal and the practices the Qur'ān suggests.

The Qur'ān

The angel Jibrīl first commanded Muḥammad, 'Iqra'!' (Recite!), and the culmination of the recitations that Muḥammad communicated over the next twenty-two years became the Qur'ān (literally 'recitation'). The complete text includes 114 chapters or *sūrāh*s. This text has a number of significant features.

Revelation

Most Muslims understand the Qur'ān to be the revealed word of Allāh communicated to Muḥammad by Jibrīl and related by Muḥammad to Muslims who recorded it in writing. Arabs in seventh-century Arabia had scant access to paper, and so Muslims recorded the revelations on whatever they had available which might be paper, leather, or even bone. Most Muslims understand the revelation as deriving from a Heavenly Book written in Arabic. The elegance and sophistication of its poetry demonstrate for many that this text could not have originated from the illiterate Muḥammad. Many understand the inimitability of the Qur'ān as demonstrative of its unique nature and authorship. The Qur'ān appears to understand itself in this way as well when it challenges its detractors: 'If you are in doubt of what We have revealed to Our votary, then bring a *sūrāh* like this and call any witness, apart from God, you like, if you are truthful' (2.23). This notion of the inability to produce any text equal to the Qur'ān has also informed the long-standing injunction against declaring a rendering of the Qur'ān into another language as a translation. The conceit of a translation is that it places into another language the meaning and form of a text. Many Muslims argue that this is not possible with the Qur'ān because its Arabic, composition, and meaning are inexorably interlinked.

Most Muslims understand that, as revelation, the Qur'ān must be safeguarded against any corruption that might affect the text. The history of the three previously revealed books, their careless treatment, and the distortions that ultimately misled their communities required Muslims to go to great lengths to protect this final revelation. And so the third caliph, ʿUthmān, oversaw the final arrangement of the Qur'ān and the destruction of alternative editions so that the Qur'ān appears the same in any house or mosque in India, Asia, or any other continent. Although print technology makes the publication of the Qur'ān a relatively inexpensive proposition today, the practice continues that some Muslims memorize the entire text. They obtain the title *ḥāfiẓ* ('protector').

Themes

The Qur'ān arrived in portions over two decades, often directly addressing the current social or military conditions that the *ummah* was confronting at a specific time. This is most clearly evident in the contrast between the Makkan and Madinian verses. The verses revealed in Makkah to a nascent community underscored themes of warning and exhortation. Specifically, these verses warned of the Day of Judgement and the individual accountability each person would undergo. This contrasted pointedly with Arab traditions that eschewed an afterlife and focused on the individual's accountability to the tribe and the tribe's accountability for each of its member's actions. One gets the impression that the Qur'ān's original verses sought to compel nonbelievers to embrace Islam with dire warnings that they otherwise would suffer the consequences that Allāh, the Judge, would levy.

The verses revealed to Muḥammad in Madinah addressed the very different situation the *ummah* experienced once it transformed from a movement into a society in its adopted home. These focus on the ordering of society on domestic and social levels while also exhorting Muslims to be brave in the face of violent oppression. These verses also stress the notion of 'signs' provided by Allāh that demonstrate Allāh's presence and involvement in history for the benefit of believers. Nature represents the first sign Allāh provided humanity. The balance, regularity, and intricacy of nature all demonstrate the involvement of a creator.

Referentiality

'This is The Book free of doubt and involution, a guidance for those who preserve themselves from evil and follow the straight path,' *āyāt* 2.2 explains. As revelation, the Qur'ān demonstrates an awareness of the book that it is, the audience it addresses, and the sense of purpose that informs it. Much of the Qur'ān appeals to Muslims who are exhorted and encouraged to various efforts. In some places, the Qur'ān appears to address non-Muslims with its warnings of imminent and long-term dangers caused by either their lack of belief and obstruction (in the case of polytheists) or their corrupt beliefs and resistance (in the case of Jews and Christians). Overall, although the revelations continued for more than two decades, various verses reflected an assumption that they cohered together.

Arrangement

Although the Qur'ān includes many narratives of events understood to have occurred in a specific order, it is neither arranged as a narrative nor in chronological order of its revelation. Instead, after the first *sūrāh*, the remaining *sūrāh*s are organized from longest first to shortest last. Each *sūrāh* is known by a name that derives from some unique feature of the chapter, undoubtedly to act as a mnemonic device for those who memorized the text in its entirety.

The first chapter of the Qur'ān is known as the *ṣūrat al-fāṭiḥah* (Chapter of the Opening). Neither the first revealed (that was *sūrāh* 96) nor the longest (*sūrāh* 2), it acts as a distillation of the entire book.

> In the name of Allāh, most benevolent, ever-merciful
> All praise be to Allāh, the Lord of all the worlds,
> Most beneficent, ever-merciful,
> King of the Day of Judgement.
> You alone we worship, and to You alone we turn for help.
> Guide us [O Lord] to the path that is straight,
> the path of those You have blessed,
> not of those who have earned your anger,
> nor those who have gone astray.

The first verse, known as the *bismi'llāh*, represents a prayer unto itself. Just as most *sūrāh*s begin with this verse, so new endeavors too are often initiated with its recitation. It dedicates the text or act 'in the name of Allāh.' The next four verses describe Allāh in praise, explicating the basic characteristics of the singular god who Muslims worship, the final yet compassionate judge. The exhortation of the concluding four verses expresses the Muslim faith that their god is involved in their lives and has a way that has been sanctioned but that not all follow. The Fātiḥah, the first or opening *sūrāh*, expresses the essence of the Qur'ān through its orientation to Allāh in the voice of the faithful who recognize a path made apparent by the One God's direct guidance.

Demonstrating how many Muslims incorporate Qur'ānic elements directly into their lives, the Fātiḥah often acts as a prayer in its entirety. For instance, after a Muslim's death, he or she is buried with it read over the grave. Then, each month for the first year, close relatives will visit the gravesite and recite the Fātiḥah again. Not uncommonly, children continue this annually at their parents' graves.

If the first *sūrāh* reflects the entirety of the Qur'ān in its most reduced form, the second *sūrāh* demonstrates the general features of the Qur'ān. Generally, it can be divided into three components. In the first, the text refers to itself and its audience, as has been quoted earlier. Like the Fātiḥah, it also refers to those who have failed to listen to Allāh's message. In the second, examples from the lives of the prophets and others illustrate humanity's repetitive failures to abide by their God's will despite the multiple demonstrations of divine power. It advances this theme with a reflection on the individual's journey from prenatal nonexistence to birth to death to resurrection: 'Then how can you disbelieve in God? He gave you life when you were dead. He will make you die again then bring you back to life: to him then you will return' (2.28). The chapter then continues on with examples of humanity's failures citing Iblīs (a satanic being), Ādam and his wife, Mūsā (Moses) and the children of Israel, and ʿĪsā (Jesus) and the people of the Book. Although this list follows a generally recognized chronology of the lives of these prophets, the text's compilers clearly do not intend to provide an overall narrative of these lives. Rather, the text appears to assume its audience's familiarity with the various stories, as indeed seventh-century Arabs apparently were. In fact, Arabs understood their lineage as deriving from Ibrāhīm (Abraham) just as Jews did. However, the two groups differed as Arabs traced their genealogy through Ibrāhīm's son Ismāʿīl (Ishmael) and Jews through Isḥāq (Isaac). More generally, the stories of the prophets apparently required, and received, little elaboration for the Qur'ān's initial audience. Therefore, the prophets served as familiar examples and illustrations for the novel themes expressed in the *sūrāh*s. The final section of the *sūrāh* concludes with a consideration of a range of prescribed and proscribed behaviors in the realms of diet, justice, fasting, pilgrimage, wine, marriage, and money.

Of course, despite the centrality of the Qur'ān, or, rather, because of it, the Qur'ān required interpretation. Although the text is ideally understood to be as transparent in meaning as it is sophisticated in its poetry, it like all verbal expressions requires interpretation because it cannot of itself speak. Traditions of interpretation (*tafsīr*) evolved over time and commonly drew first on the *sunnah* of the Prophet as the baseline of interpretation. That the Prophet had been the original interpreter of the text to Muslims only stood to reason considering his intimacy with the revealed word. Upon his death, his *sunnah* became important not only to describe as many details as possible of this exemplary figure's life but also to better understand the book he helped bring to humanity.

Ḥadīth

Toward this aim, various individuals began to collect *ḥadīth* ('reports') about Muḥammad as remembered by those who knew or encountered him. Two centuries after Muḥammad's death, the effort to collect *ḥadīth* culminated with compilers such as Abū-l-Ḥusayn Muslim (d. 875) and Muḥammad Ibn Ismāʿīl Bukhārī (d. 870) who traveled throughout Mediterranean and West Asian regions to record as many as possible. Gradually a system of collecting *ḥadīth* coalesced that took into account the volatile nature of memory and assessed not only the individual *ḥadīth* and its reporter but also all the individuals who served as links in the chain of its transmission. A 'science of humans' developed that maintained written biographies of the reporters with details including their family origins, general character, closeness to Muḥammad, and, most importantly, the trustworthiness of their memory.

Two parts, therefore, composed each *ḥadīth*: the *isnād* (chain of transmitters) and *matn* (main text). So, for example, the following *ḥadīth* – regarding Muḥammad's practice of reciting the Fātiḥah *sūrāh* of the Qur'ān in each part of *namāz* or the formal prayer – states: 'ʿAṭā reported it on the authority of Abū Huraira who said: Recitation Sūraṭ al-Fātiḥa in every (rakʿah) [part] of prayer is essential. (The recitation) that we listened to from the Apostle of Allāh (may peace be upon him) we made you listen to it. And that which he recited inwardly to us, we recited it inwardly for you' (Muslim 1990, 1: 218). The *isnād* in this case would link Imām Muslim (who compiled the collection in which this report appears) to ʿAṭā who communicates what Abū Hurayrah has heard from Muḥammad himself. The *matn* includes the discussion that follows. Should someone question the authenticity of this claim based on the quality of the *isnād*, they only have to check one of the biographical volumes that qualify each link in the chain of transmission. This genre of literature would inform the skeptic that Abū Hurayrah's real name was ʿAdb al-Raḥmān ad-Dawsi, although he went by ʿAbd Shams before his conversion to Islam at which point he took the name of either ʿAbd Allāh or ʿAdb al-Raḥmān. The biography includes such minutiae about individual transmitters that one learns that Abū Hurayrah received that name because he played with a kitten while goat herding! More importantly, the biographies record that when he arrived in Madinah in CE 629, Abū Hurayrah had no responsibilities to distract him away from his rapt attention to Muḥammad. Because of his excellent memory (an obviously critical characteristic for a transmitter), about 3,500 *ḥadīth*s have been narrated on his authority (Muslim 1990, 1: 3fn7). With this attention to the details of Muḥammad's *sunnah*, those who observed his life, and those who communicated those observations, it comes as no surprise that a host of ancillary literatures developed to support knowledge about Muḥammad. Besides the *ḥadīth* collections and transmitter biographies, these included histories and 'divine sayings' (*ḥadīth qudsi*) of Muḥammad.

The compilers arranged the *ḥadīth* according to themes, such as faith, purification, prayer, and warfare. In this form, the Ḥadīth literature offered a compendium of reports on specific topics that could be compared in the search for an answer to a particular question regarding proper conduct or belief. Muslim communities have differed in their assessment of the various reporters and the collections themselves. Most Sunnīs rely heavily on the reports of ʿĀ'ishah who, as Muḥammad's youngest and favorite wife after Khadījah's death, is understood to offer a favored eyewitness to the life of Muḥammad. However, Shiis tend to ignore her reports as her opposition to ʿAlī's claim to the caliphate mars her reputation in the eyes of many. Regardless of which collections have been used, the Ḥadīth tradition has featured prominently in Muslim efforts to discern the best way to live according to the will of Allāh.

One report, in particular, demonstrates the balance between Allāh's command and compassion as well as the role of the Ḥadīth literature to supplement the Qur'ān. It reports that, after his ascension, as Muḥammad returned from visiting Allāh, Mūsā asked him how many prayers Allāh had commanded Muslims to make daily. 'Fifty,' was Muḥammad's reply. Mūsā explained that Muḥammad needed to return and ask for a lower number because fifty prayers a day would be too onerous. Muḥammad did so and, upon his return, was questioned by Mūsā once again. Muḥammad explained that Allāh had reduced the original fifty daily prayers to forty but, at Muḥammad's urging, then to ten fewer. Muḥammad persisted until Allāh required five. Mūsā exclaimed that this would still be too difficult, but Muḥammad replied that he did not dare ask for anything less. This *ḥadīth* demonstrates a number of important dimensions of Muslim practice and literature. First, the *ḥadīth*'s importance derives at least in part from the lack of specificity regarding prayer in the Qur'ān. Although the text exhorts Muslims to pray as part of the 'five pillars,' it provides no details about the prayer such as its frequency. The Ḥadīth literature complements the Qur'ān by detailing the number of times Muḥammad prayed and the manner of the action. Second, the *ḥadīth* reflects an understanding of Allāh as compassionate and unwilling to set requirements that would be too burdensome for the believers. Muslims should wait until they are capable to perform a prescribed duty before doing so. The young, the ill, and the elderly are all exempt from requirements that cause duress until the time, if possible, for them to do so.

The five pillars

The Qur'ān emphasizes a variety of beliefs and practices.

> Piety does not lie in turning your face to East or West. Piety lies in believing in God, the Last Day and the angels, the Scriptures and the prophets, and disbursing your wealth out of love for God among your kin and the orphans, the wayfarers and the mendicants, freeing the slaves, observing your devotional obligations, and in paying the *zakāh* and fulfilling the pledge you have given, and being patient in hardship, adversity, and times of peril.
>
> (2.177)

However, no uniformity characterizes such lists as they appear in the Qur'ān. This underlines the fact that for all the Qur'ān provides for Muslims, it offers neither a detailed nor systematic outline for devotional or community life. This demonstrates why the early *ummah* considered the development of supplemental literature a necessity.

Compensating for the Qur'ān's lack of specificity in many topics, certain *ḥadīth* clearly delineate the five components of Muslim life central to 'the straight path,' which have come to be known as the 'five pillars of Islam.' Indeed, the very first *ḥadīth* in the collection Ṣaḥīḥ, Imām Muslim relates how 'Umar ibn al-Khaṭṭāb remembered that a man (whom Muḥammad recognized as Jibrīl) asked the Prophet to tell him about Islam. 'The Messenger of Allah (may peace be upon him) said: Al-Islam implies that you testify that there is no god but Allah and the Muḥammad is the messenger of Allah, and you establish prayer, pay Zakāt, observe the fast of Ramaḍān, and perform pilgrimage to the (House) if you are solvent enough (to bear the expense of) journey' (Muslim 1990, 1: 2). These have come to be known as the five pillars of Islam or the *arkān*. We shall examine each in turn.

Shahādah

The declaration of faith exactly states the central tenets of belief for almost all Muslims: '*lā ilāha illa'llāh, Muḥammadun rasūl Allāh*' (There is no god but God, and Muḥammad is the Messenger of God). In keeping with the revelation itself, the Muslim's religious emphasis begins with Allāh who, as Allāh's name implies, is 'the One' (and only One). Yet the special prophethood of Muḥammad (whose *rasūl* status elevates him above all but the three other prophets who delivered books to humanity) must be mentioned because of his role in communicating the perfect revelation but whose importance entirely derives from God. Many Muslims accept the recitation of the *shahādah* as a proclamation of one's embracing of Islam.

Ṣalāh/Namāz

As mentioned earlier, this formal prayer is ideally performed five times daily, although many who identify themselves as Muslims do so with far less regularity, if at all. Almost all Muslim women in India pray at home if they do not work outside the house, while men have the option of praying at home or at work or in a mosque. Many Muslims consider social interactions between unrelated men and women as potentially dangerous – morally and physically – and so mosques that accommodate both genders must have some form of separation. Although in some parts of India, Ladakh for instance, men and women may pray together (perhaps in separate rooms, perhaps in one room divided by a sheet), most mosques exclude women for lack of an appropriate space for them. That is to say that because almost all Muslims in India live in patriarchal communities which define the public sphere as the realm of the man and the domestic for the woman, Muslims have constructed mosques as public spaces reserved for men. Those who do not practice *namāz* (the Persian-derived term more commonly used than the Arabic *ṣalāh*) daily may be more likely to do so on Friday when all the men assemble for the noonday prayer. Most Muslims understand this time to be the most important one to perform *namāz* together because Friday, according to the term used in the Islamic calendar, is 'the day of the congregation.' Cities and villages often have a designated *jumah masjid* (congregational mosque) in which Muslim men assemble for these prayers. At the end of the Friday prayers, the assembled listen to a sermon given by the prayer leader (*imām*) for that day.

Whenever and wherever it is performed, the ritual remains basically the same. A *muezzin* performs the call to prayer (Urdu: *azān*; Arabic *nadhān*) from the *minār* (English: minaret) attached to the mosque. Previously, Muslims built *minār*s large enough to accommodate a staircase by which the *muezzin*s ascended to ensure that their call would be heard at a distance. Today, loudspeakers commonly replace the muezzin's labored climb five times a day. Many smaller mosques include a *minār* big enough for nothing more than loudspeakers. The calls announce the five prayer times: sunrise, midday, afternoon, sunset, and evening. Whether in a mosque or at home, hearing the call or watching the time, a Muslim proceeds to perform a series of ablutions (Urdu: *wuzū*) in which he or she cleans hands, mouth, forearms, and feet. This purifies the Muslim in preparation for prayer to Allāh. No matter where they pray, Muslims stand side-by-side where room allows it. In a mosque, the congregation follows the lead of the *imām* (leader) who stands in front and begins the prayer by calling out its different parts. These involve the specific bodily postures of standing, bowing, kneeling, and prostrating with head to ground. Prayer ends with a ritual greeting to those on either side of the Muslim who may take this time to supplicate or praise Allāh using the more informal *du'ā'* style of prayer.

Ṣawm

The month of Ramaḍān (many Indian Muslims refer to it as Ramẓān) represents the celebration of the revelation of the Qur'ān because in this month, in CE 610, Allāh revealed the first verse to Muḥammad. Many Muslims celebrate this dimension by reading the Qur'ān regularly throughout the month. Some Qur'āns are specially divided into thirty portions to facilitate this. At least equally prominent in this month, fasting occupies most Muslims' efforts. From before sunrise to just after sunset, Muslims forego any drink or food, using this opportunity to call to mind the suffering of the poor. This sacrifice becomes more acute in the years when this month on the Islamic calendar occurs in the summer as the days are longer and the weather warmer (the Islamic calendar operates on a lunar system, and so its months annually shift relative to the seasons). Although some will even avoid swallowing their own saliva, many describe the experience as liberating and that it brings them so close to Allāh that they do not feel any discomfort.

As with most of the other pillars of Islam, *ṣawm* (fasting) includes an important social dimension. At the conclusion of every day, everyone gathers for *iftar*, a special meal marking the breaking of the fast. Generally, the family gathers and eats together (whereas often men would be served by the women who prepare the meal first and eat last) around a large spread of different foods. Customarily, the meal begins with dates because Muḥammad enjoyed them especially. Non-Muslim friends may be invited as well. For obvious reasons, the final day of Ramaḍān means a particularly special celebration. Whatever benefits may be claimed from the fasting, the return to the rest of the year's routine is welcome. Even before the first sliver of the moon is seen following the new moon ending the month, families make preparations for 'Īd al-Fiṭr so that on the day after the sighting, everyone who can afford it dons new clothes. The men proceed to the *'idgah* – an enclosed field reserved specifically for the communal prayer of the two annual 'Īds ('Īd al-Fiṭr, 'feast of breaking fast,' and 'Īd al-Aḍḥā, 'feast of sacrifice'). This *namāz* ends with everyone hugging one another and saying ''Īd mubārrak' (congratulations on the 'Īd). Children enjoy special treats, and family members visit one another and friends.

Zakāh

The Qur'ān and Ḥadīth include many passages exhorting social justice, especially care for the orphans and the impoverished. *Zakāh* works to provide for the distribution of wealth and for the protection of the less well off in society. It ideally amounts to a 2.5 percent annual levy on the total wealth of individuals comfortable enough to afford it. Muḥammad institutionalized the practice (mentioned in the Qur'ān, later detailed in the Ḥadīth) a few years after arriving in Madinah. Premodern governments operating under an Islamic ideology commonly collected the *zakāh*, but the introduction of secular states led to a decline in its collection. It no longer exists as an operation of government in India.

Ḥajj

Pilgrimage to Makkah composed part of the religious lives of the polytheist Arabs in pre-Islamic Arabia. Muḥammad's cleansing and rededication of the Kaʿbah reoriented it solely toward Islamic practices. Even before this event, its centrality for Muslims was encouraged when Muḥammad, as directed by a Qur'ānic verse, shifted the direction of prayer away from Jerusalem (an orientation they shared with the Jewish tribes of Madinah) toward Makkah.

Historically, the *ḥajj* has served to bring Muslims from throughout the world into contact with one another annually and communicate this experience to the people of their homelands upon their return. The *ḥajj* unites Muslim social memories of the lives of the prophets with the landscape on which they purportedly lived. With the increased communications and transportation systems of today, more than 2 million Muslims arrive every year (more than 100,000 from India) at the beginning of the month on the Islamic calendar specifically designated for the *ḥajj* (pilgrimage to Makkah during any other month is designated *ʿumrah*). During the ten or so days of the *ḥajj*, pilgrims will circumambulate the Kaʿbah, the reconstruction Ibrāhīm and Ismāʿīl accomplished on the spot where Ādam built the first mosque; run between the two hills where Hagar once desperately sought water for her dying son Ismāʿīl: stand on Mount Arafat where Ādam and his wife Ḥawwā' reunited following their dispatch from Paradise; and walk in the city where the final prophet, Muḥammad, lived most of his life.

The incorporation of the individual Muslim into the larger *ummah* occurs not only through ritual reenactment but dress as well. As though in recognition of the dual ideal nature of the *ummah*, male pilgrims dress themselves in two lengths of plain white cloth that signal the equality of all humans before Allāh, while women may wear their native clothes (so long as they are appropriately austere) in recognition of the diversity of cultures in which Muslims live. Upon their return home, pilgrims often accept the honorific title *ḥajjī* ('one who has performed the *ḥajj*') as a marker of their accomplishment.

Muḥarram

The commemoration of the martyrdom of Ḥusayn and his companions plays an important, annual part in the lives of many Indian Muslims. Although many Muslims object to the celebration of individuals – whether it be a Ṣūfī on his *urs* (death day) or even Muḥammad on his birthday, Mawlid an-Nabī – Shiis consider Muḥarram a crucial commemoration. The death of the Prophet's grandson at the hands of a Muslim army summons waves of lament for a terrible tragedy experienced anew through the symbols and rituals of participants focused in a procession fueled by pathos. Despite the particularly special meaning Ḥusayn has for Shii as the rightful successor to the Prophet and one of the infallible *imāms* (of which there were only seven or twelve depending on the specific tradition), some Sunnīs too participate in the commemorations. In some places without any Shii, Sunnīs take responsibility for the procession. It is not surprising that this charged atmosphere has been one of the most frequent environments for Hindu–Muslim conflict as the processions move through shared public space in cities and villages, past temples, shrines, and sacred trees that if treated in a manner considered inappropriate may incite a defensive response. Such is not, however, usually the case as demonstrated in the example of one contemporary Muḥarram procession.

In Dehradun, at the edge of the foothills of the Himālayas, the Muḥarram procession has yet to be seen but tens of thousands of Muslims line its expected route. As it arrives, very tall poles bearing black standards precede the slowly moving crowd that barely fits through the numbers swelling the roadside. Atop the standard is a symbolic outstretched hand, each finger representing one member of the cherished family: Muḥammad, his daughter Fāṭimah, her husband ʿAlī, and their sons Ḥasan and Ḥusayn. Behind them a horse draped in a bloodstained cloth suggests Ḥusayn's horse dappled by his blood. Finally, a *taʿziyah* (replica of Ḥusayn's tomb in Karbalāʾ) is carried aloft by a group of men. Occasionally the procession halts, and a circle of primarily young men forms. They whip themselves with chains or slap their chests in an attempt to draw blood in order to feel an empathetic connection to their slain *imām*. From the balconies above, women and girls watch, drawn by its passion and spectacle, before it moves off down the dusty street.

Ṣūfī poetry

Among literature significant to Indian Muslims, Ṣūfī poetry cannot be overlooked. As described in the previous section, Ṣūfīs have molded the shape of many South Asians' religious lives by providing a language of devotion, an avenue to Islam, and a model for the devotee. Some of these Ṣūfīs have written important treatises on their mystical relationship with Allāh, but their most enduring and widespread impact has been through the devotional poems that they have crafted, which have inspired Muslims and others for centuries. The first significant Ṣūfī treatise crafted in South Asia, Abū-l-Ḥasan ʿAlī al-Hujwīrī's *Kashf al-Mahjūb li-Arbāb al-Qulūb* (The Unveiling of the Hidden for the Lords of the Heart), may still be studied 1,000 years after its formulation, but relatively few Indian Muslims know of it. However, the poems performed in the *dargāh*s (tombs) of Ṣūfī saints remain the most celebrated because of the significance of these shrines for the lives of so many Muslims and others. Rich in metaphor and imagery, these poems compel many of their readers, reciters, and audience members to engage a mystical reality distinct from the everyday world. The best-known form of Ṣūfī devotional performance is *qawwālī*. Every Thursday night at *dargāh*s large enough to attract them, *qawwāl*s perform for devotees. Some become entranced because of the presence of the *pīr*'s ('respected leader') tomb and the power of the music. A few may begin to clap and dance to the *qawwālī*, perhaps even be taken into momentary ecstasy by the experience.

Institutions and practices

The arrival of Muslim rulers in the Middle Period (fifteenth to eighteenth century CE; eighth to tenth century AH) introduced the widespread support of Islamic institutions and practices as never before. Just as earlier kingdoms defined themselves as supportive of a Brāhmaṇ-derived order in which legitimacy was expressed by Brāhmaṇic ritual confirmation of the status of the king and patronage to temples, Muslim rulership did not automatically erase Hindu institutions. However, it did displace many of these institutions with systems of rule that made claims to legitimacy based on an Islamic, not Brāhmaṇic, order. Nevertheless, many Brāhmaṇic institutions continued to receive state support as Muslim rulers sought to demonstrate the worth of their rule to their non-Muslim subjects.

No central institutions characterize Islam or organize the *ummah*. The ideal of a politically and religiously united caliphate faded before Muslims came to be a large population in South Asia. Although Muslim rulers often characterized themselves as the leader of a united Muslim community, they did not attempt to centralize the diverse practices of Islam. Instead, a variety of elements exist that provide Muslims with a collection of organizing and authoritative bodies, specifically the mosque, the *'ulamā'*, the Islamic education system, *dargāh*s, and *ṭarīqah*s.

The family

But before considering any of these formal institutions, perhaps the most important organizing body needs to be considered: the family. Throughout the Qur'ān, the Ḥadīth, and most Muslim communities in India, the family stands as the bulwark for the *ummah*. Such a notion appears at odds with modern assumptions that the preservation of individual rights and expressions outweighs group concerns. Nevertheless, their place in the family for most Indian Muslims – and most Indians – greatly defines who they are and how they behave. This perspective can be understood as one of the most influential dynamics in the definition of Muslim gender roles. As both the portals for the next generation and the primary caregivers for children, women have commonly borne a weighty responsibility by embodying the honor (Urdu: *izzat*) of the family. Such perspectives are less endemic in Islam as an ideology than in the cultures that have adapted Islam and justified their practices in the context of their interpretations. Perhaps the most prominent issue regarding *izzat* debated in Muslim circles pertains to the importance and rationale for *purdah*, the withdrawal of women from public view. Because the life of the Prophet, and his family, provides such an exemplar for most Muslims, it is to be expected that the controversy regarding *purdah* often gravitates toward a discussion of the conditions in the early *ummah*.

No consensus has been reached by Muslim reformers and secular scholars who have questioned whether life in the original *ummah* brought greater liberties or restrictions to Arab women.[3] However, much of the ensuing debate has wrestled with the Qur'ānic meaning of the term '*ḥijāb*' (commonly rendered into English as the misleading 'veil' but which can also mean 'curtain,' 'screen,' 'concealment,' 'headscarf,' and 'modesty') and its import to Muslim life. It does appear that however they have been interpreted later, the relevant Qur'ānic verses generally do not specifically pertain to women except one which is narrowly in regard to Muḥammad's family:

> O you who believe, do not enter the houses of the Prophet for a meal without awaiting the proper time, unless asked, and enter when you are invited, and depart when you have eaten, and do not stay on talking. This puts the Prophet

> to inconvenience, and he feels embarrassed in (saying) the truth. And when you ask his wife for some thing of utility, ask for it from behind the screen.
>
> (33.53; Altorki 1995: 324)

What appears to many Muslims as a cautionary injunction to protect the household privacy of the publicly high-profile Muḥammad was taken by other Muslims as another of the Prophet's examples to be followed universally. However, *āyāt* 24.31 demonstrates well the greater expectations of modesty placed on women than men and which should be practiced in front of nonrelated men, perhaps because of an understood need to control women as the embodiment of the family's honor. Various *ḥadīth* would elaborate on the issues of a woman's concealment, and many propound more restrictive perspectives.

Mirroring the academic situation regarding women in the early *ummah*, scholarly debate has ensued in the effort to determine whether South Asian women lost public freedoms with the advent of Muslim-dominated states in the Middle Period. The prevalence of similar *purdah* restrictions on many Hindu women today has been considered evidence by some of preexisting patriarchal limits (which would suggest that it is endemic to many South Asian cultures) and by others as the result of Muslim political dominance (suggesting an inequality inherent to Islam). Whatever its cultural origins, Muslim reformers began to mount wide-scale challenges to *purdah* beginning in the nineteenth century. Nevertheless, these ideologies of reform often promoted change in the interest of the family and for the greater fulfillment of women as mothers and wives, not in reference to greater individual freedom. For a great number of families, *purdah* represents the luxury of the economically well off. Women whose families rely on them to work in fields and factories cannot afford to remain secluded from nonfamily members. Meanwhile, men – although allowed a variety of public roles outside the family-dominated domestic sphere – are also commonly defined according to their place in the family.

The mosque

As mentioned above, the mosque provides a central location for Muslim men (and, in a very few places, women) to pray together. However, this space often serves as a gathering place for celebrations, as a place of reverie, and as a place of study. Mosque designs vary tremendously according to the local space limitations, community financial resources, and regional architectural styles. Yet they often include a walled courtyard, a central structure at one end, and a *minār*. The courtyard serves as an open space in which the faithful gather for prayers without chairs or benches. Its walls shield the individual from whatever commotion may occur in the neighborhood outside. Commonly white with bare walls and perhaps a clock for knowing the prayer times, the mosque provides a place of few distractions. At the west end of the courtyard stands a prayer hall of varying size, which allows prayers to be said indoors to avoid the rain, winter cold, or summer sun. A niche (*miḥrāb*) in the west wall of this enclosure indicates the direction of Makkah (*qiblah*). Like a gravitational pole, Makkah serves to orientate all Muslims who pray facing it.

Even after the decline of Muslim rulers who built mosques as emblems of their legitimation to rule, mosques today can play a central role in political mobilization.

For instance, the Mughal-built Jamaʿ Masjid in Delhi – meaningfully positioned across from the Red Fort with its imperial residence and at the edge of the Muslim-dominated Old City – has served as a forum for political activity. In an unexpected moment in 1920, for instance, Muslims and Hindus gathered there to mourn activists shot dead by police during a general strike against British rule organized by Mohandas Karamchand Gandhi and leaders of the Khilāfat Movement (see below). Reflecting the intercommunal nature of that movement, a Hindu was among those prompted to address the gathered assembly (Minault 1982: 70). However, mosques, even those once built as the concrete expression of a state's Islamic polity, on a day-to-day basis usually serve far less politically charged purposes, as could be seen on one day in the South Indian city of Bijapur.

A group of men sit with their backs against one of the four dozen towering pillars from which arches spring on each side. As they talk over the large Qur'ān opened on a winged, wooden bookstand, their voices dwindle in the vastness of the cavernous prayer hall. Above them, a dome caps the center of the hall, double in height from the already distant ceiling. The comforting cooling shade contrasts with the sharp sunlight of the Deccan sky that floods the courtyard outside the prayer hall. Sulṭān ʿAlī ʿĀdil Shāh I built this mosque in 1565 as the *Masjid al-jāmi* of the capital city, Bījāpūr, of his sprawling kingdom. More than 2,000 can gather inside for *namāz*. The care and commitment required to design, construct, and maintain such a sophisticated and graceful piece of architecture demonstrates the significance of mosques as emblems of rulership legitimated using Islamic symbols.

The ʿulamāʾ

Because of the importance of living according to Allāh's guidelines provided by the Qur'ān, elaborated upon in the Ḥadīth, and developed through traditional Islamic law (*Sharīʿah*), the specialists in the law have long had a prominent role among many Muslim communities. These juridical specialists, termed *ʿulamāʾ* ('learned'), have trained in one of the schools of law. However, the definition of *ʿulamāʾ* as jurists reflects the changes wrought by global European imperialism in the nineteenth and twentieth centuries, which established an hegemony that radically altered the understanding of what learning the *ʿulamāʾ* represented. For more than 1,000 years the *ʿulamāʾ* specialized not only in *Sharīʿah* and its supporting studies (for example, Qur'ān and *tafsīr*) but also in geometry, astronomy, logic, and medicine. The ascent of Western forms of knowledge eclipsed these studies just as English and French replaced many indigenous languages as the languages of learning. A decline in the number of states instituting *Sharīʿah* followed the expansion of British rule and the ascent of English law (Zaman 1995: 259–60). Many among the *ʿulamāʾ*, therefore, became less cosmopolitan and more isolated, especially in many of the schools of its instruction. This accelerated following the 1857 Rebellion, when the British state curtailed funding for *madrasah*s ('schools') for fear that the more educated an Indian might become, the more prone he or she was to nationalism (Reid 1995: 413–14). Today, some of the *madrasah*s run by *ʿulamāʾ* provide only the basics of Qur'ānic recitation (that is, proper pronunciation of Qur'ānic Arabic but not interpretation into vernacular languages) for very young children, while others include a range of subjects that might be pursued at higher levels of education.

The Ṣūfī dargāh

The final institution we will consider is the Ṣūfī *dargāh*. Ubiquitous across much of South Asia, *dargāhs* represent nodes of popular religiosity and perceived conduits of superhuman power. Individual Ṣūfīs, when a community recognizes them as spiritually powerful, have a variety of roles when alive. Parents may bring sick children, the despondent may seek insightful advice, and legal adversaries may request arbitration from a living Ṣūfī. When he or she dies, if particularly revered, the community may build a shrine to house his or her grave, patrons adding features as an indication of their devoted respect for or specific request of the dead saint or *pīr* ('respected leader'). The *dargāh* becomes a place for venerating the dead Ṣūfī and a site of superhuman power (*barakah*). Infertile women may kneel before the tomb vowing a gift to the Ṣūfī should she become pregnant, or a young person may touch their hand to the tomb's wall and then their head in veneration while praying for better school exam results. Some leave bottles of water on the tomb overnight and then administer it to the infirm as though the proximity to the tomb charged the liquid with an energy that can be consumed. Hindus, Christians, Sikhs, and others may join Muslims at the tomb because of their recognition of the power available for those who know how to access it through their devotions. Just as shrines offer a place of connection between Muslims and non-Muslims, most also provide a rare place of public worship for Muslim women. The shrines often offer separate entrances and/or prayer spaces for women and men to minimize sexual distraction. However, many Muslims dismiss the practices surrounding Ṣūfīs as, at best, superstition, and, at worst, idolatry. Yet, many defenders of these graveside devotions argue that the Ṣūfī only provides an example of true submission and performs no miracles himself or herself.

The political involvement of Ṣūfīs reflects the reverence they can command in life and death. Many of the premodern Muslim rulers sought affirmation of their mandate from Ṣūfīs and offered patronage to those who gave it. For instance, the Mughal emperor Akbar received the blessing for a son from Salīm Chishtī. When his prayer appeared answered, he not only named his son Salīm in appreciation and built a dazzling white marble shrine around the saint's tomb, he also removed his entire court from the competing imperial centers of Delhi and Agra (Ernst and Lawrence 2002: 98–99) and settled them in a new city, Fatehpur Sikri, specifically built for this purpose. Not all Ṣūfīs have willingly involved themselves in politics, however. According to one popular story, when Niẓām ad-Dīn Awliyā' (d. 1325), another member of the Chishtiyyah *ṭarīqah* (branch), was summoned by the Sulṭān to his encampment quite far away, the Ṣūfī refused to leave Delhi and attend to him. When the Sulṭān's camp was but one day's march away from its return to Delhi, the Ṣūfī was warned of the threat of the Sulṭān's punishment. Niẓām ad-Dīn famously replied, 'Delhi is still far.' His devotees have understood this as an expression of his preternatural knowledge that, that night one of the elephants of the Sulṭān's retinue would accidentally back into his tent, felling a pole that crushed the Sulṭān. Narratives demonstrating the divine punishment for political leaders who presume superiority over Ṣūfīs are familiar among devotees in many parts of the world.

The death anniversary provides an occasion for special celebration at the *dargāh*. During the *urs* ('wedding'), devotees of a *pīr* may arrive from other states or, if of high enough stature, from other countries to celebrate this day. Why celebrate a death day? Most Ṣūfīs have understood that the final communion with Allāh (*al-fanā'*) is impossible before death when the 'final veil' (to borrow one of myriad metaphors) falls. The *pīr* walks through the door to Paradise. During the *urs*, groups of devotees carry funeral shrouds, some decorated with Qur'ānic verse or geometric designs outlined in glitter, through the streets of the *pīr*'s village or city and then place them on the tomb's barrow along with garlands of flowers and incense. Group prayer around the tomb may offer a brief interlude for the day- and night-long commotion as attendees enjoy children's games, shopping from peddlers, and socializing. Throughout, *qawwāls* (performers of the Ṣūfī devotional music *qawwālī*) sing their songs, at times competing among themselves for the crowd's attention. But devotees and others need not wait until a Ṣūfīs *urs* to demonstrate their devotion or petition for help as can be seen most days at the famous *dargāh* of Niẓām ad-Dīn in Delhi.

The significance of Niẓām ad-Dīn's *dargāh* becomes apparent long before one reaches its actual grounds. The police barriers that protect the long alley leading to the *dargāh* announce that the local police station is named after him. Walking down the alley often means following a busy stream of people as they make their way through the various shops that line the route offering Qur'āns and bangles, incense and toys, and Islamic calendars and sports shoes. The way leads into a large stone-paved area surrounded by religious buildings and homes in this densely populated part of Delhi. A sign announces the offices of the descendants of Niẓām ad-Dīn's family, recognized as the custodians of his tomb and guardians of his legacy. The devotee passes a low wall enclosing a dozen or so tombs of prominent family members before arriving at the shrine itself. However grand this is, composed of a one-story building with red sandstone walls, it seems diminutive compared with the long, domed mosque that extends the length of the *dargāh* grounds. Some men sleep in the shelter it provides from the mild rain that falls. Nevertheless, the shrine itself draws most of the attention of visitors who approach it with evident veneration and respect. Removing their shoes and covering their heads, men enter the inner sanctum and pray while women do their devotions from an area separated from the men by a screen intricately carved from the red sandstone. Many leave behind ribbons and tufts of hair tied to the screen as evidence of some vow they have made there. Meanwhile two middle-aged men sit themselves in front of the *dargāh* entrance and begin to sing *qawwālī*, one pumping his accordion-like harmonium and the other playing a small set of drums, while a crowd gathers to sit and listen to the sonorous music.

Ethics and human relations

Overall, most Muslims understand that the practice of Islam involves relationships with other humans as surely as it does with Allāh. Social reformers have, at times, drawn on Islamic concepts to correct inequalities existing in their societies. In doing so, they often point to the example of Muḥammad and various Qur'ānic prescriptions and proscriptions regulating behavior as evidence of the original impulse to create an equitable *ummah* and as a source for more contemporary efforts.

The Qur'ān makes explicit that submission to Allāh requires appropriate individual and community behavior: 'Tell them: "My Lord has enjoined justice, devotion in all acts of worship, and calling upon Him with exclusive obedience" '(7.29). It balances reflections on the persecution of the early *ummah* (which followed their condemnation of the injustices of contemporary Makkan society) with requirements for behavior. Meanwhile, the Qur'ān emphasizes the responsibility of the *ummah* to 'enjoin the right and forbid the wrong' in all facets of society (such as the political, economic, and legal). Some verses condemn outright existing practices such as, as discussed earlier, female infanticide. Other passages seemingly attempt to moderate behavior that was understood, perhaps, not to be as easily halted because of its social inertia. For instance, a passage (4.3) dealing with polygyny explains that Muslim men may marry 'two, three, or four' wives and then warns that if each cannot be treated equitably, then they should marry only one. However, a later verse implies the impossibility of treating multiple wives equitably. According to the interpretation of some, these verses prohibit polygyny implicitly. Some have interpreted these verses as evidence that the early *ummah* sought to curtail a pre-Islamic Arab practice that could not be prohibited outright and that helped care for the many widows left economically helpless after their husbands' deaths protecting the *ummah* in the battles against the Makkans. Others have suggested that the Qur'ān endorses a change from pre-Islamic monogyny. Whatever the case may have been, what is clear is that the Qur'ān does not represent a legal code. In fact, less than 100 verses deal with legal matters. Instead, it acts as the guidance it describes itself as at the beginning of 'The Cow' *sūrāh* (see 2.2).

Meanwhile, the centrality of just human relations became ritualized through some of the five pillars. For instance, the institution of *zakāh* seeks to redistribute wealth to those with fewer resources, a perennial concern in the Qur'ān and the Ḥadīth. It ideally offers both support for the impoverished and a check on the materialism of the wealthy as well as a bond between these two groups. As such, it should not be considered 'charity' because it is neither voluntary nor an act of pity but rather an act of devotion and justice.

Ṣawm, or the Ramaḍān fasting, represents another of the five pillars with an implicit focus on human relations. Although Ramaḍān celebrates Allāh's revelation of the Qur'ān to humanity (and prompts Muslims to focus on this connection with God), it also involves a fast understood by many Muslims as allowing for empathy with the poor. The 'Īd al-Fiṭr celebration that concludes the month further manifests the connections and responsibilities of Muslims to others through the distribution of alms to the poor before the morning feast.

Finally, the conclusion of the *ḥajj* also involves a ritualized expression of concern for others. In memory of Ibrāhīm's willingness to sacrifice his son Ismā'īl (notice the difference from the Jewish and Christian narratives, which put Isḥāq in the son's place) to Allāh and Allāh's merciful exchange of a heaven-sent ram for the boy, Muslims conclude the ten-day period of the pilgrimage with Baqr 'Īd. This feast centrally features the meat of an animal especially slaughtered on 'Īd itself. Many families keep the animal (by tradition a goat) intended for the next 'Īd near their home so that the emotional impact of the sacrifice can be experienced fully. The butcher follows the rules of *ḥalāl* which prescribe the proper manner of slaughtering and bleeding the animal. After the sacrifice, in which a prayer recited over the animal precedes its slaughter, the meat is divided into three portions equally: one-third to the immediate family, one-third to other family and friends, and one-third to the poor. In many places, the impoverished arrive at the gates of homes engaged in their butchering and wait for the householders to offer them part of the sacrifice. Family members dispatch other pieces to homes in the area.

Mosques and *dargāh*s offer another form of giving: that of hospitality. It is generally understood that travelers can find shelter in a mosque or a *dargāh* for up to three nights. Moreover, *dargāh*s commonly operate as sites for the distribution of charity to the needy. Most *dargāh*s with sufficient resources offer a free meal daily that anyone can accept. At Niẓām ad-Dīn's shrine in Delhi, for example, a long line assembles as the distribution time arrives, stretching in front of the large mosque that stands at one side of the expansive courtyard. Meanwhile, the poor commonly line the entrances to *dargāh*s at any time of day in the hope that a generous devotee might offer them some money as they pass. These often include those unemployed due to physical disfigurement caused by accident, debilitating illness, or birth deformation.

However, the primary means by which Muslims have historically expressed their concerns for ethical behavior and human relations has been through *Sharīʿah*, Islamic law as established by Allāh. Reflecting, like most other Islamic institutions, the primacy of the Qurʾān and then the Prophet's *sunnah, Sharīʿah* attempts to provide what neither of these sources offers: a complete law code for the regulation of society and structures for legislation and adjudication. Therefore, *Sharīʿah* developed a reliance on other sources and specific traditions of interpreting them. The human effort to discern the details, extent, and application of *Sharīʿah* is called *al-fiqh*. If *Sharīʿah* is the law God intends, then *fiqh* is the human effort to understand and apply that law. The various traditions of *Sharīʿah* that developed globally among Muslims differ in two ways: the supplementary sources on which they define *Sharīʿah* and the specific intellectual tools used in *fiqh*. The *ʿulamāʾ*, as scholars of law, mediated the interpretation of *Sharīʿah* and the operations of *fiqh*. Among Sunnīs worldwide, four legal traditions developed, and two of these dominated South Asia: Mālikī in the south and Ḥanafī in the north. They differ only in the emphasis they put on various elements of legal reasoning, since they draw from the same sources and use similar legal techniques. The Mālikī school, which developed in eighth-century Arabia, relies heavily on the Ḥadīth and the practices of Muḥammad's contemporaries in Makkah. The Ḥanafī school, originating in eighth-century Iraq, relies less on these traditions and more on opinion derived from reason and analogy. This has allowed Ḥanafī decisions to demonstrate more liberal judgements in law than the Mālikī. Ultimately, Mālikī would become eclipsed in importance in South Asia, even in the south. Generally, the Shii have their own traditions of *Sharīʿah* that place special emphasis on *ijtihād* (interpretation), but, because of the lack of Shii rule on the subcontinent, they have seldom been instituted.

In the period when Muslims ruled as Islamicly legitimated leaders, they claimed legitimacy for their rule by speaking, at least in part, to the expectations of the *ʿulamāʾ*. These included the promotion of *Sharīʿah* and the protection of Islam that together defined *dār al-Islām* (the 'abode of Islam'). However, the actual implementation of *Sharīʿah* varied from ruler to ruler so that, for instance, the Mughal emperor Akbar routinely frustrated the *ʿulamāʾ* in pursuit of his own eclectic religious pursuits (which may have only been his effort to appeal to the diverse religious population he ruled) while his great-grandson Aurangzīb tended to cater to the *ʿulamāʾ* while disparaging Ṣūfīs and other forms of 'unorthodoxy.'

The decline of Islam as a political ideology on the subcontinent followed the ascent of British imperialism that introduced its own forms of law and legal reasoning based on secular, 'rationalist' models. Complementing their universal criminal law, however, the British communalized 'personal law' by establishing separate law codes governing individual affairs as defined by the religion to which the individual belongs. One British court explained this system in an 1871 legal decision: ' "While Brahmin, Buddhist, Christian, Mahomedan, Parsee, and Sikh are one nation, enjoying equal political rights and having perfect equality before the Tribunals, they co-exist as separate and very distinct communities, having distinct laws affecting every relation in life" ' (Derrett 1999: 39). The legal situation remains largely unchanged today although cases such as the Shah Bano trial (in 1985) have prompted calls for a uniform civil code that would apply to all regardless of religious community. Shah Bano sought maintenance from the husband divorcing her not according to the Muslim Personal Law that applied by precedent to her as a Muslim but according to the civil law governing all who do not claim minority status. Although the central government at first supported the decision to do so, it flipped its decision once it recognized the depth of Muslim anger regarding the situation. Many Muslims fear that such a code would subject India's Muslim minority to the legal traditions of the Hindu majority. Other Muslims call for reform of Muslim Personal Law and/or the implementation of the uniform code.

Modern expressions

Most Muslims understand Islam, like the Qur'ān, to be a creation of Allāh. Nevertheless Islam exists as a set of practices, beliefs, and sensibilities among people, and because all people live in cultures, the human expression of Islam reflects the experiences, attitudes, ideals, and concerns of the myriad cultures of which Muslims are a part. Like the societies that influence them, these expressions differ among one another and have changed over time, even as many lay claim to being the 'true' expression of the Qur'ān's injunctions and Muḥammad's example. In fact, modern expressions of Islam, even in India alone, cannot be numbered because of the amazing diversity of rituals, ideas, and communities among Muslims. In the effort of this chapter to describe Islam in India, it has necessarily emphasized a uniformity that seems apparent from a distance. However, the greater the familiarity one has with Muslim communities and individuals, the more apparent the lack of uniformity becomes. Although we can certainly claim that most Muslims recognize the supremacy of the Qur'ān and appreciate the example of the Prophet, universal claims can only be made at one's peril. Described below are some of the more significant organized expressions of Islam among modern Muslims.

First a note of caution is needed. Throughout history there have consistently been those who would critique, reinterpret, or reform contemporary forms of Islam in response to various internal social changes or external geopolitical conditions. Notably, most modern Muslims, and certainly those in India, have found themselves in a context of Western hegemony since the eighteenth century. Although the direct political and military control of South Asia that existed during the era of British imperial rule ended in 1947, Western hegemony in economic and cultural (if not political) spheres remains and has often influenced, if not inspired, some of the more recent expressions of Islam. We must beware caricaturing these expressions as only a reaction to the West – and thereby affirm a Eurocentric image of Westerners as the agents of historical change and Muslims as reactive, never innovative – yet recognize the unprecedented marriage of political and economic control with cultural persuasion that imperial Western powers have practiced. The imperially dominated necessarily responded to this pervasive situation even as they creatively promoted their own visions of Islam and Muslim life.

Muhammad Iqbal (*c.* 1877–1938) clearly exemplifies the dilemma of the colonial Muslim. He pursued advanced studies in Lahore, Cambridge, and Munich. Although originally an Indian nationalist, he came to disparage nationalism through critical reflection on the imperialism and chauvinism he believed it fostered in Europe. Instead he promoted a reformed Muslim society that would rely on *ijtihād* both to modernize Islam and to revive past ideals in contemporary Muslim societies. He understood that in this way democracy should become a fixture among Muslims. Ultimately his support for an independent Muslim state in South Asia became instrumental in the campaign to create Pakistan, in part because of his notoriety as a Persian and Urdu poet – and he remains today the most famous of all Urdu poets. Iqbal's influential vision, therefore, cannot be explained simply as the absorption of Western ideals or as a reaction against them. Instead it involves the incorporation of many divergent trains of thought into his own creative concept. However, Islamic reform pre-dated Iqbal, and the nineteenth century was a particularly busy time for Muslims who questioned the status quo and advocated changes.

The impulse to reform quickened after the failure of the 1857 Rebellion that led to the exile of the last Mughal descendant and the political disenfranchisement of many Muslim elite. In their effort to understand their collective decline, some Muslims blamed a failure in Muslim morality. Various movements sought to address this perceived condition at a time when pervasive social change challenged existing traditions and the leadership of the North Indian *'ulamā'* remained deeply disrupted by the violence of 1857–58.

Ahl-e Sunnat wa'l-Jama'āh

In response to this situation, some Indian Muslims sought to reform society by reforming individuals. That is, they sought to reaffirm a personal Muslim responsibility for living an ethical and orthoprax life. One group that attempted such reforms is commonly referred to as 'Barilwī' in India, a term members reject. The word derives from Bareilly (Uttar Pradesh), the town in which the initiator of this movement resided. Ahmad Riza Khan (d. 1921), a member of the *'ulamā'*, sought to renew Islam by prompting Muslims to remember the message Muḥammad delivered regarding the path prescribed by Allāh. Hence, the movement's name means literally 'People of the Way and the Community' (Sanyal 1996: 8–11). In part, the Ahl-e Sunnat attempts to do this through a focus on the Prophet as the exemplary Muslim who models individual responsibility while also promoting the veneration of Ṣūfī *pīr*s (Sanyal 1996: 328). Though the movement originated in a rural environment, it has become popular in urban areas of India, Pakistan, Bangladesh, the United Kingdom, and North America.

Deoband school

Another group of reformers influenced by Ahmad Riza Khan's emphasis on individual responsibility established the university Dār al-Ulum in Deoband, northeast of Delhi, in 1867. They formulated a curriculum that featured traditional Islamic Studies (such as Arabic, rhetoric, logic, *fiqh*, and medicine) to be taught in Urdu. Neither English nor Western science would be included as some Deobandis critically rejected Sayyid Ahmad Khan's perspectives (see following), although they borrowed various features from British models of educational methods and institutions. In the course of offering opinions on a wide range of issues in everyday life, Deobandis also eschewed many Muslim practices associated with Sufism (such as veneration and festivals at shrines) as dangerous accretions that misdirected the attention of Muslims (Hardy 1972: 170–71).

One of the most famous members of the Deoband *'ulamā'*, Mawlana Ashraf Ali Thanawi (d. 1943), exemplified the Deobandi goal of educating preachers, authors, and *madrasah* educators who would encourage personal reform. His *Bihishti Zewar* (Heavenly Ornaments) sought to reform society through an education that inculcates a renewed ethical sense among individual Muslim women. The book has become so popular that it continues to be published not only in multiple languages throughout South Asia but also in English in the West. Thanawi's book has been especially promoted by the Tabliqi-Islām, an outgrowth of the Deoband *'ulamā'* and perhaps the most influential Islamic movement in the world today (Metcalf 1990: 3–5). Because of its international profile – some Islamist movements such as the Taliban in Afghanistan have been inspired by Deobandi ideals – it will be considered in the next section.

At the same time as these movements developed, other Muslims promoted an acceptance of Western intellectual paradigms in the effort to maintain a place in the new social order as they found themselves overshadowed by the growing political power of the British, persuaded of their superior technological capabilities, and convinced of the need to adapt to the sociopolitical order the British were engineering.

Muhammadan Anglo-Oriental College

Sayyid Ahmad Khan (d. 1898) represents yet another social reformer struggling to adapt Islamic thought and Muslim culture to the new sociopolitical realities of British rule. Knighted for his contribution to the British Empire, Sayyid Ahmad established the Muhammadan Anglo-Oriental College in 1875 with the intention of providing Indian Muslim students an alternative to both British schools and Islamic *madrasahs*. Compelled to both critique faults in Indian culture and correct English misunderstandings about India, Sayyid Ahmad became dedicated to widening access to quality education in an attempt to correct what he saw as a lacuna in the British rule that he embraced. This education, he believed, would need to include the technological and scientific dimensions fundamental to the innovative successes of Western societies that made British domination possible. Sayyid Ahmad realized his ambitions with the college he founded (as well as the Aligarh Scientific Society he helped establish a decade earlier). Although he rejected many of the traditional subjects of *madrasah* education as antiquated and earned rebukes by some *'ulamā'*, the Islamic orientation of the education remained central. However, this religious quality, like every aspect of the curriculum, had to comply with the rationalism foundational to both Western learning and the reformed Islamic theology that he pioneered. Sayyid Ahmad believed in the inherent compatibility of the Qur'ān and Western science (Lelyveld 1978: 104–31). Reconstituted as Aligarh Muslim University, the institution Sayyid Ahmad helped found joined the ranks of national universities following Partition.

The Khilāfat Movement

The First World War ended with the defeat and disassembly of the Ottoman Empire – the largest and longest surviving of the three major Islamicate empires of the Middle Period (which included the Mughals in South Asia and the Ṣaffāvids in Persia). The Allied forces hungrily claimed the former territories for their own empires while the Ottoman heartland became the modern nation of Turkey. Yet one component of the Ottomans remained: the *khalīfah* (caliph or 'deputy'), an institution dating back to the generation immediately following Muḥammad's death that provided a political and spiritual leader for the *ummah*. Muslims throughout the world rallied to protest Allied plans to dissolve this significantly symbolic, but politically powerless, position because it represented the very last vestige of Muslim geopolitical rule under an Islamic ideology. In British India in 1919, the Khilāfat Movement sought to preserve not only the position of the *khalīfah* but also the territories of the erstwhile empire. Although often understood as a pan-Islamic effort, the movement in India, according to historian Gail Minault (1982: 1–3), only ever sought to create a domestic political constituency with the hope of this as a unifying issue. The Ali Brothers (Muhammad and Shaukat), graduates of Aligarh College, became the most prominent leaders of the Khilāfat Movement and successfully enlisted the aid of Gandhi and his Indian National Congress. The two groups equally saw the opportunity to build mass movements by defining themselves as nationalists willing and able to stand up to the British (Minault 1982: 11). The issue collapsed when the secularist Turkish leader, Kamal Attatürk, abolished the Khilāfat himself in 1924. However, the movement in British India, despite its subsequent evaporation, set the stage for future, more nationalist Muslim involvement in mass political movements (Minault 1982: 211–12).

Muslim secularism and nationalism

Forms of Muslim nationalism represent yet another modern expression of Islam. Indeed, the concept of the nation-state – a union of individual citizens who identify as a unified people associated with a specific, bounded territory – results from modern forces, first, in Europe and, then, in most of the rest of the world. As people colonized or otherwise subjugated by Europeans began to develop resistance to their dominated condition, many drew (ironically) on the ideologies of nationalism that the Europeans had introduced. Although the form may have been borrowed, the content of the nascent nationalist identities by necessity had to be indigenous if a critical mass of supporters would be attracted. As a democratic political system slowly coalesced under the conservative aegis of the British government, politicians sought to identify potential voting blocs to which they could appeal and gain votes. Not unexpectedly considering the emphasis the British put on defining Indians according to religion, some Muslims identified their coreligionists as a potentially substantial voting bloc if only they could be convinced that their 'natural' interests defined them as a united constituency. However, this cultivated unity did not necessarily include a sense of separatism. Many Muslims, particularly those in Muslim majority parts of the country who felt little threat from their Hindu and Sikh neighbors and/or a strong sense of identification with historical India, supported a united independent India as a matter of course. Mawlana Abu'l-Kalam Azad became one of the most prominent of these Indian nationalists.

Abu'l-Kalam (d. 1958) worked with Gandhi in the Khilāfat Movement before joining the Indian National Congress in the 1920s. By 1940 he was president of the Congress, and after Independence and until his death he served as India's Minister of Education. Throughout his career, he resisted the call for a separate Muslim state even as he affirmed his Muslim identity, for reasons evident in his Presidential Address of 1940:

> I am a Musalman and am proud of that fact. Islam's splendid traditions of thirteen hundred years are my inheritance. I am unwilling to lose even the smallest part of this inheritance. The teaching and history of Islam, its arts and letters and civilization are my wealth and my fortune. It is my duty to protect them.
>
> [. . .]
>
> I am proud of being an Indian. I am part of the indivisible unity that is Indian nationality. I am indispensable to this noble edifice and without me this splendid structure of India is incomplete. I am an essential element which has gone to build India. I can never surrender this claim.
>
> [. . .]
>
> Whether we like it or not, we have now become an Indian nation, united and indivisible. No fantasy or artificial scheming to separate and divide can break this unity. We must accept the logic of fact and history and engage ourselves in the fashioning of our future destiny.
>
> (Hasan 1993: 66–68)

Despite such assurances from Abu'l-Kalam, some Muslim leaders perceived that an alarming number of campaign issues promoted by Congress seemed tailored to suit the subcontinent's Hindu majority at the expense of Muslims. They began to express doubts that Muslims and their cultural traditions and values would be respected in an independent, majority-rule India and sought to rally them as a cohesive political voice. However, as the Khilāfat issue in British India had already demonstrated, the unity of Muslims could not be taken for granted due to the tremendous regional, linguistic, social, class, and *birādarī* (caste- or clan-like Muslim groups) differences. This culminated in 1940 with the decision by leaders of the All-India Muslim League like Muhammad Ali Jinnah (d. 1948) to call for a state in which Muslims would be the majority. This idea would eventually coalesce into the Pakistan movement that led to the establishment of Pakistan (with Jinnah as its first governor-general) at the same time that India won its independence. However, it is again critical to differentiate between a Muslim state and an Islamic one. Jinnah, celebrated as the Qaid-i-Azam (the Great Leader) in Pakistan to this day, helped create a secular state that ensured tolerance for all religions and was governed by civil law, not *Sharī'ah*. However, many others in the 1930s and 1940s supported the establishment of an Islamic state and distrusted the Western-educated leaders of the Muslim League, a sentiment that culminated when President Zia al-Haq, courting the *'ulamā'* to support his military dictatorship, worked to implement *Sharī'ah* in Pakistan in the 1980s.

Jamāʿat-i islāmī

One of those who rejected the call for Pakistan was Mawlānā Sayyid Abul-Ala Mawdūdī (d. 1979). In 1941, he established the Jamāʿat-i islāmī (the Islamic Party) as part of his effort to revive Islam, which he viewed as in decline. Having refused membership in both the Indian National Congress and Muslim League, Mawdūdī promoted a communalist agenda in his attempt to supplant Jinnah as the 'sole spokesman' of India's Muslims. Before Partition, he rejected nationalism and secularism. However, with the actualization of Pakistan in 1947, he moved there and shifted his platform to support an Islamic, *Sharīʿah*-bound state. For Mawdūdī, politics was inherent to Islam, and Indian Muslims needed a nation defined by an Islamic polity (Nasr 1994: 3–16). Mawdūdī's thought, especially as it developed during his years in Pakistan, has found a global audience, and he remains one of the most influential Islamic ideologues to this day. His works, translated into multiple languages, have been circulated internationally, supporters distributing them for free as far away from South Asia as the streets of Toronto.

Transmission of the tradition outside of India

Just as surely as Islam arrived from outside South Asia through the movements of Arabs, Turks, Persians, and others, its Indic forms have traveled beyond the subcontinent in the company of locals and foreign visitors. India has often been described as a vast sponge that absorbs those who enter it from beyond the isolating mountain ranges of the Himālayas and Hindu Kush. However, this metaphor fails to communicate the fluid, mobile nature of Islam and Muslim migrations that have repeatedly moved into and beyond regions, becoming inculturated in some ways yet distinct in others. These transregional flows become more apparent when we focus less on land masses and more on the large bodies of water that surround the peninsula. The Indian Ocean and Arabian Sea make readily accessible to deep water and coastal sailors the shorelines of Africa, Southeast Asia, Malaysia, and Indonesia. Of course, with the advent of air travel, these flows are freed to move in any direction.

The Indian diaspora

The earliest large-scale movement of South Asian Muslims beyond the subcontinent occurred through the migrations of labor precipitated and organized by the British Empire. Various British projects recruited Indians as indentured laborers and sponsored their relocation to the diverse corners of the empire, particularly South Africa, Nigeria, Uganda, and around the Caribbean. Additionally, Indians recruited for various armed forces also found themselves throughout the empire, although they seldom settled permanently outside the subcontinent. These populations represent the first wave of what would become a swelling global South Asian Muslim diaspora.

A second diasporic wave occurred following India's Independence with the migration of South Asians to the imperial heartland, taking advantage of Commonwealth status and relaxed immigration laws. Although South Asians had gone to Britain during the period of direct rule to participate in educational opportunities (such as Muhammad Ali Jinnah and Mohandas Gandhi, both of whom received their law training in London), most returned without settling. The immigration movements following the Second World War differed as many took permanent settlement in the British Isles having been recruited to address a domestic labor shortage. Although curtailed in the late 1960s and 1970s, the South Asian migrations, some of which entailed previously established communities in British settlements in Africa and elsewhere relocating once again, resulted in significant Indian Muslim populations throughout Great Britain (Nielsen 1995). Canada, Australia, and other parts of the Commonwealth that succeeded the dismembered British Empire also became popular destinations for Indian Muslim émigrés. Meanwhile, migration from the subcontinent to the United States began in significant numbers following Partition, although Punjabis had already begun arriving on the West Coast by 1895 (J. Smith 1999: 58). In locales where a critical mass had settled, ethnic-specific mosques have formed, while in more heterogeneous communities, Muslims from diverse backgrounds share mosques.

The Bradford community of Indian Muslims in Britain gained international visibility when some members burned copies of Salman Rushdie's *The Satanic Verses* after its release in 1989. Although protest of Rushdie's novel culminated in fatal riots in Pakistan and the Ayatollah Khomeini's *fatwā* (legal ruling) demanding Rushdie's death as an apostate, the Bradford burning caught many British particularly off guard. The event revealed a long-simmering frustration among many British South Asians that the ideals of multiculturalism had failed to protect them from discrimination and exclusion. Paradoxically, Rushdie (a London-resident immigrant from an Indian Muslim family) had sought to portray exactly this simmering dissatisfaction in his novel. However, his highly controversial use of both Western scholarship to analyze the Qur'ān and what seemed to be a satirical depiction of the Prophet Muḥammad transformed the author in the minds of many British Muslims into a symbol of the very depreciative elements in British culture that he thought he was exposing.

Among the diasporic communities of Indian Muslims, various movements have had varying degrees of success in establishing networks. The most prominent among these are the Deobandis, Ahl-e Sunnat wa'l-Jama'āh, Ṣūfī orders (especially Chishtiyyah and Naqshbandiyyah), and, perhaps most importantly, Tablīghī Jamā'at. Because the others have been considered above, we will examine only the latter.

Tablīghī Jamā'at

Mawlana Muhammad Ilyas (d. 1944) founded the Tablīghī Jamā'at in 1926 as a reformist movement that would foster imitation of the Prophet's companions. Specifically, this program entailed a personal commitment to practicing the five pillars, encouraging other Muslims to participate in mosque prayer, and a rejection of the worship of Ṣūfī *pīr*s. Their dedication to a missionary sense of *dawah* ('call') has led them to promote their Islamic vision in India, neighboring countries, and those at a distance. This vision includes a promotion of a transnational, pan-Islamic, and united *ummah* that sets itself apart from other communities in protective isolation. However, the Tablīghī Jamā'at eschews political change for gradual Muslim transformation (Munck 2001: 561–63). In 1952 Tablīghīs began their mission in the United States and represent perhaps the most influential reform group in the world.

Mawlānā Sayyid Abul-Ala Mawdūdī

The widely influential thought of Mawlānā Mawdūdī (mentioned in the previous section), on the other hand, has an implicit political agenda. Mawdūdī joins Iran's Ayatollah Khomeini and Egypt's Sayyid Quṭb as the three most influential Islamic political thinkers to propose definite programs of social change through Islamic revival. Mawdūdī's works greatly influenced Quṭb's thinking. Far beyond the Jamā'at-i islāmī movement he helped found, his ideas have inspired revivalism in North Africa, Central Asia, and Southeast Asia in part because they provide a non-Western alternative for imagining nationhood in areas profoundly challenged by Western imperialism and hegemony. Of course, the notion of the nation is itself a European concept, and it is a measure of the degree to which the West has defined a global order that the nation has become the universally accepted unit by which a sovereign state is defined. So although Mawdūdī necessarily acquiesced to the concept of nation, he did so only within an Islamic framework that rejected Western secularism and promoted a united *ummah*. He deftly crafted the use of Islamic symbols and ideology as tools for political mobilization to Indian Muslims, then Pakistanis, and finally Muslims around the globe (Nasr 1996: 3–5).

Relations with other religions

A number of staid perceptions have framed Western understandings of Islam, especially in India. Although these have been explored in detail in the second section, they must be addressed in this final section because they have most centrally had to do with relations with other religions. These relations have commonly been depicted as inherently antagonistic, fueled by a severe chauvinism regarding proper practice and belief. Although in the history of global Islam such images have been warranted at times, these occasions have been relatively few. As the previous discussion of Richard Eaton's work on Sufism demonstrated, no scenario of forced conversion could entirely account for the vast distribution, particular concentrations, and continued adherence of Muslims in South Asia – especially in areas most removed from Muslim political power like contemporary Bangladesh. These tired yet persistent images owe far more to European Christian self-perceptions and historical competition with Mediterranean Muslims than empirical information. Unfortunately, the establishment of British educational systems and historiographical projects during the centuries of British rule inculcated among many Indians the same image of aggressive and intolerant Muslims discriminating against their non-Muslim political subjects and domestic neighbors.

Histories of religion in South Asia commonly trace Islam's entrance into the subcontinent to the military incursion of 'Muslim armies' in the eleventh century. This belies the four centuries in which Muslims lived as integrated members of coastal communities in South India. Because these histories prefer to depict more dramatic conflicts than peaceful coexistence and ascribe the motivations of any who happen to be Muslim to Islamic ideology, they describe the first interactions between Muslims and other religious communities as inevitably destructive and religiously compelled. As evidence, two events have become salient among both scholars and religious nationalists. The first pertains to the collapse of Buddhism in South Asia. Attempting to explain the paradoxical disappearance of Buddhism (the third largest religion in the world today) in its country of origin, many historians have ascribed its decline to the persecutions of Muslim armies. However, evidence strongly suggests that by the eleventh century, Buddhism had contracted significantly from the widespread, popular movement it has once been into only a series of monasteries dependent entirely on court patronage for survival. When the Turko-Persians destroyed these courts and looted the monasteries for their wealth, it doomed the remains of Indian Buddhist customs. The second event taken to prove the inherent antipathy of Muslims to non-Muslim religions was the desecration of the Somnāth Temple in Gujarat by Maḥmūd of Ghazna. Modern Hindu nationalists have used this act in particular to perpetuate images of Muslims as inherently violent and anti-Hindu. Yet, as discussed in the third section, such destruction was more a political act than a sectarian one.

Nevertheless, at first glance, it would appear that Hinduism and Islam, the two predominant religions in contemporary India, could not be more ill-suited for one another. Hindus are commonly understood to accept multiple deities, use icons for prayer, and venerate cows, while most Muslims believe in one god, have an aversion to iconic worship, and enjoy beef. Yet to settle for this juxtaposition is to make two mistakes. The first is that such a formulation construes Hinduism and Islam as monolithic entities at odds with one another when, actually, neither exists in any kind of centralized, institutional form that would allow for this possibility. Second, this contrast reduces all Hindus and Muslims to a singular, mutually exclusive religious identity that disallows even the possibility of any common interest, activity, concern, or experience. In fact, during the sixteen centuries in which Muslims have lived in South Asia, they have lived in a great diversity of communities. Some, such as the large Muslim neighborhoods (sometimes referred to as *qaṣba*) of some cities, towns, and even villages, appear exclusive of non-Muslims. Yet even these do not make it possible for most Muslims to live in isolation from non-Muslims with whom they may share business interests, school classrooms, or team sports. A great many Muslims, however, live in mixed neighborhoods of villages and towns or, even if separated by neighborhood, exist in such intimate everyday interactions that isolation would be nearly impossible. In this way they not only encounter one another in tea stalls and restaurants, *bāzār* shops and theaters, buses and public parks, but they also often share certain identities that cut across religious groupings. For instance, the devotees of a particular Ṣūfī may identify themselves as Muslim, Hindu, Sikh, or Christian as they share a common devotion to the Ṣūfī whose efficacy they rely on. This dynamic is particularly obvious during the *urs* celebrations of one Ṣūfī at his tomb in a Bihar village.

The courtyard of Ghulām Sāhib's shrine buzzes with commotion as devotees and visitors pass in and out of the gates, some approaching the tomb to do obeisance, and others sitting under the canvas sheets stretched above parts of the courtyard to offer shade on this, the *urs* ('marriage') of the Ṣūfī, the busiest day of the *dargāh*'s life. Recognizing the special auspiciousness of the saint's death day, many have arrived in this North Indian village seeking help from the power that emanates from the green-domed tomb. Various *qawwāl*s take their position in the entrance to the tomb and take turns singing their sonorous music that celebrates the Ṣūfī, Allāh, and the Prophet. While strung plastic flags flutter in the slight breeze, one Hindu woman begins to moan and sway as she sits with her family in the courtyard. Soon her arms begin to flail alarmingly and her hands to shake rapidly. Those around her watch impassively, allowing the *dargāh*'s power to confront the ghost or spirit they know possesses her. They have brought the young woman here in the effort to relieve her of the suffering the intruder is causing. Perhaps they understand that the dead Ṣūfī empowers the exorcism. Some Muslim devotees would argue that only Allāh can perform such feats. Other Muslims disparage the *urs* celebration and saint worship altogether. But for the possessed woman and her family, the only thing that matters is that her proximity to Ghulām Sāhib is working. They escort her into the tomb itself – now that they have the attention of the ghost or spirit – so that they can identify it, discover its demands, and negotiate its departure while within the effective influence of the dead Ṣūfī who serves the Hindus, Muslims, Sikhs, and Christians gathered in his *dargāh* without discrimination.

History proves the presence of the multiple identities and social complexities, such as those apparent at this *dargāh*, that defy simple formulations of identity defined entirely by religion. From Islam's historical origins, the Islamic *ummah* has differentiated itself from other *ummah*s. As described in previous sections, the people of the Book (Jews, Christians, and 'Sabians') enjoyed *dhimmī* status by which governing Muslims allowed them the protection of the state, control over their community affairs, and freedom of religion but at the cost of fewer freedoms and a special tax. The *jizyah* (compensation) tax, alluded to in the Qur'ān, relieved all non-Muslim men from military service. However, those who did not belong to the people of the Book, often described as *kāfir* (unbelievers), faced far more severe restrictions, which might include prohibitions on the construction of new places of worship or repair of existing ones.

In India, during the period of states legitimated by an Islamic ideology, political attitudes toward non-Muslims wavered. Some members of the *'ulamā'* who advised rulers how to govern according to their vision of Islam recommended harsh treatment of non-Muslim subjects. However, the realities of rule and the experiences of individuals mitigated such purely ideological policies. For example, early during Mughal rule, the emperor Akbar granted Hindus *dhimmī* status on the basis of their adherence to 'the book' (that is, the Vedas – considered by few *'ulamā'* to be on par with the Qur'ān or its three preceding revelations). Even Aurangzīb, depicted as the most orthodox Mughal emperor and infamous for temple destruction and collecting *jizyah*, soon found himself financing temples and abolishing *jizyah* for the sake of both ruling the polyglot, multireligious people under his extensive political sway and encouraging Hindu and Sikh elites to help him maintain the empire as integral members of his court. The decline of the Mughals and ascent of Western legal forms ended any efforts of *jizyah* collection. Meanwhile, the coalescing of nationalist ideologies made *dhimmī* status irrelevant in the face of ideals of equality based on citizenship for all members of the nation rather than divergent responsibilities as members or not of the *ummah*.

As Abu'l-Kalam Azad's quote in the previous section demonstrates, most Muslims increasingly envisioned themselves to be as equal a part of the Indian nation as any other religious community. Although the British did not invent the notion of religious difference in India, their policies and practices went far toward engraining the notion of exclusive communalism among South Asians. While the effects of these endeavors varied among the population and certainly prompted some Hindus and Muslims to campaign for an exclusively Hindu or Muslim nationalism, others understood that Indian nationalism required a unity in the face of diversity, including religious diversity. For many, unity across lines of supposed 'religious communities' did not require much effort because their everyday lives involved it. The Pakistan movement appealed to many Muslims enough to sever these ties, especially among those suspicious of the future secularity of Indian politics. Today, ascendent Hindu nationalism threatens to imbue increasing numbers of Hindus with an exclusionary vision of their communities and nation as necessarily Hindu. Bigoted and at times volatile leaders among both Hindus and Muslims sometimes exacerbate cultural and political tensions, as seen in the 2002 Gujurat riots. Although the fabric of Indian societies demonstrates a complex and interwoven character, it is yet to be seen whether the political polarization of neighbors, classmates, customers, and competitors will succeed in sundering the everyday connections among the residents of India's cities, towns, and villages.

Suggested further readings

Ahmad and Reifeld (2004); Ali (1993); Eaton (2003); Esposito (1995, 2003); Gilmartin and Lawrence (2000); Gottschalk (2000); Haddad (1991); Hodgson (1974); Jalal (1994); Madan (2001); Martin (1985); Metcalf (1996); Mittal (2003); Muslim (1990); Pearson (1996); Tadgell (1990).

Notes

1 The Qur'ān also names 'Sabians' as people of the Book, although contemporary scholars remain unclear who is intended by the term. Most commentators identify them as Zoroastrians.

2 Throughout this chapter, whenever the word 'Prophet' is used in a capitalized form, it is in reference to the Prophet of Islam.

3 For an example of the view that Arab women lost freedoms under Islam, see Ahmed (1992). On the other hand, an argument for the improvement of women's social conditions can be seen in Altorki (1995: 323–27).

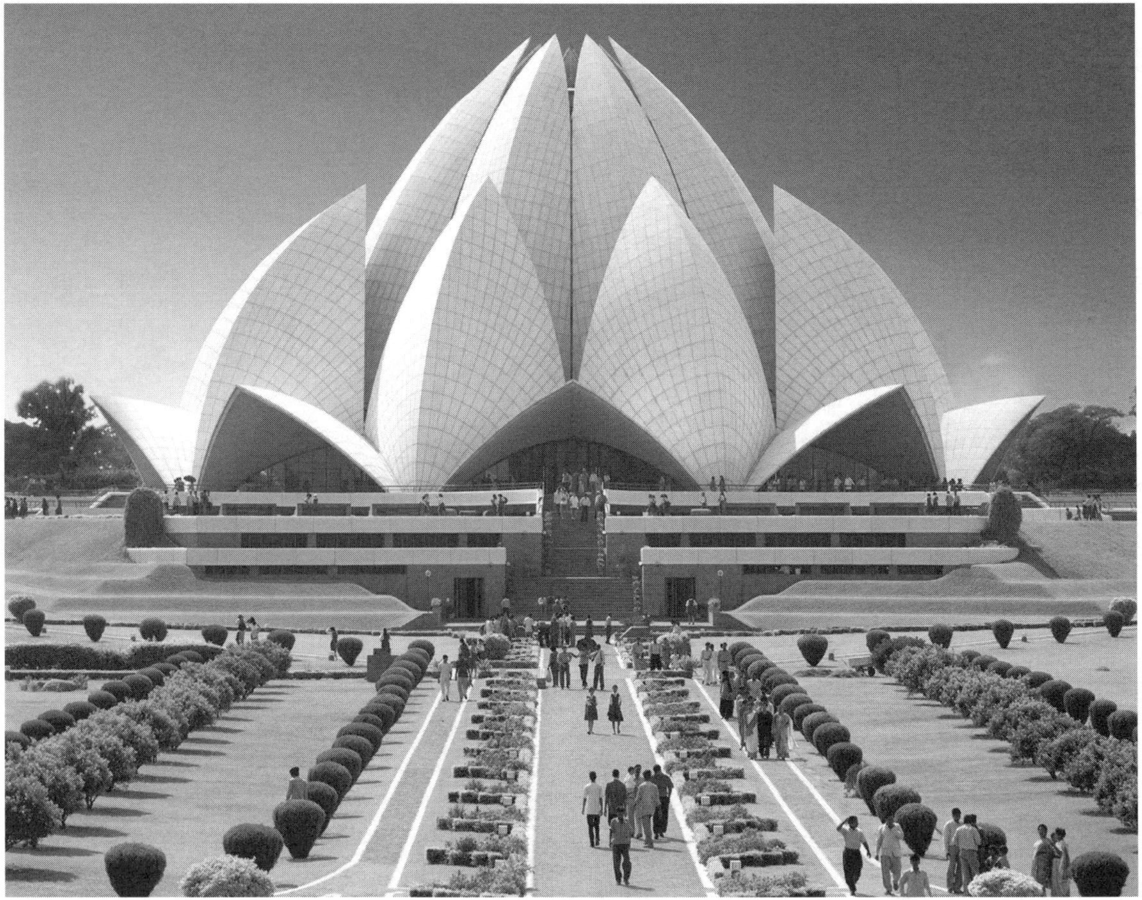

10. The House of Worship in New Delhi, popularly known as the Lotus Temple. Courtesy of Bahā'ī World News Service.

9

INDIAN BAHĀ'Ī TRADITION

William Garlington

The tradition defined

Bahā'ī is an Arabic word which means follower of Bahā'. Bahā' in turn refers to Bahā'u'llāh (the Glory of God), the title taken by the Iranian nobleman, Mirzā Husayn ʿAlī Nūrī, who in 1863 declared himself to be the latest messenger of God in a long line of such divine spokesmen. A Bahā'ī, therefore, is a person who has accepted Bahā'u'llāh's claims and, in so doing, becomes a member of the international Bahā'ī community. According to Bahā'ī authorities, as of the year 2000, the international Bahā'ī community was composed of approximately 5 million people coming from 2,100 different ethnic, racial, and tribal groups and living in over 235 countries and territories. Among these, close to 2 million are claimed to reside in the Republic of India, making the Indian community the largest Bahā'ī community in the world.[1]

Although the Bahā'ī faith originated in the predominantly Muslim country of Iran and its sacred scriptures were written in Arabic and Persian, it is important to recognize that it is not a tradition of Islam. There are several reasons for making this distinction, not the least of which was Bahā'u'llāh's claim that many of his teachings and laws superseded those found in the Qur'ān. But perhaps more importantly, Bahā'īs themselves hold to this position. Bahā'ī authors commonly refer to their faith as an independent world religion (P. Smith 1987: 3).

Cosmos and history

Tumultuous beginnings

Iran in the mid-nineteenth century was a country experiencing profound social, political, and economic changes. Contact with Western colonial nations as well as diverse internal pressures had placed great strain on traditional institutions and resulted in a number of challenges to their authority. In the religious arena there were growing messianic expectations related to the return of the Twelfth-Imām, a mystical figure who according to orthodox Twelfth-Imām Shiism (the state religion of Iran) had mysteriously disappeared in the year 873 and would one day victoriously return and usher in a period of universal peace and justice. Such ideas were particularly popular among the Shaykhī school of Twelfth-Imām Shiism whose two most prominent leaders were Shaykh Aḥmad ibn Zayn ad-Dīn al-Aḥṣā'ī (1743–1826) and Sayyid Karīm Reshti (1793–1843).

Following Reshti's death, in May 1844 a young merchant from the city of Shiraz, who had close associations with the Shaykhīs, made the first of a series of claims in which he identified himself with the messianic prophecies. His name was Sayyid ʿAlī Muḥammad, but he soon became known as the Bāb, a title that meant 'door' and referred to his station as one who was in communication with the Twelfth-Imām. He soon gathered around him a number of disciples whom he directed to spread his message throughout Iran. His popularity became widespread enough to cause both the government and ecclesiastical leaders concern, though his movement did suffer some early setbacks, as when he apparently failed to fulfill messianic prophecy by not appearing in the city of Karbalā to lead an armed uprising against the government (Amanat 1989: 252). Eventually the Bāb was arrested. Thereupon open hostilities broke out between his followers and government troops that included several major battles. These battles virtually decimated the Bābī leadership and eventually led to the government's decision in July 1850 to execute the self-proclaimed messiah.

After the Bāb's execution what remained of the Bābī community was thrown into confusion. Some elements reacted violently, as when in 1852 several followers attempted unsuccessfully to assassinate the monarch, Shāh Nāṣir ad-Dīn, while others were more quietist in orientation, pinning their hopes on a new leader who would fulfill some of the Bāb's own prophecies related to another messianic figure whom he had referred to as He Whom God Shall Make Manifest. A number of Bābīs later claimed to be this figure, but it was Mirzā Husayn ʿAlī Nūrī (Bahā'u'llāh) who was successfully able to rally the majority of Bābīs around his own claim, which he first made in Baghdad in 1863.

Bahā'u'llāh

Bahā'u'llāh's declaration coincided with his banishment from Baghdad by the order of the Ottoman Sulṭān, ʿAbd al-ʿAzīz. He and his family, along with a number of close followers, were exiled to a series of locations, the last of which was the prison city of ʿAkkā situated in the bay near Haifa in what is today the State of Israel. During this time his half-brother, Mirzā Yahyā, refused to follow him, thus creating a small schism in the community, but for the most part the majority of believers gave their allegiance to Bahā'u'llāh and in so doing became known as Bahā'īs.

As a prisoner of the Ottoman state, Bahā'u'llāh remained in ʿAkkā and its environs from 1868 until his death in 1892. During this time he dictated numerous tablets and treatises. Included among these were a series of letters to the kings and rulers of the world in which Bahā'u'llāh recognized the legitimacy of the civil state yet claimed to speak as its spiritual counselor. Among the recipients were Napoleon III, Tsar Alexander III, Queen Victoria, and Pope Pius IX. In 1873 he composed the *Kitāb-i-Aqdas* (Most Holy Book), which contained the laws and ordinances for future Bahā'ī communities.

It was also during this time that Bahā'u'llāh sent his own personal envoy to India. During the lifetime of the Bāb a few scattered Indians had become his followers. Later, several relatives of the Bāb who had accepted Bahā'u'llāh settled in Bombay, but there was no real Bahā'ī community to speak of. In 1875 Bahā'u'llāh commissioned a Ṣūfī scholar, one Jamāl Effendi, to travel to Bombay and proclaim his message. Jamāl remained in the subcontinent and Southeast Asia for close to twenty years.

During this time he traveled the length and breadth of India speaking to both English and Indian dignitaries as well as to reform groups such as the Brāhmo Samāj and Theosophical Society. This elitist approach was one that would dominate Bahā'ī teaching activity in India for nearly the next 100 years.

International expansion

Bahā'u'llāh was succeeded by his eldest son, Abbās Effendi (1844–1921), who after a brief power struggle with his half-brother, Muḥammad 'Alī, took the title 'Abd al-Bahā' (Servant of Bahā'). In 1894 the new leader, still a prisoner of the Ottoman state, commissioned a Lebanese believer to introduce the Bahā'ī faith into the United States. When 'Abd al-Bahā' regained his freedom as a result of the Turkish defeat in the First World War, he personally traveled to North America and Europe to help fortify the young Bahā'ī communities. Near the end of his life 'Abd al-Bahā' was also planning a teaching trip to India but ill health prevented the journey. He did, however, direct a number of important Persian and Western emissaries to the subcontinent to guide local communities and encourage teaching activity. As a result of their influence, by 1911 a nationwide teaching campaign was organized by the Indian Bahā'īs, and despite its failure to gain more than a handful of believers, it was a significant step forward in the development of a sense of national Bahā'ī identity. It was also during this period that a number of Indian Zoroastrians in Bombay became Bahā'īs. Their role in community organization and teaching work would remain significant throughout the following decades.

In his *Will and Testament*, 'Abd al-Bahā' appointed his grandson, Shoghi Rabbani (1897–1957), to the position of Guardian of the Bahā'ī faith. During his years of leadership Shoghi Effendi, as he is more commonly known in the Bahā'ī community, began constructing a coherent administrative system of local, national, and international institutions designed to link the various Bahā'ī communities throughout the world. He not only helped national Bahā'ī communities design and implement numerous teaching campaigns, he also made a conscious effort to wean the community from much of its Islamic heritage and identity.

In India the years of the guardianship were marked by increased community organization and teaching activity. Local communities were established in forty-five towns and cities, and a national administrative body, the National Spiritual Assembly, was created. In the area of publishing, many Bahā'ī books were translated into several Indian languages, including Hindi, Gujarati, Bengali, Sindhi, and Urdu, and a Bahā'ī periodical, *Kaukib-i-Hind*, was launched. Throughout the period Shoghi Effendi (1970: 59) emphasized the continual need for Indian Bahā'īs to share the message of their faith, and to this end, in 1953, he organized an international Bahā'ī conference in New Delhi that was attended by 450 delegates from numerous countries throughout the world. This conference helped increase local teaching activity, and by the time of Shoghi Effendi's death in 1957 there were approximately 1,000 Bahā'īs in India (Garlington 1977: 103).

Shoghi Effendi died without an heir, and consequently in 1957 the institution of the guardianship came to an end. Shoghi Effendi's personal secretary, Mason Remey, later claimed that he was the new Guardian and formed a small schismatic group that today is known as the Orthodox Bahā'ī faith, but the number of followers he was able to attract was minimal, and the Bahā'ī community remained essentially intact. For the following six years the faith was guided by a special group of twenty-seven believers known as Hands of the Cause, who had been appointed by Shoghi Effendi to help him oversee the Bahā'ī community's international affairs. Then in 1963 Bahā'ī delegates from all the countries in which Bahā'ī national communities had been established convened in London to elect the first Universal House of Justice. This body of nine men was recognized as the divinely guided and infallible source of Bahā'ī leadership. Its headquarters was established in Haifa, Israel.

It was under the leadership of the Hands of the Cause that mass teaching was first employed in India, and this process was continued when the mantle of Bahā'ī leadership switched to the Universal House of Justice. Starting in 1960 in the state of Madhya Pradesh, Bahā'īs began focusing their energies on the rural areas. In a series of teaching efforts that lasted most of the decade, emphasis for enrollment was placed on belief in Bahā'u'llāh's messianic claims rather than on intricate knowledge of the religion's history, doctrines, and laws. In response, tens of thousands of villagers accepted the message. Over the following decades additional teaching campaigns were carried out in other regions of the country with similar results, and consequently by the mid-1990s the Indian Bahā'ī community claimed over 2 million adherents.

All the prophets are one

The two metaphysical doctrines that constitute the cornerstones of Bahā'ī theology are the unity of God and the unity of the prophets. In the *Kitāb-i-Īqān* (Book of Certitude) Bahā'u'llāh (1960: 98) refers to God as an unknowable essence who is exalted beyond every human attribute. All things are known by God, but God is concealed from all men. Through the divine will the universe was created, although its creation had no beginning in time and shall have no end. Since it is impossible for created things to comprehend the divine essence, from time to time prophet messengers, or manifestations, are sent forth who serve as liaisons between God and creation. It is only through these manifestations that Man can know of the divine will. 'He Who is everlastingly hidden from the eyes of men can never be known except through His Manifestations' (Bahā'u'llāh 1969: 49). Furthermore, the relationship between God and a manifestation is one of revelation and not of incarnation; the divine reveals itself through the manifestation but does not take human form.

According to the Bahā'ī doctrine of progressive revelation, during the evolution of human history God's will has been revealed by a series of manifestations who are in essence one and the same. 'Abd al-Bahā' ('Abdu'l-Bahā' 1964: 178) likened the manifestations to mirrors which have a specific individuality but reflect the same sun. Included among the manifestations are Abraham, Moses, Zoroaster, Buddha, Kṛṣṇa, Christ, Muḥammad, the Bāb, and Bahā'u'llāh. In the course of revealing the divine will, they also act as the catalysts for the advancement of civilization. The civilizations which their revelations foster are relative to time and place, but they are bound by a fundamental unity of spirit. As the most recent manifestation, Bahā'u'llāh is believed to be the architect of a unified world civilization which is presently in the process of unfolding.

In terms of Bahā'ī activity in India, the inclusion of Kṛṣṇa by 'Abd al-Bahā' and Shoghi Effendi on the list of recognized manifestations has been extremely important since it has allowed Bahā'īs to claim Hinduism as a divinely inspired religion. This in turn has created what one might call a cultural bridge between religious traditions, whereby Bahā'ī teachers can speak from a position grounded in religious acceptance rather than religious superiority (Garlington 1984: 174). In this vein, Bahā'u'llāh is presented as the latest manifestation whose religion will not only fulfill the prophecies of Judaism, Christianity, and Islam but also accentuate the lasting spirit of Hinduism.

One of the key conceptual vehicles for identifying Bahā'u'llāh with Kṛṣṇa has been the *avatāra* doctrine. *Avatāra* means descent or a coming down, and in Hindu Vaiṣṇava theology refers to an incarnation of Viṣṇu. According to the most popular classification there have been nine *avatāras* of Viṣṇu. Included among these incarnations are Rāma, Kṛṣṇa, and the Buddha. Although strictly speaking Bahā'īs do not believe in the doctrine of incarnation, in India Bahā'u'llāh is often referred to as an *avatāra*. And just as Kṛṣṇa's purpose for entering the material world was the maintenance of justice, so Bahā'u'llāh is presented as performing a similar task. In this regard Bahā'īs often point to the following passage from the *Bhagavad Gītā*: 'Whenever there is a decline of righteousness and a rise of unrighteousness, O Bharata (Arjuna), then I send forth Myself. For the protection of the good, for the destruction of the wicked and for the establishment of righteousness, I come into being from age to age' (4.7–8). Consequently, the Guardian of the Bahā'ī faith could refer to Bahā'u'llāh as the 'Immaculate Manifestation of Krishna' (Shoghi Effendi 1965: 95).

The other Hindu *avatāra* who sometimes receives mention in Indian Bahā'ī discourse is Rāma. He is not officially considered a manifestation, in that neither Bahā'u'llāh, nor 'Abd al-Bahā', nor Shoghi Effendi made specific reference to him, yet his role in popular Hinduism as well as his Vaiṣṇava theological connections with Kṛṣṇa have resulted in what might be called legitimization through association. As an example of this process, in a speech given in Gwalior in 1964, Shoghi Effendi's widow, Rūhīyyih Khānum, openly implied Rāma's position as a manifestation by listing him alongside the prophets Kṛṣṇa, the Buddha, Jesus, and Moses (Nakhjavani Nd: 138–39).

Within the Hindu *avatāra* tradition there are also references to a tenth, or future *avatāra*, named Kalkī, who is mentioned in several of the Purāṇas as the one who will appear at the end of the Kali Yuga to restore righteousness. While Kalkī has never assumed a place of extreme importance in orthodox literary Hinduism, A. L. Basham (1967: 309) pointed out that many uneducated Hindus take Kalkī very seriously, and Bahā'īs have made use of this popular belief by specifically identifying the eschatological figure of Kalkī with Bahā'u'llāh. In this context Bahā'u'llāh's appearance in nineteenth-century Iran is presented as the end of the Kali Yuga and the beginning of a new age in the history of humankind. Through Bahā'u'llāh the same divine force that was manifest in Kṛṣṇa is once again seen as communing with humankind and reestablishing the eternal truths of religion. Perhaps the best example of such cross-cultural eschatology can be seen in several verses of an Indian Bahā'ī song (*bhajan*) entitled 'Kalki Avatāra':

> Refrain—Arise O children of India, the Kalki *avatāra* has come.
> Viṣṇu's *avatāra* has come with the name Bahā'u'llāh.

Nowhere in the entire world can the influence of religion be seen.
The wicked have obtained everything
The truthful have lost everything
According to the *Gītā*, the time of Viṣṇu's *avatāra* has come—Awake (refrain)

The *Gītā* has said when circumstances are such
Religion will once again be reestablished, just as it is happening today.
In order to save righteousness Kalki *avatāra* has come—Awake (refrain)

Foolish people have not recognized that Viṣṇu's *avatāra* has come again.
Rādhā and Arjuna knew that Bahā'u'llāh was the Lord's new abode
The eternal has once again manifested himself—Awake (refrain)

Ethics and human relations

At the heart of Bahā'ī social philosophy lies the concept of the oneness of humankind. 'Abd al-Bahā' designated it the foundation of the faith of God, and Shoghi Effendi (1965: 216–17) referred to it as the most vital of all the principles found in Bahā'u'llāh's tablets. According to this ideal, all people, regardless of race, ethnicity, gender, religious background, or social standing, are believed to be equal in the eyes of God. They may differ in their potential capacities, and they will of necessity attain to different intellectual and economic stations in life, but they are all children of the same creator. The social principles of the Bahā'ī faith are therefore an extension of its metaphysical beliefs: the emphasis placed on the oneness and unity of the Godhead results in a corresponding drive toward unity in the human sphere. In the words of Bahā'u'llāh: 'Ye are the fruits of one tree, and the leaves of one branch' (1969: 218).

The primary adjunct to the concept of the 'oneness of humankind' is the elimination of all prejudice. Ideally, Bahā'ī communities should be constantly striving to abolish all notions of basic human inequality at both the individual and structural levels. The standard was set by 'Abd al-Bahā': 'Therefore no one should glorify himself over another; no one should look upon another with scorn and contempt, and no one should deprive or oppress a fellow creature' ('Abdu'l-Bahā 1964: 110).

It would seem apparent that the ideal of human equality as expounded in the concept of the oneness of humankind was a significant factor underlying the presentation of the movement by Bahā'ī teachers in India over the past several decades. Here reference is made to the large numbers of low-caste villagers who were originally attracted to the message (Garlington 1977: 105). From this perspective, the Bahā'ī faith would be seen as a vehicle through which people from various points on the social spectrum could interact with one another on the basis of human dignity. As to the actual impact this ideal has had on local Indian Bahā'ī communities, however, there is less certainty. While there is a lack of extensive anthropological data in this regard, the experience of other religious movements in India (Buddhist, Christian, and Islamic), as well as limited information from a number of Bahā'ī communities in Madhya Pradesh in the 1970s, would lead one to tentatively conclude that Bahā'ī egalitarian ideals have to varying degrees become compartmentalized.

Compartmentalization, or the bracketing of certain behaviors into specific frames of social reference, has been seen by numerous anthropologists to be an essential dynamic within Indian social systems (Singer 1972: 320). When compartmentalization is at work, behaviors that would not be acceptable in one social setting might well be seen as acceptable in another. For example, contact with certain objects, or association with certain people, might be acceptable outside of the village setting, say, on a bus or in a factory, but prohibited within it. In terms of the Bahā'ī faith, this would mean that for many of those who have professed belief in Bahā'u'llāh, egalitarian ideals would be more likely to be expressed in specific Bahā'ī frames of reference (a Bahā'ī meeting or devotional session) than in more conventional settings where the behavioral influence of traditional institutions related to caste and kinship would prevail. Moreover, since Bahā'ī administrators and teachers have generally adopted a policy of gradualism which has not demanded that new members immediately cast off traditional patterns of behavior, they have in essence taken advantage of the compartmentalization process. Therefore, even though Bahā'ī social teachings are essentially transcaste in outlook, except within a specifically Bahā'ī context, there does not seem to have been any militant attempt to purge new believers of conventional caste behavior. Among those believers in India who have more established Bahā'ī identities (such as families that can trace their Bahā'ī roots back more than one generation), one would expect to find behavior based on Bahā'ī social principles to be less compartmentalized, although even here differences, depending on the configuration of a number of social factors, including ethnicity, educational level, and economic status, should be expected.

Scriptures and sacred places

To Bahā'īs the writings of Bahā'u'llāh are considered revealed scripture. These writings are composed of several books as well as hundreds of tablets and epistles, many of which have not yet been published. Bahā'u'llāh's core text, the *Kitāb-i-Aqdas* (Most Holy Book), contains the laws and ordinances that are the spiritual and legal bedrock of the Bahā'ī community; his *Kitāb-i-Īqān* (Book of Certitude) is an explanation and exploration of the allegorical nature of revealed scriptures; while the *Seven Valleys* and the *Four Valleys* are examples of his mystical prose. Perhaps the most widely used text, however, is a compilation of his writings entitled *Gleanings From the Writings of Bahā'u'llāh* that contains selections from a variety of sources and has been translated into numerous languages worldwide.

The writings of 'Abd al-Bahā' have a sacred character to them as well. Although they are not considered revelation, 'Abd al-Bahā's position as the official interpreter of Bahā'u'llāh's writings, and the perfect exemplar of his teachings, accounts for this elevated status. Like his father's writings, most of these documents took the form of personal correspondence. Many of the letters have been compiled into distinct volumes like *The Tablets of 'Abd al-Bahā' Abbās*. Outstanding among 'Abd al-Bahā's independent treatises are his *Will and Testament*, which attempts to ensure the continued legitimization of Bahā'ī authoritative institutions, and *The Secret of Divine Civilization*, which deals with the science of politics. In addition, a collection of his table talks entitled *Some Answered Questions* focuses on theological and philosophical issues.

In the role of Guardian of the Bahā'ī faith Shoghi Effendi was designated by 'Abd al-Bahā' as the official living interpreter of the Bahā'ī scriptures. Whereas his writings in this capacity are not believed to be revelatory in nature, they are considered authoritative. In addition to his numerous interpretive writings (published, for example, in a volume entitled *The World Order of Bahā'u'llāh*), Shoghi Effendi penned an official history of the Bahā'ī faith, *God Passes By*.

The two most sacred places in the Bahā'ī world are found in Israel. The golden-domed shrine of the Bāb, which contains the remains of 'Alī Muḥammad, is situated on Mount Carmel in Haifa, while the tomb of Bahā'u'llāh is located at Bahji near 'Akkā. Despite the fact that pilgrimage is not a religious requirement in the Bahā'ī faith, these sites have become focal points of visitation for a large number of Bahā'īs from all parts of the world. Mount Carmel also houses the permanent headquarters of the Universal House of Justice. In recent years it has become the center of significant architectural projects, and the terraced gardens that adorn its hillsides have become internationally renowned.

In addition to the two shrines in Israel, the Bahā'īs have constructed seven Houses of Worship throughout the world, with at least one building located on each continent. Each temple has a different architectural style, but common to all structures are their nine sides and central dome, which symbolize the diversity, and yet oneness, of humanity. The first House of Worship in the West was completed in 1953, in Wilmette, Illinois, USA, on the shores of Lake Michigan. Subsequent temples have been built in Kampala, Uganda; Sydney, Australia; Frankfurt, Germany; Panama City, Panama; Apia, Western Samoa; and New Delhi, India. All Houses of Worship are open to people of every religion.

Because the large majority of Indian Bahā'īs cannot afford a pilgrimage to Haifa, the New Delhi House of Worship has become the primary sacred site for the Indian Bahā'ī community. The temple was completed in 1986 on the outskirts of the nation's capital and has won numerous architectural awards. Designed around the indigenous image of the lotus flower, the forty-meter-high structure is composed of twenty-seven freestanding, marble-clad petals arranged in clusters of three to form the traditional nine sides found on all Bahā'ī temples. Since it is open to the public as well as to the Bahā'īs, the New Delhi House of Worship has become a major tourist attraction drawing over 2.5 million visitors a year. On some Hindu holy days it has attracted as many as 100,000 visitors.

Institutions and practices

Membership in the Bahā'ī community requires a willing submission to the laws and ordinances set down by Bahā'u'llāh. As mentioned earlier, Bahā'u'llāh's laws for his faith are codified in the *Kitāb-i-Aqdas*. While certain of these laws are designed for future implementation, a number are considered binding for the contemporary community. The more significant of these include individual daily prayer (noncongregational); annual nineteen-day period of fasting (daylight hours from March 2 through 20); monogamy (divorce is allowed but not encouraged); parental agreement of both partners before marriage; burial of the dead; and the writing of a will. Among the more important prohibitions are murder, theft, adultery, slave trading, monasticism, use of intoxicants, and the public confession of sins. Beyond acceptance of these communal laws, Bahā'īs are expected to adhere to the laws of the sovereign states in which they reside. Except where it would require the denial of one's faith in Bahā'u'llāh, obedience to government is required.

The occasion on which members of Bahā'ī communities gather for communal worship is called the Nineteen Day Feast. As its name indicates, this gathering takes place at the local level every nineteen days and is composed of devotional, administrative, and social segments. During the devotional section individuals take turns reading or reciting prayers and verses from the sacred writings. Since there is no priesthood in the Bahā'ī faith, there is no designated leader of prayer. Similarly, there is no communal prayer whereby all believers recite the same verses in unison. Since the spiritual power of music is also appreciated, it is not uncommon to find musical selections during Nineteen Day Feast devotional sessions.

In keeping with the Bahā'ī faith's overall approach of not emphasizing ritual activity, its two prominent passage-rite ceremonies, marriage and burial of the dead, are relatively unstructured in nature, the former calling for only a brief statement of the couple's acceptance of God's will, and the latter requiring the recitation of a short obligatory prayer along with certain details regarding the preparation of the body. In a like manner, Bahā'ī holy day ceremonies are generally lacking in prescribed formats. In most cases they involve the saying of prayers and the reading of specific scriptural passages related to each event. At many of these occasions sharing of food is also common. The most significant Bahā'ī holy days include Nō Rūz, the Persian New Year (March 21); Ridvān, the anniversary of Bahā'u'llāh's declaration (April 21); the declaration of the Bāb (May 23); the ascension of Bahā'u'llāh (May 29); the martyrdom of the Bāb (July 9); the birth of the Bāb (October 21); the birth of Bahā'u'llāh (November 12); the day of the covenant (November 26); and the ascension of ʿAbd al-Bahā' (November 28).

Like the compartmentalization of behaviors related to Bahā'ī social principles, it can be expected that the degree of implementation regarding Bahā'ī laws, devotional activities, ceremonies, and holy days varies among Indian believers according to a number of variables, the most important of which are generational and geographical. Those believers who have been raised in Bahā'ī families or who live in urban areas where local Bahā'ī community institutions and modes of communication are better developed would be more likely to demonstrate such behaviors on a regular basis than either first-generation Bahā'īs or the rural followers who have declared their membership during the last few decades. Indeed, Bahā'ī administrators have been aware of this urban/rural lacuna since the beginning of the mass teaching campaigns in the early 1960s and have made attempts to bridge it through the development of a number of educational institutions, including teaching institutes, traveling teachers, and model villages. An example of such an institution is the Indore Teaching Institute that was established in 1962. Taking in groups of selected villagers for three- to four-day training sessions, the institute was designed to deepen them in a number of the above-mentioned Bahā'ī behavioral norms in the hope that upon returning to their communities, the villagers would in turn help educate their fellow believers (Garlington 1984: 167).

Bahā'ī polity

The Bahā'ī faith eschews communal political involvement and forbids its members from playing an active role in party politics. Yet, as a distinct religious organization, it has developed a number of administrative institutions and political mechanisms that help shape and determine the nature of internal decision-making processes. Furthermore, in several of their writings both Bàhā'u'llāh and 'Abd al-Bahā' freely commented upon the formation and structure of a future Bahā'ī world commonwealth (Cole 1998: 80–90).

The current Bahā'ī administrative system is organized on three levels: local, national, and international. In every local community where nine or more Bahā'īs reside an institution known as a Local Spiritual Assembly is established. The assembly, which was ordained by Bahā'u'llāh, consists of nine individuals who are elected annually by popular vote. In addition to acting as arbiters of local problems and disputes, assembly members are responsible for organizing teaching, devotional, and educational activities at the local level.

The institution that directs national affairs is known as the National Spiritual Assembly. As is the case with local assemblies, these bodies consist of nine believers who are democratically elected annually by convention delegates. Every five years all the members of national assemblies throughout the world elect the Universal House of Justice that oversees Bahā'ī activities at the international level. Unlike local and national assemblies, only men can serve in this institution.

Running parallel to the elected institutions are a number of appointed administrative positions. In descending order of authority, they are the Hands of the Cause, the Continental Boards of Counselors, and the Auxiliary Boards. Individuals assigned to these institutions counsel and advise both the elected institutions and individual believers in all matters pertaining to the Bahā'ī faith. The Hands of the Cause (appointed by Shoghi Effendi) work at the international level; counselors (appointed by the Universal House of Justice) perform at the national level; while board members (appointed by counselors) work within specific countries.

While there are democratic principles at work in terms of both electoral and consultative procedures, it would be incorrect to perceive Bahā'ī administrative institutions solely in the light of democratic ideals. In the first place, they are all subservient to the revealed laws and teachings of Bahā'u'llāh as interpreted by 'Abd al-Bahā' and Shoghi Effendi. Only the Universal House of Justice has the right to legislate, but even this supreme institution cannot change the divine text. Second, once elected, assembly members are not responsible to those who elect them. Individual voting records are not kept; only the decision of the assembly as a whole is reported. In conjunction with this protection of individual conscience, Bahā'ī elections should ideally contain no campaigning or electioneering. There are no candidates; voters at each level simply cast their ballots for the nine individuals they feel will best serve the community. The nine people with the highest number of votes form the new institution. This last measure is designed to rid the community of internal political bickering, though in practice it often favors the re-election of incumbents.

There are currently tens of thousands of registered local spiritual assemblies in India. Whereas this figure may not accurately reflect the actual number of actively functioning assemblies, Bahā'ī administrators and teachers in India have placed great emphasis on consolidation plans designed to foster and develop as many of these institutions as possible. During the early years of mass teaching, a sustained effort was made to educate assembly members from the rural areas in the proper methods of assembly formation and operation by encouraging them to attend either specially designed courses at teaching institutes or mock assembly sessions in specific villages.

India's first National Spiritual Assembly was elected in 1923. At that time it was responsible for Bahā'ī affairs in both India and Burma. Due to the Partition of

British India into the sovereign nations of India and Pakistan, in 1947 this assembly was also put in charge of Bahā'ī activities in Pakistan. A separate National Spiritual Assembly was created for Pakistan in 1957, and the National Spiritual Assembly of Burma was established in 1959. The headquarters of the National Spiritual Assembly of India is located in New Delhi. In recent years Bahā'ī administration in India has become more decentralized with the creation of State Bahā'ī Councils which micro-manage Bahā'ī affairs in their appropriate states. These councils have under their wing a number of regional committees that provide much of the organization for grassroots propagation and consolidation activities. In addition to national, state, and regional bodies, there are currently four counselors who have the responsibility of overseeing Bahā'ī administrative affairs in India.

Relations with other religions

The impact of Hinduism

There have been Bahā'īs in India for over 100 years, yet it has been during the last several decades that the impact of Hinduism on the community has been most dramatically felt. This has been primarily the result of the decision of Bahā'ī leadership to actively teach the faith in rural areas of the country where any hope for success would require a presentation of the Bahā'ī message that made use of Hindu symbols and concepts. This strategy has in turn resulted in a greater Hinduization or Sanskritization of Bahā'ī discourse, literature, and art forms. In this regard, it is not uncommon to see such terms as Avatāra or Bhagvan Bahā' used in Bahā'ī communications, and in both Bahā'ī books and pamphlets one can find direct references to Hindu themes and idioms. For example, *Kalki Avātara kī Khoj* (In Search of the Kalkī Avatāra) is an attempt to prove Bahā'u'llāh's identification with the Kalkī *avatāra* through an examination of eschatological passages in numerous Hindu texts. In this connection it should also be noted that there appears to have been a fairly deliberate attempt made by Bahā'ī teachers to distance the movement from any Islamic identification. A good example of this approach can be seen in the Hindi translations of Bahā'ī scriptures which are so heavily Sanskritized as to make it difficult to recognize their Arabic or Persian antecedents. Then there are the Bahā'ī devotional songs (*bhajan*) which have sprung up in recent decades, some of which make free use of various Vaiṣṇava figures and symbols, especially those related to Kṛṣṇa (Garlington 1982: 43–49). Finally, as mentioned earlier, the Bahā'ī House of Worship in New Delhi is constructed in the form of a lotus, a symbol often related with the Hindu goddess Lakṣmī.

Even the question of Bahā'ī identity in India may be said to have been influenced by Hinduism. Since the Bahā'īs have not demanded that new declarants formally negate their own religious traditions nor radically depart from more conventional forms of behavior, it would not be surprising if many of those who have declared their belief in Bahā'u'llāh do not see themselves so much as belonging to a new religion as adding a new component to their traditional belief system. In this sense acceptance of Bahā'u'llāh would fit into that category of Indian religious experience called *bhakti*.

Bhakti traditions have flourished in India for centuries, and many of them have had as part of their internal dynamic transcaste attitudes. However, their primary concern has not been social change but devotion to a specific god or *avatāra*. While they may have been aware of the conditions of the depressed, they tended to represent a 'new symbolic language for the aspirations of the depressed rather than any fulfilment of these aspirations' (Forrester 1977: 45). Such a model would seem to fit well with the experiences of large numbers of Indian Bahā'īs and may be one reason why the number of Bahā'īs as recorded by the official Government of India Census remains in the thousands rather than the millions.

Interreligious dialogue and social development

One of the basic principles of the Bahā'ī faith is the oneness of religion. From the time of the religion's inception the idea of interreligious dialogue has been championed. In the *Kitāb-i-Aqdas* we find Bahā'u'llāh (1992: 75) enjoining his disciples to consort with the followers of all religions. Similarly ʿAbd al-Bahā' is recorded as saying: 'All must abandon prejudices and must even go into each other's churches and mosques, for, in all of these worshiping places, the Name of God is mentioned. Since all gather to worship God, what difference is there?' (cited in Fazel 1997: 131). ʿAbd al-Bahā' put this injunction into practice during his trip to the West where in both Europe and North America he met and exchanged views with leaders of various religious communities.

Since the time of ʿAbd al-Bahā', participation in interreligious events and organizations at the international, national, and local levels has been a common occurrence for Bahā'ī communities. The most visible examples would be their involvement in the World Congress of Faiths, the Conservation and Religion Network of the World Wide Fund for Nature, the World Conference on Religion and Peace, and World Religion Day. Directly related to this participation is the Bahā'ī Peace Program, which calls on the world's religious leaders to dialogue on the issue of how to eliminate religious strife. On this issue the Universal House of Justice has commented that theological differences will have to be submerged in a spirit that advocates the advancement of human understanding and peace (Fazel 1997: 136).

Historically, the Indian Bahā'ī community has consistently been involved in interreligious dialogue. As far back as 1910 the Bahā'īs sent a representative to an All-India Religious Convention held in Allahabad (Garlington 1997), and over the following decades there were numerous interchanges with such groups as the Brāhmo Samāj, Ārya Samāj, and Theosophical Society. In recent years the focal point of interreligious contact has been the Bahā'ī House of Worship (Lotus Temple) which is open to all the communities of India and whose structure is symbolic of religious unity.

Somewhat tangential to the theme of interreligious dialogue, but intricately related to the Bahā'ī Peace Program, is the relatively recent commitment by Bahā'ī communities to the implementation of social and economic development projects. Two outstanding examples of this approach in India can be seen in the Barli Vocational Institute for Women in Indore, Madhya Pradesh and the New Era Development Institute in Panchgani, Maharashtra. Both institutions are dedicated to the vocational training of underprivileged villagers. In Indore special attention has been given to tribal women. Groups of twenty women are enrolled in three-month courses that have focused on sewing and dressmaking. The Panchgani Institute currently provides training in a variety of vocational areas, including diesel mechanics, motorcycle repair, data processing, refrigeration and air conditioning repair, radio and television servicing, agriculture and animal husbandry, and primary and preprimary teacher training. At both sites courses in literacy, hygiene, and moral education supplement the curriculum.

Prospects for the future

As the new millennium dawns the Bahā'ī faith finds itself confronting several important challenges. Internationally it has to deal with the persecution of believers in its homeland of Iran.[2] Then there is also the question of community development. The last century has witnessed a continued increase in Bahā'ī teaching efforts worldwide, but at present there are more adherents in Asia and Africa than in the West, and, as is the case in India, many of these individuals are not well versed in the fundamentals of Bahā'ī religious life. If these numbers are to reflect any degree of social reality, there will have to be intensive educational programs on a much larger scale than currently exist. Finally, like other religions, the Bahā'ī community is not immune to internal debate. In recent years some of the more significant issues have included the male-only restriction to membership of the Universal House of Justice, prepublication review by Bahā'ī institutions of articles and books on the Bahā'ī faith written by adherents, and, especially in India, the relative distribution of community resources related to social and economic development projects. Consequently, the twenty-first century could prove to be a critical one for the Bahā'ī faith in that it may well determine whether the community will hover like other new religious movements on the peripheries of the more established traditions or evolve into the category of world religion toward which both its leadership and rank-and-file membership aspire.

Suggested further readings

Amanat (1989); Bahā'u'llāh (1963); Cole (1998); *The Divine Art of Living* (1965); Garlington (1977, 1984, forthcoming); Momen (1997); Nakhjavani (Nd); P. Smith (1987).

Notes

1 The Bahā'ī statistics for both India and the world are based on the number of signed declarations of belief and do not necessarily indicate the number of active participants within the religion. Moreover, the latest Indian census records only 5,700 individuals as claiming a Bahā'ī identity.

2 During its short history the Iranian Bahā'ī community has experienced periods of intense persecution. The most recent outburst began following the 1979 Iranian Revolution. Examples of such persecution include imprisonment, destruction of property, and occasionally execution.

Part Three

BEYOND THE INTRODUCTION

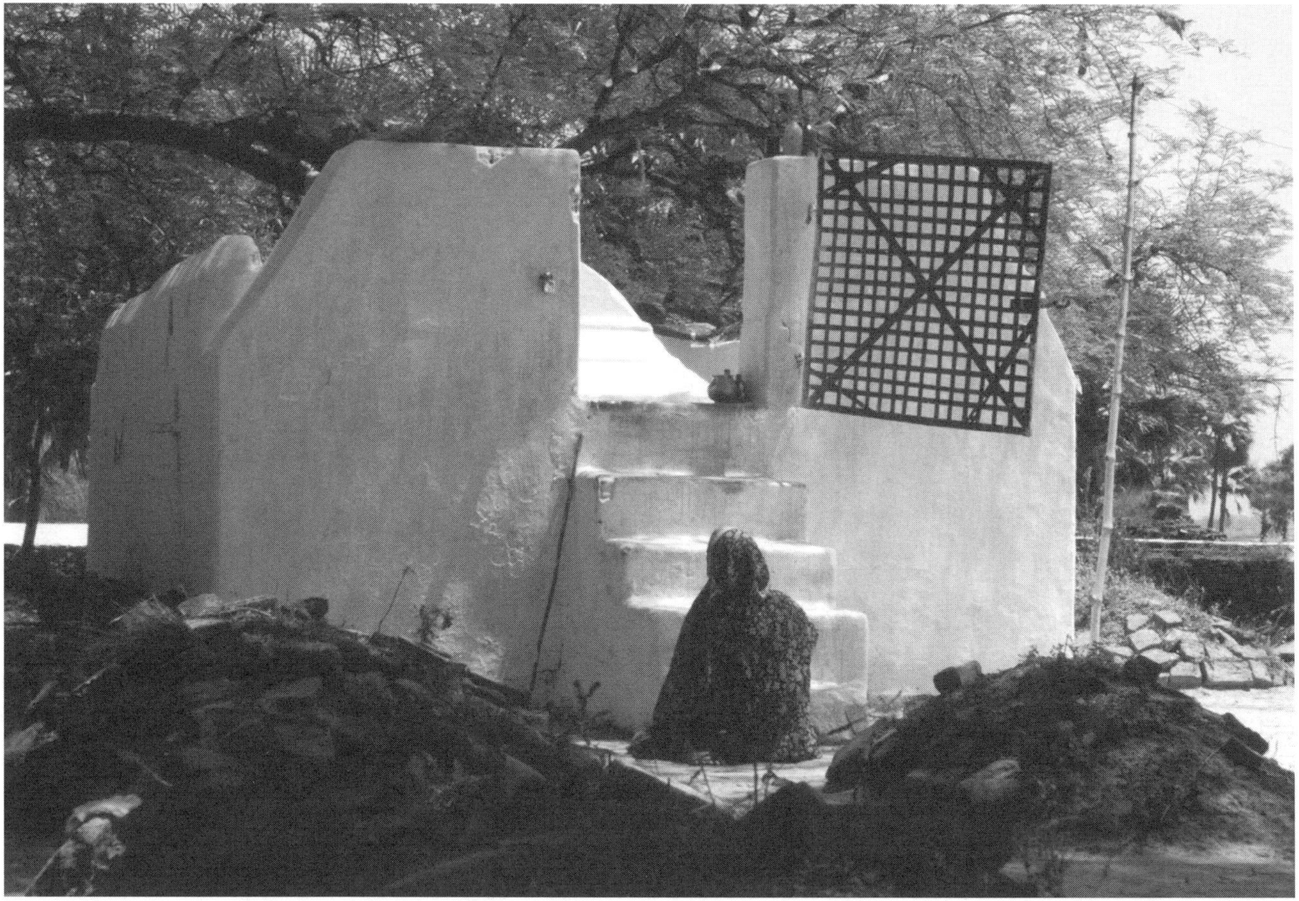

11. A woman, her religion unknown, seated in prayer at the tomb of a Ṣūfī saint in a village in Bihar. Courtesy of Professor Peter Gottschalk.

10

CONTESTED CATEGORIES AND ISSUES IN INTERPRETATION

Carl Olson

The other chapters in this book introduce various religions of India or South Asia. Those chapters, and this one, were composed during what many would call a poststructural, postmodern, or postcolonial era. Whatever the label, the period through which we are currently passing is characterized by calling into question all categories, definitions, and assertions. This means that basically accepted notions are actively doubted – such as that Hinduism and Buddhism are world religions or even that we can distinguish religion (or a religion) from everything else. Within such a skeptical and ambivalent era, the context from which one writes is crucially important – in particular whether one writes as an insider or an outsider. The insider/outsider problem raises questions about objectivity, subjectivity, interpretive presuppositions, authenticity, and fundamental fairness in relation to the focus of one's study. These problems are connected to issues of cross-cultural sensitivity and the question of whether (and, if so, how) it is possible to grasp ideas and practices that are totally foreign to a scholar. If a scholar is an outsider to the religious tradition being studied, this fact also raises questions about the nature of the comparative method.

This final chapter proposes to examine some of these methodological issues for this book and others like it that use the talents of Western scholars to examine foreign religious traditions. The chapter will be intentionally critical of some of the issues and figures covered. The criticisms, biases, and presuppositions in this chapter are mine, and they should not be attributed to the authors of the other chapters on the various religions of India or South Asia. I will begin by examining some key terms and categories used in this book, the position of the scholar is examined next with respect to the insider/outsider problem, the importance of interpretation is considered, and the role of comparison because of its long use in the study of foreign religions. Because the chapters of this book concentrate on the various religious traditions, it is essential to focus on the context in which this scholarship occurs at the present moment. It is, therefore, vital to examine the Orientalist critique of the study of non-Western cultures and how it gives birth to postcolonial studies. Finally, this chapter will conclude with a look at the use of the representational mode of thinking.

The problematic nature of religion

Religion is an elusive notion to define in such a way that it can be applied cross-culturally to all religions. We delude ourselves into believing that we know what it is and that we can recognize it when we see it. But our attempts to precisely define it cross-culturally tend to fail. Inspired by a thinker such as René Descartes (1596–1650) and his development of a method of doubt in order to find certainty and first principles, some Western scholars were inspired to search for the origins of religion. The quest for the origins of religion by such scholars as Edward B. Tylor (1832–1917), James George Frazer (1854–1941), and Andrew Lang (1844–1912) also demonstrated the influence of the theory of evolution advocated by Charles Darwin and Herbert Spencer. A pioneer in the field of anthropology, Tylor argued that animism was the basis for religion, which originated in a belief about the continuing existence of souls of deceased creatures. These ghostly spirits represented the origin of supernatural beings. According to Tylor, it was possible to find traces of animism in the religions of the present. Frazer, who was most famous for his voluminous work entitled *The Golden Bough*, which eventually grew with the publication of new editions to twelve volumes, traced the origins of religion to totemism, whereas magic represented an earlier stage of evolution in comparison to religion, which will itself be replaced by science in his conception of human evolution. Finally, in contrast to Tylor and Frazer, Lang argued that there were primitive tribes devoid of any religion. Lang also criticized other theories for relying on weak sources.

The understanding of religion was also shaped by the efforts of Immanuel Kant (1724–1804) and Friedrich Schleiermacher (1768–1834), who identified religion with the feeling of absolute dependence. In his own quest for certainty, Kant distinguished between theoretical reason and practical reason as part of his efforts to discern the relationship of knowledge to reality. Although a person can know things that appear in space and time, Kant argued that we cannot know metaphysical reality or what he called ideas such as the soul or God. Kant wanted to maintain a distinction between the phenomenal world (appearance) that we can know and reality (the noumenal or the thing-in-itself) that we cannot know, although there is synthetic a priori knowledge (valid independent of empirical observation) such as mathematics that is unconditioned by experience. The influence of Kant and Schleiermacher is evident in the theory of religion espoused by Rudolf Otto (1869–1937) in his classic book *The Idea of the Holy*. Otto argued for the necessity of investigating the nature of religious experience, which he identified with the experience of the holy, before examining religious expression. For Otto, the origins of religion can be discovered in a human being's emotions, and he grasps the holy as an a priori category under the influence of the reworking of Kant's philosophy by Jakob Fries (1773–1884), who did not follow Kant's treatment of a priori categories as ideal and devoid of cognitive content until shaped by sensory experience. In summary, the effort to develop a viable definition of religion was shaped by Enlightenment thought in the West.

The attempt to find an adequate definition of religion continued into the mid-twentieth century when the German theologian Paul Tillich (1886–1965) identified religion with a person's ultimate concern. Due to its more neutral and less prejudicial nature, this definition enjoyed wide acceptance for a time because it could be used in a cross-cultural way without inflicting harm on other religions. In spite of the acceptance of Tillich's definition for a time, other voices called the category of religion into question.

Concurrent with the period of Tillich's influence on the field of religion, two important textbooks appeared: *Man's Religions* (1949) by John B. Noss and *The Religions of Man* (1958) by Huston Smith. The use of noninclusive language in the titles is indicative of the time period in which these two authors were writing, although more recent editions of these books correct this defect. By the late 1950s, these two texts were widely adopted by college instructors teaching introductory level courses on world religions. Their widespread use reflects the fact that they were the best available texts at the time.

Noss' book is more comprehensive than Smith's and very different in style. Noss' book is an historical treatment of various religions with lots of names, dates, and other data. In the preface to the first edition of the book, Noss, writing in an impersonal third-person style, states that the book was written to meet two needs: to serve as an introduction to the world's religions that describes and interprets material based on original sources; and to present the various religions in their historical context. Noss (1949: xiii) anticipates that his book will have an uneven quality for some readers. What Noss implies, although he does not explicitly admit it, is that it is impossible for one human being to become an expert in all the religions encompassed by his book. Nonetheless, the commercial success of Noss' book is evident by its appearance in an eleventh edition that is now coauthored by his son David S. Noss and retitled *A History of the World's Religions*.

Nine years after the publication of Noss' book, Huston Smith published his book as partially a reaction to the approach taken by Noss. In the preface to the first edition of his book, Smith tells a reader what his book is not. It is not a textbook in the history of religions, and he refers in a footnote to Noss' book as an excellent example of such a textbook. Smith decides to reduce historical facts to a minimum because he is more concerned with ideas and meaning. Second, Smith admits that his book is not a comprehensive view of the religions because of their diverse nature and even the diversity that one can find within a particular tradition. This aspect makes selection unavoidable for the scholar, and he admits to not discussing strange practices, which suggests that he may have been offering a sanitized or idealized version of a religion. Smith confesses that his book is not comprehensive because each religion combines universal principles and local contexts. The principles are more important to Smith than the context of a particular religion. Finally, Smith's (1958: 2–4) book does not assume that one religion is better than another, which is a major attitudinal advance over the motivation of many previous authors of books in the area of comparative religion.

After informing his reader about what his book is not, Smith proceeds to inform his reader about three characteristics of the book. Smith claims that the book seeks to embrace the world, even though this wish must remain frustrated due to human finitude. Smith wants his readers to be world citizens, and he quotes approvingly a statement by Socrates about being a citizen of the world. In his vision, Smith foresees an overcoming of the barriers that separate East and West with each party borrowing from the other and exchanging mutual help. Second, Smith admits that he takes religion seriously. Smith writes personally of using religions of others for assistance with major questions about life. Finally, Smith claims that his book is a sincere effort to communicate. In a statement that seems directed at Noss, Smith says, 'Religion is not primarily a matter of facts in the historical sense; it is a matter of meanings' (1958: 12). Smith wants to communicate more than just the details about the various religions.

Instead of the impersonal and detached approach of Noss, Smith provides his reader with his personal vision. Smith confesses that he envisions listening to the voices of God-seekers, which he conceives as a universal fellowship, as motivation for writing his book. Smith also tells us that his book is about the 'best values,' although he does not tell us on what basis he makes such judgments. When Smith asserts that his book is about religions that are alive, he also claims that these religions confront an individual with a choice: 'It calls the soul to the highest adventure it can undertake, a proposed journey across the jungles, peaks, and deserts of the human spirit. The call is to confront reality, to master the self' (H. Smith 1958: 11). Some scholars advocating a strictly scientific approach to the study of religion would view such a statement as a hidden theological agenda and purpose for studying religion. A scholar such as Smith might respond that such scientific-oriented scholars want to denude religion of existential meaning, bleed it of its vitality, and transform it into a museum artifact. Thereupon, people can see it objectively and not have to interact with it in a personal way, because it ceases to speak to them or to challenge them.

In contrast to Noss, Smith wants his reader to become existentially engaged with the various religions in his book, whereas Noss is more comfortable with descriptively presenting historical data. The major difference between Noss and Smith resides, however, with the latter's use of empathy. Smith is probably the first scholar to enter empathically so many different religious traditions so successfully. It should come as no major surprise that both books are still in print, although there are many competitors in the marketplace.

In his book entitled *God and the Universe of Faiths* (1973), John Hick attempts to account for the various world religions by recounting that they were formed within the context of two cradles of civilization – Mesopotamia in the Near East and the Indus Valley of northern India, both of which manifest devotion to nature deities and spirit worship. These civilizations existed long before there were identifiable religions and gave birth to a surge of religious creativity and growth, from about 800 BCE onward. This 'Axial Age' creativity is responsible for the origin of the world's religions in a series of revelatory experiences occurring over a 500-year period that was followed by time gaps filled later by Christianity and then Islam.

According to Hick, God did not reveal the various world religions all at once but gave partial revelations at different times and places to diverse peoples. The various forms of the revelations conformed to the diverse mentalities of the recipients of the revelations, and these developed into world religions. It is impossible to claim that all world religions are equally valid, but the extent to which these revelations have sustained people over time is indicative of their genuine nature. Each of them is incomplete and imperfect because no single religion can represent the vastness of ultimate reality. Hence all religious traditions are in contact with the same ultimate reality, even though each religion represents a different experience of that unfathomable and all-surpassing reality.

Hick also envisions a future time when world religions will gradually become a global community and the great religions will cease to be rivals. They will unite to resist the worldwide wave of secularism, although differences among the world's religions will continue. In the end, religion will disappear into the eternal life where there will be no need for any of the world's religions because their goal would have been attained.

Tracing the evolution of the term 'religion' (*religio*) in the West as used by scholars such as Noss, Smith, and Hick, Wilfred Cantwell Smith in his book *The Meaning and*

End of Religion (1963) demonstrated how the term changed meanings during its history, how it became intellectualized, and the way that it became associated with Western religious polemics and apologetics. If the notion of religion originated in the West, does this mean that a scholar cannot apply the term to a foreign culture? If a scholar pluralizes the term, then it seems to refer to something abstract, impersonal, and reified. The use of the term 'religions' reflects a process of external classification and renders the subject into something generic. The confusion initiated by the imprecise term and the way that it distorts what it studies render it useless and unnecessary from Smith's perspective. However, Smith's suggestion that 'faith' would be a preferable substitute for 'religion' has not been widely embraced by scholars because the notion of 'faith' presents its own set of problems particularly with traditions that are not based on faith.

Frustration with lack of success in finding an acceptable definition of religion has led to some concessions by some scholars. John Hick concludes in his book *An Interpretation of Religion* (2004), for instance, that religion cannot be defined and its plural nature ('religions') does not share a common essence, although he does claim that it can be described. Reflecting the influence of the philosopher Ludwig Wittgenstein and his notion of family resemblance, Hick argues that religions do have commonalities and differences not unlike members of a family. Something that all religions have in common is a concern with the 'real,' which represents Hick's attempt to find something that fits into a cross-cultural context for theistic and nontheistic traditions. This does not mean that various traditions do not find different ways to experience, respond to, and conceive of the real. In a similar fashion to Tillich's notion of ultimate concern, Hick is attempting to devise a neutral language for an elusive subject.

Rather than searching for an adequate term to identify and define, Jonathan Z. Smith thinks that it is impossible to search outwardly and internally for religion because there is no data for it. Smith does not mean to imply that there are no expressions, phenomena, or experiences that may be termed religious. He intends to assert instead that religion is created by the reflective imagination of the scholar as he or she compares and generalizes about his subject. If it is the scholar that creates the category of religion, then it cannot possess any independent existence by itself (J. Smith 1982: xi). In short, Smith claims that religion is a human construct made by academic types of individuals. Does this imply that the religions of India covered in this book are imaginative fabrications of the scholars who have written the chapters? What the authors of the various chapters have written does have a basis in empirical reality. Hindus, Jainas, and Buddhists do live their lives according to certain convictions and patterns of behavior as do people in the West.

Scholars of religion are victims of a certain terminological vagueness with respect to the nature of religion, and there is a real question about whether the term 'religion' can be used with any precision when applied to other cultures. It is possible to accept Smith's suggestion that we become aware that religion itself is a construct of academic life, but this acknowledgement does not lead us to a more satisfying definition, although it does render us more honest with ourselves. Maybe, we are forced to admit that both locally and cross-culturally we are stuck with something that is just too elusive to define. The obscure nature of religion suggests that it is never exactly right here for us. The elusive nature of religion and its disappearance from our grasp, because it is continually slipping away, can be understood as its tendency to withdraw from us. We need not lament the withdrawal if it allows phenomena to appear. Even if religion is not completely present, 'what religion is about is not elsewhere' (M. Taylor 1999: 1). Because religion is a slippery subject and most often we cannot be certain about where to find it, we can look within our own culture and that of others with a sense of adventure and the excitement of uncertainty. The possibilities of our failure are increased by the nature of the subject, but we also run the risk of discovering much about the other and in turn something about ourselves. The study of religion is dangerous and risky. The potential rewards for taking the risk can also be great for our self-understanding and for our understanding of the behavior of others.

Problems of terminology and categories

If the term 'religion' is problematic, it is also challenging to name the religion of the other. Since Westerners were comfortable with the terms 'Judaism' and 'Christianity,' they assumed that foreigners shared such a tendency to name the religion that they practiced. Until influenced by the West, people in India did not call their religion, for instance, Hinduism or Buddhism. It is very probable that there was no need to give it a name except for the benefit of outsiders. The term '*dharma*' (law, teaching, way of life) is probably the closest to an equivalent in Indian language to the meaning of 'religion' in the West.

The term 'Hindu' can be traced, for instance, to a Persian word ('hind') that is related to the Indo-Āryan term '*sindhu*' for a river in the Indus Valley of northern India. During the eighth century CE, invading Muslim tribes used such a term to differentiate themselves from the indigenous people in the trans-Indus region. By the fifteenth century, the term is used by Śrīvara, a Śaiva historian, to distinguish natives of India from the several waves of arriving Muslims. This practice was continued in Sanskrit and Bengali sources for the purpose of differentiating groups of people (O'Connell 1973: 340–44). By the end of the eighteenth century, the British adopted the term 'Hindoo' or 'Hindu' to identify the people of 'Hindustan.' After indigenous writers appropriated the term, it became widely accepted in India during the nineteenth century. Around this period, Indians were seeking to establish their own national identity in response to colonial domination by Western powers, although at first they did not use the term for narrowly religious purposes.

The more narrowly religious implications for the term 'Hinduism' owe their origin largely to so-called Orientalists and the scholarly work that they accomplished on the basis of Judeo-Christian presuppositions about the nature of religion (Kopf 1980: 502). This makes 'Hinduism' a scholarly abstraction created by the West. In a sense, one can argue that this abstraction was *imposed* on Indian culture. Nonetheless, some of India's indigenous people found it to be a cultural and political advantage to have their own recognized religion. What may have begun as an ahistorical abstraction became the name for a world religion along with others, and at first upper-class members of Indian society and then others embraced it. Moreover, this invented 'Hinduism' became part of a growing nationalist consciousness during the nineteenth century (King 1999: 103–107). This scenario suggests an initial external process of abstraction followed by an indigenous acceptance and political utilization of 'Hinduism' as a term of identification.

Taking the scholarly origins of 'Hinduism' into account, its original purpose for designating a geographical area and its plural nature lacking a simple unity, there are some scholars who think that it is not a useful term to refer to a single unified religion (Stietencron 1989: 20). Another scholar argues that it is possible to use the authority of the Veda to determine the identity of a Hindu as someone who accepts this literature as revealed (B. Smith 1989: 26). A critic of this assertion counters that there is no common religion in India because there are many different paths, doctrines, philosophies, or traditions, which renders using the Vedas as a measure for Hinduism inadequate (Michaels 2004: 18). This does not entail that 'Hinduism' is a meaningless term. Underlying the apparent pluralism of Indian culture, there is common social consensus that the different cults and sects are interchangeable and possess an underlying identity (Michaels 2004: 19).

Even with all the problems associated with the term 'Hinduism,' there are some scholars who think that it is a useful construct and well worth retaining. If the Sanskrit equivalent of 'Hindu' is *hindutva* or *hinduta*, these terms suggest a particular way of being in the world or, more specifically, a distinctive type of mentality that is paradoxical (Lipner 1996: 124). The retention of the term 'Hindu' is practical so long as it is used to refer to the culture in a nonessentialist manner that does not turn it into a static essence. Lipner (1994: 6) views 'Hinduism' as a term that conveys a sense of family resemblance.

While disagreeing with aspects of Lipner's position because of a danger that it could lead to misunderstanding, King (1999: 108) agrees about keeping the term 'Hinduism' for its usefulness on an introductory level, because of the advent of religious movements that approximate the term coined by Orientalists, and with an acknowledgment that the term represents something pluralistic with ruptures and discontinuities rather than a single, static, unchanging entity.

If the term 'Hinduism,' a religion without a specific founder, is problematic, can this also be true of a path such as Buddhism with an actual founder or at least someone who inspired a religion? Although it can be agreed that the historical Buddha founded a monastic community, it is another thing altogether to claim that he established a religion. It can, however, be asserted that he taught a *dhamma* or *dharma* (doctrine), which is a term closest in meaning to the Western notion of religion. The term 'Buddhism' originated in the West from the minds of scholars. Even long after the death of the historical Buddha, we lack any definitive evidence that Tibetans, Indians, Sinhalese, or Chinese referred to or conceived of themselves as Buddhists before Westerners gave them this label (King 1999: 144). Because the scholarly study of Buddhism evolved from earlier studies of Indology, Sinology, and classical philology, the term 'Buddhism' may not be an adequate one to capture the incredibly rich variety of cultural phenomena and levels of discourse associated with it. Does this mean that the term should be discarded? Since many people in the East and West use the term to define their religiosity at the present time, and since the term is pragmatically useful in a general way, it seems appropriate to use it while remembering that it is not completely adequate.

When using categories such as Hinduism or Buddhism, it is important to keep in mind that categories in general and these in particular do not possess rigid boundaries. Any category entails a range of degrees of membership within it. Thus some members of a category are more prototypical than others. It is also possible for members of a category to be related to other members of the same category, even though they share no common elements (Lakoff 1987).

Insider/outsider problem

Issues of terminology are directly related to the standpoint of the scholar. Because all scholars write or speak from some standpoint or perspective, it makes a big difference if one speaks about a religious tradition as an outsider (*etic*) or an insider (*emic*). Some would argue that only a member of a religious tradition, or insider, could speak with genuine authority about a particular tradition. There is certainly some validity to this position. But a cursory examination of insiders would reveal that there is much about their own tradition of which they are totally unaware and experience may vary from one insider to another. Therefore, an empathetic outsider should not be dismissed so quickly. After reading the earlier chapters in this book, it should be obvious that a religious tradition has more than a single voice, even those traditions founded by or traced to a specific individual. These various voices offer their own interpretations of their inherited traditions, which often result in new understandings of the tradition. An outsider studying and interpreting a particular tradition offers another kind of perspective that is not inferior or superior to that of the insider. It is just a different perspective in which the insider will be able to recognize his or her tradition, if the outsider is successful. If the insider cannot recognize his or her tradition as interpreted by the outsider, then there might be a problem associated with misinterpretation, misunderstanding, distortion, or outright deceit. For that matter, an insider as much as an outsider could have a political agenda, for instance, that distorts the formative tradition for short-term political gain. Does this suggest that a selected insider should represent the group experience? This is not necessarily the case according to Lipner, who exposes a potential problem:

> And even if it were agreed that some particular individual was entitled to represent the group, the description of a collective experience must be sufficiently critically detached from each individual's particular experience so as to represent what is shared in such a way that each individual of the collective recognizes his or her own experience in the representation. But to adopt this stance of critical distance is to begin to adopt the stance of the observer or so-called outsider parallel to the 'objective' stance of the scholar. At which point the insider is becoming an outsider, and the argument is being turned inside out.
>
> (2004: 16)

For a fuller grasp of a religious tradition, the problem identified by Lipner seems to suggest that both insider and outsider perspectives are needed in order to counterbalance and correct each other.

If both kinds of perspectives are useful, is it possible to bring the insider/outsider positions into even closer proximity? The outsider, for instance, can adopt a position of empathy with the religion of the other. Empathy (fellow feeling) attunes a scholar's cognitive faculties, especially his or her imagination, to enter the religious world of the other (Lipner 2004: 22). A scholar immersing himself or herself in the language, history, literature, and cultural context of the religion being studied makes this approach possible. In order to overcome the cultural barrier between the insider and outsider, the former can adopt a more relativistic and open stance and reject any absolutist perspective that might suggest that the viewpoint of the outsider is erroneous. The adoption of this type of procedure for both parties would increase the chance for achieving fruitful dialogue and mutual understanding.

Either the outsider or insider standpoints can lead to ethnocentrism. Is there anything that can be done to avoid the danger of falling into ethnocentrism? In order to overcome ethnocentrism, the philosopher Charles Taylor argues that we may have to 'relativize features of our own self-understanding that we cherish' (1995: 149). This cannot occur by following the model of natural science, but we must rather follow a comparative model. Taylor explains: 'That is because we make the other intelligible through our own human understanding' (1995: 150). Taylor means this in the sense of liberating the other by allowing the other to stand apart from us on his or her own. Then we seek to take into account the self-understanding of the other, and this enables us to move toward a broader understanding that is neither complete nor final and may lead in the direction of some newer and better understanding. What we gain in overcoming ethnocentrism is achieved by including the other in our understanding (C. Taylor 1995: 151). It is important to reiterate that this wider understanding owes its origin to comparison, which makes the comparative method crucial in understanding the other and overcoming ethnocentrism. Taylor summarizes his position in the following way: 'Precisely the aim of the comparative exercise is to enable us to understand the other undistortively, and hence to be able to see the good in their life, even while we also see that their good conflicts with ours' (1995: 62–63).

Another way to deal with the insider/outsider problem is offered by Gavin Flood when he argues that all understanding is dialogical, which possesses important implications for the study of religion. Flood shifts focus from consciousness, experience, and inner states to the sign, which locates religion more securely within culture and history that reflects better its narrative character. His emphasis on the narrative character of religion reconfigures the insider/outsider problem by transforming it into competing narratives (Flood 1999: 118). The cultural stories are both lived and told within time. This point enables us to recognize that insider/outsider narratives 'exist through time and are subject to constant revision and reassessment in new situations' (Flood 1999: 148).

As Paul Ricoeur (1984–88) makes clear in his three-volume work on narrative, it is inextricably connected to time and history. A narrative approach to a religious tradition can have the advantage of avoiding imposing a Western method upon another religious culture. A narrative approach by an outsider to a tradition such as Buddhism would follow the practice of members of the tradition by telling stories (Olson 2005: 2). Therefore, the narrative approach is grounded in the culture being studied, uses a method already utilized by members of that culture itself, and reduces the imposition of outside categories that might make good sense within the context of the outsider but would distort the context of the insider.

Issues of interpretation

Whether approaching a particular subject as an insider or an outsider, scholars who have contributed to this book encountered various texts, beliefs, and phenomena that called for interpretation and possibly comparison with phenomena from different religious traditions in order to understand what they encountered. The study of any religion is intimately connected to the art of hermeneutics. As the chapters of this book make clear, scholars of religion describe, explain, and interpret in the service of reaching understanding about a specific religion. Although explaining, describing, and interpreting can be distinguished as separate activities of a scholar, they are also interconnected (Gadamer 1982: 31; Ricoeur 1976: 72). As a scholar describes and explains his or her subject with the aim of making it more intelligible, his or her descriptions and explanations involve interpretations. Therefore, description, explanation, and interpretation are three interconnected activities that are directly connected to understanding in the sense that all three become part of what is actually comprehended (Gadamer 1982: 359). Scholars do not attempt to describe and explain everything because of limitations associated with space. Thus some discretion is exercised about what to emphasize for an intended audience. These intentional choices by scholars about what is extraneous and what is significant are also part of the process of interpreting and understanding.

Even if there is a certain amount of guesswork at the beginning of the process of encountering various religious phenomena because of difficulties associated with discerning the intention of a writer or performer in a religious rite, for instance, understanding gets created by the three activities of explaining, describing, and interpreting in the sphere of meaning. The actualization of meaning by a scholar is an act of appropriation, an event in the present moment that reveals possible ways of viewing the object of study. This new way of perceiving is analogous to a fusion of horizons between the researcher's world and the world of the religious other (Gadamer 1982: 273; Ricoeur 1976: 93). It is ideally possible for researchers to arrive at a moment when they come to understand not only something about the religion of another person but in the process also something more about themselves. The activities of describing, explaining, and interpreting should be kept separate from making judgments about the truth (or falsity) of the phenomena being studied (Clarke and Byrne 1993: 74). By offering judgments about the truth of a religious phenomenon or belief, one violates one's role as an impartial scholar. Rather than sitting in judgment about true or false aspects of a religion, the scholar's task is to strive for knowledge and understanding.

Interpretation represents an instance of understanding as applied to texts (Ricoeur 1976: 73). When a scholar interprets a text he or she does not simply repeat what the original author intended to say, which is ultimately beyond the reach of the interpreter. Although any interpretation involves a certain amount of guesswork about the original intention of an author, an interpretation nevertheless generates 'a new event beginning from the text in which the initial event has been objectified' (Ricoeur 1976: 75). This process does not imply that all interpretations are equal; it does, however, suggest that some are more probable than others within hermeneutical circles or interpretive contexts because a text presents certain interpretive limits.

When an interpreter encounters another religion he or she sets forth on an adventure that is risky because one is confronted with numerous strange situations during the course of his or her investigations that can be extremely complex and need to be interpreted in order to be understandable. It is possible that one could lose one's way through the labyrinth of understanding. There is a danger of getting absorbed by the subject and losing one's critical perspective. During the interpreter's adventure, he or she is potentially shaped by his or her interpretations and reinterpretations of topics such as life, death, myth, love, or hate. The boundary situations that the interpreter encounters will challenge him or her to rethink his or her own ontological situation. If an interpreter finds it difficult to get started or loses his or her way, it is possible to get started or to rediscover one's way by utilizing the method of comparison.

The use of comparison is characteristic of ordinary learning. It is not unusual to compare a strange or new thing, event, or experience with a similar thing, event, or experience from our body of knowledge or past experience. Although comparison does not give us new knowledge per se, it can help us to comprehend something new or strange by incorporating it into our ongoing pattern of life experiences. In short, comparison helps us to cope with the incongruities of our existence and helps us to make sense of the world within which we reside (Doniger 1998: 28). Unfortunately, some scholars have misused comparison as a method by attempting to discover timeless essences and to make broad generalizations of dubious merit about the universal structures of human meanings and symbols. In other words, some scholars using comparison have been motivated to seek similarities to the detriment of differences between religions.

A number of scholars have provided advice about the proper use of comparison. Jonathan Smith (1982: 21–24) wants to limit the use of comparison to cultural items that are spatially and temporally contiguous. Kurt Rudolph (1992: 53–65) wants to use comparison to arrive at more defined distinctions that will lead to better organization of material, classification of it, and to fuller understanding of it. Sam Gill (1994: 965) warns that comparison must not be used to make phenomena conform to a pre-existing paradigm, while William E. Paden (1997, 2000) calls for a 'new comparativism' that will reveal both similarities and differences, avoid being static and essentialistic, exercise self-control, and be more multiaspectual than prior forms of comparison.

Edward Said and Orientalism

Western scholarship concentrating on the East and the aftermath of colonialism has given rise to a reaction that can be called the Orientalist critique and postcolonial studies. Although Orientalism is a term of Western origin, Edward Said recaptured the term for his own critical purposes. In turn, Said's work helped to give birth to postcolonial theory among scholars. We will deal with each reaction to Western scholarship separately and critically by concentrating on the method used by participants. This approach will allow us to focus on some problems associated with the methods used by different writers.

As part of his method, Said empties the term 'Orientalism' of its previous content as a way of referring to academic studies of the Middle East and Asia. He revises it to suggest scholarly work that is unsympathetic and hostile toward Oriental (i.e., Near Eastern and all Asian) people. If we examine the historical meaning of the term, we find that earlier it represented a school of painting in Europe, and it was later a branch of scholarship composed mostly of philological efforts to recover, examine, interpret, and publish ancient and traditional texts. During the summer of 1973, the term was discarded at the Twenty-ninth International Congress of Orientalists in Paris. The term was, however, retrieved from the garbage heap of history by Said to be used for what Bernard Lewis (1993: 100–101, 104) has sharply characterized as polemical abuse and the demonization of Western scholars.

According to Said, the intellectual creation of the so-called 'Hindu' or 'Muslim' is a social and mental construct of Western scholars that can be called Orientalist. By this, he means that Orientalism is a body of theory and practice that represents a style of Western scholarship that has been used by its practitioners as a tool to dominate, particularize, divide, and restructure Oriental things into components that can be more easily managed and manipulated by outsiders. This is done with the intention of imposing hegemony based on the assumed superiority of European ideas over the backward ideas and practices of 'the Orient.' This style of scholarship is directly connected to a long history of Western domination and exploitation of Oriental cultures. From the perspective of the present moment, this helps to explain the current plight of these denigrated cultures. Said expresses it this way: 'The relationship between occident and Orient is a relationship of power, of domination, of varying degrees of a complex hegemony' (1979: 5). Orientalist scholarship embodied within itself racism, ethnocentrism, imperialism, and convictions about Western superiority. The guilty Western scholars did not objectively describe what they witnessed in the Orient but rather recreated an image of the Orient, which assumed the guise of an unchanging premodern entity.

Said's basic criticism is that this creation is a representation that does not accurately reflect the reality actually found in cities, towns, and villages of real people throughout the Orient. The Orientalist style of representation of people living in the Orient is a product of a mode of thinking that is fundamentally flawed, derogatory, and illusory. Moreover, the caricature of the Oriental person created by Orientalist scholarship is designed to control such a person both politically and socially. Said correctly calls our attention to a past tradition of racism, ethnocentrism, and imperialism of Western scholars. Thus, we are in his debt for correcting deficiencies within Western scholarship.

Unfortunately, Said creates a false caricature of Western scholarship as Orientalist by means of his own representations. Why would he fall prey to the same transgressions as some Westerners? Why would he create a false representation of the work of all Western scholars working on Eastern cultures? The answer to this question can be found by looking at his adaptation and use of the poststructural methodological approach of Michel Foucault and at the French scholar's political agenda.

Texts, power, and discourse

Said's understanding of the nature of texts and power has been shaped by his reading of Michel Foucault's work. From the perspective of Said, it is significant that Western scholars have described the Orient in books. According to Said's (1979: 93) understanding of Foucault's notion of a text, over time a book assumes a greater authority and utility than the actual phenomena that it allegedly describes. This scenario creates a crisis for those being described because readers are shaped by what they have read. Not only does the reader become what he or she reads, the books themselves create the knowledge and reality that they allegedly describe. This produces a tradition or a way of looking at foreign cultures that establishes a set of constraints upon thought and sets limitations on what can be examined in an unprejudiced way. According to Said, Orientalism is a political vision of reality that promotes difference between the common and the foreign that degenerates into an antihuman attitude on the part of its practitioners.

Once the vision of Orientalism is accepted and embodied within a text, it is extremely difficult to change the picture of the East created by the Westerners because the vision contained within the text constrains any subsequent interpretation. Said asserts, 'This means that a text has a specific situation, placing restraints upon the interpreter and his interpretation not because the situation is hidden within the text as a mystery, but rather because the situation exists at the same level of surface particularity as the textual object itself' (1983: 39). Endorsing what he considers the perspicacity of Nietzsche on this subject, Said concludes that texts are basically instruments of power. Within the context in which Orientalism developed, texts served the hegemonic interests of Western political powers that promoted an unequal relation between themselves as the colonizers and oppressors over the colonized and oppressed Orient. The lives of texts, for Said, are not in any sense real but are rather matters of force and conflict: 'Texts incorporate discourse, sometimes violently' (1983: 47). Implied in the argument of Said is the fact that a text, although it is an instrument of power and can keep one in bondage, can also be used as a liberating power to free the oppressed. And this assumes, of course, that the texts have readers.

Intertwined with Foucault's notion of text is an understanding of discourse that is also appropriated by Said. Discourse is concerned, for instance, with social subjects and the kinds of consciousness that are created by ideologies, which are grounded in economic or class relations. This process occurs by means of a circulating power that shapes the social subjects by means such as regulation, construction, and exclusion. These forms of knowledge render possible what can be said and what cannot be said (Foucault 1972: 21–39). Foucault's notion of discourse undermines the Marxist's notion of ideology. But it is inseparable from the formation of a discipline and the shaping of the object studied by a particular discipline.

Said also adopts Foucault's assertion that discourse always involves some kind of violence. What this means is that discourse imposes its linguistic order on the world. For Said, Orientalism is a violent form of discourse that represents a kind of Western projection onto the Orient in an attempt to govern it (1979: 95). In short, Orientalist discourse is a form of knowledge that is utilized to control the other by creating representations of the Orient that are dependent upon Western institutions, traditions, social conventions, and accepted modes of understanding to be effective. Said understands the creation of Orientalism as a repetitive process of more representations that take their reality from the authority embodied within textual repetition. Thus Said (1979: 322) cannot and does not want to claim that there is a real or true Orient because it is a construction by Orientialists that stands for an ideological representation lacking any genuine reality.

Said and his critics

Said shares with Foucault (1980: 142) a conviction that culture is a repressive means to power. It is certainly true that a particular culture can become oppressive and even tyrannical. Said's view, however, is too one-dimensional because he neglects the ways in which cultures can act as bearers of symbols, values, customs, institutions, and meanings for their adherents. Since there is an inevitable tyranny built into the fabric of any culture for Said, it is impossible for any group to legitimate its cultural identity. John McGowan indicates that such a stance 'has the advantage of undermining (delegitimating) all existent social forms but points only to an anarchic "politics of difference" as an alternative' (1991: 172). Nonetheless, Lisa Lowe (1991: ix–x) questions Said's assumption that Orientalism monolithically constructs the Orient as the other of the Occident. Along similar lines of criticism, David Smith (2003: 49) claims that there is no evidence that Orientalists who were doing linguistic and textual study served colonial purposes and that the conquerors and exploiters did not have any interest in or sympathy for such scholarly work. Moreover, Rosane Rocher (1993: 215–49) criticizes Said for creating a single discourse of social and intellectual identities that are undifferentiated within time and space. The postcolonial scholar Homi Bhabha (2004: 72) shares Rocher's concern about the totalizing aspect of Said's argument and his assumption that the West had an unequivocal intention that has been realized through its discursive representations. According to Robert Young, the totalizing effect of Said's model of Orientalism prevents him from offering an alternative to the phenomenon that he criticizes and makes it impossible for him to solve the problem of how he can separate himself from the coercive structures of knowledge. The result is that Said repeats the structures that he censures. He does not offer any alternative forms of knowledge due to his inability to deal rigorously with the problem of method (Young 1990: 127–29).

Bernard Lewis shows that Said gives his reader a restricted version of the Orient, and Lewis undermines the impression that Said gives of presenting a totalistic picture. According to Lewis, Said bases his notion of Orientalism exclusively on the Arabic Middle East. Furthermore, Said neglects to include the Germans among the practitioners of the Orientalist disciplines, and his work reveals a 'lack of knowledge of what scholars do and what scholarship is about' (1993: 108). Besides demonstrating contempt for modern scholarship on the Arabs, Lewis accuses him of composing science-fiction history and using lexical Humpty-Dumptyism (that is, it means whatever I say it does).

Said's notion of discourse has been subjected to criticism, too. Bhabha (2004: 86), for instance, finds his notion of discourse too determining, univocal, and uniform because it undermines the complexity of the writers covered by him. Young does not like the way that Said makes broad historical generalizations based on his reading of a limited number of literary texts. Young also thinks that Said's approach dehistoricizes texts and treats them synchronically and ahistorically, which undermines history as a field of objective research. This scenario would suggest that all knowledge is relative. Said also contradicts himself when he claims that the Orient is a misrepresentation of the real but acknowledges that it is impossible for anyone to depict other cultures accurately in any case (Young 2001: 39–91).

Other scholars have criticized Said on epistemological grounds. Wilhelm Halbfass (1991: 12) cannot understand how it would be possible for a Westerner to study another culture without preconceptions and to eliminate all nonindigenous categories of understanding from one's study of another culture. He does not think that the representation of an Oriental culture could be freed of all constructs, because of the internal superimpositions that tend to derive from different forces, with any culture (Halbfass 1991: 13). From a different perspective, Catherine Gallagher describes succinctly the epistemological impasse that Said has created: 'He writes of distortions of reality while denying the existence of a reality beneath the distortions. He notes that knowledge is always bounded by place but insists that there is an epistemological locus of displacement called exile' (1985: 37).

In sharp contrast to Said, J. J. Clarke finds a wide range of attitudes embodied within Orientalism that are affirmative and that demonstrate an attempt by the West to integrate Eastern thought into its intellectual concerns. Unlike what Said might claim, Clarke thinks that these more affirmative attitudes toward the Orient cannot be explained as matters of 'power' and 'domination.' If one views Orientalism as simply a ruling imperialist ideology, then this would miss its role in the Western context as 'a counter-movement' that has tended to subvert entelechy, albeit not a unified or consciously organized one, which in various ways has often tended to subvert rather than to confirm the discursive structures of imperial power (Clarke 1997: 9). Clarke acknowledges that the reaction of Westerners to the East at times was largely patronizing, chauvinistic, and racist. And yet Westerners have also exhibited a fascination with the East that has manifested itself in a tendency to romanticize and idealize the East and contributed to a much more positive misrepresentation and oversimplification of it. Clarke criticizes Said for the narrowness of his explanation, a tendency to reductionism, and for ignoring the complexity of the motivations for Orientalism. What Said fails to acknowledge is that 'Eastern ideas have been used in the West as an agency for self-criticism and self-renewal, whether in the political, moral, or religious spheres' (Clarke 1997: 27). Clarke goes on to argue that Orientalism has served as a corrective mirror in the West that 'provides a conceptual framework that allows much fertile cross-referencing, the discovery of similarities, analogies, and models; in other words, the underpinning of a productive hermeneutical relationship' (1997: 27).

Clarke goes astray, however, when he agrees with Said that all human knowledge is political. This is a very universal type of assertion that is not supported by common sense and ordinary experience. It is only necessary to call attention to the apolitical nature of mathematics and scientific discoveries in DNA research, for instance, to refute such an argument. Of course, mathematical and scientific knowledge can be used for political purposes. But this is another issue. If Said is rightly opposed to broad generalizations about the Orient, it is inconsistent of him and of Clarke to claim that all human knowledge is political.

Without mentioning him specifically, Hugh Urban points to a deficiency in the work of Said, when he depicts those who are colonized as passive, unreflective, and submissive subjects. Referring to the Indian colonial context, Urban argues that Indians did not simply accept the imaginary representations projected upon them. Indians could appropriate and subvert representations and transform them into anticolonial uses. Citing the mimetic use of the image of the goddess Kālī, Urban observes: 'Within the colonial imagination, the native is often represented as the negative antitype of the colonizer: conceived as savage or feminine, the native embodies the irrationality and backwardness against which the colonizer imagines himself. Yet particularly in cases like the terrifying goddess Kālī, this image often becomes a frightening mirror that reflects back the colonizer's own deepest fears, fantasies, and dangerous desires' (2003: 88). For critics like Urban who claim that his analysis of Orientalist discourse does not leave sufficient room for genuine dialogue and constructive interaction, Said responds in his more recent book *Culture and Imperialism* (1993) with his notion of 'discrepant experiences,' which are experiences that expose the limitations of such abstract concepts as 'East' and 'West.' 'Discrepant experience' suggests the possibility of recognizing a world order that respects differences of all kinds (Said 1993: 31–43). Nonetheless,

Said's response in *Culture and Imperialism* is more of a beginning rather than a guideline for a real constructive interaction between the parties.

A critical look at Said's political agenda

There is a certain irony contained in Said's discussion of Orientalism. He was a Palestinian and member of the so-called Third World, who used some of the philosophical notions of Foucault and Nietzsche to develop his own theory. To criticize Western scholarship, it may seem ironic that Said would rely upon theories from former European colonial cultures. But according to Said's philosophical hero, Foucault (1980: 52), knowledge is power and it tends to be coercive in order to gain control. Said's intention is to use his knowledge to control Western views of the East. What we have in Said's analysis of Orientalism is a clever attempt, by a self-portrayed powerless person, to turn the tables on the powerful. By using Western philosophers to construct his argument and not something from the East, Said indirectly confirms the prejudice of so-called Orientalists about the East, that it possesses nothing of enduring intellectual value to offer to the Western mind. Moreover, Said's characterization of Orientalism functions in his work as a kind of evil bogeyman, which may remind one of religious fundamentalism in America and its polemic against secular humanism for its alleged godlessness and divinization of human beings.

The way Said adapted Foucault's notion of power presents additional problems. Foucault conceives of power as a force that circulates like an air-conditioning system. In contrast, Said understands power as hierarchical and as something imposed from above by a superior person, institution, or nation upon inferiors. If Said were to accept Foucault's own model of power, he would have to admit that people and cultures of the Orient do possess power. In fairness to Said, I think that he came around to this position in his more recent book *Culture and Imperialism* where he discusses the active resistance by non-Western indigenous people that he admits to having left out of his earlier book on Orientialism.

Besides the problematic reworking of Foucault's notion of power, another problem with Said's poststructuralist/postmodern approach to comparative studies is his concept of culture, which for him means a system of discrimination and evaluations. Said tends to conceptualize culture in terms of power relationships. When a particular group in a given country identifies itself with the prevailing cultural milieu, that culture tends to become tyrannical. 'And it also means that culture is a system of exclusions legislated from above but enacted throughout its polity, by which such things as anarchy, disorder, irrationality, inferiority, bad taste, and immorality are identified, then deposited outside the culture and kept there by the power of the state and its institutions' (Said 1983: 11).

By a continual process of differentiation of itself from what it perceives to be different from itself, a culture protects and conforms itself and gains hegemony over its society and state. Thereby, it vindicates its power over everything different (Said 1983: 14). Again, we witness the influence of Foucault's (1980: 142) view of culture as a repressive means to power. Although it is true that a given culture can become oppressive and even tyrannical, Said's view is too one-dimensional because he neglects the way in which culture can act as a bearer of symbols, values, customs, institutions, and meanings for its adherents. Since there is an inevitable tyranny built into the fabric of any culture for Said, it is impossible for any group to legitimate its cultural identity.

Within the context of his argument about failings of Orientalism, Said's use of spatial metaphors (for example, distance, exile, and margins) is instructive because it indicates that he favors models of escape and supposes that criticism should take place between culture and system within individual consciousness, which he imagines to be distanced from both of them. These spatial metaphors are problematic in association with the notion of the other: 'To put it another way, to imagine the other as distant and separate is profoundly undialectical' (McGowan 1991: 175). It is a strategy that places the scholar-critic beyond the nexus of social relations.

Said's postcolonial children

In his award-winning novel *Midnight's Children* (1980), Salman Rushdie's main character named Saleem Sinai opens the narrative by reflecting on the moment of his birth. He tells the reader that he was born in the city of Bombay at midnight on August 15, 1947 at the precise instant of India's Independence. Outside the nursing home of his birth, there are large crowds celebrating the momentous moment as fireworks explode in the sky. Saleem humorously confesses: 'Soothsayers had prophesied me, newspapers celebrated my arrival, politicos ratified my authenticity. I was left entirely without a say in the matter. I, Saleem Sinai, later variously called Snotnose, Baldly, Sniffer, Buddha and even Piece-of-the-Moon, had become heavily embroiled in Fate – at the best of times a dangerous sort of involvement. And I couldn't even wipe my own nose at the time' (Rushdie 1980: 7). In a sense Rushdie's character is calling attention to the moment of transition between the colonial period and the postcolonial era in India.

According to some scholars, colonialism was a time of subjugation by Western political powers, whereas postcolonialism is a period during which those who previously were subjugated can respond critically to their trials. According to Bhabha, postcolonial criticism emerges from the colonial context and testimony of Third World countries. They interrupt and interact with modern ideological discourses that attempt to maintain previously hegemonic interrelations as the norm. Moreover, postcolonialists 'formulate their critical revisions around issues of cultural difference, social authority, and political discrimination in order to reveal the antagonistic and ambivalent moments within the "rationalization of modernity" ' (Bhabha 2004: 171). In addition, postcolonialists examine issues like loss of meaning, hopelessness, and other kinds of social pathology. Finally, postcolonial theory reminds us of the persistent neocolonial relations with the present (Bhabha 2004: 6).

Adding to the points made by Bhabha, Gayatri Chakravorty Spivak (1999: 172) draws a useful distinction between internal and external colonization. If the latter represents the domination of the space of others elsewhere, internal colonization refers to patterns of exploitation and domination of disenfranchised groups within a world-dominating country like the United States or Britain. Spivak draws another distinction between colonialism and neocolonialism. Colonialism is a European creation stretching from the mid-eighteenth to mid-twentieth centuries, whereas neocolonialism represents an economic, political, and cultural development in the twentieth century in the aftermath of the disparate dissolution of the territorial empires. Finally, postcolonialism describes the present global condition.

If economic interests motivate colonialism, postcolonialism is a result of reaction and resistance to colonialism and imperialism, which is a deliberately state-sponsored policy. By intermingling the past (colonialism) and the present (imperialism), postcolonial theory focuses on the active transformation of the present from the domination of the past (Nandy 1983, 1987). In addition to acts of historical retrieval, postcolonial theory also attempts to dislocate, undermine, and displace Western knowledge about the Oriental other. According to Robert Young, the basic presupposition about the operation of postcolonial theory is that 'intellectual and cultural traditions developed outside the West constitute a body of knowledge that can be deployed to great effect against the political and cultural hegemony of the West' (2001: 65). In addition to replacing the heritage of colonialism, postcolonial theorists want to decolonize the West.

Along with the work of Frantz Fanon in books like *The Wretched of the Earth* published in 1961 that analyzes the relation between violence and national consciousness and *Black Skin, White Masks* published in 1963 that studied the effects of race within colonial and postcolonial contexts, Said's work has given impetus to the development of postcolonial studies. Within the context of this field, there is not a single postcolonial theory or a single person that speaks for the entire field. This lack of consensus creates a situation that tends to be confusing to those outside of the discussion. Different authors offer diverse definitions of notions like imperialism, colonialism, and postcolonialism. The 'postcolonial situation' is a reference, for instance, used to describe a global condition. After examining and comparing different nations and cultures, this condition may reflect an unequal distribution of the situation. Due to the diversity of postcolonial studies, just two figures will serve as representative examples of the children of Said and Fanon. They are Homi Bhabha and Gayatri Chakravorty Spivak.

In his work *Location of Culture* published in 1994, Bhabha utilizes a methodological combination of deconstruction, psychoanalysis, literary and historical criticism. He (Bhabha 2004: 1) views the present moment as characterized by transition, disorientation, lack of direction, and restlessness. He seeks those 'in between' locations of time and space where one can develop new strategies for individual and communal selfhood.

Without replicating or inverting its character, Bhabha wants to create alternatives to the prevailing culture. He (Bhabha 2001: 39) introduces his notion of 'vernacular cosmopolitanism' that originates with his insistence on a continuation of an anti-colonial struggle that will coordinate local concerns with international political relevance. Bhabha's notion of cosmopolitanism, which is paradoxically formulated, envisions the postcolonial subject gaining real political power from a complicit relationship between colonial and neocolonial discourses. This process renders the postcolonial subject an historical person. In addition, as the postcolonial subject also becomes a contemporary with others, his or her local situation starts to exert an international influence.

Bhabha's vision also includes the ideal of a subaltern secularism, which emerges from the limitations of liberal secularism and 'keeps faith' with those communities and individuals that have been denied and excluded from the egalitarian and tolerant values of liberal individuals. Furthermore, Bhabha explains, 'Such secularism does not assume that the value of freedom lies within the "goodness" of the individual; freedom is much more the testing of boundaries and limits as part of a communal, collective process, so that choice is less an individualistic internal desire than it is a public demand and duty' (2001: 51). His stress on subaltern studies is an attempt to remove the center of theoretical knowledge from the grasp of the West. This can only be accomplished by shifting the writing of history away from its traditional representational mode of thinking.

Spivak shares many of the same concerns as Bhabha, but she uses a different set of methodological approaches that combines deconstruction, feminism, and Marxism. By using this combination of approaches to the subject of postcolonialism, Spivak confesses to being a *bricoleur* (using what is at hand). This suggests that a reader will not discover a master discourse or critical taxonomy in her work. Much like Jacques Derrida, Spivak does not assume or promote a constructive philosophical position that she would then defend from critics. By using a combination of feminism, Marxism, and deconstruction, her purpose is to retain the discontinuities and complexities that she discovers and exposes.

In what may seem very Daoist, Spivak argues that postcolonial intellectuals must 'unlearn' theoretical and privileged positions. Such a call suggests that postcolonial intellectuals must initially rid themselves of biases, prejudices, and preunderstandings that they bring with them to their work (Spivak 1985b: 120). A problem with such an argument in the case of Spivak is that the notion of intellectual 'unlearning' exposes a basic contradiction within her position because her anti-individualism conflicts with her assumption about the fundamental homogeneity of the subject. Moreover, her call for the intellectual to 'unlearn' is rather utopian (Young 1990: 170).

Another problem arises with Spivak's (1985a: 130) assertion that history is a process of epistemic violence. By epistemic violence, she means the construction of a specific representation of an object of study. Any object can be constructed without any existence or reality beyond its specific representation. Such a representation usually consists of an historical narrative from a Western perspective. To counteract the Western representation, Spivak wants to produce a new narrative about how the Third World was itself created as a representation for the West and for itself. Within the context of such a discussion and using her feminism, Spivak claims that the Third World woman cannot speak. There is a danger in this claim because Spivak suggests that she is constructing herself as a spokesperson and representative for the Third World woman. Moreover, Spivak idealizes, essentializes, and turns the Third World Woman into an icon that she intends to contest from the start (Gandhi 1998: 8). If this is the case, she is also rather presumptuous because she possesses an elitist status by virtue of her position at the Ivy League research institution Columbia University, even if we consider her origins. In short, Spivak herself is not a Third World woman, although her empathy for them is certainly commendable.

If her feminism does not mesh easily with her use of the deconstructive method of Derrida, this is equally true of Spivak's Marxism, which is invoked in part for political effect and renders her method inconsistent. Her use of Marxism makes her approach inconsistent because Spivak wants to use essentialism and universals in certain situations in a strategic way. This approach conflicts with her use of the deconstructive method that seeks to undermine all universals and essentialisms. In the final analysis, deconstruction, Marxism, and feminism do not go together comfortably. By trying to use all three approaches, this shows an ambivalence toward giving up all 'isms' on her part, and it essentially contradicts her deconstructive method. Does this make her a 'halfway' deconstructionist? Based on the position of Derrida, I do not think that it is possible to be a 'halfway' deconstructionist.

There is also a certain amount of irony associated with Spivak's use of Marxism because it possesses a long history of involvement in anticolonial struggles. And yet Marxism is itself the historical ideology of political imperialism as used by the former Soviet Union as it colonized the countries of Eastern Europe. Of course, Spivak would want to distinguish her brand of Marxism from its orthodox European type. She suggests using Marxism as a means of critiquing the objective material conditions in former colonial countries with an analysis of the subjective effects of the material conditions. Nonetheless, postcolonial thinkers like Spivak do little to expose the causes of the poor material conditions of former colonial subjects and do not offer ways to bring about change (Young 2001: 7).

By means of her three-pronged approach, Spivak joins political company with the subaltern from her perspective. In fact, she attempts to create a literary insurgency that is highly political. Moreover, she wants to create a crisis within historiography in order to counter its hegemonic tendency. We are impelled to ask the following question: Is her Marxist politicization of postcolonialism an improvement over the representations that she seeks to deconstruct? With her revolutionary rhetoric, she talks in a Marxist political spirit, but she does not walk with the subalterns from her ivy perch at Columbia University. With her heavily laden, dense, and obscure deconstructive, Marxist, and feminist jargon, it is highly unlikely that she could adequately communicate with any subaltern subject. In contrast to scholars like Spivak, there are others that have joined the subaltern and build homes and schools for them in rural India.

Representations and representational thinking

Said, Spivak, and Bhabha share a common concern. They stand opposed to Western representations of the East in part because the representations created by Western scholars possess no reality. Poststructural/postmodern thinkers like Foucault and Derrida influenced the thinking of such postcolonial scholars. In this section of the chapter, I want to examine critically the genealogical approach of Said and Foucault. I then want to turn critical attention to Derrida's method of deconstruction and its use by Bhabha and Spivak.

With respect to Said, a person can ask the following question: Has he created a concept, representation, or 'ism' with his notion of Orientalism? I raise this question within the context of the writings of a person who informs us that he is opposed to representations and the type of thinking upon which they rest. Said's adoption of Foucault's notion of genealogy represents an attempt to overcome the representational mode of thinking. In order to respond to the question raised, I propose to briefly review Foucault's method of genealogy.

For Foucault, the history that we inherit is not a body of facts but rather a collection of interpretations of various kinds that continue into the future. Therefore, it is not possible to reach any layer or level of primal, untainted material using scientific or research tools. Why is this the case? Even the most primary historical data is a product of interpretation according to Foucault (1967: 189). A scholar must also become aware that history is made difficult because it stands within an interconnected web of power relations. One cannot find a place outside of this interconnection from which to make an accurate analysis. An aspiring historian is also unable to account adequately for the paradoxical nature of the discontinuity of history because such an historian describes what he or she perceives from his or her perspective.

In order for an historian to grasp what is occurring, Foucault turns to Nietzsche and his notion of genealogy in order to complement his earlier archaeological method with the purpose of developing a new theory of discourse. In contrast to his earlier use of archaeology, genealogy widens one's analysis of a particular topic by concentrating 'on the forces and relations of power connected to discursive practices; it does not insist on a separation of rules for production of discourse and relations of power' (Davidson 1986: 227). This position implies that a purely descriptive history is useless as Nietzsche contends in his work *The Gay Science*. Nietzsche is primarily interested in appreciating and defending the differences that are found by demonstrating the plurality of human histories. Nietzsche, Foucault, and Said agree that genealogy is not a mere search for origins but instead is more akin to a process of unmasking and stripping away pretensions of universality. For Foucault, genealogy is a diagnostic approach that focuses on the interrelations of power, knowledge, and the human body. Foucault adopts this method because he is concerned with discontinuity, differentiations, dispersion, and mutations that are neglected and forgotten aspects of history.

As the genealogist attempts to discern the punctuating gaps of history, Foucault refers to an effective history (*wirkliche Historie*) that is not associated with metaphysics, acknowledges no absolute, does not claim to be objective, and is without constants. This type of radical history makes no truth claims and recognizes that all knowledge is relative (Foucault 1977: 152–57). Foucault is opposed to notions of method, starting point, and theory. Within the Nietzschean spirit, Foucault's adoption of genealogy suggests that he wants to abandon objectivity and any vision of objective truth.

Moreover, genealogy allows Foucault to emphasize differences, discontinuities, and divisions within history and culture, which makes it a heterological approach that discovers the weak points of rationalism, separates history from metaphysics, and acknowledges no absolutes (Foucault 1977: 153). Foucault focuses on the interrelations of power, knowledge, and the human body by standing within the interconnected web of power relations at the current moment and acknowledging the relative nature of all knowledge.

Using Foucault's notion of genealogy, Said explores patterns, traces developments, and sketches values in transition. At the same time, Said constructs a representation of the West that he calls Orientalism. This construction stands in sharp contrast to his attempt to overcome the representational mode of thinking. As I have argued in another work, Foucault himself does not overcome the representational mode of thinking, and the same can be affirmed of Said (Olson 2000). Said gives us an unbalanced, distorted, incomplete, and highly politicized construction that is only partially real. In addition, his adoption of the method of genealogy from Foucault gives his reader something more akin to fiction than historical analysis. Of course, the use of genealogy presupposes that historical objectivity is impossible anyway and that historians are really constructing fiction. Therefore, there is an indefinite multiplicity of interpretative possibilities. This attitude results in either a fictitious relationship to the truth or a dismissal of it (MacIntyre 1990: 205). Foucault admits to doing this, but I am not certain that Said is as publicly honest as Foucault. Hans G. Kippenberg claims that such postmodern thought is reminiscent of the crisis of historicism about 100 years ago. Both are connected to the insight that historical descriptions contain a strong subjective aspect and are thus handicapped. This calls into question any distinction between correct and incorrect representations of the past and its distant data (Kippenberg 2002: 188) and has important implications for representational thinking.

Like Foucault, Said claims to be opposed to representational modes of thinking. However, his creation of the notion of Orientalism ironically is a product of a kind of representational thinking. Said is opposed to the Western creation of the Orient. Yet, he creates a caricature of the West likewise grounded in a representational mode of thinking.

In contrast to Said's adoption of the method of genealogy from Foucault, Bhabha and Spivak use Derrida's notion of deconstruction. Derrida admits to following and continuing the work of Martin Heidegger, although he wants to bring the efforts of Heidegger to completion by deconstructing the presence of the present because the representational mode of thinking is shaped by presence. Deconstruction is an ambiguous term that suggests the disarranging of the construction of terms in a sentence and disassembling the parts of a whole (Derrida 1987: 387–88). Derrida denies that deconstruction is a particular event, a human act, or an operation. However, its goal is to locate an instance of otherness within a text that reflects a logocentric conceptuality and then to deconstruct this conceptuality from the standpoint of alterity. This is a procedure that suggests obtaining a position of exteriority with respect to that which one is deconstructing. This position of alterity is a form of writing that is accomplished on the margin of the text. Without waiting for any conscious deliberation by a person, deconstruction does occur as an event that enables it to deconstruct itself (Derrida 1987: 391). Derrida suggests that deconstruction is not a method because it is not reductive like an ordinary method; it is also not a nonmethod because it does not advocate uncontrollable free play.

According to Derrida, deconstruction is like an *exergue*, which is an inscription on the face of a coin or at the beginning of a book. It suggests functions associated with making something evident, a bringing forth or displaying. Similar to an inscription, deconstruction possesses value within a context or in a series of possible substitutions of inscriptions (Derrida 1987: 392). Since whatever is inscribed is located within a chain related to other items, any external difference is also part of an internal process in which the interval or difference between items divides the items within itself. Whatever differences and contradictions are encountered by means of the process of deconstruction, the person using the method does not attempt to overcome these internal differences, but he or she wants to maintain these heterogeneities. Therefore, deconstruction functions in Derrida's works in a parasitic manner because it preys on other readings or interpretations in an endless process.

Because deconstruction erases positions as they are immediately established, it is antidialectical in the sense that it destroys any progress of the dialectic, whereas Marxist philosophy is fundamentally dialectical and akin to Hegelian philosophy. If Marxism does not truly exist without its dialectic, this raises the following question: Can a person using a Marxist analysis continue to be a deconstructionist without contradiction? This is precisely the conundrum facing Spivak. Although the deconstructive approach of Spivak does a good job of deconstructing colonial categories, her usage of the method does not result in newer or more adequate categories. This is partly a shortcoming of the method of deconstruction and its parasitic nature and tendency to repeatedly prey on a text.

The notion of deconstruction, which is not truly a method or a nonmethod for Derrida, is subject to other types of criticisms. Deconstruction leads, for instance, to a radical skepticism that refuses to recognize the common world that everyone shares in order to create a better world (Putnam 1992: 140). There is also an exaggerated importance placed upon metaphysics by postmodernists who falsely assume that it forms the basis of Western culture. In turn, the deconstructive stance suggests that the destruction of its metaphysical basis would result in the collapse of Western culture (Putnam 1992: 124). Moreover, the attempt by deconstructionists to obliterate old hierarchies tends to upset the traditional distinctions between different subjects like philosophy and literature and disrupt such distinctions as equal/unequal, community/discord, uncoerced/coerced, and other such distinctions. By potentially creating a fluid cultural situation, this does not mean that anything worth affirming would emerge from this flux other than deconstruction itself and subjectivity (Taylor 1989: 489). Thus some critics perceive a loss rather than any worthwhile gain to be made by using deconstruction.

Beyond prejudices

Even though Said exposes the false ideas, presuppositions, and stereotypes that Western scholars formed of the Orient, his work exemplifies his own prejudices. The West is depicted as responsible for the current problems of the East because Western ideas and attitudes have undermined traditional Eastern cultures by enslaving them and making them feel inferior. To turn his own postmodern perspective against him, it can be stated that Said's work becomes an artifact or an episode in the history of Eastern responses to Western views of the Orient. Thus the stereotypes and prejudices of Western scholars of the Orient are supplemented in Derrida's sense of the term – an addition to, a surplus – by Said's equally stereotypical, prejudicial, and political work.

Nonetheless, Said's work makes an important contribution by exposing the shortcomings of a nonscholarly style of Orientalism. Thus Said teaches us lessons about how not to do cross-cultural scholarship. His work should not, however, intimidate those doing research on the East, even though his political objective is to accomplish just that condition and to deter scholars from doing cross-cultural studies in a stereotypical fashion. Certainly, scholars should avoid perpetuating cultural stereotypes that have no basis in reality. As I have argued, Said is, however, just as guilty of using hermeneutics for political purposes as those figures that he discusses in his books. Unfortunately, he neglects to mention those Orientalists who made important contributions to our knowledge of the Orient and embraced elements of Oriental culture in their personal lives because they recognized its enduring value. Both sides – East and West – need to make new beginnings.

Because Said contributes to exposing the wrong ways for Eastern and Western cultures to encounter each other, we owe him a debt of gratitude. We can repay him by doing work that is more self-conscious of our biases and strives to be fair with the treatment of the subject of our study. But we must also be aware that Said's work is a clever attempt to turn the tables on Western scholars and intimidate them with the power of his own text. Said confesses to the personal nature of his work when he writes, 'In many ways my study of Orientalism has been an attempt to inventory the traces upon me, the Oriental subject, of culture whose domination has been so powerful a factor in the life of all Orientals' (1993: 60). Since he is convinced that a text is an instrument of power, Said (1993: xxiii) attempts to use this power against the West in spite of his claims to be a marginal person caught between two cultures. In his attempt to repay the West for injustices inflicted on the East, Said reveals the political agenda of his work, which serves as an excellent example of hermeneutics used for political purposes. In the case of postcolonial thinkers, they are caught between a politics of structure and fragmentation (Gandhi 1998: 167).

And although Bhabha and Spivak call for a fuller appreciation and acceptance of differences, their use of deconstruction leads to similar problems with respect to method and politics. Like Said, Bhabha and Spivak adopt methods from Western thinkers and not Third World thinkers. In other words, Bhabha and Spivak claim to speak for the non-Western other, but they use methods devised by Westerners. This gives the impression of contradicting and undermining their purposes. Bhabha tells his reader that he wants, for instance, 'to rename the postmodern from the position of the postcolonial' (2004: 175). But he is using Western methods to do the renaming. Thus he is not using the discourse of the Third World to rename the postmodern.

In summary, many Westerners reacted to the East in patronizing, chauvinistic, and racist ways, while others were also fascinated with the East, which manifested itself in a tendency to romanticize it (Clarke 1997). This latter tendency contributed to a systematic misrepresentation and oversimplification of it. Thus it is important to avoid narrow explanations, a tendency to reduce complex issues, and ignoring the complex nature of the motivations for Orientalism. Said's position and that of Bhabha and Spivak tend to neglect the role of Eastern culture in the process of renewal and self-criticism for those in the West. Possibly, Rushdie's main character sums it up best when he refers at the end of *Midnight's Children* to immortalizing his memories by sharing his tale with readers, even though distortions are possible. He summarizes the situation in the following way: 'We must live, I'm afraid, with the shadows of imperfection' (1980: 585).

Suggested further readings

Flood (1999); Hinnells (2005); King (1999); Kippenberg (2002); McCutcheon (2004); Paden (2000); J. Z. Smith (1982); W. C. Smith (1963).

REFERENCES

ʿAbdu'l-Bahā. 1964 [1930]. *Some Answered Questions: Collected and Translated from the Persian of ʿAbdu'l-Bahā* (trans. Laura Clifford Barney). Wilmette: Bahā'ī Publishing Trust.

Abrahams, Margaret. 1995. 'Ethnicity and Marginality: A Study of Indian Jewish Immigrants in Israel.' *South Asia Bulletin, Comparative Studies of South Asia, Africa and the Middle East* 15, 1: 108–23.

Ahmad, Imtiaz and Helmut Reifeld, eds. 2004. *Lived Islam in South Asia: Adaptation, Accommodation and Conflict*. New Delhi: Social Science Press.

Ahmed, Leila. 1992. *Women and Gender in Islam: Historical Roots of a Modern Debate*. New Haven: Yale University Press.

Ali, Ahmed, trans. 1993 [1984]. *Al-Qur'ān: A Contemporary Translation*. Princeton: Princeton University Press.

Altorki, Soraya. 1995. 'Women and Islam: Role and Status of Women.' *In* John L. Esposito, ed., *The Oxford Encyclopedia of the Modern Islamic World*, 4: 323–27. New York: Oxford University Press.

Amanat, Abbas. 1989. *Resurrection and Renewal: The Making of the Babi Movement in Iran, 1844–1850*. Ithaca: Cornell University Press.

Babb, Lawrence A. 1996. *Absent Lord: Ascetics and Kings in a Jain Ritual Culture*. Berkeley: University of California Press.

Bahā'u'llāh. 1960 [1931]. *The Kitāb-i-Iqān: The Book of Certitude* (trans. Shoghi Effendi). Wilmette: Bahā'ī Publishing Trust.

Bahā'u'llāh. 1963 [1932]. *The Hidden Words* (trans. Shoghi Effendi with the assistance of some English friends). Wilmette: Bahā'ī Publishing Trust.

Bahā'u'llāh. 1969 [1939]. *Gleanings from the Writings of Bahā'u'llāh* (trans. Shoghi Effendi). Wilmette: Bahā'ī Publishing Trust.

Bahā'u'llāh. 1992. *Kitāb-i-Aqdas: The Most Holy Book*. Haifa: Bahā'ī World Center.

Banks, Marcus. 1992. *Organizing Jainism in India and England*. Oxford: Clarendon Press.

Barrett, David B, George T. Kurian, Todd M. Johnson, eds. 2001 [1983]. *World Christian Encyclopedia: A Comparative Survey of Churches and Religions in the Modern World*. Volume 1 of 2: *The World by Countries: Religionists, Churches, Ministries: India*, 359–71. Oxford: Oxford University Press.

Bartholomeusz, Tessa J. 1994. *Women Under the Bo Tree: Buddhist Nuns in Sri Lanka*. Cambridge: Cambridge University Press.

Bartholomeusz, Tessa J. 1998. *Buddhist Fundamentalisms and Minority Identities in Sri Lanka*. Albany: State University of New York Press.

Bartholomeusz, Tessa. 2002. *In Defense of Dharma: Just-War Ideology in Buddhist Sri Lanka*. London: RoutledgeCurzon.

Basham, A. L. 1967 [1954]. *The Wonder That Was India: A Survey of the Culture of the Indian Sub-Continent Before the Coming of the Muslims*. London: Sidgwick and Jackson.

Bayly, Susan. 1989. *Saints, Goddesses, and Kings: Muslims and Christians in South Indian Society, 1700–1900*. Cambridge: Cambridge University Press.

Bhabha, Homi K. 2001. 'Unsatisfied: Notes on Vernacular Cosmopolitanism.' *In* Gregory Castle, ed., *Postcolonial Discourses: An Anthology*, 39–52. Oxford: Blackwell.

Bhabha, Homi K. 2004 [1994]. *The Location of Culture*. London: Routledge.

Bhatti, Anil and Johannes H. Voigt, eds. 1999. *Jewish Exile in India 1933–1945*. New Delhi: Manohar.

Bilimoria, Ardeshir N. and Dinshah D. Alpaivala. 1898. *The Excellence of Zoroastrianism* (*The Religion of the Parsis*). Bombay: Printed at the Jamsetjee Nesserwanjee Petit Parsi Orphanage Captain Printing Works.

Blavatsky, Helena P. 1960 [1877]. *Isis Unveiled: A Master-Key to the Mysteries of Ancient and Modern Science and Theology*. 2 vols. Pasadena: Theosophical University Press.

Bond, George. 1988. *The Buddhist Revival in Sri Lanka: Religious Tradition, Reinterpretation, and Response*. Columbia: University of South Carolina Press.

Bose, Sugata and Ayesha Jalal. 2004 [1998]. *Modern South Asia: History, Culture, Political Economy*. London: Routledge.

Boyce, Mary. 1975. *A History of Zoroastrianism*. Volume 1: *The Early Period*. Leiden: E. J. Brill.

Boyce, Mary. 1979. *Zoroastrians: Their Religious Beliefs and Practices*. London: Routledge & Kegan Paul.

Boyce, Mary, ed. and trans. 1984. *Textual Sources for the Study of Zoroastrianism*. Manchester: Manchester University Press.

Boyd, Robin H. S. 1979 [1969]. *An Introduction to Indian Christian Theology*. Madras: The Christian Literature Society.

Bukhari, Saleem. 2002. 'Hajj by the Numbers.' *Saudi Aramco World*, 53, 3: 27.

Caillat, Colette and Ravi Kumar. 1981. *The Jain Cosmology*. New York: Harmony Books.

Carrithers, Michael and Caroline Humphrey, eds. 1991. *The Assembly of Listeners: Jains in Society*. Cambridge: Cambridge University Press.

Chaudhuri, K. N. 1990. *Asia before Europe: Economy and Civilisation of the Indian Ocean from the Rise of Islam to 1750*. Cambridge: Cambridge University Press.

Choksy, Jamsheed K. 1989. *Purity and Pollution in Zoroastrianism: Triumph over Evil*. Austin: University of Texas Press.

Clarke, J. J. 1997. *Oriental Enlightenment: The Encounter Between Asian and Western Thought*. London: Routledge.

Clarke, Peter B. and Peter Byrne. 1993 [1992]. *Religion Defined and Explained*. New York: St Martin's Press.

Cole, Juan R. I. 1998. *Modernity and the Millennium: The Genesis of the Baha'ī Faith in the Nineteenth-Century Middle East*. New York: Columbia University Press.

Cole, W. Owen. 1982. *The Guru in Sikhism*. London: Darton, Longman, & Todd.

Cole, W. Owen. 1984. *Sikhism and Its Indian Context, 1469–1708: The Attitude of Guru Nanak and Early Sikhism to Indian Religious Beliefs and Practices*. London: Darton, Longman, & Todd.

Collins, Steven. 1982. *Selfless Persons: Imagery and Thought in Theravāda Buddhism*. Cambridge: Cambridge University Press.

Collins, Steven. 1990. 'On the Very Idea of the Pali Canon.' *Journal of the Pali Text Society* 15: 89–126.

Cone, Margaret and Richard F. Gombrich, eds. and trans. 1977. *The Perfect Generosity of Prince Vessantara: A Buddhist Epic*. Oxford: Clarendon Press.

Coningham, Robin A. E. 1995. 'Monks, Caves and Kings: A Reassessment of the Nature of Early Buddhism in Sri Lanka.' *World Archaeology* 27, 2: 222–42.

Cook, F. C. 1884. *The Origins of Religion and Language*. London: John Murray.

Cooper, John and Judy Cooper. 2002. 'The Life-Cycle of the Baghdadi Jews of India.' *In* Shalva

Weil, ed., *India's Jewish Heritage: Ritual, Art and Life-Cycle*, 100–109. Mumbai: Mārg Publications.

Cort, John E. 1990. 'Models of and for the Study of Jains.' *Method & Theory in the Study of Religion* 2, 1: 42–71.

Cort, John E. 2001. *Jains in the World: Religious Values and Ideology in India*. New York: Oxford University Press.

Daniel, Ruby and Barbara C. Johnson. 1995. *Ruby of Cochin: An Indian Jewish Woman Remembers*. Philadelphia: The Jewish Publication Society.

Das, C. R. 1996. 'Israel's Jews from India.' *The Eastern Anthropologist* 49, 3–4: 317–48.

Davidson, Arnold I. 1986. 'Archaeology, Genealogy, Ethics.' *In* David Couzens Hoy, ed., *Foucault: A Critical Reader*, 221–33. Oxford: Blackwell.

Dempsey, Corinne G. 2001. *Kerala Christian Sainthood: Collisions of Culture and Worldview in South India*. Oxford: Oxford University Press.

Denny, Frederick Mathewson. 1994 [1985]. *An Introduction to Islam*. New York: Macmillan.

Derrett, J. Duncan M. 1999 [1968]. *Religion, Law, and the State in India*. Delhi: Oxford University Press.

Derrida, Jacques. 1987. *Psyché: Inventions de l'autre*. Paris: Galilée.

Desai, Boman. 2001 [1988]. *The Memory of Elephants*. Chicago: University of Chicago Press.

Devasahayam, V., ed. 1997. *Frontiers of Dalit Theology*. Madras: Indian Society for Promoting Christian Knowledge.

Dhalla, Maneekji Nusservanji. 1972 [1914]. *Zoroastrian Theology: From the Earliest Times to the Present Day*. New York: AMS Press.

The Divine Art of Living: Selections From the Writings of Bahāu' llāh and'Abdu' l-Bahā. 1965 [1944]. Wilmette: Bahā'ī Publishing Trust.

Doniger, Wendy. 1998. *The Implied Spider: Politics and Theology in Myth*. New York: Columbia University Press.

Dubois, Abbé J. A. 1977. *Letters on the State of Christianity in India in which the Conversion of the Hindoos is Considered as Impracticable to which is Added a Vindication of the Hindoos Male and Female in Answer to a Severe Attack Made Upon Both by the Reverend* (ed. Sharda Paul). New Delhi: Associated Publishing Press.

Dundas, Paul. 1992. *The Jains*. London: Routledge.

Eaton, Richard. 1993. *The Rise of Islam and the Bengal Frontier, 1204–1760*. Berkeley: University of California Press.

Eaton, Richard, ed. 2003. *India's Islamic Traditions, 711–1750*. New Delhi: Oxford University Press.

Eck, Diana L. 1985 [1981]. *Darśan: Seeing the Divine Image in India*. Chambersburg: Anima Books.

Elgood, Heatner. 1999. *Hinduism and the Religious Arts*. London: Cassell.

Engineer, B. A. 1918. 'Advancement of Religion: An Article Contributed to the Dastur Hoshung Memorial.' Bombay: K. R. Cama Oriental Institute. Typescript.

Ernst, Carl W. and Bruce B. Lawrence. 2002. *Sufi Martyrs of Love: The Chishti Order in South Asia and Beyond*. New York: Palgrave Macmillan.

Esposito, John L., ed. 1995. *The Oxford Encyclopedia of the Modern Islamic World*. 4 vols. New York: Oxford University Press.

Esposito, John L., ed. 2003. *The Oxford Dictionary of Islam*. New York: Oxford University Press.

Ezekiel, I. A. 1966. *Sarmad (Jewish Saint of India)*. Punjab: Radha Soami Satsang Beas.

Ezra, Esmond David. 1986. *Turning Back the Pages: A Chronicle of Calcutta Jewry*. 2 vols. London: Brookside Press.

Farmer, B. H. 1983. *An Introduction to South Asia*. London: Methuen.

Fazel, Seena. 1997. 'Interreligious Dialogue and the Bahā'ī Faith: Some Preliminary

Observations.' *In* J. A. McLean, ed., *Revisioning the Sacred: New Perspectives on a Bahā'ī Theology*, 127–52. Los Angeles: Kalimāt Press.
Firth, Cyril Bruce. 1976 [1961]. *An Introduction to Indian Church History*. Madras: The Christian Literature Society.
Fischer, Michael Max Jonathan. 1973. 'Zoroastrian Iran between Myth and Praxis.' PhD Dissertation. Chicago: University of Chicago Library.
Flood, Gavin. 1999. *Beyond Phenomenology: Rethinking the Study of Religion*. London: Cassell.
Folkert, Kendall W. 1993. *Scripture and Community: Collected Essays on the Jains* (ed. John E. Cort). Atlanta: Scholars Press.
Forrester, Duncan B. 1977. 'The Depressed Classes and Conversion to Christianity.' *In* G. A. Oddie, ed., *Religion in South Asia: Religious Conversion and Revival Movements in South Asia in Medieval and Modern Time*, 35–66. New Delhi: Manohar.
Forrester, Duncan B. 1980. *Caste and Christianity: Attitudes and Policies on Caste of Anglo-Saxon Protestant Missions in India*. London: Curzon Press.
Foucault, Michel. 1967. 'Nietzsche, Freud, Marx.' *In, Nietzsche, Proceedings of the Seventh International Philosophical Colloquium of the Cahiers de Royaumont, 4–8 July*, 183–200. Paris: Editions de Minuit.
Foucault, Michel. 1972 [1969]. *The Archaeology of Knowledge and The Discourse on Language* (trans. A. M. Sheridan Smith). New York: Pantheon Books.
Foucault, Michel. 1977 [1971]. 'Nietzsche, Genealogy, History.' *In* Donald F. Bouchard, ed., *Language Counter-Memory, Practice: Selected Essays and Interviews* (trans. Donald F. Bouchard and Sherry Simon), 137–64. Ithaca: Cornell University Press.
Foucault, Michel. 1980. *Power/Knowledge: Selected Interviews and Other Writings 1972–1977* (ed. Colin Gordon; trans. Colin Gordon, Leo Marshall, John Mepham and Kate Soper). New York: Pantheon Books.
Framjee, A. 1841. *The Hadie Gum Rahan: Or, a Guide to Those Who Have Lost their Way, Being a Refutation of the Lecture Delivered by the Rev. John Wilson*. Bombay: Bombay Samachar Press.
Fuller, C. J. 2004 [1992]. *The Camphor Flame: Popular Hinduism and Society in India*. Princeton: Princeton University Press.
Gadamer, Hans-Georg. 1982 [1960]. *Truth and Method* (trans. Garrett Barden and John Cumming). New York: Crossroad.
Gallagher, Catherine. 1985. 'Politics, the Profession, and the Critic.' *Diacritics* 15, 2: 37–43.
Gandhi, Leela. 1998. *Postcolonial Theory: A Critical Introduction*. New York: Columbia University Press.
Garlington, William. 1977. 'The Bahā'ī Faith in Malwa.' *In* G. A. Oddie, ed., *Religion in South Asia: Religious Conversion and Revival Movements in South Asia in Medieval and Modern Time*, 101–17. New Delhi: Manohar.
Garlington, William N. 1982. 'Bahā'ī Bhajans.' *World Order* 16, 2: 43–49.
Garlington, William. 1984. 'Bahā'ī Conversions in Malwa, Central India.' *In* Juan R. Cole and Moojan Momen, eds., *From Iran East and West*, 157–85, 196–98. Los Angeles: Kalimāt Press.
Garlington, William. 1997. 'The Bahā'ī Faith in India: A Developmental Stage Approach.' *Occasional Papers in Shaykhī, Bābī and Bahā'ī Studies*, no. 2. Accessed on-line at <http://www.h-net.org/nbahai/bhpapers/india1.htm>.
Garlington, William. Forthcoming. *The Bahā'ī Faith in India: An Historical Study*. Los Angeles: Kalimát Press.
Gethin, Rupert. 1998. *The Foundations of Buddhism*. Oxford: Oxford University Press.
Gill, Sam. 1994. 'The Academic Study of Religion.' *Journal of the American Academy of Religion* 42, 4: 965–75.
Gilmartin, David and Bruce Lawrence, eds. 2000. *Beyond Turk and Hindu: Rethinking Religious Identities in Islamicate South Asia*. Gainesville: University of Florida Press.

Gombrich, Richard. 1966. 'The Consecration of a Buddhist Image.' *The Journal of Asian Studies* 26, 1: 23–36.
Gombrich, Richard F. 1988. *Theravāda Buddhism: A Social History from Ancient Benares to Modern Colombo*. London: Routledge & Kegan Paul.
Gombrich, Richard and Gananath Obeyesekere. 1988. *Buddhism Transformed: Religious Change in Sri Lanka*. Princeton: Princeton University Press.
Gommans, Jos. 1998. 'The Silent Frontier of South Asia, *c.* A.D. 1100–1800.' *Journal of World History* 9, 1: 1–23.
Goodall, Dominic, ed. and trans. 1996 [1966]. *Hindu Scriptures*. London: J. M. Dent.
Goodman, Hananya, ed. 1994. *Between Jerusalem and Benares: Comparative Studies in Judaism and Hinduism*. Albany: State University of New York Press.
Gottschalk, Peter. 2000. *Beyond Hindu and Muslim: Multiple Identity in Narratives from Village India*. New York: Oxford University Press.
Grafe, Hugald. 1990. *The History of Christianity in Tamilnadu from 1800 to 1975*. Bangalore: Church History Association of India.
Grewal, J. S. 1991. *The Sikhs of the Punjab*. Cambridge: Cambridge University Press.
Grewal, J. S. 1998. *Contesting Interpretations of the Sikh Tradition*. New Delhi: Manohar.
Grimes, John. 1996 [1988]. *A Concise Dictionary of Indian Philosophy: Sanskrit Terms Defined in English*. Albany: State University of New York Press.
Haan, Michael. 2005. 'Numbers in Nirvana: How the 1872–1921 Indian Censuses Helped Operationalise "Hinduism".' *Religion* 35, 1: 13–30.
Haddad, Yvonne Yazbeck, ed. 1991. *The Muslims of America*. New York: Oxford University Press.
Halbfass, Wilhelm. 1991. *Tradition and Reflection: Explorations in Indian Thought*. Albany: State University of New York Press.
Hallegua, Samuel H. 2002. 'The Marriage Customs of the Jewish Community of Cochin.' *In* Shalva Weil, ed., *India's Jewish Heritage: Ritual, Art and Life-Cycle*, 60–67. Mumbai: Mārg Publications.
Hansen, Bent Smidt. 1998. *Dependency and Identity: Problems of Cultural Encounter as a Consequence of the Danish Mission in South India Between the Two World Wars*. St Hyacinthe: World Heritage Press.
Hardy, Peter. 1972. *The Muslims of British India*. Cambridge: Cambridge University Press.
Hasan, Mushirul, ed. 1993. *India's Partition: Process, Strategy and Mobilization*. Delhi: Oxford University Press.
Hedlund, Roger E. 1999. 'Indian Instituted Churches: Indigenous Christianity Indian Style.' *Mission Studies* 16, 1: 26–42.
Herodotus. 1987. *The History* (trans. David Grene). Chicago: University of Chicago Press.
Hick, John. 1973. *God and the Universe of Faiths*. New York: St Martin's Press.
Hick, John. 2004 [1989]. *An Interpretation of Religion: Human Responses to the Transcendent*. New Haven: Yale University Press.
Hinnells, John R. 1996. *Zoroastrians in Britain: The Ratanbai Katrak Lectures, University of Oxford 1985*. Oxford: Clarendon Press.
Hinnells, John R., ed. 2005. *The Routledge Companion to the Study of Religion*. London and New York: Routledge.
Hodgson, Marshall. 1974. *The Venture of Islam: Conscience and History in a World Civilization*. 3 vols. Chicago: University of Chicago Press.
Holdrege, Barbara A. 1996. *Veda and Torah: Transcending the Textuality of Scripture*. Albany: State University of New York Press.
Hudson, D. Dennis. 2000. *Protestant Origins in India: Tamil Evangelical Christians in India, 1706–1835*. London: Curzon Press.
Al-Hujwīrī, 'Alī ibn 'Uthman al-Jullabi. 1990 [1911]. *The Kashf al-Majhub* (trans. Reynold A. Nicholson). Karachi: Darul-Ishaat Urdu Bazar.

Humphrey, Caroline and James Laidlaw. 1994. *The Archetypal Actions of Ritual: A Theory of Ritual Illustrated by the Jain Rite of Worship*. Oxford: Clarendon Press.
Huntington, Susan. 1990. 'Early Buddhist Art and the Theory of Aniconism.' *Art Journal* 49, 4: 401–408.
Insler, S. 1975. *The Gāthās of Zarathustra*. Tehran-Liège: Bibliothèque Pahlavi.
Isenberg, Shirley Berry. 1988. *India's Bene Israel: A Comprehensive Inquiry and Sourcebook*. Berkeley: Judah L. Magnes Museum.
Isḥāq. 1987 [1955]. *The Life of Muhammad: A Translation of Isḥāq's Sīrat Rasūl Allāh* (trans. A. Guillaume). Karachi: Oxford University Press.
Jaini, Padmanabh S. 1979. *The Jaina Path of Purification*. Berkeley: University of California Press.
Jaini, Padmanabh S. 1991. *Gender and Salvation: Jaina Debates on the Spiritual Liberation of Women*. Berkeley: University of California Press.
Jalal, Ayesha. 1994 [1985]. *The Sole Spokesman: Jinnah, the Muslim League and the Demand for Pakistan*. Cambridge: Cambridge University Press.
Johnson, Barbara C., ed. 2002. *Oh Lovely Parrot: Jewish Women's Songs from Kerala* (trans. Barbara C. Johnson and Scaria Zacharia). Jerusalem: Jewish Music Resource Center.
Jondhale, Surendra and Johannes Beltz, eds. 2004. *Reconstructing the World: B.R. Ambedkar and Buddhism in India*. New Delhi: Oxford University Press.
Jussay, P. M. 1982. 'The Songs of Evarayi.' *Pe'amim* 13: 45–160.
Kabīr. 1986 [1983]. *The Bījak of Kabir* (trans. Linda Hess and Shukdev Singh; Essays and Notes by Linda Hess). Delhi: Motilal Banarsidass.
Kalupahana, David J. 1976. *Buddhist Philosophy: A Historical Analysis*. Honolulu: University of Hawaii Press.
Kamenetz, Rodger. 1994. *The Jew in the Lotus: A Poet's Rediscovery of Jewish Identity in Buddhist India*. San Francisco: Harper.
Kapstein, Matthew T. 2000. *The Tibetan Assimilation of Buddhism: Conversion, Contestation, and Memory*. New York: Oxford University Press.
Katz, Nathan. 2000. *Who are the Jews of India?* Berkeley: University of California Press.
Katz, Nathan and Ellen S. Goldberg. 1993. *The Last Jews of Cochin: Jewish Identity in Hindu India*. Columbia: University of South Carolina Press.
Kelting, M. Whitney. 2001. *Singing to the Jinas: Jain Women, Mandal Singing and the Negotiations of Jain Devotion*. New York: Oxford University Press.
King, Richard. 1999. *Orientalism and Religion: Postcolonial Theory, India and 'The Mystic East'*. London: Routledge.
Kippenberg, Hans G. 2002 [1997]. *Discovering Religious History in the Modern Age* (trans. Barbara Harshaw). Princeton: Princeton University Press.
Kopf, David. 1980. 'Hermeneutics Versus History.' *Journal of Asian Studies* 39, 3: 495–506.
Laidlaw, James. 1995. *Riches and Renunciation: Religion, Economy and Society among the Jains*. Oxford: Clarendon Press.
Lakoff, George. 1987. *Women, Fire and Dangerous Things: What Categories Reveal about the Mind*. Chicago: University of Chicago Press.
Lala, R. M. 1981. *The Creation of Wealth: A Tata Story*. Bombay: IBH Publishing.
Lala, R. M. 1984. *The Heartbeat of a Trust: Fifty Years of the Sir Dorabji Tata Trust*. New Delhi: Tata McGraw-Hill.
Lelyveld, David. 1978. *Aligarh's First Generation: Muslim Solidarity in British India*. Princeton: Princeton University Press.
Lentin, Sifra Samuel. 2002. 'The Jewish Presence in Bombay.' *In* Shalva Weil, ed., *India's Jewish Heritage: Ritual, Art and Life-Cycle*, 22–35. Mumbai: Mārg Publications.
Lewis, Bernard. 1993. *Islam and the West*. New York: Oxford University Press.
Lipner, Julius J. 1994. *Hindus: Their Religious Beliefs and Practices*. London: Routledge.

Lipner, Julius J. 1996. 'Ancient Banyan: An Inquiry into the Meaning of "Hinduness".' *Religious Studies* 32: 109–26.
Lipner, Julius J. 2004. 'On Hinduism and Hinduisms: The Way of the Banyan.' *In* Sushil Mittal and Gene Thursby, eds., *The Hindu World*, 9–34. London: Routledge.
Lopez, Donald S., ed. 2004. *Buddhist Scriptures*. New York: Penguin Books.
Lorenzen, David N. 1999. 'Who Invented Hinduism?' *Comparative Studies in Society and History: An Historical Quarterly* 41, 4: 630–59.
Lowe, Lisa. 1991. *Critical Terrains: French and British Orientalisms*. Ithaca: Cornell University Press.
Luhrmann, T. M. 1996. *The Good Parsi: The Fate of a Colonial Elite in a Postcolonial Society*. Cambridge: Harvard University Press.
Luhrmann, T. M. 2002. 'Evil in the Sands of Time: Theology and Identity Politics among the Zoroastrian Parsis.' *Journal of Asian Studies* 61, 3: 861–89.
MacIntyre, Alistair C. 1990. *Three Rival Versions of Moral Enquiry: Encyclopedia, Genealogy and Tradition*. Notre Dame: University of Notre Dame Press.
McCutcheon, Russell T. 2004. ' "Religion" and the Problem of the Governable Self: Or How to Live in a Less than Perfect Nation.' *Method & Theory in the Study of Religion* 16, 2: 164–81.
McCutcheon, Russell T. 2005. *Religion and the Domestication of Dissent: Or, How to Live in a Less than Perfect Nation*. London: Equinox.
McGowan, John. 1991. *Postmodernism and Its Critics*. Ithaca: Cornell University Press.
McLeod, Hew. 1997. *Sikhism*. London: Penguin.
McLeod, W. H. 1989. *The Sikhs: History, Religion, and Society*. New York: Columbia University Press.
McLeod, W. H. 1999. *Sikhs and Sikhism: Gurū Nānak and the Sikh Religion; Early Sikh Tradition; The Evolution of the Sikh Community; Who is a Sikh?* New Delhi: Oxford University Press.
McLeod, W. H. 2003. *Sikhs of the Khalsa: A History of the Khalsa Rahit*. New Delhi: Oxford University Press.
Madaan, Davinder Kumar. 1997. 'SAARC: Origin and Development.' *In* Verinder Grover, ed., *Encyclopedia of SAARC Nations*, 1 of 7: 634–70. New Delhi: Deep & Deep Publications.
Madan, T. N., ed. 2001 [1976]. *Muslim Communities of South Asia: Culture, Society and Power*. New Delhi: Manohar.
Marshall, John, ed. 1931. *Mohenjo-dara and The Indus Civilization: Being an Official Account of Archaeological Excavations at Mohenjo-dara Carried Out by the Government of India Between The Years 1922 and 1927*. 3 vols. London: Oxford University Press.
Martin, Richard, ed. 1985. *Approaches to Islam in Religious Studies*. Tucson: University of Arizona Press.
Masani, Ervad Phiroze Shapurji. 1917. *Zoroastrianism Ancient and Modern: Comprising a Review of Dr Dhalla's Book of Zoroastrian Theology*. Bombay: Ervad Phiroze S. Masani.
Metcalf, Barbara Daly. 1990. *Perfecting Women: Maulana Ashraf Ali Thanawi's Bihishti Zewar. A Partial Translation with Commentary*. Berkeley: University of California Press.
Metcalf, Barbara Daly, ed. 1996. *Making Muslim Space in North America and Europe*. Berkeley: University of California Press.
Michaels, Axel. 2004 [1998]. *Hinduism: Past and Present* (trans. Barbara Harshav). Princeton: Princeton University Press.
Minault, Gail. 1982. *The Khilāfat Movement: Religious Symbolism and Political Mobilization in India*. New York: Columbia University Press.
Mistree, Khojeste P. 1982. *Zoroastrianism: An Ethnic Perspective*. Bombay: Zoroastrian Studies.
Mistry, Rohinton. 2002a [1987]. *Tales from Firozsha Baag*. Toronto: Penguin.
Mistry, Rohinton. 2002b. *Family Matters*. New York: Alfred A. Knopf.
Mittal, Sushil, ed. 2003. *Surprising Bedfellows: Hindus and Muslims in Medieval and Early Modern India*. Lanham: Lexington Books.

Mittal, Sushil and Gene Thursby, eds. 2004. *The Hindu World*. London: Routledge.

Modi, Jivanji Jamshedji. 1885. *The Religious System of the Parsis: A Paper*. Bombay: Modi.

Momen, Moojan. 1997. *A Short Introduction to the Bahā'ī Faith*. Oxford: Oneworld.

Munck, Victor C. de. 2001 [1975]. 'Sufi, Reformist and National Models of Identity: The History of a Muslim Village Festival in Sri Lanka.' *In* T. N. Madan, ed., *Muslim Communities of South Asia: Culture, Society and Power*, 555–78. New Delhi: Manohar.

Mundadan, A. Mathias. 1989 [1984]. *History of Christianity in India*. Volume 1: *From the Beginning up to the Middle of the Sixteenth Century (up to 1542)*. Bangalore: Church History Association of India.

Muslim, Imām. 1990 [1971]. *Ṣaḥīḥ Muslim: Being Traditions of the Sayings and Doings of the Prophet Muḥammad as Narrative by His Companions and Compiled Under the Title Al-Jāmi'-Uṣ-Ṣaḥīh*. 4 vols. Lahore: Shaikh Muhammad Ashraf.

Nakhjavani, Violette. Nd. *Amatu'l-Bahā' Visits India*. New Delhi: Bahā'ī Publishing Trust.

Nandy, Ashis. 1983. *The Intimate Enemy: Loss and Recovery of Self Under Colonialism*. Delhi: Oxford University Press.

Nandy, Ashis. 1987. *Traditions, Tyranny and Utopias: Essays in the Politics of Awareness*. Delhi: Oxford University Press.

Narayanan, M. G. S. 1972. *Cultural Symbiosis in Kerala*. Trivandrum: Kerala Historical Society.

Nasr, Seyyed Vali Reza. 1994. *The Vanguard of the Islamic Revolution: The Jama'at-i Islami of Pakistan*. Berkeley: University of California Press.

Nasr, Seyyed Vali Reza. 1996. *Mawdudi and the Making of Islamic Revivalism*. New York: Oxford University Press.

Neill, Stephen. 1970. *The Story of the Christian Church in India and Pakistan*. Grand Rapids: William B. Eerdmans Publishing.

Neill, Stephen. 1984. *A History of Christianity in India: The Beginning to AD 1707*. Cambridge: Cambridge University Press.

Neill, Stephen. 1985. *A History of Christianity in India, 1707–1858*. Cambridge: Cambridge University Press.

Nielsen, Jørgen S. 1995. 'Great Britain.' *In* John L. Esposito, ed., *The Oxford Encyclopedia of the Modern Islamic World*, 2: 69–72. New York: Oxford University Press.

Noss, John B. 1949. *Man's Religions*. New York: Macmillan.

Nye, Malory. 2003. *Religion: The Basics*. London: Routledge.

Oberoi, Harjot. 1994. *The Construction of Religious Boundaries: Culture, Identity, and Diversity in the Sikh Tradition*. New Delhi: Oxford University Press.

O'Connell, Joseph T. 1973. 'The Word "Hindu" in Gauḍiya Vaiṣṇava Text.' *Journal of the American Oriental Society* 93, 3: 340–44.

O'Flaherty, Wendy, ed. and trans., with Daniel Gold and David Shulman. 1988. *Textual Sources for the Study of Hinduism*. Manchester: Manchester University Press.

Olson, Carl. 2000. *Zen and the Art of Postmodern Philosophy: Two Paths of Liberation from the Representational Mode of Thinking*. Albany: State University of New York Press.

Olson, Carl, ed. 2003. *Theory and Method in The Study of Religion: A Selection of Critical Readiness*. Belmont: Thomson/Wadsworth.

Olson, Carl. 2005. *The Different Paths of Buddhism: A Narrative-Historical Introduction*. New Brunswick: Rutgers University Press.

Omvedt, Gail. 1994. *Dalits and the Democratic Revolution: Dr Ambedkar and the Dalit Movement in Colonial India*. New Delhi: Sage Publications.

Paden, William E. 1994 [1988]. *Religious Worlds: The Comparative Study of Religion*. Boston: Beacon Press.

Paden, William E. 1997. 'Elements of a New Comparativism.' *Method & Theory in the Study of Religion* 8, 1: 5–14.

Paden, William E. 2000. 'Elements of a New Comparativism.' *In* Kimberly C. Patton and

Benjamin C. Ray, eds., *A Magic Still Dwells: Comparative Religion in the Postmodern Age*, 182–92. Berkeley: University of California Press.
Parfitt, Tudor. 2002. *The Lost Tribes of Israel: The History of a Myth*. London: Weidenfeld & Nicolson.
Parry, Jonathan. 1986. 'The Gift, the Indian Gift and the "Indian Gift".' *Man* (n.s.) 21, 3: 453–73.
Parry, R. B. and C. R. Perkins. 1987. *World Mapping Today*. London: Butterworth.
Patel, J. M. Framjee. 1905. *Stray Thoughts on Indian Cricket*. Bombay: Times Press.
Pearson, Michael N. 1996. *Pilgrimage to Mecca: The Indian Experience, 1500–1800*. Princeton: Markus Wiener.
Prothero, Stephen. 1996. *The White Buddhist: The Asian Odyssey of Henry Steel Olcott*. Bloomington: Indiana University Press.
Putnam, Hilary. 1992. *Renewing Philosophy*. Cambridge: Harvard University Press.
Raj, Selva J. and Corinne C. Dempsey. 2002. *Popular Christianity in India: Riting Between the Lines*. Albany: State University of New York Press.
Reid, Donald Malcolm. 1995. 'Educational Institutions.' *In* John L. Esposito, ed., *The Oxford Encyclopedia of the Modern Islamic World*, 1: 412–16. New York: Oxford University Press.
Reissner, H. G. 1950. 'Indian-Jewish Statistics (1837–1941).' *Jewish Social Studies* 12: 349–66.
Reynolds, Frank E. 1997. 'Rebirth Traditions and the Lineage of Gotama: A Study in Theravāda Buddhology.' *In* Juliane Schober, ed., *Sacred Biography in the Buddhist Traditions of South and Southeast Asia*, 19–39. Honolulu: University of Hawaii Press.
Reynolds, Frank E. and Jason A. Carbine, eds. 2000. *The Life of Buddhism*. Berkeley: University of California Press.
Ricoeur, Paul. 1976. *Interpretation Theory: Discourse and the Surplus of Meaning*. Fort Worth: Texas Christian University Press.
Ricoeur, Paul. 1984–88 [1983–85]. *Time and Narrative* (trans. Kathleen McLaughlin and David Pellauer). 3 vols. Chicago: University of Chicago Press.
Robb, Peter. 2002. *A History of India*. New York: Palgrave.
Robinson, Richard H., Willard L. Johnson, and Thanissaro Bhikkhu (Geoffrey DeGraff). 2005 [1970]. *Buddhist Religions: A Historical Introduction*. Belmont: Thomson Wadsworth.
Rocher, Rosane. 1993. 'British Orientalism in the Eighteenth Century: The Dialectics of Knowledge and Government.' *In* Carol A. Breckenridge and Peter van der Veer, eds., *Orientalism and the Postcolonial Predicament*, 215–49. Philadelphia: University of Pennsylvania Press.
Roland, Joan G. 1989. *Jews in British India: Identity in a Colonial Era*. Hanover: University Press of New England.
Roland, Joan. 2002. 'The Contributions of the Jews of India.' *In* Shalva Weil, ed., *India's Jewish Heritage: Art, Ritual and Life-Cycle*, 110–21. Mumbai: Mārg Publications.
Rudolph, Kurt. 1992. *Geschichte und Probleme der Religionswissenschaft*. Leiden: E. J. Brill.
Rushdie, Salman. 1980. *Midnight's Children*. New York: Alfred A. Knopf.
Russell, James R. 1987. *Zoroastrianism in Armenia*. Cambridge: Harvard University Department of Near Eastern Languages and Civilizations and National Association for Armenian Studies and Research.
Said, Edward W. 1975. *Beginnings: Intention and Method*. New York: Basic Books.
Said, Edward W. 1979 [1978]. *Orientalism*. New York: Vintage Books.
Said, Edward W. 1983. *The World, the Text, and the Critic*. Cambridge: Harvard University Press.
Said, Edward W. 1993. *Culture and Imperialism*. New York: Vintage Books.
Sanyal, Usha. 1996. *Devotional Islam and Politics in British India: Ahmad Riza Khan Barelwi and His Movement, 1870–1920*. Delhi: Oxford University Press.
Schopen, Gregory. 1990. 'The Buddha as Owner of Property and Permanent Resident in Medieval Indian Monasteries.' *Journal of Indian Philosophy* 18, 3: 181–217.

Schopen, Gregory. 1991. 'Archaeology and Protestant Presuppositions in the Study of Indian Buddhism.' *History of Religions* 31, 1: 1–23.

Segal, J. B. 1967. 'The Jews of Cochin and their Neighbours.' *In* H. J. Zimmels, J. Rabbinowitz, and I. Feinstein, eds., *Essays Presented to Chief Rabbi Israel Brodie on the Occasion of his Seventieth Birthday*, 381–97. London: Soncino Press.

Seneviratne, H. L. 1978. *Rituals of the Kandyan State*. Cambridge: Cambridge University Press.

Sheleg, Yair. 2000. *The New Religious Jews: Recent Development among Observant Jews in Israel*. Jerusalem: Keter Hebrew.

Shoghi Effendi. 1965 [1944]. *God Passes By*. Wilmette: Bahā'ī Publishing Trust.

Shoghi Effendi. 1970. *Dawn of a New Day*. New Delhi: Bahā'ī Publishing Trust.

Silliman, Jael. 2001. *Jewish Portraits, Indian Frames: Women's Narratives from a Diaspora of Hope*. Hanover: University Press of New England.

Singer, Milton. 1972. *When A Great Tradition Modernizes: An Anthropological Approach to Indian Civilization*. New York: Praeger Publishers.

Singh, Harbans. 1983. *The Heritage of the Sikhs*. New Delhi: Manohar.

Singh, Harbans, ed. 1992–98. *The Encyclopaedia of Sikhism*. 4 vols. Patiala: Punjabi University.

Singh, Nikky-Guninder Kaur. 1993. *The Feminine Principle in the Sikh Vision of the Transcendent*. Cambridge: Cambridge University Press.

Singh, Nripinder. 1990. *The Sikh Moral Tradition: Ethical Perceptions of the Sikhs in the Late Nineteenth/Early Twentieth Century*. New Delhi: Manohar.

Singh, Pashaura. 2000. *The Guru Granth Sahib: Canon, Meaning, and Authority*. New Delhi: Oxford University Press.

Singh, Pashaura. 2003. *The Bhagats of the Guru Granth Sahib: Sikh Self-Definition and the Bhagat Bani*. New Delhi: Oxford University Press.

Smith, Bardwell L., ed. 1978. *Religion and Legitimation of Power in Sri Lanka*. Chambersburg: Anima Books.

Smith, Brian K. 1989. *Reflections on Resemblance, Ritual, and Religion*. Oxford: Oxford University Press.

Smith, David. 2003. 'Orientalism and Hinduism.' *In* Gavin Flood, ed., *The Blackwell Companion to Hinduism*, 45–63. Oxford: Blackwell.

Smith, Huston. 1958. *The Religions of Man*. New York: Harper & Row Publishers.

Smith, Jane I. 1999. *Islam in America*. New York: Columbia University Press.

Smith, Jane Idleman and Yvonne Yazbeck Haddad. 1981. *The Islamic Understanding of Death and Resurrection*. Albany: State University of New York Press.

Smith, Jonathan Z. 1982. *Imagining Religion from Babylon to Jonestown*. Chicago: University of Chicago Press.

Smith, Peter. 1987. *The Babi and Baha'i Religions: From Messianic Shiʿism to a World Religion*. Cambridge: Cambridge University Press.

Smith, Wilfred Cantwell. 1963. *The Meaning and End of Religion: A New Approach to the Religious Traditions of Mankind*. New York: The Macmillan Company.

Spivak, Gayatri Chakravorty. 1985a.'The Rani of Sirmur.' *In* Francis Barker, Peter Hulme, Margaret Iversen, and Diana Loxley, eds., *Europe and Its Others: Proceedings of the Essex Conference on the Sociology of Literature*, July 1984, 1 of 2: 128–51. Colchester: University of Essex.

Spivak, Gayatri Chakravorty. 1985b. 'Can the Subaltern Speak? Speculations on Widow Sacrifice.' *Wedge* 7, 8: 120–30.

Spivak, Gayatri Chakravorty. 1999. *A Critique of Postcolonial Reason: Toward a History of the Vanishing Present*. Cambridge: Harvard University Press.

Sreekala, S. 1995. 'Israel in the Perception of Indian Jews: A Case Study of Bene Israel.' PhD Dissertation. New Delhi: Jawaharlal Nehru University Library.

Stietencron, Heinrich von. 1989. 'Hinduism: On the Proper Use of a Deceptive Term.' *In*

Günther D. Sontheimer and Hermann Kulke, eds., *Hinduism Reconsidered*, 11–27. New Delhi: Manohar.

Sweetman, Will. 2003. ' "Hinduism" and The History of "Religion": Protestant Presuppositions in the Critique of the Concept of Hinduism." *Method & Theory in the Study of Religion* 15, 4: 325–53.

Tadgell, Christopher. 1990. *The History of Architecture in India: From the Dawn of Civilization to the End of the Raj*. New Delhi: Viking.

Tambiah, S. J. 1970. *Buddhism and the Spirit Cults of North-East Thailand*. Cambridge: Cambridge University Press.

Taylor, Charles. 1989. *Sources of the Self: The Making of the Modern Identity*. Cambridge: Harvard University Press.

Taylor, Charles. 1995. *Philosophical Arguments*. Cambridge: Harvard University Press.

Taylor, Mark C. 1999. *About Religion: Economies of Faith in Virtual Culture*. Chicago: University of Chicago Press.

Taraporewalla, D. 1987. 'The Knowledge of Religion among Parsi Zoroastrians in Bombay.' PhD Dissertation. Bombay: University of Bombay Library.

Taraporewalla, I. J. S. 1965 [1926]. *The Religion of Zarathushtra*. Bombay: B. I. Taraporewalla.

Thackston, Wheeler M., trans., ed. and annotator. 2002. *The Baburnama: Memoirs of Babur, Prince and Emperor*. New York: The Modern Library.

Thangaraj, M. Thomas. 1971. 'The History and Teachings of the Hindu Christian Community Commonly Called Nattu Sabai in Tirunelveli.' *Indian Church History Review* 5, 1: 43–68.

Thangaraj, M. Thomas. 1994. *The Crucified Guru: An Experiment in Cross-Cultural Christology*. Nashville: Abingdon Press.

Thapar, Romila. 1973 [1963]. *Aśoka and the Decline of the Mauryas*. New Delhi: Oxford University Press.

Thapar, Romila. 1978. *Ancient Indian Social History: Some Interpretations*. New Delhi: Orient Longman.

Thekkedath, Joseph. 1982. *History of Christianity in India: From the Middle of the Sixteenth to the End of the Seventeenth Century (1542–1700)*. Bangalore: Theological Publication in India.

Thursby, Gene R. 1992. *The Sikhs*. London: Brill.

Thursby, Gene R. 1993. 'Recent Sikh Scholarship: Sikhism in Religions Studies.' *Religious Studies Review* 19, 1: 36–41.

Trainor, Kevin. 1997. *Relics, Ritual, and Representation in Buddhism: Rematerializing the Sri Lanka Theravāda Tradition*. Cambridge: Cambridge University Press.

Umāsvāti. 1994. *That Which Is: Tattvartha Sutra* (trans. Nathmal Tatia). San Francisco: Harper Collins.

Urban, Hugh B. 2003. *Tantra: Sex, Secrecy, Politics, and Power in the Study of Religion*. Berkeley: University of California Press.

Vallely, Anne. 2002a. *Guardians of the Transcendent: An Ethnography of a Jain Ascetic Community*. Toronto: University of Toronto Press.

Vallely, Anne. 2002b. 'Ethical Discourses among Orthodox and Diaspora Jains.' *In* Michael Lambek, ed., A *Reader in the Anthropology of Religion*, 555–69. Oxford: Blackwell.

Veer, Peter van der. 2002. 'Religion in South Asia.' *Annual Review of Anthropology* 31: 173–87.

Vimadalal, Jal Rustamji. 1967. *What A Parsee Should Know*. Bombay: Vimadalal.

Wagoner, Philip. 2003. 'Fortuitous Convergences and Essential Ambiguities: Transcultural Political Elites in the Medieval Deccan.' *In* Sushil Mittal, ed., *Surprising Bedfellows: Hindus and Muslims in Medieval and Early Modern India*, 31–54. Lanham: Lexington Books.

Warder, A. K. 1970. *Indian Buddhism*. Delhi: Motilal Banarsidass.

Webster, John C. B. 1992. *A History of the Dalit Christians in India*. San Francisco: Mellen Research University Press.

Weil, Shalva. 1982. 'Symmetry between Christians and Jews in India: The Cnanite Christians and the Cochin Jews of Kerala.' *Contributions to Indian Sociology* 16, 2: 175–96.
Weil, Shalva. 1994. 'Yom Kippur: The Festival of Closing the Doors.' *In* Hananya Goodman, ed., *Between Jerusalem and Benares: Comparative Studies in Judaism and Hinduism*, 85–100, 293–95. Albany: State University of New York Press.
Weil, S. 1996. 'Religious Leadership vs. Secular Authority: The Case of the Bene Israel.' *The Eastern Anthropologist* 49, 3–4: 301–316.
Weil, Shalva. 2002a. 'Bene Israel Rites and Routines.' *In* Shalva Weil, ed., *India's Jewish Heritage: Ritual, Art, and Life-Cycle*, 78–89. Mumbai: Mārg Publications.
Weil, Shalva, ed. 2002b. *India's Jewish Heritage: Ritual, Art and Life-Cycle*. Mumbai: Mārg Publications.
Weil, Shalva. 2003. 'Dual Conversion Among the Shinlung of North-East India.' *Studies of Tribes and Tribals* 1, 1: 43–57.
Williams, Paul with Anthony Tribe. 2000. *Buddhist Thought: A Complete Introduction to the Indian Tradition*. London: Routledge.
Williams, Raymond Brady. 1996. *Christian Pluralism in the United States: The Indian Experience*. Cambridge: Cambridge University Press.
Wilson, John. 1847 [1839]. *The Doctrine of Jehovah Addressed to the Pársís: A Sermon Preached on the Occasion of the Baptism of Two Youths of that Tribe, May MDCCCXXXIX*. Edinburgh: William Whyte & Co.
Wilson, Liz. 1996. *Charming Cadavers: Horrific Figurations of the Feminine in Buddhist Hagiographic Literature*. Chicago: University of Chicago Press.
Writer, Rashna. 1993. *Contemporary Zoroastrians: An Unstructured Nation*. Lanham: University Press of America.
Young, Robert J. C. 1990. *White Mythologies: Writing History and the West*. London: Routledge.
Young, Robert J. C. 2001. *Postcolonialism: An Historical Introduction*. Oxford: Blackwell.
Zaehner, R. C. 1961. *The Dawn and Twilight of Zoroastrianism*. New York: Putnam.
Zaman, Iftikhar. 1995. '"Ulamā': Sunnī'ulamā'.' *In* John L. Esposito, ed., *The Oxford Encyclopedia of the Modern Islamic World*, 4: 258–61. New York: Oxford University Press.
Zelliot, Eleanor. 2004. 'B. R. Ambedkar and the Search for a Meaningful Buddhism.' *In* Surendra Jondhale and Johannes Beltz, eds., *Reconstructing the World: B. R. Ambedkar and Buddhism in India*, 18–34. New Delhi: Oxford University Press.

INDEX